BORDER WAR
FOOTBALL
1891 - 2009

SHAWN BUCHANAN GREENE

VIRIDIS PUBLISHING, Saint Louis, Missouri • www.ViridisPublishing.com

HOW THE BOOK CAME TO BE

In 2006, I chose to write a book regarding the oldest, current Thanksgiving Day football game West of the Mississippi River. Although only a high school game, attendance varies between 5,000 to 10,000 on any given year. With the 100th anniversary of the game arriving in 2007, my book received quite a lot of attention and I believed that it was enjoyed by the alumni of those two schools.

Of course, many of the alumni from my school also played for the University of Missouri and, dare I acknowledge it, Kansas. That game was the oldest Thanksgiving Day game until it was rescheduled to not occur on Thanksgiving Day.

Regardless, I thought to duplicate what I had done for the Turkey Day Game book and apply it to my collegiate alma mater... Kansas! In effect, I wanted a book that summarized the game's information by decade and had plenty of personal accounts of the game's history. What I already knew from my previous book was that you did not have to necessarily play in the game to be a part of it.

This book is a labour of love and there are many that I want to thank for their help in its creation: Joe Jordan, Dan Thompson, Doug Harris, Mike Reid, Letha Johnson, Rebecca Schulte, Todd McCubbin, Kevin Corbett, Malcolm Gibson, my old friend James Meng, my old roomates Brian Hamilton (and family) and Monika Fischer, Devin Sauer, and Alex Hamilton (for giving me a complimentary beer or two at Free State Brewing Company on research stops in Lawrence).

I hope that the game is a joyous celebration for you now and forever.

Shawn Buchanan Greene
Principal Author
Kansas Alumnus 1991

DEDICATION

This book is dedicated to the memory of all Tigers and Jayhawkers matriculated or adopted, who with unrivalled spirit, created and continue the second oldest football tradition in the United States.

It is with pride and honour that this book is put to print the most detailed photographic history of Missouri and Kansas football thereby ensuring that they shall not be lost or forgotten.

PUBLICATION STAFF

Author. . . . . Shawn Buchanan Greene

Editor . . . . Monika P. Fischer

Book Design . . . . Martin Taylor

Dust Jacket Artist . . Marilynne G. Bradley

Logo Design . . . . Mark Arnold

Photo Editor . . . . Martin Taylor

Dust Jacket Design . . . . Martin Taylor

Publisher . . . . Viridis Publishing LLC

TABLE OF CONTENTS

CONTRIBUTING AUTHORS

 Edger Henry Summerfield Bailey, Ph.D.
Kansas Professor 1881-1931

 James Aloysius Bernard Bausch
Kansas Alumnus 1931

 Frank Wilson Blackmar, Ph.D.
Kansas Professor 1909

 Chad Ernest Bryan
Kansas Alumnus 1992

 Chester L. Brewer
Missouri Football Head
Coach 1911-1913
Missouri Athletic Director
1910-1917, 1923-1935

 John M. Burnam, Ph.D.
Missouri Professor 1896

 Joseph R. Childs
Kansas Alumnus 1971

 Paul J. Christman, Junior

 Victoria Lee Christman

 Tilghman R. Cloud
Missouri Alumnus 1924

 Kevin J. Corbett
Kansas Alumnus 1988
President, KU Alumni
Association

 Jane Faurot Hazell
Missouri Alumna 1955

 John Frier, Junior
Missouri Alumnus 1950

 James Edger Gibson
Missouri Alumnus 1902

 Joseph R. Gilman, Junior
Kansas Alumnus 1950

 Shawn Buchanan Greene
Principal Author
Kansas Alumnus 1991

 John Phillip Hamel
Missouri Junior 1915

 Stan Hamilton
Kansas Alumnus 1955

 Mark D. Hersey, Ph.D.
Kansas Alumnus 2006

 Chip Hilleary
Kansas Alumnus 1993

 Thomas S. Hudson
Missouri Alumnus 1915

 Darl Anthony James
Kansas Alumnus 1916
Kansas Football Captain
1915

 Don C. Johnson
Missouri Alumnus 1972

 Albert Rutherford Kennedy
Kansas Alumnus 1898
Kansas Football Head
Coach 1904-1910

 Frank H. King
Missouri Alumnus 1916

 Henry N. Kuhlmann, Junior
Missouri Alumnus 1959
Missouri Football Assistant
Coach 1966-1970

 Edward J. Leland
Missouri Alumnus 1899

 Lori Lincoln Grizzel

 Charlie W. Lovelace
Kansas Alumnus 1904

 Tom Mahoney
Missouri Alumnus 1927

 John H. McCool
Kansas Alumnus 2002

 Todd A. McCubbin
Missouri Alumnus 1995
Executive Director, Mizzou
Alumni Association

Park McGee
Kansas Alumnus 1956

 John F. McLean
Missouri Instructor 1905

 Gentry Moss Moellenhoff

 Charles R. Nathan
Missouri Alumnus 1930

 Clarke G. Oberheide

 John H. Outland, M.D.
Kansas Alumnus 1896
Kansas Football Head
Coach 1901

 Duke N. Parry
Missouri Alumnus 1920

 Marion L. Plessner
Missouri Alumnus 1931

 Orville H. Read
Missouri Alumnus 1933

 William W. Roper
Missouri Football Head
Coach 1909

 Tony Sands
Kansas Alumnus 1992

 Jay Simon
Kansas Alumnus 1940

 Edward B. Smith
Missouri Alumnus 1921

 Ralph H. Turner
Missouri Alumnus 1915

 Dick Walt
Kansas Alumnus 1957

 Betty Lou Dobson
Kansas Alumna 1955

 John R. Weisenfel, J. D.
Missouri Alumnus 1971

 Frank X. Zuzulo
Missouri Alumnus 1937

The Kansas-Missouri rivalry is not only a heated contest between two storied universities, but it also chronicles a period of American history routed in bloodshed on the state border.

As time has past, the Border War name has been replaced with the Border Showdown but the rivalry between the schools remains as intense as any rivalry in the country. For Kansas alumni and fans, Missouri is our rival; not Kansas State as some might think. The rivalry brings out the best of both schools' teams whenever they compete – often with epic endings and national implications.

It has taken many, many decades, but both schools have subscribed to the fact that an intense rivalry has ample room for good sportsmanship. Games seen in the national spotlight may well bear witness to insensitive barbs at one another, but the truth of the matter is the Kansas-Missouri rivalry is steeped in both dislike and respect for the opponent. A good day for Kansas is when Missouri loses. A great day for Kansas is when a Missouri loss comes at the hands of the Jayhawks. That will never change!

Rock Chalk, Jayhawk!

Kevin J. Corbett
President
Kansas University Alumni Association

For more than 100 years, one game has been circled on football schedules in both Missouri and Kansas each and every year. The annual game between the Tigers and the Jayhawks is one of the great rivalries in college sports today. Fitting of the Nation's second-most-played rivalry and oldest west of the Mississippi River, the series is dead even at 54-54-9 through 119 meetings (of course, I am using the Mizzou record book!).

The rivalry has been intense throughout the years but I often hear students and alumni talk about how exciting it is to be a part of it. Beating Kansas is something that unites all Mizzou fans and friends and I am sure it is the same way for Kansas fans. The stories of the games have taken on a life of their own.

In 1911, MU Athletic Director Chester Brewer wanted so badly to create a home field advantage in Columbia that he called all alumni to "come home" for the game. That turned out to be the world's first home-coming celebration and has become the most cherished annual tradition for the Mizzou family.

The games have created many memorable moments on both sides. For Mizzou, the 2007 match-up with both teams nationally ranked in the top five is likely the most memorable. The game in Kansas City's Arrowhead Stadium, not only propelled the Tigers to the number one position in the national polls, but kept our bitter rivals from reaching the top spot and secured the ultimate bragging rights.

While the victory was sweet, it was most memorable because of the atmosphere it created. It was truly electric. Two football teams, two states, two rivals, coming together in the perfect storm of circumstances to battle it out, winner-take-all style on a national stage. The atmosphere was so worthy of the rich history between the universities and was the perfect way to celebrate the storied rivalry.

It may not get any better than that but if the rivalry teaches us anything, we all know that anything can happen when the Tigers and Jayhawks face off.

Go Tigers!

Todd A. McCubbin
Executive Director
Mizzou Alumni Association

BORDER WARS

The story of the states of Missouri and Kansas began when the territories separated in 1821 as part of the Missouri Compromise of 1820. Missouri, until that time, was considered in part both lands of the combined states in a much larger Missouri Territory, with the Kansas portion of the territory being occupied of mostly aboriginals known as the Kansa. The territory of Missouri, similarly, was named for a French mispronunciation and misspelling of the Illiniwek word for their neighbours west across the great river, "Mizuria," meaning "big canoe people." The endonym of the "Mizuria" people was "Niuachi" and they, along with the Kansa and another well known tribe, the Niukansa, known by the exonym "Osage" by French and English explorers and settlers, were, unlike the Illiniwek, of similar language and culture, being of the Oceti Sakowin (Seven Council Fires) known in English as the "Sioux," another French generated term.

William T. Anderson

Prior to 1820, the land that was soon to be the State of Missouri was being settled by slave-owning Southerners who brought their slaves with them from the South. The Missouri Compromise allowed Missouri to enter the Union as a slave state, provided that slavery was prohibited in the former Louisiana Territory north of the parallel 36.5 degrees North, except within the boundaries of the proposed State of Missouri. Between the years of 1821 and 1854, many treaties were enacted with the aboriginal residents of Kansas relocating many of them outside of the territory. In 1854, the new Kansas-Nebraska Bill repealed the Missouri Compromise and allowed for the residents of the Kansas Territory to determine if they would join the Union as a free or slave state. This caused a rush from southern proslavery and northern abolitionist settlers to the territory to control its politics. The ideological conflict between the two opposing factions resulted in violence, which culminated in "border wars" between the abolitionist residents of Kansas and the proslavery residents of Kansas and Missouri. The conflicts between the two factions were ongoing from 1854 until 1856 when the level of lawlessness brought Federal troops to the Kansas Territory to end the violence. In 1858, the people of Kansas rejected a proslavery constitution that included a provision for slavery, which initiated the end of the proslavery movement in Kansas. On January 29, 1861, Kansas was admitted to the Union as a "Free State," just prior to the outbreak of the Civil War.

Prior to the Civil War in 1839, the Missouri Legislature passed the Geyer Act to establish funds for a state college in Missouri.

William C. Quantrill

Missouri State College became the first public college west of the Mississippi River. In the year of its founding, the citizens of the City of Columbia and Boone County pledged $117,921 in cash and land to have the college located south of Columbia's downtown. The land was owned by James S. Rollins, who is known as the "Father of the University." Because of the association of the Louisiana Purchase to President Thomas Jefferson, the design of the school was based upon the original plans that Jefferson had made for the University of Virginia. During the Civil War, the board of curators suspended operations of the college for a brief time because of the low enrollment and because the residents of Columbia formed a home guard that was based at the College to defend against Confederate guerrillas, led by William T. "Bloody Bill" Anderson. The home guard, known as the "Fighting Tigers of Columbia," defended the City of Columbia, the surrounding area and the college during the Civil War against Anderson and all other similar groups, who desired to plunder the city and college.

Prior to Bill Anderson commanding his own guerrilla company, he was a lieutenant of another noted Missouri Confederate guerrilla leader, William C. Quantrill. Quantrill is notoriously known for his August 21, 1863 massacre of 200 men, women, and children in his raid of the City of Lawrence, Kansas. Lawrence, for a long time, was known as a base of operations for abolitionist forces during the earlier Border Wars between Missouri and Kansas, when Kansas was still a territory; a key militant faction of the forces being known as the "Jayhawks." During the Civil War, the Jayhawks participated in the war on the side of the Union as a guerrilla group. The fictional "Jayhawk" bird is thought to have originated from settlers as a cross between two real birds; the blue jay and the sparrow hawk.

At the conclusion of the Civil War in 1865, Kansas University was founded by the citizens of Lawrence under a charter from the Kansas Legislature. The former governor of Kansas, Charles Robinson and his wife Sara donated 160,000 square metres of Mount Oread property, located in Lawrence, while another famed politician, Amos Adams Lawrence, made many large financial donations. Both Charles Robinson and Amos Adams Lawrence founded the City of Lawrence, it being named for the latter. Their similarities and differences now intertwined inextricably in a myriad of ways, the states, people, and universities of Missouri and Kansas were now destined to compete in a new type of border war in twenty-five years.

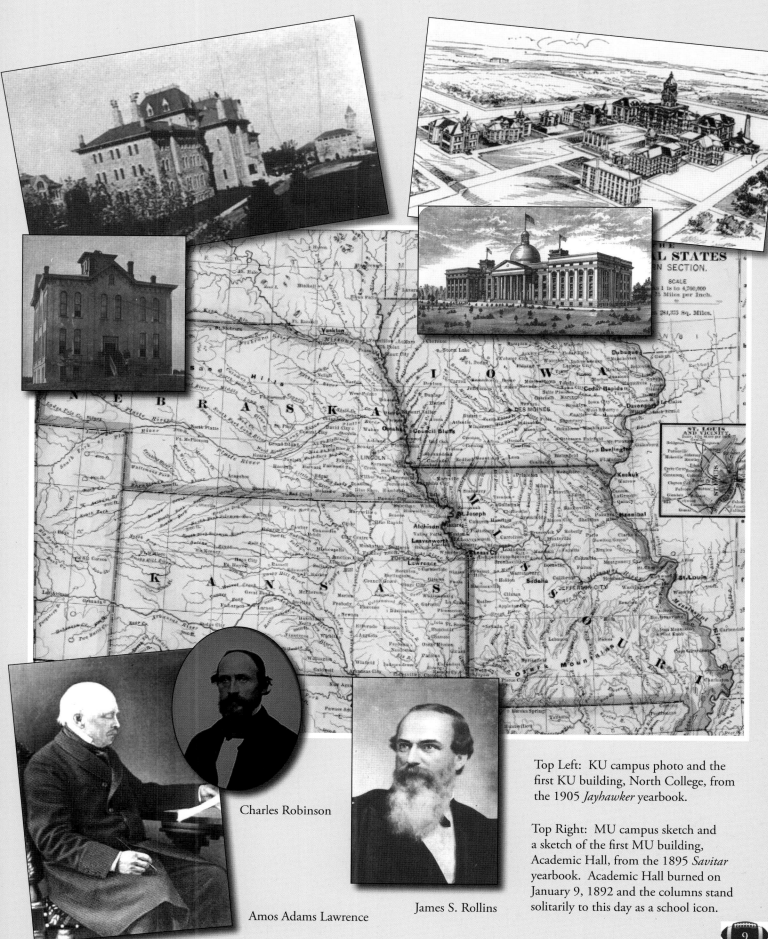

Charles Robinson

Amos Adams Lawrence

James S. Rollins

Top Left: KU campus photo and the first KU building, North College, from the 1905 *Jayhawker* yearbook.

Top Right: MU campus sketch and a sketch of the first MU building, Academic Hall, from the 1895 *Savitar* yearbook. Academic Hall burned on January 9, 1892 and the columns stand solitarily to this day as a school icon.

Football that is played in America began as an incident occurring in 1823 in Rugby, England, during an interclass game of football. In the game, one of the players became frustrated by his lack of skill at kicking the ball and, picking it up, ran with it. Despite it being against the rules, the advantages of carrying the ball led to the adoption of this type of play at Rugby in 1841 and became known as Rugby football. In America, Rugby football began to use a system of lines and zones that resembled a gridiron. For this reason, the game in America and Canada later became known as gridiron football and in America and Canada was later shortened to the term "football." The name of the game that did not permit the use of hands became known as soccer, taken from the term "association football." In the United Kingdom, and most other countries of the world, the name of rugby and gridiron, or in many cases it is referred to as American football, apply to the games that utilize hands, whereas the original form of the game that does not utilize hands retains the name of football. Oddly, in English speaking former colonies of England, each country uses the term "football" for whichever version of the game is the most popular. For example, Canadians and Americans refer to gridiron football as "football," and call association football "soccer." Australians and New Zealanders also refer to association football as "soccer." However, in Australia both the games of rugby football and a derivative game called Australian rules football are played. In Australia, Australian rules football is called "football" and the other two games are called "rugby" and "soccer."

The first football game in the United States was played in November, 1869, in which Rutgers defeated Princeton playing the game under the rules that did not involve the use of hands. In 1874, McGill University of Canada played Harvard University, the first half of the game being played under the original rules and the second half played under the rules innovated in Rugby. The following year was a Rugby rule game between Yale and Harvard, which appealed greatly to the Yale players. As a result, an association of five colleges was formed in 1876 to play Rugby rule football. As time evolved with the game of football in America and Canada, before the beginning of each contest the players would agree upon which of the various rules known for play would be used, which is how the game of gridiron football evolved differently from that of Rugby Union Football.

In September, 1890, physics professor Austin Lee McRae of Missouri State University, the school having by this time replaced the word "college" in its name, visited Washington University in Saint Louis, Missouri and was informed of the desire of the students there to participate in athletic competitions with Missouri State University. Shortly after his return to the Missouri campus, a meeting was organized on October 10 to discuss the purpose and feasibility of starting an athletic association. At the meeting, it was decided that due to the lack of funds available to them and also due to student apathy that a general athletic association could not be formed but it was determined that they would organize a "foot ball" team and use it as the nucleus for a future athletic association. Also, the name of the team was decided to be the "Tigers" in honour of the Fighting Tigers of Columbia and the colours of Black and Gold were selected for the team. Three days later, on October 13, 19 students formed a "Foot Ball Association" and indicated their willingness to try for a place on the team. In this their first year, the Varsity Eleven played their first game on October 20 against a picked team of 13 students of Missouri State University, winning the game 22-6. As had been previously planned, the Missouri State University varsity football team played Washington University at 3:00 p.m. at their campus on Thanksgiving Day, November 27, losing the contest 28-0. Finally, the Missouri Varsity Team played a final game of the season on December 1, 1890 against a squad composed of Missouri State University engineering students, who felt that the wrong eleven member squad had been sent to Washington University. The Missouri Varsity Team won the game soundly 90-0, with a special notation being made in the Missouri State University yearbook, "Note – The ball leaked badly was the reason so few goals could be kicked."

The rules governing the game at this time came from the Intercollegiate Football Association, which assigned five points for a field goal, four points for a touchdown, known in rugby football as a try (on goal), and two points for a conversion, drop kick, or safety. A conversion in gridiron football at this time was awarded by taking the football back 5 yards from where the touchdown was scored and then kicking it through the uprights as a place kick. Additionally, the game only required five yards for a first down and a team was only given three downs to do it.

The success of the Foot Ball Association caused it to clear $100 above expenses and resulted in the formation of the Athletic Association occurring on December 15, 1890. The creation of the Athletic Association at the University caused the equipping of a baseball team, the creation of a tennis tournament, and a track and field event, all causing the Curators of Missouri State University to set apart grounds for use as an athletic field. Finally, the funds also provided for the printing of the first annual of the Missouri State University, recording its deeds of the 1890-91 school year.

Across the border in Kansas, a team was also formed for the first time in 1890 at Kansas University. The first coach of the team was Will J. Coleman, a student who played center on the team. The team duplicated the same efforts of their Missouri counterparts, playing three games and winning one. The first game played by the Kansas football squad was against nearby Baker University in Baldwin, Kansas on November 22. Kansas lost the game 22-9 and played five days later in Kansas City against the Kansas City Young Men's Christian Association, which they again lost 18-10. Kansas' final game of the season was against Baker University again, this time played in Lawrence. This final game of a limited season gave the Jayhawks their first win of the season and their first ever in their history. Similar to Missouri State University, the team adopted the name of their Civil War fighting force, "Jayhawks," and selected the colours of Crimson and Blue to represent them on the football field. Originally, the colours of Kansas were Blue and Yellow and it is conjectured that Crimson was later adopted by the University because the football team adopted it as their colour. The commonest given theory for the football team using this colour is that their first athletic field, McCook Field, was funded by Colonel John James McCook, who was a graduate of Harvard Law School and the Crimson was therefore sported to honour his ties to Harvard.

With the establishment of football at both colleges and each carrying a 1-2 record, Missouri and Kansas would the next year engage in the first Border War since Kansas was a territory on much different terms and, in doing so, the Tigers and Jayhawks would engage in the oldest Turkey Day game rivalry west of the Mississippi River and the second oldest collegiate rivalry in the United States.

THE 1890S...

Twenty-five years after the end of the Civil War, America's pioneer era had matured and was transitioning into a new one. Because currency could still be redeemed for silver and gold, an economic depression struck the United States caused by the Panic of 1893, when a run on the gold supply reached its statutory limit in the Federal Reserve. Motion pictures evolved from inventions introduced during the Civil War era, such as the zoetrope and the praxinoscope, to individual component images being captured and stored on a reel of film and signifying the beginning of soundless "moving picture shows." In 1895, physicist Wilhelm Rontgen discovered electromagnetic radiation in a wavelength range, known commonly as an x-ray. A year later, scientist Henri Becquerel discovered radioactivity. By the end of the decade, the United States engaged in two brief wars with Spain and the Philippines, defeating both with relative ease.

The first meeting between Missouri and Kansas occurred on Saturday, October 31, 1891 – Halloween, at Exposition Park in Kansas City. The reason that the two teams selected Kansas City is that it served as the best neutral location for the two teams. Kansas won the first battle between the two schools 22-10 before an estimated crowd of 2,000 attendees. Each school had a new coach at the helm of the team, Hal Reid for Missouri and English professor Edwin M. Hopkins for Kansas. In the early years of football between the schools, it would be nearly yearly or every couple of years that the head coach would change for both schools for various reasons, but usually due to the coaches' expense for a sport that was considered by the universities a recreational hobby.

Although teams travelled by train, the main local mode of transportation was still by foot and horse, the invention and patenting of the first internal combustion flat engine of the automo-

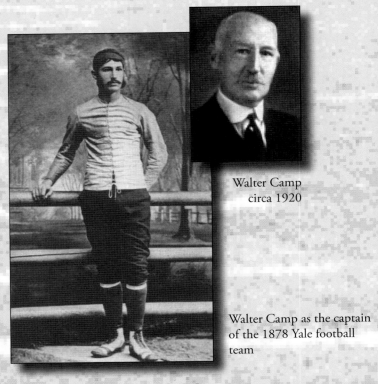

Walter Camp
circa 1920

Walter Camp as the captain of the 1878 Yale football team

bile occurring in 1896. Travel for the two teams, therefore, could be relatively expensive for that time and time-consuming affairs. All games, save one, between Missouri and Kansas occurred in Kansas City until the Missouri Valley Intercollegiate Athletic Association passed a rule prohibiting schools from having contests anywhere but on school campuses.

In 1892, the Border War Game between Missouri and Kansas became a Thanksgiving Day game, featured as a season-ending climax for the two schools. This year, Missouri had its first mascot in a bulldog named "Grover Cleveland." Both Thanksgiving Day games and bulldog mascots were becoming common components to the game of football at this time, with a Thanksgiving "Turkey Day" game serving other eastern rivals as the climax to their seasons.

The year of 1892 is also significant because that is the year that football began to formerly transform from the game of rugby. Yale's first coach, Walter Chauncey Camp, known as the "Father of American Football," in 1888 had advocated several changes to the game of rugby in order to improve it. Over a twenty-year period of time, the changes that occurred in the game as a result of Camp's suggestions included; the invention of a two-point "safety" for tackling an opponent in their end zone, the replacement of the "scrum" with a "scrimmage" and a field dividing "line of scrimmage," a system of "downs" for advancing the ball, which originally was three downs to make five yards for

The Missouri Tigers in an informal team photograph in 1890

a renewed series of downs, the lessening of 14 players per team on the field to 11 and the organization of a seven-man offensive line and a four-man backfield.

In 1895, Missouri had a new coach at their helm C. D. "Pop" Bliss, who had come to Missouri from Yale. The field on which the team played was changed to run East-West, with the Rollins family paying part of the cost for the grading and drainage of the field. A track was installed around the football field and, for the first time, bleachers were erected, 600 on the southern side for the home team and 250 for the visiting team on the northern side. The curators had wrought-iron gates erected around the field, enclosing it for the first time and they also named the field after the family that had contributed so much to the University and the field's development-Rollins Field.

Pop Bliss was a former star player from Yale and he imposed perhaps the strictest rules for players up to that point, forbidding them from smoking and drinking and the players were also

"Pop" Bliss

forced into curfews. Bliss' discipline worked for the team, the season ending 7-1, defeating Kansas 10-6 in their fifth game of the series. Unfortunately for Missouri, despite beating Kansas, the Western Football Association inexplicably awarded Kansas the title of the Big Four Conference Champion because Missouri had lost a conference game to Nebraska. Kansas' 6-1 record also was a conference loss coming from Missouri, which caused Missouri to strongly consider leaving the league.

Pop Bliss' leadership came at a stiff price at that time for a coach, $500-$700 a month, causing his departure from the team after one season. He was replaced by another Yale athlete, Frank Patterson. Patterson was reported to have been a popular person amongst his team and did not seem to be as strict as his predecessor, both in regards to Bliss' previously established social rules for the players and in regards to the rules set forth by the league and the school. During the 1896 season, the antics of the team included the slugging of an official at a game, an unauthorized trip to Texas and Mexico, and the use of players that were not enrolled at the school, which was acknowledged, at least in part, in the seven-page description in the *Savitar* yearbook; "The M. S. U football team started on the longest and most interesting trip ever taken by an American college football team. Little idea did they have as they volleyed forth their farewell, Tiger, Tiger, M. S. U., of the great deeds they were destined to accomplish or the awful consequences that were to follow their acts of youthful

indiscretion."

Missouri ended the 1896 season 7-5, but earned five of their victories as part of their excursion to Texas and Mexico. The failure of the season and the team's exploits in Texas and Mexico caused the University of Missouri to take control of intercollegiate athletics for the first time, so that they could make the decisions for the football team. Despite a faculty movement to eliminate athletics from Missouri, athletics and the football team were allowed to continue at the behest of Missouri State University President Richard Jesse, however, Coach Patterson was fired and the team captain, Tom Shawhan, and the team manager, George H. English, were suspended indefinitely for their roles in managing the team and for taking the unauthorized trip to Texas and Mexico, which the University Council had previously forbade them from doing. Until the incidents of the 1896 season, the University and the University Council had no real power over the Athletic Association, causing the team to take the trip to Texas and Mexico on their own initiative, despite the University Council's refusal to authorize the trip when presented to them by Patterson. The Athletic Association president was also replaced with a newly titled Director of Athletics.

At Kansas, a great deal of concern was also developing regarding its football program. Initially, Kansas' teams were ones that were played strictly by students, who did so successfully, but in 1893 and 1894 the teams did not fair as well, prompting alumni to intervene. As a result, Kansas boosters began recruiting paid athletes and also saw that academically ineligible and players that were not enrolled at the University be allowed to play on the team.

Changing control of the program at Missouri saved its demise, but it did not save it from Kansas. In 1899, the series between the two teams stood at 7-2, fa-

"Hurry-up" Yost

vouring Kansas. Kansas had at its helm a first, one-year coach who would later join the College Hall of Fame for his long and storied career with the University of Michigan, Fielding Harris "Hurry Up" Yost. Yost earned his nickname from the term that often preceded his instructions to his players, "Hurry up and..." Yost's Kansas team in 1899 beat Missouri 34-6, and became the school's first undefeated and untied season.

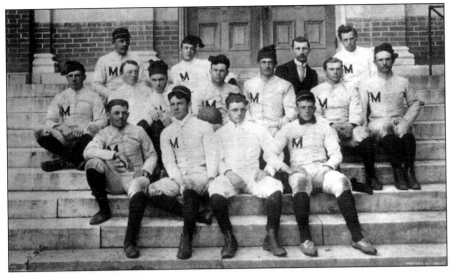

MU Football Captain
William Robinson Littell

Missouri Football (1-2) - Head Coach Austin Lee McRae

(Unordered) Captain William Robinson Littell, Benjamin Franklin Goslin, George Pentzer Whitsett, Aytchmonde Perrin Shull, William Pleasant Records, William Edward Gordon, Charles Alexander Keith, Dennis William Kane, Mordecai Miller Maughs Bogie, Daniel Lee Shawhan, Burton Maude Thompson, Benjamin Richard Graham, John Harry La Motte, James Milton Denny, Henry Roberts Terrill, Harris Lancaster Moore, Oliver Neal Axtell.

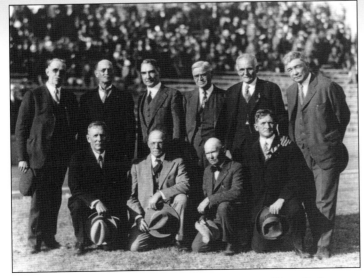

(Left) Although a team photograph was never made in 1890, some Kansas football players reunited 40 years later in 1930. Will J. Coleman was a player and served as the team's coach that first year.

KU Football Captain
Howard Peairs

Kansas Football (1-2) - Head Coach Will J. Coleman

(Roster) Cook, LE; Champlin, LT; Frederick; LG; Coleman, C; Captain Peairs, RG; Huddleston, RT; Hogg, RE; Williamson, QB; Sherman, HB; Kinzie, HB; Dyer, FB. Substitutes: Baldridge, Kutz, Case, Hudson.

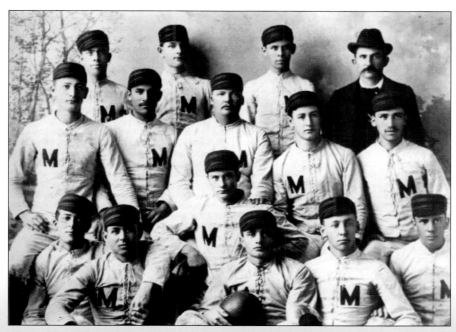

Missouri Football (3-1) - Head Coach Hal Reid

MU Football Captain
Curtis Hill

KU Football Captain
Wilbur John Kinzie

Kansas Football (6-1-1) - Head Coach Edwin Mortimer Hopkins

(Roster) Fred Dobson, LE; F. S. Jewett, LT; C. W. Frederick, LG; Will J. Coleman, C; A. E. Huddleston, RG; G. Mendell, RT; W. H. H. Piatt, RE; O. K. Williamson, QB; Wilbur Kinzie, HB; A. F. Sherman, HB; A. R. Champlin, HB; Archie Hogg, FB. Substitutes: Howard Peairs, RG; R. D. Brown, C; W. H. Kutz, Chas. W. Baldridge, Dean Foster, R. D. Brown, Paul Hudson, John Mustard. Thornton Cook, LE.

MU Football Captain
Daniel Lee Shawhan

Missouri Football (1-2) - Head Coach E. H. Jones

KU Football Captain
Wilbur John Kinzie

Kansas Football (7-1) - Head Coach Alvin Wayland Shepard
Western Intercollegiate Association Champion
Row 1: L. W. Springer, O. K. "Swede" Williamson. Row 2: Coach Alvin Wayland Shepard, M. B. Mendell, A. E. Huddleston, A. R. Champlin, Will J. Coleman, Wilbur John Kinzie, W. A. Matteson. Row 3: F. A. Lutz, Foster, W. H. H. Piatt, Bert "Shorty" Hammill, Manager Moody, Chester W. Dumm, Foster, Hickey. Not Present: O. C. Hill, W. H. Kutz, Hugh Means, W. E. Higgins.

Missouri Football (4-3) - Head Coach Harry Orman Robinson
Western Intercollegiate Association Co-Champion

MU Football Captain
Charles E. Young

Kansas Football (2-5) - Head Coach Alvin Wayland Shepard
Western Intercollegiate Association Co-Champion
Row 1: Captain Champlin, Williamson, Shepard, Will McMurray. Row 2: Johnson, Harvey, Griffith, Coleman, Mattison, Art McMurray, Wilson. Row 3: Armour, Jantzen, Steinberger, Piatt, Hamill, Manager Moody, Rothrock, Shellenbarger.

KU Football Captain
A. R. Champlin

Missouri Football (4-3) - Head Coach Harry Orman Robinson
Western Intercollegiate Association Co-Champion

MU Football Captain
Charles E. Young

Kansas Football (2-3-1) - Head Coach Hector W. Cowan

KU Football Captain
O. K. Williamson

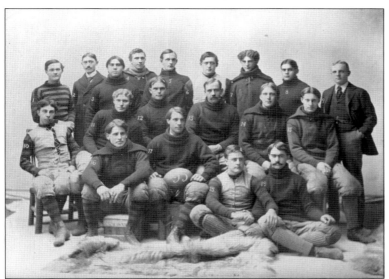

**Missouri Football (7-1) - Head Coach Clifford Douglas Bliss
Western Intercollegiate Association Co-Champion**

MU Football Captain
Charles E. Young

**Kansas Football (6-1) - Head Coach Hector W. Cowan
Western Intercollegiate Association Co-Champions**
(Unordered) Burney, Pope, Gump, Mastin, Nester, Cowan, Palmer, Hamill, Piatt,
Kennedy, Walken, Mitchell, Stone, Hill, Griff, Williamson, Outland, Fletcher,
Crooks, Gaines, Griffith.

KU Football Captain
W. H. H. Piatt

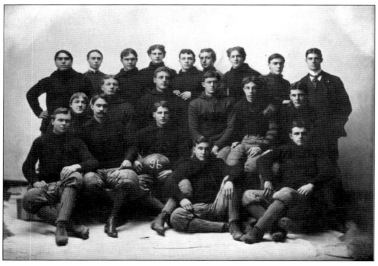

Missouri Football (7-5) - Head Coach Frank M. Patterson
Row 1: Swearingen, Evans, Captain Shawhan, Hall, Jones. Row 2: Blanton, White,
J. Hill, A. Hill, Sinnett, Corrigan. Row 3: McAlester, English, Conley, Dowdall,
Brandon, W. Hill, Tucker, Perry, Coach Patterson.

MU Football Captain
Thomas Redmon Shawhan

Kansas Football (7-3) - Head Coach Hector W. Cowan

KU Football Captain
B. D. Hamill

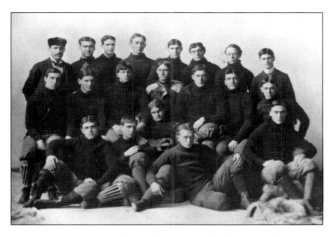

Missouri Football (5-6) - Head Coach Charles Young
Row 1: Jones, Bungard, Liggett, Cramer, Perry. Row 2: Harris, Corrigan, Parker, Howard, Captain Hill, Killiam, Gentry. Row 3: Coach Young, Phillips, Crawford, Woodson, Robertson, Troy, Kirk, Dewey.

MU Football Captain
Adam Hill

Kansas Football (8-2) - Head Coach Wylie G. Woodruff
Row 1: Simpson, McKay, Spear, Buzzi. Row 2: Teas, Walker, Captain Kennedy, Poorman, Hess.
Row 3: Coach McKinnie, Wheeler, Blockberger, Boigts, Mosse, Games, Avery, Woodruff.

KU Football Captain
Albert Rutherford Kennedy

MU Football Captain
Thomas P. Howard

Missouri Football (1-4-1) - Head Coach David Lewis Fultz
(Unordered) Captain Howard, McCaslin, Harris, Houx, Parker, Hunter, Dunn, Mossman, Harding, Kramer, Cooper, McAlester, Jenkins, Corrigan, Kirk, Jewett, Peper, Mills, Liggett, Keenan.

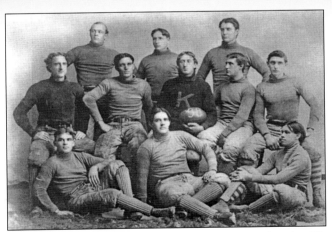

KU Football Captain
Arthur St. Leger Mosse

Kansas Football (7-2) - Head Coach Wylie G. Woodruff
Row 1: Row 1: Silvers, Woodward, Owen. Row 2: Avery, Buzzi, Captain Mosse, Tucker, Simpson.
Row 3: Smith, Wilcox, Hamill.

Missouri Football (9-2) - Head Coach David Lewis Fultz

MU Football Captain
John Kramer

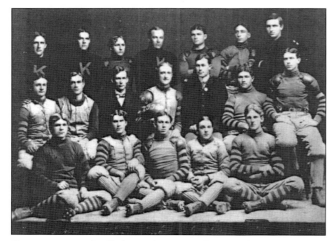

Kansas Football (10-0) - Head Coach Fielding Harris Yost

KU Football Captain
Hubert Avery

FOOT BALL ASSOCIATION

The following named students of the M. S. U. assembled on the evening of October 10th, 1890, for the purpose of considering the feasibility of starting an Athletic Association in the University: G. P. Whitsett, B. M. Thompson and W. P. Records, L., S., '92; W. R. Littell, C. A. Keith, D. W. Kane and A. P. Shull, L. S., '91; C. Hill, W. E. Gordon and D. L. Shawhan, Eng., '93; and H. L. Moore, Acad., 93.

Dr. A. L. McRae was present and stated that while in St. Louis recently he had talked with some of the students of Washington University, and that they were anxious to meet the students of the M. S. U. in athletic contests.

After discussing the situation and considering the various obstacles in the way of such a movement, it was voted as the sense of the meeting that owing to the lack of funds and to the general apathy in regard to athletic among the students, it would be impossible to form a general athletic association at that time but that a special effort be made to organize a foot ball team to form the nucleus of a future athletic association. Various committees were appointed and the meeting adjourned to meet again Monday night.

At the meeting Monday night, October 13th, 1890, the following named students signified their willingness to join a foot ball association and to try for a place on the team:

LAW SCHOOL

'91.	'92.
William Robinson Littell.	George Pentzer Whitsett.
Charles Alexander Keith.	Burton Maude Thompson.
Dennis William Kane.	William Pleasant Records.
Aytchmonde Perrin Shull.	Mordecai Miller Maughs Bogie.

ENGINEERING SCHOOL.

'92.	'93.
Samuel Farder Crecelius.	Curtis Hill.
Oliver Frank Ray.	William Edward Gordon.
	Daniel Lee Shawhan.

ACADEMIC SCHOOL.

'92.	'93.
James Milton Denny.	Harris Lancaster Moore.
John Harry LaMotte.	Jesse James Duncan.

'94.
Benjamin Richard Graham.
Mark McCausland Anderson.

An organization was effected by the election of the following officers:

Austin Lee McRae, *President*.
Samuel Farder Crecelius, *Secretary*.
Dennis William Kane, *Treasurer*.

It was voted that a team be organized to play Washington University at St. Louis on Thanksgiving Day, 1890.

William Robinson Littell was elected Captain, and A. L. McRae, Manager, of the team.

Executive Committee.

A. L. McRae.	W. R. Littell.
C. A. Keith.	G. P. Whitsett.
B. M. Thompson.	

The general management and raising the necessary funds for uniforming the team was placed in the hands of the executive com[m]ittee.

The Foot Ball Association cleared one hundred dollars above expenses, and, at a meeting of the members held December 5th, 1890, it was voted to turn this money over to the students of the University for the purpose of forming a general athletic association. This proposition being accepted by the students, Messrs. Keith, Whitsett and Bogie were appointed a committee to frame a constitution for the new association. The report of the committee was adopted December 12th, and the Athletic Association duly organized December 15th, 1890, by the election of a president, vice-president, secretary, treasurer and eleven class directors.

At the beginning the Association was badly handicapped by having no athletic field or gymnasium facilities. In spite of these difficulties, a base ball team was equipped which has won two out of four games played during the year; a tennis tournament for the championship of the University, and a University field day meeting were held; the Board of Curators have set apart grounds for an athletic field. Finally the publication of a College Annual has been inaugurated.

Written for the 1891 Athletic Association Yearbook

(The background is a photograph of Austin Lee McRae)

BIRTH OF A RIVALRY

At first glance, the Kansas-Missouri football rivalry would appear to have all the ingredients of any great gridiron rivalry. In the first place, it has proven to be remarkably even. As of the 2007 season when the 116th game in the series was played, the second oldest Division IA rivalry stood but one game in the Jayhawks' favor at 54-53-9. However, since Kansas was compelled to forfeit its 1960 victory, Missouri fans can reasonably claim that the series stands in their favor at 54-53-9.

Further, through the years the underdog has come out on top nearly as often as the favorite, which is quite possibly the signature characteristic of classic gridiron rivalries. Although a favored Missouri team soundly defeated Kansas in November, 2006, the last few years provide ample evidence of this. In 2005, for instance, the Tigers had entered the game as six point favorites but wound up losing to the Jayhawks 13-3.

Likewise, in 2004 the Jayhawks defeated their archrivals 31-14 despite entering the game as nine and a half point underdogs and the 2003 contest saw an unranked Kansas squad knock off a ranked Missouri team that the Las Vegas oddsmakers favored by more than 10 points. What is more, the rivalry has roots that stretch back as far as "Bleeding Kansas," a prologue to the Civil War, well before the first football game was played on any college campus.

In short, the Kansas-Missouri rivalry has everything associated with the great collegiate football rivalries except for one thing: maniacal, unbridled passion. Fans of the Tigers and Jayhawks don't spend 364 days talking about the previous match up and anticipating the next showdown. Most sports fans in Lawrence live for March, not for September, which is hardly surprising since Kansas has developed into a "basketball" rather than a "football school." This was not, however, always the case. There was a time when fans of the flagship universities of Missouri and Kansas thought football was the quintessential college sport, when fans of the defeated team could not shrug their shoulders at yet another loss and console themselves because their team had played hard.

The heyday of the football rivalry between Missouri and Kansas came in the first few decades of the 20th century when the game had fewer rules, less protective equipment and served as a proving ground for the players' masculinity rather than as a cash cow feeding network television and university coffers. It was a rivalry, which thanks to the legacy of historical antipathy between the residents of Kansas and Missouri had seemed old at its very beginning. It witnessed its first tussle in Kansas City's Exposition Park on Halloween Day 1891 when the Jayhawker and Tiger gridiron squads re-ignited a "Border War" which had lain dormant since before the start of the Civil War.

As the *Lawrence Journal-World* pointed out in the days lead-

ing up to the first football clash between Missouri and Kansas, the prospect of a Tigers-Jayhawkers tangle had "awaken[ed] a great deal of interest" among the alumni of the two schools and throughout the region. This might be expected since Lee's surrender to Grant at Appomattox had taken place scarcely a quarter century earlier, and undoubtedly many still lived who had donned either gray or blue uniforms and had been witnesses to the events of Bleeding Kansas. But even many of those too young to remember Quantrill's raid on Lawrence or the theft of Missourians' property by Jayhawkers, found themselves intrigued by the match up.

Not surprisingly, the weeks leading up to the contest had seen the regional papers cover virtually every aspect of the impending clash. Sketches of the 14 players from each squad, the 11 starters and three reserves, had appeared in various Kansas and Missouri publications. Although no formal line was set, the match was pretty well handicapped. The Missouri eleven had less experience than their opponents from Lawrence, but were a shade heavier and didn't have the sorts of injury problems that burdened Kansas, which would be forced to take the field with its best player sidelined. John Kinzie, the captain of the Jayhawkers, had been hurt in an intra-squad scrimmage and "was not sufficiently recovered … to play." On top of that, two other Kansas starters were hurt but capable of playing. Despite these medical casualties, however, consensus opinion favored Kansas in the showdown.

On the Thursday before the first Kansas-Missouri gridiron contest, the *Kansas City Star* reported, "All the preliminaries for the opening game of the Missouri and Kansas series of football matches [had been] completed." The University of Kansas squad had received its first crimson uniforms three days prior to the Saturday clash and so would be sporting them for the first time in the Jayhawker-Tiger showdown that was to launch the University's second football season. Crimson had been selected as the University's "athletic color" earlier in the month, while the official school colors still remained yellow and blue. Transportation concerns had been ameliorated when, recognizing the appeal of the game, all of the rail lines connecting Lawrence to Kansas City offered specials on their tickets. The Wyandotte and Northwestern road would claim the lion's share of the business as it dropped its rates first, to one dollar for a round trip ticket. The other lines would eventually match the price, but by then they had lost their chance at snaring a significant portion of the Lawrence-Kansas City traffic.

Arranging the "preliminaries for the opening game of the Missouri and Kansas series" had proven somewhat more difficult for the men from Columbia since they had had to make all of their arrangements for the game without the support of the university they represented. Indeed the University of Missouri's "faculty and president" were "opposed to the team [going] to Kansas City" to meet the Jayhawker squad and consequently had not even proven amenable to furnishing the squad with "a room [on campus] in which to hold a mass meeting to arouse enthusiasm for the game." Nonetheless, the Tigers had made reservations at the Centropolis Hotel, vowed to bring pro-Missouri "rooters" with them, and were "confident of winning the game."

At 6:30 Friday evening, the night before the game, the Missouri squad quietly disembarked from their train and made their way to the hotel. Less than 12 hours later, the first fans arriving from Columbia would shatter the stillness of the Halloween morning by shouting "Rah! Rah! M.S.U.! Missouri University! Ray! Rah! Rue!" By 9:45 on Saturday morning, it was Kansas' turn to arrive, and downtown Kansas City rang with Kansas' "Rock Chalk" cheer as the men from Lawrence and 200 or so students, including, as the *Kansas City Star* noted, "about thirty ladies," made their way to the Coates House, which was to serve as "University headquarters" for the game. As one of the most conspicuous manifestations of university pride, college cheers were taken very seriously at that time. Indeed, the Friday edition of the *Kansas City Star* had published the words to both the Missouri and Kansas cheers as an aid for those planning to attend the following day's contest. Meanwhile, other Missouri and Kansas fans trickled into the city through various means, including five determined Kansas students who lacked the money to purchase a rail ticket and had walked the 39 miles [63 km] from Mount Oread to Exposition Park.

Nonetheless, most of those who filled the bleachers as the inaugural Tiger-Jayhawker football game prepared to get underway that afternoon called Kansas City home. The *Kansas City Star* estimated that about 300 of the approximately 3,000 people who attended the first game had actually come from Lawrence. As the University of Missouri was farther from the field than was Kansas, it seems unlikely that more than that number arrived from Columbia. Thus perhaps only one quarter of the fans watching the showdown were from either college town.

The Kansas contingent made its way to Exposition Park first "and promptly took possession of the west bleachers." In contrast to the University of Missouri's official lack of support for the game, Kansas Chancellor Francis Snow and about 15 other faculty members from Lawrence ranked among those bedecked with crimson ribbons, sashes and neckties. At that time, of course, standard attire for sporting events was more formal than the present-day. Women generally wore dresses and men wore suits and hats. Thus support for the University wasn't demonstrated through sweatshirts and T-shirts, but rather through ribbons of the school's color adorning the hair of

women and hats of men as well as through sashes and neckties.

As Kansas supporters "yelled themselves hoarse" Missouri fans flooded into the stadium and soon the "college cries of the rival universities filled the air," Taunts arose as well, especially from the Missouri "rooters" who jeered the "Kansas crowd with the epithet 'Rainmakers,'" a mocking reference to the ongoing and largely unsuccessful attempts of the Sunflower State to artificially increase precipitation through such means as planting trees and setting off explosions. Kansas professor Lucien Blake recently had publicized his theory that exploding a squadron of small balloons in the atmosphere would produce the necessary conditions to cause rain.

Lucien Ira Blake

At 2:40 in the afternoon, 10 minutes later than the scheduled kickoff time, the event which "for the past three weeks … [had] been the sole topic [of discussion] in college circles in both states" got underway. Things started off poorly for the Jayhawkers as Missouri won the toss, consequently chose to defend the south goal, and claimed the first possession. On their first play, the Tigers reeled off a long run that brought them into Kansas territory. Three plays later, a Missouri halfback slipped around the left end and galloped in for a touchdown. The Missouri kicker, however, "made a sorry attempt, kicking too low" and so Missouri led 4-0. At the time, a touchdown was worth four points, a field goal five points and a conversion two points.

Kansas rebounded quickly. On their next possession, the Jayhawkers plunged into the end zone for a score, tying up the game, but they were just beginning. The men from Lawrence managed two more touchdowns before the half and were about to score another when time was called. As it was, after the men in crimson had crossed the goal line for their third score, fullback Archie Hogg converted the only "extra point" of the day to give the Jayhawkers a 14-4 lead.

Archibald Hogg

Hogg had also set up the score by kicking the ball into the end zone where one of his teammates fell on it. This, of course, would not be allowed today, but the rules of football at the time differed but little from those of rugby. Indeed on the day of the game, the *Kansas City Star* announced, "American Rugby rules [would] govern the match." Despite the fact that half time "probably prevented the Kansans from scoring another touchdown," the west bleachers were "one mass of waving streamers of bloody hue, while the Kansas University cry filled the air."

After the 10-minute break, the Tiger squad apparently regrouped as it stopped Kansas for several consecutive Jayhawker possessions. Unfortunately for the men from Columbia, they couldn't take advantage of Kansas' stalled offense. When Missouri's starting left end went down with a sprained ankle, Kansas' Hogg, who was the hero of the game, swept around the left side for a touchdown; extending his team's advantage to 14. A few minutes later, the Kansas fullback made "the most brilliant play of the game" when he fielded a punt, feinted as if he intended to kick it back down the field, tucked the ball away and rolled down the sideline for a score.

Trailing by 18 points, the "Missourians grew desperate and did what they should have [done] earlier in the game, go through by mere force of weight." Just before the final whistle blew, Kansas allowed a Tiger back to roll "out from under the struggling heap of humanity clear of the bunch and [score] Missouri's second touchdown."

When the game ended in a 22-8 Kansas victory, a "mighty yell went up from the Kansas delegation and they broke into the field and carried off the victorious team while the Missouri eleven quietly disappeared." In the hours after the game, delirious Jayhawker supporters, "enveloped in crimson bunting," paraded through the streets of Kansas City lifting their beloved "Rock Chalk" cry time and again.

When the team returned to Lawrence at 10:00 that night, "an enthusiastic reception committee" greeted its members. Chancellor Snow and a number of professors, who had apparently returned earlier than the team, led the throng awaiting the victorious squad. The crowd "marched through town and proceeded to celebrate the great victory by bonfire," which was held in South Park at the "urgent request of the mayor, who stated that the city had no fire protection." The celebration of the Jayhawker triumph over the Tigers and of Halloween continued long after the fire had been reduced to smoldering coals. The exuberant students, the *Lawrence Journal-World* informed its readers, remained "out all night doing considerable harmless mischief."

Francis Huntington Snow

"A return game," the *Kansas City Star* reported on the Monday after the game, had been "talked of for Thanksgiving Day," but the talk of such a rematch did not come to fruition, at least for that year. Indeed, although 1891 and 1892 saw the football Jayhawkers roll up an impressive record of 14-1-1, neither year saw a Thanksgiving Day clash between Missouri and Kansas. In 1893, however, the squads from Lawrence and Columbia initiated a tradition of Turkey Day battles held for many years

afterward and establishing itself and the oldest Thanksgiving Day game west of the Mississippi River.

By Mark D. Hersey, Ph.D.
Kansas Alumnus 2006
Written for This Week in KU History
www.KUHistory.com

TRUMAN AND THE TIGERS

Shortly after the first football team was formed in 1890, the athletic committee chose to adopt the team name "Tigers" in recognition of the Civil War militia organized to repel the expected attack of "Bloody Bill" Anderson and his Confederate guerilla force, though the attack never came.

Originally, the Tigers were depicted in various nameless incarnations, but a contest was finally held to name the tiger in 1984. The winning name was "Truman," after the Missouri politician, President Harry S. Truman.

By Shawn Buchanan Greene
@$%#&! Alumnus 1991
Written Monday, November 3, 2008

Despite protestations from her Jayhawker father, the Tiger may have this girl's tail.

THIRTY YEARS OF RIVALRY

The close of the 1920 gridiron season marked the thirtieth milestone of Varsity football at the University of Kansas. Although the game was first played here in the early eighties, it was not organized nor did it come to stay as a collegiate sport until 1890.

During this 30-year period Kansas has had two all-victorious teams, in 1891 and in 1908. The first football association to which the University belonged was the Triangular League with Washburn and Baker, but this was dissolved in 1893 by the withdrawal of Washburn, Iowa, Missouri, Nebraska and Kansas composed the Interstate Association, organized in 1892, and in 1907 K. U. became a member of the Missouri Valley Conference, the present organization.

The team of 1890, of which no group photograph is in existence, won two of its three games. The first K. U. football game was played Nov. 22, 1890, on a Massachusetts street vacant lot, between 14th and 15th. Kansas defeated Baker, 22 to 9, in the historic opening game. The feature of the combat was the first field goal in Missouri Valley history, made by Sherman, Kansas right half. The Baker team could not fathom the new play, and stood looking on while it was being made.

Though Baker, the great rival in those days, is officially credited with the final game of the season, no Kansas rooter would admit the victory. Coleman, K. U. center, ran 107 yards to a touchdown, but was called back and informed that one of the officials had called the game. The Kansas rooters swarmed on the field and the game ended.

Prof. Edwin M. Hopkins, still at the University as a professor of English, was the first football coach and manager. The three games of 1890, according to him, were merely preliminary, since football on an organized, scheduled basis did not begin till 1891. It was at about this time that Uncle Jimmy Green, as a member of the Athletic Board, began to be interested in the game and won his title, "The Dean of Football," which he bore till his death, in 1919.

On the back of a picture in the trophy room at the gym is the inscription: "Kansas University Football Team which Won Renown in the Fall of 1891, not Being Defeated Once." Then follows a record of seven victories, including two games with Baker, two with Washburn and the first Missouri battle. Lawrence business men presented the team with gold watch fobs in honor of their showing, which it will be noted bear the inscription "First Season."

The first Kansas-Missouri game was played in Kansas City Oct. 31, 1891, and resulted in a 22 to 8 victory for K. U. The write-up in the *Kansas City Star* of next day gives an interesting picture of the game as played thirty years ago. It begins:

About the time the shadows of the tall grandstand had crept to the outer edge of Exposition Park yesterday afternoon a crowd of 22 young men, dressed in parti-colored uniforms, might have been seen piled in a heap three or four yards from the place that marks the home plate of the baseball diamond. Crimson and black stockinged legs stuck out at various angles, heads covered with crimson and old gold and black caps bobbed in and out and hands waved in the air signals of distress.

Now and then one of the young men would jump up and fall back uttering a yell of exultation. At length a shrill whistle sounded. A voice called "Time!" and the mass of men immediately dissolved into 22 different people. The ones uniformed in the white suits and crimson stockings were picked up by a crowd of yelling people who bore them off on their shoulders shouting "Rock Chalk! Jay Hawk! K. U.!" The others, dressed in white uniforms, black stockings and old gold caps, walked off the field by themselves and the long-lookcd-for game between the elevens representing the two universities was over.

1891 KU gold watch fob
presented to each player

Typical of early football tactics is the following from the same article:

> The Missourians formed a V with "Baby" Rummans in the center and the ball in Bradley's hands. Amid the encouraging shouts of their supporters, both teams rushed solidly into each other. When the Missourians had finished shoving the ball was 20 yards from where the play started.

The game was much rougher than at present, and was played in 45-minute halves. Substitutions were not permitted except in cases of serious injury or disqualification. The ball was put into play by a species of kick-off in which the kicker touched the ball with his foot, then picked it up and carried it. Interference usually assumed the form of a flying wedge.

1892 KU backfield: (L-R) Champlin, Williamson, Piatt, Kinzie.

Thirty years have seen sweeping changes in the game inaugurated here by the pioneers of 1890 and 1891. It has become the major college sport, with its season the most prominent activity of every year. A more humane though no less virile game than in those days, it has been expanded to a scale they never dreamed of.

Every supporter of the team that is now will hope these veterans of the days that were can be present at the formal opening of the new memorial stadium. It is only fitting, as has been proposed, that these men who built McCook and laid the foundation of the great Jayhawk spirit should be guests of honor at the opening of an era for their Alma Mater as great as any they ever imagined in their pioneer beginnings.

Written for the 1921 Jayhawker *Yearbook*

Kansas against Baker, in Lawrence, December 8, 1890

The first uniforms were for the most part made by the mothers of the players, and were of white canvas. In 1891 the Athletic Association furnished uniforms, the men to supply their own shoes. The suits cost about $4. The players wore crimson serge caps with peaks of a style affected by other football teams of the period. Protective gear such as is worn now was unknown in those days and according to the early day players would have been scorned.

James J. McCook of New York made a considerable donation to the athletic fund in 1891, and the playing field purchased from ex-Governor Robinson was named in his honor. The players themselves did all the manual labor in fitting up the field. They also erected the first grandstand, which stood at the northwest corner.

TURKEY AND CRANBERRY SAUCE

While many families in Kansas City dined on turkey and cranberry sauce in the warmth of their houses, a steady, cold wind whipped through the bleachers of the city's Exposition Park, making it difficult for the 3,000 or so people watching the inaugural Kansas-Missouri Thanksgiving Day football game to keep warm. Despite the weather, the *Lawrence Journal-World* and *Evening Tribune* boasted the following day that the game "was witnessed by the biggest crowd ever gathered for an athletic event in the west." This probably was a bit of an exaggeration, since the turnout differed little from that of the two previous encounters of the football squads.

A number of prominent state officials, including Kansas' Populist Governor Lorenzo D. Lewelling, had turned out to watch what was already a bitter football rivalry. As fate would have it, the Kansas supporters would have little to cheer about. The hated Tigers of Missouri would overwhelm the Jayhawker squad and earn their first gridiron victory against Kansas.

Lorenzo Lewelling

Little went right for the men from Lawrence that day. Less than two minutes into the game, Missouri's star, a fellow by the name of Thompson, broke through Kansas' line "as though it was made of paper instead of bone and muscle," blocked a punt, scooped up the ball and returned it for a touchdown. Surprised by their early good luck, the Missouri fans "roared forth with 'Tiger! Tiger! M.S.U.!'" While the Kansas players tried to regroup, "canes were broken, hats were thrown and Missouri went wild." The ensuing kick made the score 6-0 in favor of the Tigers. At the time, a touchdown was worth four points and the kick after two.

Taken aback, the Jayhawkers promptly gave their fans something to cheer about as well when they proceeded to drive the ball inside the Missouri five-yard line on the ensuing possession. However, the Kansas men squandered the opportunity by fumbling away their possession. After getting the ball back the Kansas eleven again drove to the Tiger's goal line, but the squad from Columbia made a determined stand and forced Kansas to surrender the ball on downs. Finally, after holding Missouri, the Jayhawks managed a touchdown but missed the ensuing kick, and so trailed 6-4. A promising Missouri drive was interrupted by halftime, but in spite of the reprieve the men from Lawrence still found themselves behind on the scoreboard.

The second half would prove equally disappointing for Kansas. In their frustration and eagerness to defeat the Tigers, they were penalized time and again for being off sides. Several times during the second half the game was stopped for injuries,

although in an era in which football provided an opportunity for young men to prove their masculinity and toughness, the hurt players were not inclined to leave the field. A Missouri player, for example, "went down with his leg badly sprained," but after being attended to by a doctor, "pronounced himself all right" and returned to the contest. After his return, tempers began to flare and "some of the players took occasion to indulge in a little fist fighting." As such scrapping befitted a rivalry game, the referees didn't penalize anyone.

In "one of the mix-ups," a Kansas player by the name of Coleman got his nose so badly broken that his "face was covered with blood and he looked like a prize fighter who had just been knocked out." Like his injured Missouri counterpart, however, Coleman insisted on staying in the game. However, when he was again bloodied, Coleman was helped to the sidelines and replaced by a teammate named Harvey, whom the Lawrence Journal-World identified as "the colored boy." The newspaper, revealing the racial biases of many Kansans at the time, continued that the presence of Harvey on the field "weakened the team" and helped spell doom for his Jayhawkers.

With about ten minutes left in the game, Missouri scored another touchdown and converted the kick as well, increasing the Tiger lead to eight. Down by at least two scores, the Kansas squad began "playing without hope" and Missouri might have won by a final score of 18-4 if the referee had not ruled that time had expired before the team from Columbia crashed across Kansas' goal line on the last play of the game. Thus Kansas' season ended on a loss, and worse, with a record of 5-2, the Jayhawkers had allowed Missouri to tie them for the Western Inter-collegiate Football Association crown.

Disappointed by the defeat and unwilling to concede that their rivals had fielded a better team, students on Mount Oread and other Jayhawker supporters hunted around for excuses. Some blamed the overconfidence of the Kansas eleven, while others found the cause of the failure in the fact that the team had no real coach. A fellow by the name of A. W. Shephard served both as the team's right end and its coach. Others looked to the injuries that had prevented two of Kansas' starters from competing at all and forced Coleman from the game.

Further, added Jayhawker apologists, the team had not been adequately rested following its "severe drubbing at the hands of Michigan" the prior week, and consequently no team "member was in good condition" for the showdown with the Tigers in Kansas City. The previous year, Kansas had allowed its second teamers to play at Baker the week before the Missouri game and "had saved her best men for [the] all important game" against Missouri. In words that would echo through much of the twentieth century, the *Lawrence Journal-World* declared that for Kansas to field a winning team in subsequent years, it would need to "work harder, practice more, play better, talk less and get a coach."

Although Kansas lost the first Thanksgiving Day game held in Kansas City, the men from Mount Oread would dominate this holiday series in the Midwest metropolis until its abrupt end in 1910. In the 17 gridiron contests between the Tigers and Jayhawks held in Kansas City on Thanksgiving Day between 1893 and 1910, the University of Kansas lost only four, also winning a Turkey Day showdown held in Saint Joseph, Missouri in 1907. Despite the lopsided nature of the rivalry early on, by 1906 the *Kansas City Star* could rightly assert that the annual Thanksgiving Day clash had come to play so prominent a part in buttressing the universities' pride that the students and alumni of the two schools gave "thanks on that day because there [was] such a game as football."

By Mark D. Hersey, Ph.D.
Kansas Alumnus 2006
Written for This Week in KU History
www.KUHistory.com

From the late 1870s through the mid-1890s, the official colors of the University of Kansas were sky blue and corn yellow. The derivation of these original choices remains uncertain. One account indicates Kansas' first graduating class made the selection. Another explanation suggests that Kansas' first Board of Regents, which had modeled its charter on the one used by the University of Michigan, adopted that school's colors as well. Wherever these first colors came from, little use was made of them prior to the inception of intercollegiate athletics at Kansas in 1890. When Kansas athletic teams started facing off against rival squads from other universities, however, greater attention was turned to the color question.

By the fall of 1891, the University's athletic board was debating changing the yellow and blue to a less delicate palette that would show fewer stains of the sort so frequently acquired in games of football and baseball. The board sought a single, distinguished, and somewhat darker color. Since certain elements at Kansas were then imbued with the belief that the school could become the "Harvard of the West," it is perhaps not surprising that crimson was selected in October 1891.

When word leaked that a change in Kansas' athletic colors was imminent, some students began to object. An open letter to the *University Weekly Courier* argued against the new colors, noting that crimson represented nothing in Kansas, while sky blue symbolized the skies of the state's open prairie and the yellow stood for its abundant production of grain. Such objections did not last long. Shortly after the announcement of the switch, the *University Weekly Courier* proposed a showdown between the advocates of the yellow and blue and those of the crimson at the annual Thanksgiving Day football game between Kansas and Missouri in Kansas City. Proponents of each choice were invited to show up wearing their preferred color combination. Crimson adherents turned out in greater numbers than their rivals. Kansas, incidentally, won the game, scoring a 22-8 victory.

The matter was put to rest, at least temporarily. For nearly five years, Kansas athletes sported crimson uniforms. Sometime in 1895, however, a rumor swept through campus that people back East believed Kansas' choice of crimson belied a larger tendency of the University to imitate Harvard. A series of defiant editorials in Kansas publications revealed the degree to which these accusations touched a nerve. One commentary, for example, contended Kansas owed "nothing to Harvard." Nonetheless, it added, "Why not be original?" when choosing the school's athletic colors.

Some members of the University administration turned to prominent New York attorney John J. McCook, who had given money to build the school's first full-fledged athletic field after delivering Kansas' 1890 commencement address. The fact that

McCook had received his law degree from Harvard may actually have played a role in Kansas' choice of crimson in 1891, since his donation was made at the same time the color issue was first being debated.

McCook proved willing enough to offer advice concerning the adoption of new colors and suggested Kansas adopt either Crimson and Blue or Crimson and Black. Though his first proposal was ultimately chosen, it was by no means the only one offered. One suggestion called for simply changing the crimson to red, while another correspondent advocated the adoption of the "brown and yellow of the sunflower." The person who offered this idea added the caveat that "care should of course be taken to select pleasing and harmonious shades of these often ugly colors."

By late May 1896, Kansas' athletic board had settled on crimson and blue. This selection scuttled any lingering concerns about imitating Harvard, but it did open Kansas to the charge that it had merely adopted the colors of another Ivy League school, the University of Pennsylvania. Nonetheless, the *University Weekly Courier* praised the new combination as "a striking one," and disingenuously maintained that "so far as we know [the combination is] not used by any other university."

The selection of Crimson and Blue was not unanimously popular. In a letter to the Graduate Magazine, one disgruntled alumnus asserted the "change was made in a misguided effort to flatter our patron saint, Colonel McCook." He was joined in his objections by a reasonably large contingent of students. In a letter to the editor of the *University Weekly Courier*, one student praised the class of 1896 for refusing to decorate the chapel for its graduation with anything other than crimson and lamented the "high-handed proceeding" that had resulted in the introduction of crimson and blue. Like the disgruntled alumnus, he argued that the athletic board had sought only to "curry favor with a certain Yale man [by which presumably he meant McCook]." The writer then maintained that the colors had not legally been changed since the student body had not been consulted and proceeded to launch a call to boycott the new colors at future athletic events.

Interestingly, the editor responded to this complaint by agreeing that Kansas' official colors had not been changed and technically remained Sky Blue and Corn Yellow, but acknowledged that the athletic board had acted within its powers in changing the athletic colors. On September 27, 1896, Kansas wore the colors of Crimson and Blue for the first time on their uniforms and by the end of that fall semester, which as fate would have it turned out to be an excellent one for Kansas' football squad, the matter was firmly settled as students ceased objecting to the new colors. Indeed, Innes,' a Lawrence department store, could advertise that

it carried the "Kansas colors adopted by the Athletic Association [sic]" in "shades peculiar to [the] University of Kansas [and] very different from Harvard and Yale colors." Thus by the end of the autumn of 1896, crimson and blue had become the University's official athletic colors. Since they happened to be the combined colors of Harvard and Yale, a myth arose that crimson and blue were chosen to assuage the Yale alumni among Kansas' faculty who had endured a difficult time embracing the hues of their alma mater's chief rival.

The alteration in the colors wrought changes beyond those affecting the tones of the uniforms in which Kansas athletic teams took the field. It also made necessary an alteration in the university's "Alma Mater" song, which prior to 1896 had been Yellow and Blue. The tune, of course, remained the same, but then the tune had not originated in Lawrence. An absent-minded Kansas music professor and Dean of the School of Music named George B. Penny, a former Cornell man, had "borrowed" it from Cornell's alma mater, "Far Above Cayuga's Waters." Penny was so absent-minded that he was reputed to have once boarded a train and completely forgotten that he had left his horse tied up at a train station. Only a telegraph to a friend enabled him to rescue "the beast from a death by starvation."

George B. Penny

By itself, crimson did not fit the tune, and thus Yellow and Blue continued to be sung at Kansas gatherings after the transition to crimson uniforms in 1891, which explains the *University Weekly Courier*'s assertion in 1896 that Kansas' official colors were still yellow and blue. Because crimson has two syllables like yellow, however, when it was paired with blue, the song could remain essentially the same by substituting crimson for yellow. This was done within a few years and so it remains today.

By Mark D. Hersey, Ph.D.
Kansas Alumnus 2006
Written for This Week in KU History
www.KUHistory.com

SOME M. S. U. YELLS.

Tiger! Tiger! M. S. U.
Rah! Rah! Rah! Mis-sou-ri!
M. S. U. Ni-ver-si-ty,
Hu-rah! Hi-rah! Yes-sir-ree.
Who are we! Who are we!
We are a push from Missouri.
We are the stuff. That's no bluff.
We play football and never get enough.
Rock Chalk Johnnie
Jay Hawker too,
Better get a hustle on you
P. D. Q.
Rock Chalk Johnnie,
Jay Hawk Florence.
Go get a hump on you
Back to Lawrence.

Ray! Ray! Ray!
Whop! Hoop! Whoop!
Did you see the Tigers
Put Kansas in the soup?

Halla-baloo! Keneck! Keneck!
Halla-baloo! Keneck! Keneck!
Look at the man, look at the man,
Look at the Kansas man.

Written for the 1896 Savitar *Yearbook*

The 1896 MU Glee Club

COLLEGE SONG.

"There was a Jayhawk,
    That's mostly talk,
And it flapped its wings and crowed about K. U.
    But now it keeps still,
    Because it feels ill,
For the Tigers showed the Jay a thing or two.

"The bird cried Rock Chalk
    And likewise Jayhawk,
And said a word or so about K. U.,
    But on Thanksgiving
    It gave up living,
For the Tigers showed the Jay a thing or two.

"When dewy eve came
    To mark the great game,
Our glorious team went out to see a show,
    As they loved the muses
    As well as bruises,
It was to the Auditorium they did go.

"Camille D'Arville,
    She is a marvel,
With her magic kiss she makes a fellow – young,
    But Captain Charley
    He did not parley,
For Charley did not need to be made – Young.

"Good Captain Piatt,
    He raised no riot,
He refused to make a speech for K. U.'s sake,
    But when persuaded,
    The gallant Jay said,
That the Kansas team had no remarks to make."

Composed by members of the Missouri Glee Club
Written for the 1896 Savitar *Yearbook*

HOW WE SENT THE K. U.'S BACK.

The Kansas game was a glorious one,
And a great and lasting work was done,
When the M. S. U.'s old gold and black
Proudly sent the K. U.'s back.
The people from o'er two great states,
Passed in thousands through the gates,
Fathers and mothers in droves like cattle,
Came to see their sons do battle.
The day was cold, the field was mud,
But the Tigers fought for fame and blood.
The throng it cared not for the weather,
While the maidens spoke to one another
Of the tall and handsome men,
And pointed to our center Ben.
Then arose a deaf'ning shout,
That made each one look round about,
The reason was that on the field,
The tigers came, and not to yield.
The hour came on when it was time
For every man to fall in line;
And now each patriot held his breath,
But not from fear of pain or death,
The coin was tossed and Kansas won,
But then who cares how that was done;
For it was such a little thing,
We knew it could no vantage bring.
Right soon the fight in noble style,
Was waxed warm in little while;
When lo! By chance a man got loose,
And past our line without a truce
Adown the field he went like mad,
And women cried, Oh my! How bad;
But noble hearts do not despair,
Nor even did those ladies fair;
But on he went with break-neck speed,
And sore indeed became our need.
Brave Captain Young pursued in haste,
Though once his labor went to waste;
Yet on and on the fleet one went,
Till it would seem his strength was spent.

Now soon there came upon the scene,
One all bedecked in whitest sheen;
No one can guess how fast he ran,
In fact he was the very man
On whom Missouri staked her cash,
Nor would I say the deed was rash.
But in less time than words can tell,
The race did end with magic spell;
For on the Kansan's brawny neck,
Great Brigham's hand created wreck.
Then the play more fierce went on,
No man could doubt our game was won,
For there lives no soul so dead,
That would not wish his state ahead.
The Jayhawks, though, with one wild scream,
Made a point for the K. U. team;
It was their last, it was their best,
For the M. S. U. made all the rest.
The game then grew so hot and fast,
The Kansans knew the die was cast,
While Shawhan tore around the end.
"To touch a down" you may depend.
The cheers were lusty, deep, and loud,
A cause we had for being proud,
For now the goal, with easy kick,
Was made by Price, who knew the trick.
From that the Tigers had their way,
And Young made such a brilliant play,
That if before ther'd been a doubt,
It vanished with a joyous shout,
As past the goal he took the ball,
To make a score deciding all.
And so we did the Kansans fix,
The day was ours by ten to six.
If you should as why thus in verse,
I chose this story to rehearse,
The only answer I could give,
Is that so long as mortals live,
The story shall be often told;
How proudly waved the black and gold,
When by the Tiger's fierce attack,
We bravely sent the K. U.'s back.

Composed by Moreau
Missouri Glee Club
Written for the 1896 Savitar *Yearbook*

JAYHAWK JUBILEE

The smiling Jayhawk originally drawn by Harold "Hal" Sandy in the mid-1940s is perhaps Kansas' most recognizable symbol. It may also rank as one of the University's wisest investments. Sandy sketched his version of the Kansas mascot as a means of financing his last two years of education on Mount Oread, producing it in decal form and retailed it on campus and around Lawrence. Following his graduation in 1947, Sandy sold the copyright to his bird to the Kansas Union Bookstore for $250, which he thought at the time was a substantial amount of money.

Since then, of course, Kansas has plastered Sandy's Jayhawk on an endless array of apparel and merchandise, making millions of dollars in the process. Thus it was only fitting that Kansas marked the 50th anniversary of this avian emblem with a parade down Jayhawk Boulevard in Sandy's honor on September 12, 1996. Although the smiling Jayhawk was the only cartoon Sandy ever drew for money, it was hardly the first iteration, or the last, for that matter, of this most peculiar collegiate mascot.

The terms Jayhawk and Jayhawker have been virtually synonymous with Kansas and Kansans since the Territorial period, but their etymology is, at this juncture, virtually unknowable. Numerous sources have provided "authoritative" explanations of the origin of the word. However, the accounts seldom correlate well and often contradict each other. Depending on whom one might be inclined to believe, the term was coined in 1848 or 1849 or perhaps somewhat earlier or maybe a shade later. Similarly, the mythical bird was a combination of the blue jay, a territorial and often aggressive bird, and the sparrow hawk, a bold and fearsome predator, or maybe of some other kind of jay and some other kind of hawk. According to one version, an Irishman by the name of Pat Devlin coined the term following his one-man plundering raid on a camp of Missouri "Border Ruffians" at the outset of the period now known as "Bleeding Kansas," When asked how he had pulled it off, he bemusedly replied that he had not stolen anything, but that his horse, however, was apparently akin to a bird called a jayhawk that lived in his native Ireland and "just took things."

By another account, the term jayhawk owes its provenance to a group of people passing through Kansas on their way to California during the gold rush who witnessed a group of blue jays drive a hawk from the sky. Still others credit it to Pat Devlin, but under different circumstances, or trace its origins to different individuals or groups altogether.

Of course, it is equally possible that the term had less precise origins and merely reflected the biases of pro-slavery Kansans and their Missouri brethren. Indeed the "jay" part of the term might represent a backhanded insult to the New England emigrants to Kansas whom Missourians considered "greenhorns," for such was one of its slang meanings.

It is even possible that the term had its origin as a pejorative for the theft or liberation of slaves. That Jayhawkers separated slaves from their owners, often at the point of a gun, is not a matter of historical debate. Indeed in a letter written to the United States Secretary of War Edwin M. Stanton in 1862, Union General Henry Halleck complained that the chief occupation of the "Kansas Brigade" under noted Jayhawker James Henry Lane, the United States Senator from Kansas known as the "Grim Chieftain" whom Lincoln had granted a commission as a brigadier general of volunteers, was not the waging of war but "the STEALING OF NEGROES." The "evidence of their crimes," added Halleck, who made this charge prior to the Emancipation Proclamation, was "unquestionable."

Thus it might well be that much like a chicken hawk derived its name from stealing poultry, the jayhawkers may have derived their name from stealing "jays," i.e. a derogatory term for blacks, since jays belong to the same family as crows. This semantic slight then would be to the slaves rather than the free-staters, much as the segregation laws enacted in the decades following emancipation would be dubbed Jim Crow laws as an insult to the freedmen and their children.

Much then is unknown about the term's origins. What is known, however, is that on the eve of the Civil War the term came to be applied, primarily in an uncomplimentary sense, to anti-slavery free-staters who engaged in various guerilla skirmishes and vigilante activities against Missouri's Border Ruffians. Given the Jayhawkers' somewhat complicated legacy, it is not surprising that historians have alternately celebrated and condemned them.

While they generally opposed slavery and fought to keep it out of Kansas, a meritorious service, many were also antiblack as well as anti-slavery, and their guerrilla war tactics often differed little from those of the Border Ruffians, hardly commendable activities. Western novelists such as Louis L'Amour used the term Jayhawkers as a synonym for tough "bad guys," and western movies such as The Outlaw Josey Wales reflect a similar understanding of them. In fact, most dictionaries define jayhawking as a slang term for stealing or raiding. Nonetheless, the fact that Jayhawkers opposed slavery has mitigated, at least to some degree, some of their lawless activities and has stood them in somewhat higher stead than their Border Ruffian counterparts.

Regardless of the merits of the original Jayhawkers, the ultimate Union victory and the abolition of slavery caused free-staters, and Kansans in general, to pride themselves on the moniker. Thus it was that in 1886, Kansas Professor E. H. S. Bailey incorporated the term Jayhawk into the University science club's cheer, which soon evolved into the Rock Chalk, Jayhawk chant, and represented the first manifestation of the Jayhawk on Mount Oread.

It would not be the last. Songs would be written about the mythical bird, which also would lend its name to numerous University publications and clubs. With the Jayhawk already shrouded in legend and folklore, more myths would be added, some inadvertently, and some, like, Kirke Mechem's booklet, "The Mythical Jayhawk," deliberately written tongue in cheek. And so over time, the Jayhawk would come to serve as the most widely recognizable symbol of the state's flagship university.

Perhaps it is surprising then, that it was not until 1912, the same year that George "Dumpy" Bowles wrote "I'm a Jayhawk," that a caricature of the Jayhawk first became widely accepted as an emblem of the University. Prior to that, the University's athletic teams had no set mascot for sporting events. Apparently a bulldog was the most commonly used mascot as it appeared on Kansas pennants and post cards, but it was hardly the only one used.

The members of the 1909 football team, for instance, each contributed a dime a week to the feeding of Don Carlos, "a very substantial porker" from a farm in Leavenworth. An assistant coach donated what the *Kansas City Star* referred to as "his pigship" to the team at the beginning of the season. The squad apparently even purchased a "gaudy suit of KU colors" for their pig prior to their annual Thanksgiving Day clash with Missouri in Kansas City's Association Park. Thus for at least one season, the University could boast a Jayhawker pig as its mascot.

Although the caricature sketched by Kansas student Henry Maloy in 1912 with his quasi-human appearance, complete with shoes rumored to be worn in order to better kick the Missouri Tiger, gained widespread backing, evidence suggests it was not the   first popular iteration of the Jayhawk, and support for it was not universal. In December 1916, the *University Daily Kansan* ran an article about a group of disgruntled alumni who objected to "the conventional twentieth century Jayhawker" and sought to "revive the original Jayhawker with the jay bird body, hawk head, and eagle beak." Indeed the student newspaper quoted a "prominent cartoon advertiser and sign painter" who prognosticated that the "Jayhawker... of the

1912

future will be of the original type of the bird" with a black body and head and long, hooked, yellow beak. Of course, the sign painter's prediction proved to be errant, but the fact that disgruntled alums called for the revival of an older characterization of the Jayhawk indicates that there had likely been drawings of the mythical bird before that of Maloy. That the "original" Jayhawk had a black body and head might lend further credence to the idea that the term Jayhawker originated in the theft of slaves.

Those objecting to Maloy's cartoonish Jayhawk apparently represented a small minority. His long-legged bird remained the University's unofficial mascot for the remainder of the

1920

1910s. The first of several attempts to improve the caricature of the Jayhawk came in 1920. Although this version was blue rather than black, it looked much more like the "original Jayhawk" described by the disgruntled alumni in 1916 as it sat perched on a KU monogram, looking dignified with its hooked "eagle's" beak.

That version of the Jayhawk, however, was short lived and was replaced in 1923 by a Jayhawk as cartoonish as Maloy's, although with short, rather than, long legs and without   any shoes. It had, as the Kansas Alumni magazine pointed out, "a quaint, duck-like" essence. The third alteration in the Jayhawk of the 1920s to win widespread acceptance came in the year of the great stock-market crash. The 1929 Jayhawk, which had been designed by an artist in the employ of the Alumni Club of Kansas City, stood in what might be described as a boxer's pose and served as the University's mascot for the next 12 years.

1923

This is not to say that the 1930s added nothing to the legacy of the Jayhawk. As the nation suffered through the Great Depression, a Kansas student by the name of Ray Senate designed a version of the mythical bird that looked as though it had fallen on hard times with much of the rest of the country. For reasons that are fairly obvious, the featherless bird with the long face and sad eyes, sapped of its spunk and fight, never won widespread acceptance.

In 1932, following his return from a Central American expedition, Dr. Richard Sutton presented "a real, honest-to-goodness Jayhawk in everything but name" to Chancellor E. H. Lindley. The *University Daily Kansan* asserted that the mounted toucan was a "replica" of the University's mascot, "except for the coloring, which is yellow and black instead of crimson and blue." It also maintained that a Kansas fraternity had once had such a bird, which unfortunately had "passed away dramatically" following a loss to Missouri in their 1928 gridiron match up. That toucan "was reported to have died of shame and a broken heart."

1929

When the Great Depression gave way to the Second World War, a Kansas student by the name of Eugene "Yogi" Williams who served as a cartoonist for the *University Daily Kansan*, *Jayhawker*, and *Sour Owl*, sketched a Jayhawk that quickly gained popularity. His "Fighting Jayhawk," as it became known, was aptly named. It wore a scowl to match its ruffled tail feathers and appeared even more aggressive than its immediate predecessor. Notably, it drew upon Maloy's 1912 Jayhawk inasmuch as the University's mascot donned shoes for the first time in more than two decades.

1941

Williams' fighting Jayhawk, however, barely outlived the war before a new caricature of the University's mascot won widespread acceptance. In 1946, a Kansas student by the name of Harold "Hal" Sandy designed a "smiling Jayhawk" which fit the happy mood of a victorious United States. The 1946 Jayhawk looked much like the "Fighting Jayhawk," except, of course, for its smile and friendlier demeanor.

A quarter century later, a KU student by the name of

1946

Amy Sue Hurst jokingly mentioned the idea of having a small Jayhawk follow the University mascot around to Eldon Puett, who served as the University's Jayhawk at athletic events. She claimed to have gotten the idea from the decals on cars where there was one big Jayhawk and several small ones "following" it. Puett, in turn, was enamored of the idea and suggested it to the Kansas Alumni Association, which also liked the concept but lacked the funds for another Jayhawk costume. Hurst spent the summer building such a costume and then donated it to the University, which in turn invited her to wear it at sporting events. "Baby Jay" was "hatched" at halftime of Kansas' Homecoming victory over Kansas State on October 9, 1971, and has since served as a second mascot.

The addition of "Baby Jay" notwithstanding and despite occasional attempts to introduce new versions of the University's mascot, the Jayhawk designed by Sandy has proved much more durable than any of its predecessors.

By Mark D. Hersey, Ph.D.
Kansas Alumnus 2006
Written for This Week in KU History
www.KUHistory.com

2005

THE JAYHAWKER AND THE SAVITAR

When yearbooks first started getting published across the United States they were often done sporadically, usually reliant upon funding and student desire. The first yearbook published at Kansas was *The Heirophantes* in 1874. In sporadic years until 1901 the Kansas yearbook had a multitude of names decided by that year's class:

1874   *The Heirophantes*
1882   *The Kansas Kikkake*
1883   *The Kansas Cyclone*
1884   *The Cicada*
1889   *The Helianthus*
1893   *Quivera*
1895   *Annus Mirabilis*
1896   *The Kwir Book*
1897   *Senior Annual of the Class of '97*
1898   *The University that Kansas Buill*
1899   *The Oread*
1900   *The Galaxy*
1901   *The Jayhawker*

In 1901 *The Jayhawker* debuted at Kansas and the annual kept that name and has published an annual continuously since that time until 2008. Waning student interest in the *Jayhawker* caused the yearbook's demise for one year in 2008. Howev-er, the yearbook was rescued in no small measure by

Dave Mucci, KU Memorial Unions Director; Tom Johnson, advisor in the Union Programs office; and Mike Reid, Director of Marketing for the Kansas Union, who also had a 2008 issue of the *Jayhawker* published in 2009.

At Missouri, the first yearbook published by the school was done by its newly inaugurated Athletic Association in 1891, bearing no name. On January 9, 1892, Missouri's Academic Hall burned to the ground. To this day, the columns still stand and have become an icon to the institution. The burning of the building caused many administrative problems, which caused the delay of a second annual until 1895. The yearbook was named for the Indian solar deity, Savitar, which is thought to have been chosen as a reference to the burning of Academic Hall and the annual's birth "to enlighten and to delight, to inspire and to guide." No doubt, Savitar being a black and gold deity may also have influenced the naming of the annual, *Savitar*. In 2006, waning student interest ended its publication.

Following, is the history of the Border War Game as told by the schools' yearbooks:

SAVITAR 1896 – BORDER WAR 1895

Missouri won the toss and kicked off far toward the north goal and quickly gained the ball on downs. Repeated short gains were made but not enough to score. The ball changed hands two or three times, when Outland, Kansas' swift half back, helped by good interference and better holding (as was admitted by the umpire), made a long run of eighty-five yards. Every one supposed he was good for a touchdown; for he was a fine runner, had pulled away from Young, and on that muddy field was ten yards ahead of everyone else. But big Frank Brigham showed a sensational burst of speed and overhauled the fleet Kansas boy. After two or three downs more a double pass secured a touchdown, which yielded a goal and Missouri was clouded in sorrow. Shortly after the next kickoff, when Missouri earned the ball, Shawhan worked the old fake kick for twelve yards and a touchdown right through the line. Tie score! And Missouri's hopes bright. Time was soon called for that half.

It was clear that Missouri's line was almost impenetrable and only a fluke could now give Kansas a victory. But could Missouri score again? During the intermission, Bliss used some very, very emphatic language to his boys and they reappeared ready to do or die.

Kansas made a poor kickoff, Ben Thompson stopping the ball at ten yards' distance. Then came a series of plays never to be forgotten by any Missouri enthusiast. My blood runs faster while these words come from my pen. For in spite of Kansas" vaunted fast play Missouri's was faster still. Bang! crash! smash! This side and that; through the line, around the end, between end and tackle, went Young, Shawhan, and Allee. Finally old Charley Young went for the Kansas goal on the last down with five yards to gain, fell two feet short on his face in that slime of mud and mortar. All is over! Missouri's hopes have perished! Stop; just that instant Price and Thompson are there, they turn Young over and actually slide him across the line. Score, Missouri, 10; Kansas, 6.

During the remainder of the half there was no excitement till Kansas made a twenty yard run through the line and was barely stopped three yards' from goal by Allee. Now came Missouri's gallant stand for fifteen minutes with the enemy just in sight of Canaan but destined never to cross. Kansas tried McAlester, won three yards, tried him again and lost three, tried Gibson twice without gain and it is Missouri's ball. It now weighed twenty pounds or so. Allee was weary with many a hard kick, his feet were covered with mud, but the line held solid like a stone wall and the ball flew twenty yards away. Kansas comes back five yards, the line still holds and while we are in agony of expectation, wondering what threat timekeeper means by waving and swinging his arms, at last we know; 'time's up" and Missouri wins!! My hat was a wreck.

"That last gallant stand," says Mr. Bliss, "is the finest thing I ever saw on the gridiron."

By John Miller Burnam, Ph.D.
Missouri Faculty, Assistant Professor
Latin Language and Literature

SAVITAR 1897 – BORDER WAR 1896

[There is no description of the game. Kansas won 30-0.]

SAVITAR 1898 – BORDER WAR 1897

Then came a week's hard practice on Rollins field, coached by the '95 team. Rapid development was evident because all recognized that the time for the crucial test of nerve and training was fast approaching. And when on Thanksgiving Day the light line of Missouri held like a wall against the beef of Kansas, and they took us "down the line" with the small score of 16-0, each Missouri player felt in his heart that we had won a victory.

SAVITAR 1899 – BORDER WAR 1898

The practice games at Fayette were without accident and put us in form for the Thanksgiving game. On that day the icy condition of the field gave K. U. the advantage of her superior weight and her heavy guard-back plays, which at least cost us two scores. So the season of '98 closed, not as a brilliant campaign, but as the best we could possibly do under the circumstances.

OREAD 1899 – BORDER WAR 1898

The Thanksgiving game at Kansas City is always the event of the season. Missouri put up a fine game, but was unable to score against the Jayhawkers. As usual, this game was characterized by clean, gentle- manly playing on both sides. The final score was 12 to in favor of Kansas.

By Edward J. Leland
Kansas Football Manager
Kansas Law School Alumnus 1899

SAVITAR 1900 – BORDER WAR 1899

The foot ball season, as seen by the list of games and the points won and lost, was brilliant in the beginning, shone splendidly at the noonday of its career, was overclouded for a moment in the afternoon, but, alas, the sun of our success set just three hours too soon. Had it continued to shine, we would tell the story of the great game at Kansas City on Thanksgiving [Day]. It didn't, and we give no description. On that day, however, the Jayhawkers [were] abroad in the land, his mouth did continue to go, and there was none to stop him. Verily did the Puke feel sick at heart and   worthy of his name.

THE 1900S...

As America's pioneer past began to fade and transition into the beginning of the modern era, a ragtime piano player named Scott Joplin moved to Saint Louis, Missouri in 1900 and composed some of his best known works; The Entertainer, Elite Syncopations, March Majestic, and Ragtime Dance. Also in 1900, the Democratic National Convention came to Kansas City and nominated William Jennings Bryan for President. A few years later on December 17, 1903, a pair of brothers, Orville and Wilbur Wright, took flight at Kitty Hawk, South Carolina and, before the end of the decade, Henry Ford introduced the Model T automobile to the public, which started the popular usage of the machine.

In the 1900s, Kansas dominated the newly named University of Missouri six games to two with two games ending in ties. The 1900 Thanksgiving Day game was expected to be a win for Missouri, had its newly hired Faculty Manager, Clark Wilson Hetherington, not suspended two of the Missouri players for being academically ineligible. The game, held before 8,000 attendees, ended in a 6-6 tie, the points for Kansas being scored by reserve halfback, Ernest Cosmos "Ernie" Quigley, who would later be a well known baseball National League umpire and Midwestern collegiate football and basketball referee. Quigley's resume as a sports official is quite extensive, culminating in his becoming the athletic director at the University of Kansas from 1944-1950 and having Kansas' first baseball field named after him-Quigley Field.

Until 1905, football as a national sport had become increasingly rough and dangerous with 18 deaths occurring in that year alone, creating a popular demand for rule changes. President Teddy Roosevelt got involved and invited representatives of the big three schools, Harvard, Yale, and Princeton, to the White House to convince them of the need for rule changes. As a result, the national Football Rules Committee was formed and acted with the creation of a set of rules that would allow for more action and scoring, while also achieving a greater degree of safety for the players. Of the changes, three were the most important; the introduction of the forward pass, the change from five yards to ten yards to achieve a first down, and the banning of mass formations and group tackling.

In two years time, Clark Hetherington transitioned from Faculty Manager to Missouri Athletic Director. Hetherington was born in Minnesota in 1870, but was raised in California. He graduated from Stanford University in 1891 with a degree in Health and received a Master of Physical Training from Whittier State School. He also received a degree of Psychology from Clark University. Hetherington viewed athletics as an educational ve-

hicle for students and believed strongly in competition between schools in athletics. Hetherington espoused many theories about athletics which today still prove relevant; the primary of these being the differentiation between amateur and professional athletics and the importance of intercollegiate competition. His strong views caused him in December, 1905 to initiate a discussion with several regional schools regarding the creation of an athletic conference. On January 12, 1907, representatives from the University of Missouri, Kansas University, Washington University, Nebraska University and the University of Iowa met at the Midland Hotel in Kansas City to develop the newly created Missouri Valley Intercollegiate Athletic Association. Among those in attendance from the University of Kansas was Director of Physical Culture, James A. Naismith, the inventor of basketball and the football helmet.

The early football power of the Missouri Valley Intercollegiate Athletic Association was Nebraska, who won or tied nine of the conference titles in the Conference's first 11 years. In 1908, Kansas had its second undefeated and untied team in the school's history, winning that year's Missouri Valley Intercollegiate Athletic Association title. The team had its longest serving coach at that time, Albert Rutherford "Bert" Kennedy, who had served the team as quarterback for the teams of 1895, 1896, and 1897. Kennedy became head coach of the Jayhawks in 1904 and served the team in that position until 1910.

Although Bert Kennedy was quite a success at Kansas, earning a 53-9-4 total record, and as of 2008 having the most wins of any Kansas football coach and the second highest winning percentage at .833, a large part of his success was due to a remarkable athlete named Tommy Johnson who played at quarterback for the years 1908, 1909, and 1910 and was also Kansas' first basketball All-American. During his term at quarterback, Tommy Johnson was the star on a team that over three years amassed a 23-2-1 record and also earned the team its second undefeated and untied season in 1908. While as a freshman quarterback, Tommy Johnson got the better of Missouri to accomplish the undefeated and untied season, regrettably and tragically, it was the football game against Missouri that would get the better of him in his next two encounters with that team.

Not having beaten the Jayhawks since 1901, Missouri's professor of Greek and perhaps Missouri's first athletic historian, W. G. Manly, headed to New England to recruit a new coach, finding one in William W. "Bill" Roper. Roper was born in Philadelphia in 1880 and played football, basketball, and baseball at Princeton University, graduating in 1902. He obtained a law degree from Virginia University and shortly after began coaching at Princeton. Roper has been described as an emotive coach, his teams reflecting his attitude. Upon his arrival in Columbia, Bob Broeg wrote in his book, *Ol' Missou: A Century of Tiger Football*, "It was at the now-deserted Wabash station in 1909 that William W. Roper stepped off the train, greeted by 400 students. Roper's first words, to the delight of his welcoming committee, were: 'I understand you want to beat Kansas.'"

Both Kansas and Missouri went to Kansas City for the Border War Game as unbeaten teams in 1909; Kansas 8-0 and Missouri 6-0-1. In the game, Missouri edged Kansas 12-6, due to an outstanding performance by Theodore Edward Dupuy "Ted" Hackney, who scored two field goals in the first two minutes of the game and accounted for 7 of Missouri's 12 points. Johnson, on whom the entire Kansas team relied, suffered a concussion in the first half of the game on a punt return and remained in the game the entire first half, unable to communicate intelligibly

to any of the players or even remember any of the plays that he called as quarterback. At halftime, the team physician, John Outland, asked Coach Kennedy to remove Johnson, who overruled the doctor. The victory allowed Missouri to give Kansas its only loss of the season and caused Missouri to have its first unbeaten team, albeit not untied, in school history and also earned Missouri the Missouri Valley Intercollegiate Athletic Association football championship title. The celebration was so raucous by the Missouri players and fans that a goalpost was broken and a hapless, black chicken was found and crucified upon it, in lieu of a Jayhawk, and paraded around the field for an hour.

Those that tried for a position on the 1905 Missouri Tiger team.

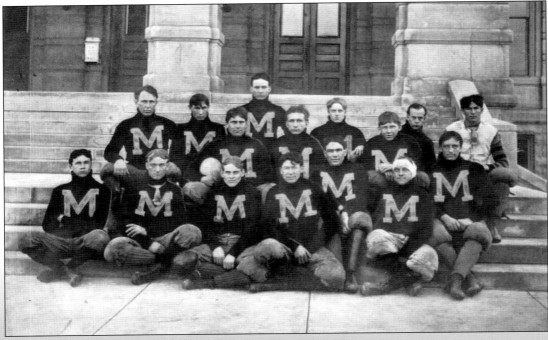

MU Football Captain
Carl Kruse

Missouri Football (4-4-1) - Head Coach Fred Murphy
Row 1: Douglass, Cooper, Houx, Dunn, Washer, Yant, Ellis. Row 2: Hayes, McMurtry, Captain Kruse, Smith, Thurman, Saunders, Anderson, Murphy, Craig.

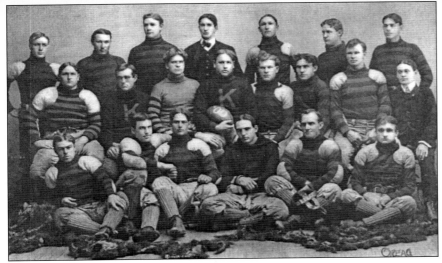

KU Football Captain
Charles Wilcox

Kansas Football (2-5-2) - Head Coach Charles Boynton
Row 1: Vincent, Quigley, Breese, Botsford, Elder, Copping. Row 2: Allphin, Jenkinson, Algie, Captain Wilcox, Schrant, Odle, Pouppert, Manager Davis. Row 3: Hart, Morton, Powell, Coach Boynton, Blockberger, Tucker, Black.

MU Football Captain
Charles Washer

Missouri Football (2-6-1)- Head Coach Fred Murphy

Row 1: B. Houx, L. M. Anderson, Perry, Frazier, McCaslin, Coach Murphy. Row 2: I. Anderson, Jesse, Captain Washer, Gordon, Coe. Row 3: Arnold, Ellis, Nick Hall, Hoff, Playter, Laudon, Hogan, Forrester, Anamosa, Bennet, Birney, Moore.

KU Football Captain
Julian Jenkinson

Kansas Football (3-5-2) - Head Coach John H. Outland

Missouri Football (5-3) - Head Coach Patrick John O'Dea
Row 1: Abner Birney, W. H. Hayes, George Anamosa, L. W. Smith, Carl Hoff, Lucien Childrens, T. B. Perry, H. C. Ardinger, E. B. Smith, Hans Wulff, R. H. Jesse, J. F. Hogan, Jas. Landon.

MU Football Captain
Tom M. Ellis

KU Football Captain
Wilbur D. Vincent

Kansas Football (6-4) - Head Coach Arthur H. Curtis
Western Inter-State University Association Champions
(Unordered) Richardson, Ackerman, Allen, Peters, Brummage, Algie, Hicks, Pooles, Reed, Jenkinson, Captain Vincent, Love, Etchens, Cock, Mosher, Russell, Nicols, Scott, Hart, Thornberry.

Missouri Football (1-7-1) - Head Coach John F. Mclean
Western Inter-State University Association Co-Champions

MU Football Captain
Abner Cassidy Birney

KU Football Captain
Alpha Brumage

Kansas Football (6-3) - Head Coach Harold S. Weeks
Western Inter-State University Association Co-Champions
(Unordered) Manley E. Michaelson, Carl Ackerman, Emile Bruner, Harry Allen, C. Prentice Donald, Albert Hicks, John Fleischman, Arthur Pooler, W. H. Chappell, William Rice, Captain Alpha Brumage, James Woodford, Charles Ise, Chester Cook, Arthur Griggs, T. J. Strickler, John Greenlee, Harry L. Heinzman, Coach Harold Weeks.

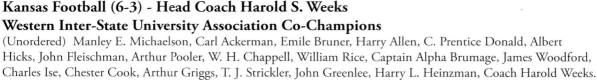

Missouri Football (3-6) - Head Coach John F. Mclean
Western Inter-State University Association Co-Champions
(Unordered) Captain Homer Haggard, H. W. Anderson, H. Akerson, J. W Bryant,
M. Currie, A. F. Forster, L. H. Gentry, D. K. Hall, L. H. Hedrick, E. C. Moor-
house, C. Nichols, E. F. Salisbury, B. W. Tillman.

MU Football Captain
Homer H. Haggard

Fourteenth Annual Game

KANSAS

vs

MISSOURI

Thanksgiving Day
1904

Rock-Chalk!
Jay-Hawk!!
K. U.!!!

Tiger!
Tiger!!
M. S. U.!!!

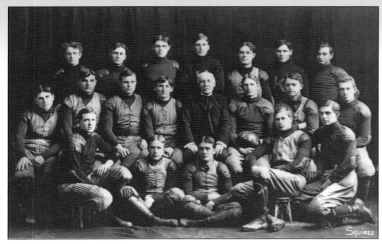

Kansas Football (8-1-1) - Head Coach Albert Rutherford Kennedy

KU Football Captain
Albert Hicks

Missouri Football (5-4) - Head Coach John F. Mclean
Western Intercollegiate Association Co-Champions

(Unordered) Captain Harvey Anderson, Eugene Salisbury, Oscar Brockmeyer, Harry Rutherford, Aubrey Frazier, Carl Hoff, Richard Jesse, Charles Leaphart, Lucius Childers, Curry Potter, Casper Rucker, Edwin Miller, B. W. Tillman.

MU Football Captain
Harvey W. Anderson

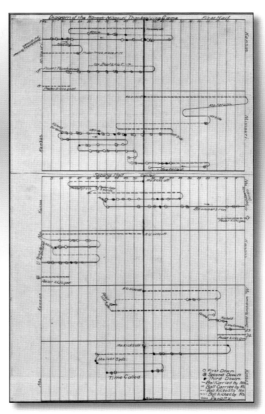

1905 game diagram

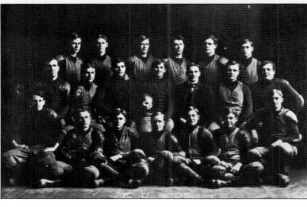

Kansas Football (10-1) - Head Coach Albert Rutherford Kennedy
Western Intercollegiate Association Co-Champions

(Unordered) Reed, Milton, Heinzman, White, Brunner, Donald, Rouse, Captain Pooler, Hart, Myers, Miller, Waring, Angney.

KU Football Captain
Arthur C. Pooler

Missouri Football (5-2-1) - Head Coach William James Monilaw
(Unordered) Captain B. W. Tillman, E. L. Miller, H. K. Rutherford, F. C. Livingston, D. V. Graves, W. L. Driver, A. N. Bobbit, W. J. Carothers, Harry Tidd, J. P. Nixon, Harry, Rue, Prewitt Roberts, Burr Douglass, E. E. Zook, E. D. White, Jewett.

MU Football Captain
B. W. Tillman

Kansas Football (7-2) - Head Coach Albert Rutherford Kennedy

KU Football Captain
C. P. Donald

Missouri Football 7-2) - Head Coach William James Monilaw
Row 1: Crain, Alexander, Rutherford, Captain E. L. Miller, Deatherage, Driver, Sigler, Manager Ebright, Coach Monilaw. Row 2: Axline, Ristine, Carothers, Nixon, Kurtz, Graves, Roberts, Anderson.

Kansas Football (5-3) - Head Coach Albert Rutherford Kennedy
Row 1: Rice, Steele, White, Crowell, Angney, Miller. Row 2: Priest, Forter, Milton, Captain Rouse, Reed, Carlson, Lamb. Row 3: Coach Kennedy, Dennis, Ranson, Caldwell, Stephenson, Wood, Coach Parry.

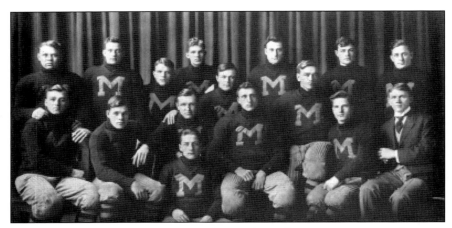

Missouri Football (6-2) - Head Coach William James Monilaw
(Unordered) Captain E. L. Miller, D. V. Graves, W. L. Driver, J. R. Bluck, H. W. Anderson, A. G. Alexander, K. P. Gilchrist, C. L. Ristine, W. N. Deatherage, D. M. Nee, E. M. Ewing, R. W. Roberts, W. J. Carothers, Allen Wilder, H. S. Grove, H. W. Crane.

MU Football Captain
Edwin Lee Miller

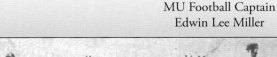

Tigers Mascot
William Wells

KU Football Captain
George F. Crowell

Kansas Football (9-0) - Head Coach Albert Rutherford Kennedy
Missouri Valley Champion
Row 1: Rice, Myers, Fink, Steele, Carlson, Pleasant, Bond. Row 2: Waring, Manager Landson, Coach Kennedy, Captain Crowley, Coach Mosse, Reed, Caldwell, Ford. Row 3: Newbold, Wood, Randall, Johnson, Stephenson, Dahlene, V. Wood, Spear, Hennessy.

Missouri Football (7-0-1) - Head Coach William W. Roper
Missouri Valley Champion
(Unordered) Captain Carl Ristine, George Alexander, Henry Crain, William Deathrage, Warren Roberts, Henry Gove, Joseph Bluck, William Saunders, K. P. Gilchrist, Edward Klein, Arthur Idler, Frank Thacher, Glen Shuck, Ewart Johnson, John Care, Eugene Hall, Lloyd Curtis, James Pixlee, Theodore Hackney.

MU Football Captain
Carl C. Ristine

KU Football Captain
Carl A. Pleasant

Kansas Football (8-1) - Head Coach Albert Rutherford Kennedy
Row 1: Dahlene, Ford, Bond, Johnson, Heil, Abernathy, Magill. Row 2: Lynch, Randall, Carlson, Mosse, Captain Pleasant, Coach Kennedy, Caldwell, Ammons. Row 3: Wilhelm, V. Smith, Lovett, Maxwell, R. Smith, Stephenson, Davidson, Spear, Brownlee.

TOUCHDOWNS AND TRAGEDY

He was Kansas' first truly great athlete and has been dubbed "the Original KU Legend" by institutional historians.

As starting quarterback for three years, he led his team to a record of 23-2-1; as a basketball player, he was honored as the University's first All-American on the hardwood. He died a year after his last football game for the University of Kansas having left a legacy as impressive as any subsequent Kansas athlete. In 1920 Kansas Director of Athletics "Phog" Allen recognized the accomplishments of his former basketball teammate when he briefly considered naming Memorial Stadium after him. At a ceremony honoring him in 1935, flags flew at half-mast and former teammates reminisced about his greatness.

His name was Tommy Johnson and on this day in 1909 in a football game against Nebraska, he made a run that transformed him from an excellent quarterback into an institutional icon.

VANQUISHED

They came 'mid the flourish of trumpets,
As they did the year before.
They though to awe with throat and jaw.
They howled as the dogs of war,

They came with banners flying;
They were loud in their champions' praise,
For they had no doubt they would put to rout,
The vanquished of others days.

The day of the year is upon us,
The battle royal is here,
And the coolest heart gives a sudden start,
When the chosen few appear.

There they go like a shot from a cannon
Look! The foe falls beneath their tread,
And they forge their way to the fortress gay,
Flying the blue and red.

Might has come; the battle is over,
And Missouri has won the day.
Kansas may talk but when Tigers eat chalk,
Old Kansas has nothing to say.

Written for the 1902 Savitar *Yearbook*

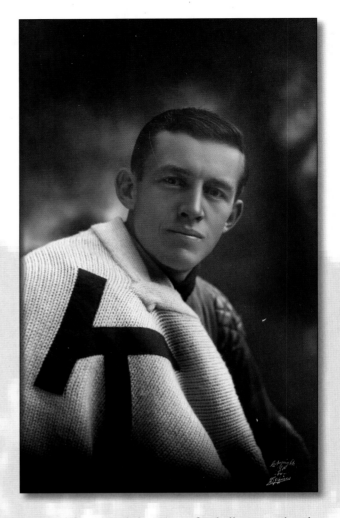

Johnson had first joined the Kansas football team – then known as the Jayhawkers – in 1908. The 5 foot 11 inch, 160-pound [180 cm, 72 kg] quarterback promptly led them to an undefeated season, only the second in the school's history. Consequently, Kansas fans cherished similarly high expectations for the 1909 season, and by mid-October, they had not been disappointed.

Indeed, a *Lawrence Daily Journal* article on October 18, 1909, about Kansas' defeat of the Kansas State Agricultural College Aggies was headlined simply "Ever Victorious." According to the article, Johnson had provided the only score for his team when he returned a fumble for a touchdown. His play had enabled the men from Mount Oread to escape Manhattan with a 5-3 win despite the fact that they had been "clearly outplayed." (At the time, a touchdown was worth five rather than six points.) The triumph over Kansas State was Kansas' 13th consecutive victory and extended the already impressive winning streak of the Jayhawks, who had not lost a game since November 16, 1907.

The following day, Lawrence's evening paper began looking ahead to a game against Nebraska that was still nearly three weeks away despite the fact that Kansas had to play both Washington University (Saint Louis) and Washburn University in the interim. The paper recognized what most fans of the Missouri Valley Conference already realized – that the Jayhawker-Cornhusker game would be the year's most important conference game. Interestingly, however, the article included the comments of an "Ann Arbor man who [had] played football" at the University of Michigan, and who had watched the Jayhawks' game against the Aggies. The former Wolverine criticized Kansas' team for being slow, lacking cohesion, and depending too heavily on its star. He further predicted, "When a team puts on a good defense" against Johnson, Kansas would prove unable to "win the game."

After throttling Washington University and Washburn by a combined score of 40-0, the Kansas team began its preparations for Nebraska. Supporters of both schools could hardly have been more excited. By the Thursday before the big game, students on Mount Oread had already clad themselves in crimson and blue and begun a push to send as many Kansas fans to the game as was humanly possible. For those fans that could not make it to Lincoln, the *Kansan* had decided to provide regularly updated reports of the game at the chapel.

"Heretofore," the student paper advertised, "no free reports of the big games have been given on the hill." Nonetheless, so important was the game to the University that despite the "considerable expense" it entailed, the *Kansan* thought it vital to host such an event. On Friday afternoon the University held a mass meeting at which Chancellor Frank Strong, football coach Bert Kennedy, Dr. James Naismith, and others detailed "how and why [Kansas] must beat Nebraska." After the meeting, the University's gridiron representatives prepared for their trip.

The football team arrived in Lincoln late Friday night having somehow neglected to load the trunks that held their uniforms onto the train. Conveniently, a Union Pacific passenger train was scheduled to leave for Lincoln from Lawrence the following morning and proved willing to carry the team's outfits north. Shortly before 2:00 p.m., a crowd began to assemble at the University of Nebraska's new athletic field. It was a spectacular day for football with cool temperatures and clear skies and by 2:30, roughly 6,000 fans had turned out to watch the highly anticipated match-up.

The first half amounted to a punting duel as the teams combined for a total of three first downs. The only excitement occurred when Johnson turned the corner around left end and scampered 27 yards for an apparent touchdown. As the "Kansas rooters [went] wild," the officials held a conference that culminated in a decision to penalize Kansas for holding. Predictably, as the *Lawrence Daily World* pointed out, the "Nebraska rooters

[went] crazy at this decision," while Jayhawk fans became "correspondingly quiet." (After the game, the referee reportedly concluded that he had made the wrong call and, maintaining that the touchdown should have counted, apologized to the team from Lawrence for his error.) Shortly after the touchdown was called back, the teams mutually agreed to call a timeout, "as the men were suffering from running down so many punts." Play resumed after a few minutes but the breather accomplished little in terms of injecting energy into the game.

At halftime, the teams remained deadlocked 0-0. While some of the older alumni and former players made their way to their respective teams to offer words of encouragement and inspiration, the rest of the crowd seized the opportunity to release their pent-up energy. Fans of both schools "paraded the field with the two bands leading" them as they sang school songs and shouted the yells of the university they supported.

When play resumed, it looked as though the crowd was in for another half of punting that would finally end in a game knotted at zero. The tone of the game changed when, with time winding down, Kansas forced the Cornhuskers to punt the ball yet again. This time, however, as Johnson received the ball on his own 30-yard line he began the run that would transform him into a legend. Following his blockers, he wound his way into the open field where he had proven over his career to be virtually unstoppable. Rising to their feet, the "Kansas rooters [went] wild in a veritable delirium of joy" as Johnson eluded would-be tacklers and dashed 70-yards for a score. The quarterback's touchdown, followed by his team's extra point, gave the Jayhawks a 6-0 advantage. Three possessions later, time expired and the game was over. Ecstatic Kansas fans scrambled down from the bleachers and carried the game's hero off the field on their shoulders.

Back in Lawrence, the 1,000 students who had crammed into the chapel to wait for game updates from the *Kansan* "like to tore down the building" when "the news came back from Lincoln of the Kansas victory." Students hastily organized a bonfire for that evening in Lawrence's Central Park. Merchants whose establishments were located downtown set empty, wooden boxes out along the street for the undergraduates to collect as firewood. "With each additional box that was taken to the park," the *Lawrence Daily World* reported, "another tribute was paid to those boys up in Lincoln and to 'Tommy' Johnson who had won the day."

More than 2,000 people showed up for the nighttime celebration. Speakers took their turn atop a dry goods box that acted as a podium. At one point, Chancellor Strong stepped up onto the makeshift platform and led the crowd in a "Rock Chalk" chant before telling the students that he had a "secret announcement" to make at chapel on Monday morning. The students, realizing that he intended to cancel Monday's classes, let out a roar of approval. The chancellor went on to prophesy that the 1909 team, like the 1908 version, would end the season "ever victorious."

The following morning, the team itself returned to Lawrence, where an exuberant swarm of supporters waited to greet it. Johnson had not even stepped from the train to the platform before "a crowd of admirers … grabbed him up on their shoulders and carried him to the waiting tallyho [a four-in-hand carriage]" where his other teammates soon joined him.

Taking the place of four horses, a contingent of men from Mount Oread proceeded to pull the team's carriage to the Eldridge House Hotel where Lawrence Mayor Sam Bishop welcomed the team. (In an evidently popular gesture, Hizzoner promised to spring the players from jail should they ever get in any trouble.) The gala continued as members of the victorious squad addressed the crowd. Johnson, "a real modest hero" the *Lawrence Daily Journal* commented, "merely bowed his thanks to the boys for their kind words."

Team members had a few days off as no game had been scheduled for the following Saturday. Supporters spent the week rehashing the victory and predicting that Kansas would certainly finish the season undefeated. An "ever victorious" season, however, was not in the cards for the 1909 Kansas team. On Thanksgiving Day in Kansas City's Association Park, Kansas' hated rival, the Missouri Tigers, defeated the Jayhawk team for the first time since 1901.

Johnson suffered what was probably a concussion on a punt return in the first half and, although he remained in the game was unable to communicate intelligibly with his teammates or remember which plays he had called. At halftime, former Kansas player and current team physician Dr. John Outland asked Coach Kennedy to remove the star from game for his own safety. The assistant coach and the ex-players who had joined the team at the break concurred with the doctor, but Kennedy

overruled them and asked Johnson to play in the second half.

Just as the Michigan player had predicted at the end of the Kansas State game, with their star injured, the Kansas team proved unable to win. The *Kansas City Times* suggested the loss was due in large measure to the fact that the "wobbly" Johnson had "failed to produce any of the startling runs which ha[d] set the Kansas rooters wild so many times." (Despite his injury, the elusive quarterback had managed, at one point, a 40-yard punt return.) Unable to believe their good fortune, Missouri supporters swarmed over the field after the victory, which was only their team's fourth win in 19 tries against Kansas. Tearing down a goal post, they found a luckless black hen (which was apparently the closest thing they could find to a Jayhawk), "crucified" it at the top of the post, and paraded around the field in a celebration that lasted for an hour.

That winter, having recovered from his concussion, Johnson led the Kansas basketball team to a conference title and a record of 18-1. The leading scorer on the team, his play earned for him All-American honors – the first such distinction bestowed upon a Kansas student. When the 1910 hardwood season ended, Johnson helped lead student opposition to an attempt by certain members of the Board of Regents to abolish football at Kansas and replace it with the more "civilized" game of rugby.

Both Johnson and football returned to the University for the fall semester of 1910 where he again led the team to an excellent record, although Nebraska beat Kansas that year. Thus, Kansas entered its finale against Missouri with a 6-1 record. In a game that ended in a 5-5 tie, Johnson once again suffered an injury, but this time it was more severe than a concussion.

Sandwiched between two Tiger defenders, Johnson re-aggravated a kidney condition that had plagued him as a youth. His injury rendered him unable to compete in the 1910-11-basketball season and over the course of the next year his health steadily deteriorated. On November 24, 1911, the most accomplished athlete the school had yet known died of kidney failure at a Kansas City hospital.

His alma mater did not quickly forget him. "Phog" Allen, who had been Johnson's basketball teammate during the 1905-06 season, later claimed that his preference for the name of the stadium that replaced McCook Field (the home football field of Johnson's era) would have been "Tommy Johnson Memorial Field" had the University not lost 130 students and alumni in the First World War. (In remembrance of those war dead, Kansas named the new sports venue Memorial Stadium.)

In 1935 the University of Kansas honored Johnson at halftime of the Homecoming game against Missouri. In front of a sold out crowd at Memorial Stadium, with flags flying at half-mast, former teammates celebrated him as the best athlete in Kansas history. Four years later, the *University Daily Kansan*, released a poll ranking the greatest Kansas athletes, Johnson had lost his crown, but was still in the running. The paper listed him third behind 1932 Olympic decathlon champion James Bausch and the great miler of the 1930s, Glenn Cunningham.

By the end of the century, however, memory had relegated Johnson to a more obscure corner of Kansas' pantheon of athletic heroes. When in 1999 the *University Daily Kansan* ran a series of articles on the University's leading sports stars, it did not rank Johnson even among the top 10 athletes of the past 100 years.

Given the fact that Kansas emerged as a basketball powerhouse, it is perhaps ironic that Johnson's All-American honors for his abilities on the hardwood served, in his lifetime, as a mere footnote to his gridiron career. It may be equally unexpected that the man who earned the first nationally recognized individual athletic award in the University's history and whom institutional historians have dubbed "the Original KU Legend" has not yet had his football or basketball jersey retired by the school at which he distinguished himself.

By Mark D. Hersey, Ph.D.
Kansas Alumnus 2006
Written for This Week in KU History
www.KUHistory.com

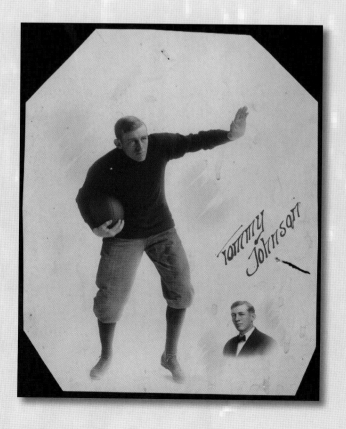

COACH A. R. KENNEDY

A. R. Kennedy, the Kansas coach for the past two seasons, is a native of Douglas [County]. He graduated from the Lawrence High School in [1895]. The following autumn he entered the University and played quarter on the team. He was captain of the team in [1897]. In [1898], Kennedy attended the University of Pennsylvania and was captain of the second eleven. The next year he played on the famous [1899] team. The next three years Kennedy spent in coaching city teams in Philadelphia, and in [1903] came to Topeka, where he tutored Washburn. Year before last Kansas secured his services and was able to turn out a very successful team. So much confidence was placed in Kennedy's ability, that his Alma Mater desired his services for another year, and the result of this season is a fitting testimonial to his work.

Written for the 1906 Jayhawker *Yearbook*

FOR THE FIRST TIME IN THE MISSOURI VALLEY CONFERENCE

For the first time in the history of football in the Missouri Valley, Kansas and Missouri universities will bring undefeated teams to Kansas City to-morrow to engage in a struggle for the championship of the conference. It is not the first time they have fought for the championship, but the first time both have been undefeated up to the final Thanksgiving day game. Nearly 18,000 tickets have been disposed of, and with perfect weather conditions predicted a record-breaking crowd may be expected. Many of these tickets have reached the hands of scalpers, and good seats are to-night selling at double the schedule prices.

The betting odds of 2 to 1 on Kansas show what the general opinion of rooters and students is regarding the outcome. For years Kansas has triumphed. One game was a tie, but in the nineteen years these teams have met in annual turkey day battle Missouri has won but three games. Kansas really has 10 per cent of the battle won before it is fought, because of the confidence of the players.

Kansas will undoubtedly rely on straight football to win. A few on-side kicks may be used if the Jayhawkers take an early lead. Kansas has the on-side kick perfected and it has worked well in former games this year. An element of luck has been with the Jayhawkers in several games, but barring this, the Kennedy aggregation has played wonderful football all season, and is entitled to credit for every victory. If the Jayhawkers win they will earn every point they make. Missouri's hopes of victory lie in the open style of play.

Roper has trained his men to use a short, snappy forward pass, which has been a success in the East, and the Tigers have his play pretty well perfected. In the on-side kick, the Tigers are really better drilled than any team in the conference. It is this play which Roper expects to put against Kansas with hopes of victory, and it is this play which the Tigers will resort to after a few scrimmages in straight football.

By St. Louis Globe-Democrat *Newspaper*
Published Wednesday, November 24, 1909

A WORD FROM THE COACHES

Don't underestimate the strength of the Tigers. That team is not going to be a mere toy in the hands of our eleven, by any means. I expect to see the machine Roper has built up make a grand fight to win this game, but I do not expect to see it succeed. We hope for a dry field, so the Jayhawks can surprise their friends by showing great speed. On straight football we are sure to win, and I can not see where Missouri can play much of anything else. The on-side kick and forward pass formations for the Missouri team are sure to be broken by us. I think the best way for Missouri to play to win is the new Roper open style. But the speedy little backs of the Tigers are too light. The line is a stone wall, but ought to crumble before the onslaught of the Jayhawkers. We have a heavy line and a fairly heavy back field. Our ends will break up any ends they attempt, and our back field is heavy enough to crack through their line.

I expect several of our big gains to be around the ends, which I believe is the weak spot in the Tiger line-up. I expect to see Johnson, our peerless quarter back, break away for some long runs, and I do not know of a Missouri man who is such a star that he can perform the feats on the gridiron which Johnson can. Johnson's headwork has been a feature of every game this season. He attempts plays which Capt. Ted Coy of Yale would not attempt and he gets away with them. He attempts plays I do not expect myself and am sometimes surprised at him, but he seldom fails to make big gains on some of his daring runs. I do not think Roper has had the material to give Missouri a winning team.

By Albert Rutherford Kennedy
Kansas Football Head Coach
St. Louis Globe-Democrat *Newspaper*
Published Wednesday, November 24, 1909

This is my first battle against Kansas. I am not familiar with former conditions in the annual game, except what I have read, and have been told. The Missouri team has been defeated so often by the Kennedy aggregation that it went East for a coach last year, and I was elected. When I reached Columbia, the first thing I was told was that the students wanted a victory over Kansas. That is why I was engaged. I am going to try to give them that victory. For eight weeks I have worked with this team, molding it into shape to beat the Jahawkers from the Sunflower State, and it is now in as good condition as I have been able to put it.

I realize that we have not as good material as we might have, but we have weeded out the best football material in the university, and if we can not win it will be because of the superiority in weight and strength of the Kansas eleven. I have seen Kansas' players. We have as good formations, and better ones in the open style of play, as much speed, if not more, and I can not see why the Tigers should swallow another defeat. I think Missouri will win by a close score, although, of course, each team has a chance.

If the Tigers do not fumble and play the brand of football they have played against Drake, it is going to be the hardest fight of the year for both elevens. A new coach can not always give a university a winner the first year, but we have won or tied every game, and I hope to break a record and give Missouri an all-victorious aggregation for my first year's work in Columbia.

By William T. Roper
Missouri Football Head Coach
St. Louis Globe-Democrat *Newspaper*
Published Wednesday, November 24, 1909

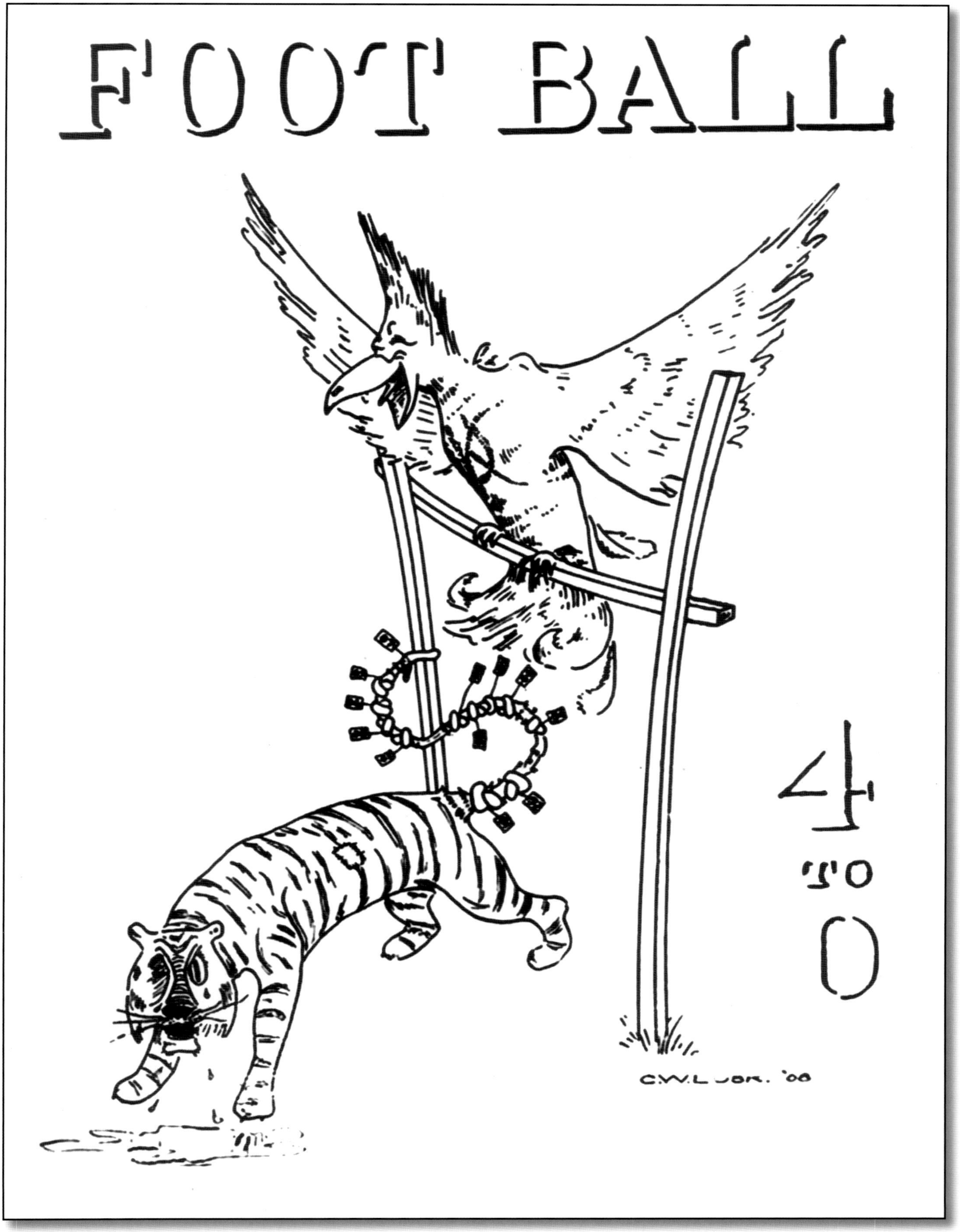

FOOT BALL

C.W.L. JR. '08

4 TO 0

From the 1908 Jayhawker *Yearbook*

THE DAY THEY ALMOST ABOLISHED FOOTBALL

Twenty seasons after its formal introduction at the University of Kansas, the game of football had plenty of fans – and plenty of detractors as well. In the former category were many Kansas students and alumni, as well as University Chancellor Frank Strong, although he did, apparently, have some reservations about the sport. But in the latter zone were J. W. Gleed and William Allen White, members of the Board of Regents and significant men in their own rights in early twentieth-century Kansas.

On January 28, 1910 in Kansas history, Gleed proposed and White seconded a motion to abolish football until the rules were changed to eliminate endemic corruption and promote player safety. Although the motion was defeated, the Board of Regents agreed that it was "opposed to the game of football as now conducted, believing it does not tend to clean athletics." For the next few months, the future of football at Kansas hung in the balance and, for a while, it almost seemed that English Rugby would replace this classic American college game.

Kansas' Athletic Association had organized its first football team in September, 1890. Despite an inauspicious inaugural season that saw the Jayhawkers lose twice to Baker, though Kansas fans claimed the second game as a victory because of some questionable officiating, students and the rest of the University faithful embraced the sport wholeheartedly.

The universities of the sort to which Kansas aspired to equal, the Ivy League schools and Michigan for instance, all maintained top-flight football teams, and so the University of Kansas' supporters believed their institution needed to develop a similarly excellent team. As a result, football came to enjoy an immense popularity at Kansas. Students, alumni, and faculty members all rallied their school spirit behind a team that over its first two full seasons, 1891-1892, enjoyed a record of 14-1-1.

These initial successes fostered the expectation that future teams would fare equally well. When this failed to happen, Kansas boosters sought other ways to help ensure gridiron victories. Kansas began recruiting paid athletes and the team allowed players who were not passing their classes, or were not enrolled students at all, to participate in the weekly games.

By 1895, the demise of the team's amateurism had bred a number of critics within the University, including English professor Edwin M. Hopkins who had served as Kansas' football coach for its very successful 1891 and 1892 seasons. Hopkins was not alone in wondering whether football on Mount Oread had come to "stand for brutality, for trickery; for paid players, for profanity, for betting before games and for drinking after them."

The brutality to which Hopkins alluded was indeed an integral part of the game as it was played in the late-nineteenth and early-twentieth centuries. Players wore very little in the way of protective gear, even spurning helmets. Compounding these problems was the fact that officials enforced what few safety rules there were rather unevenly. In 1894, for example, the officials failed to penalize Michigan's team after one of its players jumped, with both feet, on a Kansas player who had just scored a touchdown.

Two years later, a player named Bert Serf from Doane College in Nebraska was killed while making a touchdown-saving tackle against Kansas in the final minute of a game in which he had earlier been knocked unconscious. Serf's death led the *Kansas University Weekly* to conclude, "rather than allow this [sort of] danger to exist it would be better to abolish the game completely." When the paper ultimately backed off and asked instead that the Western Inter-State University Foot Ball Association, to which Kansas belonged, "adopt the needed reforms," it fell in line with the majority of the game's critics.

Chancellor
Frank Strong

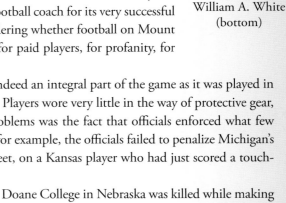

J. W. Gleed (top),
William A. White
(bottom)

Edwin M. Hopkins

But in 1901, Kansas Coach John Outland, of the Outland Trophy fame, was caught using an ineligible player with an assumed name. Criticism of the game began to mount again and continued to do so for the remainder of the first decade of the twentieth century. Much of the criticism was well deserved. After a 1903 Kansas-Nebraska game, both sides charged the other with using ineligible players and in consequence suspended all future

athletic contests between the schools. The following year, Kansas Chancellor Frank Strong had to fire Coach Harold S. Weeks for carrying on a sexual relationship with a freshman girl.

By the end of the autumn of 1905, the University was not alone in its skepticism about the benefits of football. Following that year's season, in which 18 college players from schools around the country died from injuries sustained in games and more than 150 were hurt seriously, cries for football's abolition echoed from every quarter of the nation.

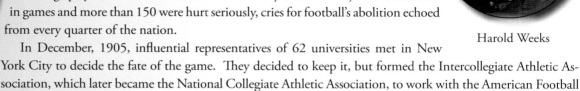

Harold Weeks

In December, 1905, influential representatives of 62 universities met in New York City to decide the fate of the game. They decided to keep it, but formed the Intercollegiate Athletic Association, which later became the National Collegiate Athletic Association, to work with the American Football Rules Committee to make the game safer. Most of the rules that were adopted early in 1906, including the legalization of the forward pass and the adoption of a neutral zone, were designed to spread out the players so that there would be fewer pileups.

John Outland

The change in the rules, coupled with Kansas' entry into the Missouri Valley Conference in 1907, eased the debate over the game's future at the University, but this was only temporary. Complaints about football cropped up again during the 1909 season when it became apparent that certain Kansas boosters were paying substitutes to cover the shifts of football players when their outside jobs interfered with practices or games. At the time, it was acceptable for college athletes to be employed, as long as they actually worked for the money. In addition, the University had broken conference rules by spending more than $400 on training tables, which regularly featured steak dinners aimed at keeping the players healthy.

The proverbial "straw that broke the camel's back" came, perhaps, in the rumor that opposing coaches had begun supplying their players with alcohol and narcotics both to ease pain and heighten energy. Thus it was that when the Board of Regents met on January 28, 1910, J. W. Gleed made a motion to abolish intercollegiate football at the university. Fellow regent William Allen White joined him in his motion.

This proposal failed to achieve majority support, but the Regents subsequently invited representatives from the other schools in the Missouri Valley Conference to a meeting scheduled for April 19 in which the matter of the "betterment of the present game" might be discussed. If the talks concluded that that the game was irretrievably corrupt, the Regents were willing to accept the substitution of English Rugby for football or mandate football's outright abolition.

In the weeks that followed, the relative merits of football were debated at all levels of the University. The Regents remained divided over the issue even after Gleed published an attack on the game in which he alluded to players who "get a passing grade without earning it" and maintained that it was not "possible for men to engage in fierce hand to hand physical struggle without arousing the smashing and destroying instinct which comes down to us from our animal ancestors."

Chancellor Strong, who favored the retention of football, wrote a letter to the American Football Rules Committee encouraging them to make substantive changes in the rules to protect collegiate players. Kansas Coach Bert Kennedy asserted that the game was no more dangerous than any other sport at the University and argued that his "football players [were] among the manliest men in the school." College Dean Olin Templin, however, hoped that rugby would replace football and insisted that "from a spectator's point of view [English Rugby was] much the better game."

Even W. H. Stubbs, the governor of Kansas, entered the fray and announced his opposition to football in April, 1910. As might be expected from a politician, he waffled somewhat. When addressing a crowd of students, he claimed to "like clean American sports," and announced that the "old American game is good enough for me."

Kansas students, for their part, almost universally favored retaining football and soon launched, as *The Kansan* reported, "an open campaign against rugby." Members of the football team, Coach Kennedy, and

Bert Kennedy

Dr. James Naismith, the inventor of basketball and Kansas' Director of Physical Culture, assisted the students in this effort. Naismith gave a resounding endorsement of the contested sport when he announced at a mass meeting that he had "always believed that football [was] the typical college game." Shortly thereafter, a "football ticket" was organized to run in student government elections, and all of its candidates won.

Olin Templin

Nonetheless, student hopes for the preservation of Kansas football began to dwindle in early April when word leaked out that Coach Kennedy would devote the team's spring practices to teaching his players the game of rugby. Within days, many students had grown downright despondent and started to assume that their cause was lost. *The Kansan* even published an article explaining the rules of rugby to the students so that they would understand what it was they had been opposing.

This "Monday mourning" turned out to be premature. On April 19, 1910, the schools of the Missouri Valley Conference voted to retain their football teams. However, the conference did institute some rules it hoped would de-emphasize the importance of football at its respective universities. The representatives of the schools banned freshmen from playing on the varsity football squad, proscribed Thanksgiving Day football games, mandated that all intercollegiate games be played on college campuses, and forbade the hiring of any coach who was not a "regular member of the teaching staff employed by the governing board of the institution, for the full academic year."

Although the changes made little difference in the questionable practices of Kansas' football team, the game was never again threatened at the University. The following year, for example, a man named Henry Ahrens "was induced to [play football for] the University by offers of payment in one fashion or another" and managed to masquerade as a law school student while he was on the team. When the matter was discovered, the Board of Regents hinted that it might again "seriously [consider] the abolition of football," but ultimately did not.

Henry Ahrens

Ironically enough, despite all of the emphasis placed on football in the early years and the cheating that accompanied it, Kansas never developed into a football powerhouse in the manner that the flagship universities of the states immediately to the north and south of Kansas did. While all this attention was focused on football, Kansas quietly developed a basketball program that would rank among the very best in the nation. If Kansas could not say it achieved the greatness of Notre Dame, Michigan, or Alabama in the sport in which it so badly wanted to excel, its ability to claim membership in the same basketball fraternity as University of California-Los Angeles, Duke, and Kentucky proved to be a more than adequate consolation prize.

By Mark D. Hersey, Ph.D.
Kansas Alumnus 2006
Written for This Week in KU History
www.KUHistory.com

James Naismith was not only the inventor of basketball. While a student and center on the football team at Springfield College, in Massachusettes, he took a football, cut it lengthwise, affixed a strap, and placed it over his head to protect his ears. Thus was recorded the invention and first use of the football helmet. James Naismith, seen left, with his football helmet.

THE JAYHAWKER AND THE SAVITAR

SAVITAR 1901 – BORDER WAR 1900

[There is no description of the game. Game tied 6-6.]

THE UNIVERSITY FOOTBALL ANNUAL 1901

KANSAS ACCOUNT:

The Texan game was played on November 23, which left only five days' preparation for the Missouri-Kansas game at Exposition Park, Kansas City, and one day being Sunday, left four days in which to prepare for the hardest game of the season, with some good men hurt at that: Buzzi, with a broken leg, and Allphin was still unable to go into a game; but on the 28th, Kansas met Missouri, and the least said about that meeting the better. Missouri winning by the score of 18 to 12; the first time since 1895, when they defeated K. U. by a score of 10 to 6. The team went to Kansas City expecting to win, and by all laws of football, Kansas should have had the odds, but they [didn't] count on the Tigers' strength or their own over-confidence. From the first kick-off until the end of the game, it was a harrowing sight to the K. U. rooters, if there were any, as the grandstand and bleachers rooted with "Tiger! Tiger! M. S. U." As one of the K. U. football boys stated, "I just didn't have energy enough to get low, I couldn't have made a touchdown if they had given me the ball, a bicycle and an open field. Maybe he couldn't ride a bicycle; any way neither he nor his team mates could play football, as was painfully witnessed by everyone; maybe they were overtrained, surely over confident.

Missouri started pounding the line at the very first, and when her backs couldn't go through it, they would go over it; and though Elder stopped them somewhat, he couldn't always get them before they gained their length. It was a clean-cut victory for Missouri, who out-played her opponents from up the Kaw, at every point. Jenkinson, the gritty Kansas Captain never gave up, and to him and Vincent, Brummage, Louthan, Dodds, Hicks and McKenna, is largely responsible the showing K. U. did make. Jenkinson's punting was far better than anything in that line he had done before during the season, and came as an agreeable surprise to the Kansas supporters. Kansas admits her clean defeat, and only hopes to regain her lost laurels next season.

By Charlie W. Lovelace
Kansas Alumnus 1904

MISSOURI ACCOUNT:

Great credit is due Mr. Fred Murphy for his excellent work in producing a team at the close of the season that showed complete reversal of form, surpassed all expectations, and caused general surprise by winning the final game of the season with Kansas.

By James Edgar Gibson
Missouri Alumnus 1902

John H. Outland's Review.

While our defeat at the hands of Missouri was unexpected to outsiders as to ourselves, yet when we consider the hard game with Texas on the Saturday before Thanksgiving, I think it need not have been so surprising. In the Texas game we were especially unfortunate in losing the services of Buzzi, left half-back, whose leg was broken. Owing to the hard condition of McCook field, numerous bruises were accumulated in the Texas game which operated against us in our Thanksgiving game. As was expected we were defeated but not disgraced at Nebraska. Considering the strength of the Nebraska team, I felt that the score was about as good as we had reason to expect. I think it would be advisable on account of the usual hard condition of McCook field the later part of the year to allow the men at least a week and perhaps ten days before the Thanksgiving game in which to recover from their bruises.

I do not wish to detract in the least from Missouri's victory. We found them stronger than we had expected and were simply out-played.

By John H. Outland
Kansas Head Coach 1901

1900S

Notes of the Game.

The Tiger did it.

Superior team-work--same old story.

Jenkinson worked hard, but it was no use.

Society was there; but the swell turnouts were few.

"Missouri wins" sounds rather queer, doesn't it?

The side lines were kept clearer than ever before.

Judge Hook, of the federal court, was an interested spectator.

M. S. U., 18; K. U., 12; every goal kicked --that's playing the game.

Kansas need not feel blue--Terrrible Terry went down and out, too.

Missouri played low, and crept along the ground. "That helped some."

The grand stand and bleachers looked like "mum's the word," but it wasn't.

Captain Casey, and twenty-five picked policemen handled the crowd in excellent style.

Missouri enthusiasm, pent up for five long years, was let loose at Exposition Park yesterday.

After the game a locomobile sped swiftly down Fifteenth with its Kansas flag at half mast.

"We've got 'em goin'," sang out a K. U. rooter as the Jayhawkers scored the first touch-down.

Both sides are agreed that the result of the game means a better one next year with stronger teams.

The team work of the Tigers was superb, as the way they went through the Jayhawkers' lines at times, showed.

The number of vehicles was smaller than usual. People seemed to prefer the grand stand; it was crowded.

The crimson and blue, and the yellow and black were about on an equal footing. They floated on all sides.

Lawson Price, the full-back and champion goal-kicker of the famous '95 team, held the line for Missouri.

From the spectator's point of view the weather was ideal. It was too mild to be called good football weather, however.

Kansas lost out on a comparatively warm day. That's what the Jayhawkers get for going up North and playing where it is cold.

"Go way back and sit down," shouted a dozen or more of the Tiger faction. "We're from Missouri, and we're going to show you."

"Which are the Kansans?" asked a late comer, edging up to the fence. "The ones coming this way," returned an enthusiastic K. U. student. "Coming this way," said a Columbia student, "look at 'em." And just then Missouri scored another touch-down.

"Exposition Park lived just long enough to see the tide turned," said an enthusiastic M. S. U. rooter at the conclusion of the game. "Yes, but one good turn deserves another," came from the K. U. corner. "That'll come next year in a new park."

Two pretty girls stood at Fifteenth and Park last evening while cars bearing the football crowd passed. One waved a black and yellow flag, and when she got a response from the car, daintily kissed her hand and bowed to the rooters.

"That ball is mighty unpopular," said a pretty girl to several young fellows who were standing with her. "See, all the players are down on it." And the young men seemingly tried to outdo each other in laughing, but it wasn't at the joke.

K. U., like the maid from the Niger,
Went smiling to ride on the tiger.
   But when it got through,
   Its looks had turned blue,
With the smile on the face of the tiger.

There once was a team from K. U.,
Which trid to "butt in" on Missou,
   But it found lines so strong,
   It adoped this song:
"We'll even things up in '02."

SAVITAR 1902 – BORDER WAR 1901
VANQUISHED

They came 'mid the flourish of trumpets,
As they did the year before.
They thought to awe with throat and jaw.
They howled as the dogs of war,

They came with banners flying;
They were loud in their champions' praise,
For they had no doubt they would put to rout,
The vanquished of others days.

The day of the year is upon us,
The battle royal is here,
And the coolest heart gives a sudden start,
When the chosen few appear.

There they go like a shot from a cannon;
Look! The foe falls beneath their tread,
And they forge their way to the fortress gay,
Flying the blue and red.
Night has come; the battle is over,
And Missouri has won the day.
Kansas may talk but when tigers eat chalk,
Old Kansas has nothing to say.

JAYHAWKER 1903 – BORDER WAR 1902

…and then came the joyous and soul-stirring finish at Kansas City on Thanksgiving. The old Tiger looked very formidable. He had learned some Kangaroo stunts, and had become fierce and confident. After one of the fiercest, cleanest games in the history of Kansas City gridiron annals, Kansas won by the unexpected score of 17 to 5. All past short-comings were forgotten. The '02 team had redeemed itself and revenged the defeat in '01, and so closed the season in a whirl of glory.

SAVITAR 1903 – BORDER WAR 1902

The Kansas game came next and the largest crowd that ever went from Columbia to Kansas City to cheer the Tigers on to victory was on hand at the new park, waving the Old Gold and Black. The betting was 10 to 7 in favor of Missouri. A crowd of 8,000 people watched the two teams fight it out. The contest was a good one, and up to the early part of the second d half the teams seemed evenly matched. But from the time that K. U. first got the ball in the second half, the game went against M. S. U. Poor team work and poor tackling were the causes of the Tigers' defeat. The men were capable of better work.

JAYHAWKER 1904 – BORDER WAR 1903

[There is no description of the game. KU won 5-0.]

SAVITAR 1905 – BORDER WAR 1904

The 1905 football season was a disastrous one. Missouri was beaten by Washington, and on Thanksgiving day was sorely trounced by Kansas. In this championship game Missouri was outclassed, Kansas going as much as thirty yards at a time by straight bucks through the Missouri line.

From the moment of the Purdue game Missouri's was a patched-up team. The patching-up process necessitated that the men be worked overtime. The men went stale, became brittle, lost their ginger and spirit. The team became disorganized. It was a sorry organization that faced Kansas Thanksgiving day to represent Missouri. We all hoped against hope that the Missouri spirit would give the men that brace so characteristic of Missouri teams in this final game. But the spirit had been knocked out of the men, the men had lost their aggressiveness, and the men were crippled.

By John F. McLean
Missouri Faculty, Instructor in Athletics

JAYHAWKER 1906 – BORDER WAR 1905
[There is no description of the game. KU won 24-0.]

SAVITAR 1906 – BORDER WAR 1905
[There is no description of the game. KU won 24-0.]

SAVITAR 1907 – BORDER WAR 1906
[There is no description of the game. Game tied 0-0.]

JAYHAWKER 1908 – BORDER WAR 1907

Sam Forter won undying fame by the work of his trusty right leg, and will go down in history as the hero of the '07 Kansas-Missouri contest

SAVITAR 1908 – BORDER WAR 1907
[There is no description of the game. KU won 4-0.]

JAYHAWKER 1909 – BORDER WAR 1908

One of the hardest games of the season was the one played with Missouri at Kansas City, coming as it did four days after the hard Iowa game.

SAVITAR 1909 – BORDER WAR 1908
[There is no description of the game. KU won 10-4.]

SAVITAR 1910 – BORDER WAR 1909
[There is no description of the game. MU won 12-6.]

CHICAGO CONFERENCE RULES.

RULE 1. No person shall participate in any intercollegiate game or athletic sport, unless he is a *bona fide* student, doing full work in a regular or special course as defined in the curriculum of his college; and no student who has participated in any intercollegiate game, as a member of the college team, shall be permitted to play on the team of any other college during the succeeding season devoted to that game; unless he has obtained a college academic degree; preparatory students shall not be eligible to membership on the college teams.

RULE 2. No person shall be admitted to any intercollegiate contest who receives any gift, remuneration or pay for his services on the college team.

RULE 3. No student shall participate in a particular sport upon the teams of any college or colleges for more than four years in the aggregate, and any member of a college who plays during any part of an intercollegiate football (or baseball) game does thereby participate in that sport for the year.

RULE 4. No student shall participate in any intercollegiate contest who has ever used or is using his knowledge of athletic skill for gain. No person who receives any compensation from the university for services rendered by the way of regular instruction shall be allowed to play on any team.

RULE 5. No student shall play in any game under an assumed name.

RULE 6. No student shall be permitted to participate in any intercollegiate contest who is found by the faculty to be delinquent in his studies.

RULE 7. All intercollegiate games shall be played on grounds either owned or under the immediate control of one or both of the colleges participating in the contest, and all intercollegiate games shall be played under student management, and not under the control of any corporation, or association, or private individual.

RULE 8. The election of managers and captains of teams in each college shall be subject to the approval of its committee on athletics.

RULE 9. College football teams shall play only with teams representing educational institutions.

RULE 10. Before any intercollegiate contest the respective chairmen of the athletic committees of the institutions concerned shall submit to each other a certified list of players, eligible under the rules adopted, to participate in said contest. It shall be the duty of the captains of the respective teams to exclude all players from the contest save those certified.

RULE 11. Athletic committees shall require each candidate for a team to represent the university in intercollegiate contests to subscribe to a statement that he is eligible under the letter and spirit of the rules adopted.

RULE 12. No person having been a member of a college athletic team during any year, and having been in attendance less than one college half year, shall be permitted to play in any intercollegiate contest thereafter until he shall have been in attendance six consecutive calendar months.

Reprinted in The University Football Annual 1901

As music transitioned to jazz and then blues, the pursuit and application of science gave way to the modern era. Despite cultural advances, such as the first United States feature film, Oliver Twist, being released and technological advances, such as Albert Einstein's publishing of his General Theory of Relativity, great monarchies of the world fell and new political orders arose as a result of European militarism and a great, world war.

In the decade of the 1910s, Missouri squeaked one more victory over Kansas in the decade 5-4 and, for the only time in the game's history between the two schools, a game was cancelled. After Missouri's enormously successful 1909 season, Bill Roper left the team because his high demand to take control of other football programs also elevated his $2,500 cost to a level that Missouri could not pay, perhaps being as high as $5,000 to retain his services for another year.

In Kansas, due to what was considered mounting corruption in the football program, J. W. Gleed made a motion in the January 28, 1910 Board of Regents meeting to abolish intercollegiate football which was seconded by regent William Allen White. While their motion did not pass, it was decided to invite the other members of the Missouri Valley Intercollegiate Athletic Association to an April 4 meeting where the betterment of football might be discussed. Although the abolishment of football was seriously considered, to the extent that the Kansas team began learning rugby football, it did not happen. In an April 19 meeting, the representatives of the Missouri Valley Intercollegiate Athletic Association voted to continue gridiron football. However, the conference did institute some new rules; freshmen were banned from playing on the varsity team, Thanksgiving Day games were prohibited, all intercollegiate games were to be held only on college campuses, and all coaches must be a regular member of the teaching staff employed by the governing board of the university for the full academic year.

Just before the 1910 football season, William M. "Bill" Hollenbeck took control of Missouri football, posting a 4-2-2 season record, which was far less impressive than what his predecessor Bill Roper had accomplished just the year prior. In the game with Kansas, however, Missouri was able to hold Kansas, the expected winner, to a 5-5 tie, causing a sensation for two years in a row by withstanding the athletic greatness of Tommy Johnson. In the game, held at Gordon and Koppel Stadium in Kansas City because the new rules voted on April 19 had not yet taken effect, Tommy Johnson was tackled by two Missouri defenders, causing the aggravation of a childhood kidney condition that had plagued him throughout his childhood. The condition became so grave that Johnson remained hospitalized for a year, causing him to miss the entire basketball season and the following football season.

The idealism of Clark Hetherington at Missouri brought intercollegiate cooperation and organization to collegiate athletics and also brought proper oversight to Missouri's football program, especially at a time of great need. However, Hetherington was more comfortable with academic pursuits and writing than dealing with people, which earned him his detractors. Continued friction with the faculty and students at the University of Missouri brought an end to Hetherington's reign. Replacing him in 1911 was Chester L. Brewer who was noted as being a very good handler of people. Brewer was born in Owoso, Michigan in 1876 and was an excellent athlete at the University of Wisconsin. He coached football at Michigan Agricultural College, now Michigan State University, for seven years before coming to the University of Missouri. Brewer viewed athletics at a university as a focal point of character building for the students and a centerpiece around which alumni could rally their support, as his article in the 1911 *Savitar* states; "The Department aims also to promote athletics in their broadest sense, not only for their physical effect but for their effect on the moral fiber of the individual. It is a fine thing to develop a body. It is even a finer thing to develop

November 12, 1912, Kansas students burn a tiger effigy on campus (top) Events at the 1912 game (bottom)

the mind, but the greater value comes in the fact that athletics develop the character, and this is what counts. Whatever may be said of men who have done their duty on 'the team,' whether it be class, department, scrub, or varsity, those men must necessarily have practiced the rugged virtues of courage, resolution, self domination the power of acting in conjunction with others, resolution to act as gentlemen; and often, what is more important, to act as men. It is these qualities which make athletics so invaluable and for these qualities athletics are a most important factor in the higher education."

......HOMECOMING AND THE GREAT WAR

In 1911, Brewer, in addition to becoming Missouri football's new head coach, promoted the first ever "homecoming" for any institution by inviting the first 1890 Missouri football team and other alumni back to Columbia in celebration of the game against Kansas. At that homecoming, members who had played for Missouri's early teams, who played when letters were not awarded, were awarded letters for their past service to the team and to the University of Missouri. The game was scheduled for the first time since 1892 on a Saturday, November 25, because of the new Missouri Valley Intercollegiate Athletic Association rule changes, which would remain in effect until 1914. On the eve of Missouri's first great homecoming, news reached the Kansas team that Tommy Johnson, who had been unable to play that season due to his injury, died in a Kansas City hospital of kidney failure. The game between Missouri and Kansas ended the next day in a 3-3 tie.

Missouri fans board the train for Lawrence in 1912

In 1912, football began to undergo changes in its play, such as the reduction of the field to 100 yards, the downs were increased from three to four and the scoring changed so that a touchdown became worth six points. In 1913, Brewer served his last year as football head coach, coaching the team to a 7-1 record and to the Co-Championship of the Missouri Valley Intercollegiate Athletic Association. Although the new Missouri Head Coach Henry F. "Indian" Schulte, who was nicknamed for appearing as an aboriginal American, took control of the team the next year, Chester Brewer stayed in his position as Director of Athletics. In 1915, Turkey Day games were once again permitted in the Missouri Valley Intercollegiate Athletic Association and a new milestone was reached when Missouri players wore numbers for the first time with the captain and end of the team, Jacob "Jake" Speelman, donning number "1."

The previous year on June 28, 1914, Archduke Franz Ferdinand was assassinated in Sarajevo causing the Great War to erupt in Europe. America's policy for the first three years of the conflict was Isolationism, but the policy changed, causing great numbers of Americans to join the war effort, greatly impacting collegiate institutions. America entered the conflict in 1917, immediately affecting collegiate attendance, but the severer effects would occur later, as the 1919 *Savitar* noted, "Despite the fact that the United States was engaged in the world conflict almost

18 months, it was only during the last year of the struggle that the athletic programs of our higher institutions of learning were vitally affected. The heroes of the diamond, gridiron, court and track responded at the first blare of the trumpet for humanity's salvation; but the athletic programs were not allowed to be seriously interrupted. They were vital in this early period of trial and were not discontinued. Thus we saw the various schools struggling throughout the seasons of late 1917 and 1918. The spring track and baseball seasons were well nigh lost in the bustle of the great overseas campaign. Prominent athletes from every branch of sport were now flocking to the colors. What teams did appear in the field were composed of young men well under the 21-31 draft bill."

Despite the end of the war nearing, the Armistice being signed on November 11, 1918, students were still drilling at the University of Missouri with the Student Army Training Corps, with honourable mention going to the students who participated in the corps and also practiced two hours a day on the gridiron. The team for Missouri was built around three remaining varsity players who had not gone to the war; Edwin L. "Bunny" Morris, quarterback; Elmer F. Edwards, halfback; John Harrison Marshall, end. The Missouri Valley Intercollegiate Athletic Association also ruled to allow freshmen to compete on the varsities so that universities could have complete teams.

The 1918 Missouri team might have competed had an awful influenza pandemic and consequent quarantine not reached Missouri and Kansas, the former being affected greater than the latter, another effect of the Great War. The entire season was a large disappointment to Missouri players and fans as each game scheduled for the team was cancelled two or three days before each contest. Kansas was more fortunate than their Missouri counterparts, in that they were able to play four games in November, winning two. Alas, for Missouri, despite the 250 hours spent practicing, not a single game was held and the majority of the team had gone to war, including the team's Captain-Elect, Henry B. Blass. Because of the shelving of the 1918 season and the loss of great players expected for that season, Missouri anticipated and succeeded in having a great 1919 football team, finishing the season with a 5-1-2 record and earning a win over Kansas and attaining its third Missouri Valley Intercollegiate Athletic Association Championship title.

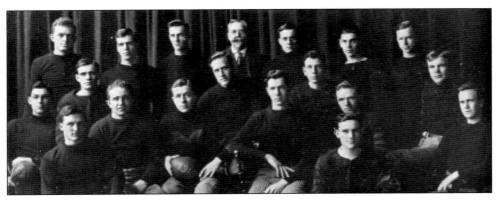

Missouri Football (4-2-2) - Head Coach William M. Hollenbeck
(Unordered) Captain Frank Thacher, Theodore Hackney, Edward Klein, Ewart Johnson, William Saunders, Frank Burress, Walter Barnes, Arthur Idler, Clarence LeMire, Lloyd Curtis, Glen Shuck, Eugene Hall, Grant Hastings, Edmund Knobel, John Mills, Paul Graves, John Miller, Proctor Thompson.

MU Football Captain
Frank Barclay Thacher

Kansas Football (6-1-1) - Head Coach Albert Rutherford Kennedy
(Unordered) Spencer L. Baird, Roy E. Spear, W. Ellis Davidson, Ralph Smith, Frank C. Lynch, Harold William Cowell, Earl F. Ammons, Tom W. Johnson, Charles Woodbury, Harold Woodbury, Henry J. E. Ahrens, William E. Price, Ben Davis, Levi L. Kabler, John Power, Glenn P. Wilhelm, Roy H. Heil.

KU Football Captain
Tom W. Johnson

Missouri Football (2-4-2) - Head Coach Chester L. Brewer
(Unordered) Captain Glenn Shuck, Theodore Hackney, Eugene Hall, Clarence LeMire, Edmund Knoble, Oscar Houston, William Blees, David Dexter, Allen Wilder, James Pixler, Grant Hastings, John Mills, Elmer Anderson, George Barton, Edgar Anderson, Robert Wilson.

Kansas Football (4-2-2) - Head Coach Ralph Waldo Sherwin
Row 1: Daniel, Heil, Davis, Coolidge. Row 2: Hoffman, Kabler, Price, Brownlee, Wilson, Woodbury, Magill. Row 3: Davidson, Hamilton, Woodbury, Green, Ammons, Sherwin, Delaney, Ahrens. Row 4: Tudor, McMillan, Schwab, Burnham, Baird, Weidlein, Bramwell.

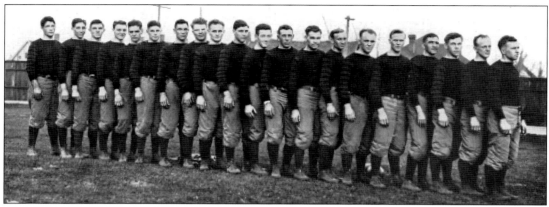

Missouri Football (5-3) - Head Coach Chester L. Brewer
Row 1: Gallagher, Kemper, Groves, Clay, Dunckel, Shepard, Knoble, Hastings Barlos, Herndon, Turkey, Captain Cap Le Mire, Duvall, Lake, Pixlee, Miller, Happ, Wiggans, McWilliams, Wilson.

MU Football Captain
Clarence Plato Le Mire

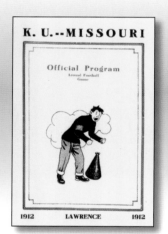

Kansas Football (4-4) - Head Coach Arthur St. Leger Mosse

KU Football Captain
Harold Brownlee

Missouri Football (7-1) - Head Coach Chester L. Brewer
Missouri Valley Co-Champion
(Unordered) Captain Robert Wilson, James Clay, Crosby Kemper, Robert Groves, Lee McWilliams, Paul Shepard, Roy Wiggans, Janes Gallagher, Arnold Zimmerman, Jacob Speelman, Frank Herndon, Joseph Moore, William Dunckel, Floyd Lake, De Witt Collins.

MU Football Captain
Robert Charles Wilson

Kansas Football (5-3) - Head Coach Arthur St. Leger Mosse
Row 1: Parker, Wilson, Russel, Greenelees. Row 2: Sommers, Martin, Cawkins, Bishop. Row 3: Detwiler, James, Coach Mosse, Captain Weidline, Coach Frank, Tudor, Steuwe. Row 4: Kane, Burton, Strothers, Keeling, Malot, Hammond, Reber.

KU Football Captain
Bill Weidlein

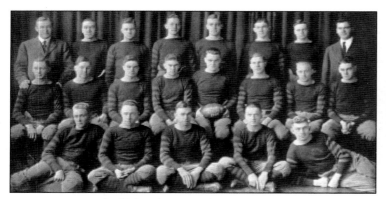

Missouri Football (5-3) - Head Coach Henry F. Schulte
Row 1: Lansing, Rutledge, Woody, Miller, Graham. Row 2: La Rue, Herndon, Collins, Shepard, Captain James Clay, Speelman, Lake. Row 3: Brewer, Wikoff, Graves, Van Dyne, Drumm, Groves, Savage.

MU Football Captain
James Ashton Clay

KU Football Captain
John Eli Detwiler

Kansas Football (5-2-1) - Head Coach Henry M. Wheaton
Row 1: Burton, Coolidge, Wood, James. Row 2: Gray, Day, Robbins, Craig, Calkins, Lamb, Kietzman, Lindsey, Roswurm. Row 3: Gross, Strother, Russell, Reber, Mulloy, Detwiler, Sproull, Coleman, McCaitlin, Keeling. Row 4: McKenney, Bohannan, Jones, Dilley, Housholder, Heath, Stryker, Kempert, Fink.

Missouri Football (2-5-1) - Head Coach Henry F. Schulte
Row 1: White, Reppy, Stankowski, Clay. Row 2: Pittam, Rider, Groves, Captain Jake Speelman, Collins, Van Dyne, Giltner. Row 3: Brewer, Preston, Muir, Coach Schulte, Hamilton, McAnaw, Coach Wilson.

MU Football Captain
Jacob Speelman

Kansas Football (6-2) - Head Coach Herman P. Olcott
Row 1: Carter, Fitzgerald, McKone, Lindsey, Fast, Wood, Todd, Kabler, Gorrill, Fletcher. Row 2: McMeel, Holt, B. Gillespie, Reber, Coach Bond, Coach Alcott, Captain James, Manager Hamilton, Neilson, Lawellin, Reedy, Hartley. Row 3: Wilson, Robbins, Palkowsky, Frost, Hammond, Bell, Heath, Groft, Keeling, Meyn, Smith, Ruble, W. R. Smith, L. Gillespie, Strother, Petterson.

KU Football Captain
Darl James

Missouri Football (6-1-1) - Head Coach Henry F. Schulte
Row 1: Rutlege, Stankowski, McMillan. Row 2: Hamilton, Rider, Preston, Groves, Muir, Macanaw, Pittam, Giltner. Row 3: Peeples, Collins, Bass, Wilder, Slusher, Viner, Coach Schulte, Coach Woody, Athletic Director Brewer. (Not Pictured: Captain Harry Lansing)

MU Football Captain
Harry S. Lansing

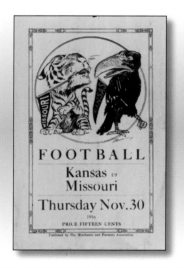

Kansas Football (4-3-1) - Head Coach Herman P. Olcott
Row 1: Arnold, Bradley, Neilson, Foster, Cowgill, Laslett, Todd. Row 2: M. Ruble, E. Smith, Gregory, Woody, Lindsey, Fiske, Shinn, Reed, Kabler, Pringle. Row 3: Hamilton, Russel, Woodward, Wilson, Palkowsky, Olcott, R. Ruble, W. Smith, Clark, Miner, Hull, Martin, Frost, Burton, Wilbur.

KU Football Captain
Adrian Hobart Lindsey

Missouri Football (3-5) - Head Coach Henry F. Schulte
Row 1: Morris, Viner, Collins, Captain Paul Hamilton, Rider, Marshall, Edwards. Row 2: Coach Groves, Chittenden, Schroeder, Kolb, Stevens, Coach Schulte. Row 3: Bass, Kirkpatrick, Urie, Berry, Slusher.

MU Football Captain
Paul A. Hamilton

Kansas Football (6-2) - Head Coach Herman P. Olcott
Row 1: Zoellner, Idol, Lonborg, Casey, Davis, Marquis, Wilson, Hilton, Russell, Laslett. Row 2: Woody, Pringle, Frost, Neilsen, Wilson, Todd, Mandeville. Row 3: Smith, Bunn, Jones, Harms, Ruble, Nettles, Hull, Olcott, Liggett, Davison, Arnold, Simon, Wenzel, Stevenson, Dietrich, Gregory.

KU Football Captain
Harry M. Neilsen

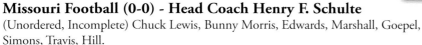
PHOTOGRAPH UNAVAILABLE

Missouri Football (0-0) - Head Coach Henry F. Schulte
(Unordered, Incomplete) Chuck Lewis, Bunny Morris, Edwards, Marshall, Goepel, Simons, Travis, Hill.

MU Football Captain-Elect
Henry B. Bass

Missouri practicing in a season where all games were cancelled

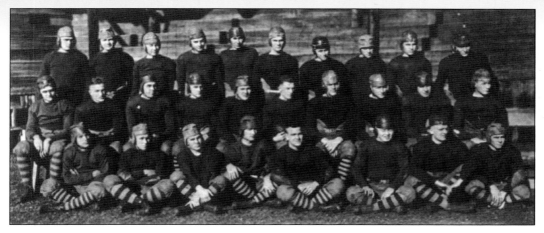

Kansas Football (2-2) - Head Coach James Bond
Row 1: Sherman, Love, unknown, Russell, Walther, McLeod, Lamb, unknown. Row 2: unknown, Simmons, Hochuli, Banta, Jones, Captain Foster, Marxen, Heizer, Mason, Rinehart. Row 3: Schnell, Rammus, Myers, Harris, Pringle, Winkler, Oswald, unknown, Bunn, Norris.

KU Football Captain
Lewis C. Foster

Missouri Football (5-1-2) - Head Coach John F. Miller
Missouri Valley Champion

Row 1: Cross, Forster, Packwood. Row: Sylvester, Kolb, Collins, Captain Anton Stankowski, Viner, Edwards, Schroeder, Leis. Row 3: Peterson, Ruth, Hardin, Redman, Bahr, Travis, Shannon. Row 4: Springgate, Andrews, Guild, Bloomer, King, Vilkas. Row 5: Coach Phelan, Hamilton, Coach Miller, Stablein, Goepel, Coach Kelley.

MU Football Captain
Anton J. Stankowski

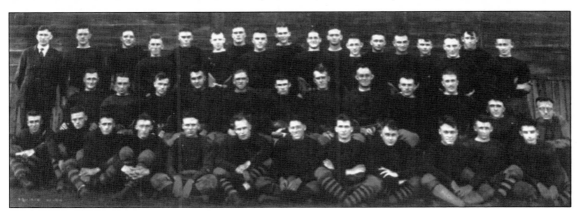

Kansas Football (3-2-3) - Head Coach Leon McCarty

Row 1: Evans, Shurtliff, Reid, Lupher, Snare, Cowgill, Woody, Wilson, Reedy, Saunders, Barter, Clarke. Row 2: Gress, Brigham, Wood, Pringle, Lonborg, Laslett, Nettels, Smith, Rinehart, Simons, Sherman, McCarty. Row 3: Allen, Lindsey, Davison, Love, Bell, Hall, Ruble, Marxen, Duff, Knoles, Bernard, Heizer, Church, Mandeville, Morrison, Hart, Kanpert, Cohn.

KU Football Captain
Howard Laslett

THE PURPOSE OF PHYSICAL TRAINING AND ATHLETICS

It is an established fact that the physical health of the individual largely determines his capacity for usefulness, and with this in mind the Department of Physical Training and Athletics aims to supply the opportunity for such physical work as is necessary to favor the attainment by the student body of a high state of physical efficiency. The Department aims also to promote athletics in their broadest sense, not only for their physical effect but for their effect on the moral fiber of the individual. It is a fine thing to develop a body. It is even a finer thing to develop the mind, but the greater value comes in the fact that athletics develop the character, and this is what counts. Whatever may be said of men who have done their duty on "the team," whether it be class, department, scrub, or varsity, those men must necessarily have practiced the rugged virtues of courage, resolution, self domination the power of acting in conjunction with others, resolution to act as gentlemen; and often, what is more important, to act as men. It is these qualities which make athletics so invaluable and for these qualities athletics are a most important factor in the higher education.

By Chester L. Brewer
Missouri Football Head Coach 1911-1913
Missouri Director of Athletics 1910 -1917, 1923-1935
Written for the 1911 Savitar *Yearbook*

FOOTBALL DURING THE FALL OF 1918

For the fist time since football originated at the University, the Tigers were not represented on the gridiron last fall. Misfortune alone seemed to doom the Herculean efforts of Coach "Indian" Schulte and his tribe of loyal pigskin chasers to appear for Missouri.

Immediately after the opening of school, Coaches Schulte and Miller of the varsity and freshmen squads respectively went to work with their usual vigor despite the fact that they hadn't the least idea what was to happen when the Student Army Training Corps was installed. A long, arduous schedule had been arranged and all was set for a big year on the gridiron, even under the adverse circumstances of war conditions. The team was granted to be much younger than ever before. A [Missouri Valley Intercollegiate Athletic Association] ruling allowed freshmen to compete on the conference varsities.

Coach Schulte had but a few stars of the freshmen team around which to build his varsity when the S. A. T. C. opened here at Missouri. Three varsity men served as a nucleus. "Bunny" Morris was back to handle the quarterback berth and Edwards and Marshall would have been at the halves. Goepel and Simons, Freshmen ends of the year before, were in school, as were Travis and Hill Tackles. In the backfield "Chuck" Lewis was the best prospect from the year previous. With several promising freshmen in school it looked as though this lineup would give Missouri a fair chance in the "Valley Title Race."

Everything was arranged for the first game of the season when the "Flu" quarantine went on. The second game and the third were postponed in the same manner, yet the team worked steadily on. Some men had left school to enlist in a favored branch of the service until there were but two or three men left, and those, freshmen from 1917. Work continued with the idea of playing the next game on the schedule, and so it went throughout the season, each game being canceled two or three days ahead of the date of the battle. Nothing could have been more discouraging. One enterprising Tiger follower has figured that some 250 hours were spent in practice but not a single game played. These men, who worked hard while in the Student Army Training Corps and then spent two hours a day out on the football field, deserve honorable mention of the highest order.

While the S. A. T. C. was in session, Coach H. F. Schulte was in charge of the athletics of the Collegiate Section, and under his direction some mighty spirited gridiron battles between companies were played. On Saturday it was usually the custom to have some sort of a track fete which consisted of many interesting events. Indoor baseball and tennis were also played to a considerable extent. The army authorities demanded that the men have at least one hour of athletics a day. We enjoy most to say that the periods of the S. A. T. C. is over and we are once again back in regular routine of affairs with plenty of "ye olde fighte." We are looking forward to the 1919 football season that we may contrast it with the last one.

Written for the 1919 Savitar *Yearbook*

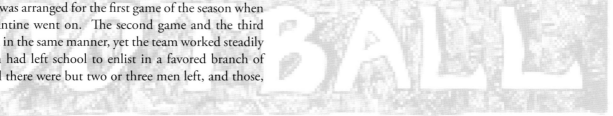

HOW AND WHEN, "ROCK CHALK" CAME INTO BEING

Professor Bailey from the 1917 *Jayhawker* yearbook

We must go back more than thirty years to learn about the beginnings of our famous yell, the "Rock Chalk" of which we are so proud. In the year 1883-'4 a Science club was started by some of the older men of the University, including Dr. E. L. Nichols, now head of the Physics department of Cornell University; Doctor Snow, the late chancellor; Professor Marvin, the late dean of the School of Engineering; E. Miller, of California, emeritus professor of Mathematics and Astronomy; and the writer, who was professor of Chemistry.

None of the above departments were at the time strong enough to support a seminar or department club, as there were only three hundred students in the University proper. Consequently the Science Club was started as a clearing house for scientific information, and also to keep the students of the sciences together. At its weekly meetings papers were read and the social side for the club was not neglected. There was an annual Science Club day, with a social gathering in the evening, and the scientific work of the year was reviewed by professors and advanced students; there were excursions to Blue Mound, Leavenworth or Kansas City. As the ladies were always in the company, these trips were very popular.

Perhaps the most famous of the "doings" of the Science Club was the unique annual banquet, known as the "It," a name proposed by Professor Martin, after we had sought in vain for an appropriate name for such a feast of jollity and wit. This was attended by members only and held in the basement of the Chemistry building, now Medical Hall. The "It" recalls many pleasant memories to the students of the Nineties. Usually after an oyster supper prepared by the expert cooks of the club, a program was "put on." The speakers told of their own discoveries (?) and burlesqued those of their colleagues.

This may seem a long introduction to the history of "Rock Chalk" but as it was originally designed for the sole use and profit of the Science Club, this seems proper. It was at one of our meetings in 1887 or '88, over our doughnuts and cider, that someone suggested that we adopt a yell. Several were presented to the club, tried and found unsatisfactory. Shortly after this meeting, early one morning, I was thinking of the matter of these words occurred to me: "Rah, Rah, Jay hawk, K. U." three times repeated, with staccato emphasis. I proposed this yell at the next meeting of the club and it was adopted. We used it

with such success on our picnics and excursions that it was soon taken up by the student body at large and made the regular yell of the University. Shortly after this, by some process of evolution, and I think at the suggestion of some of the Snow Hall men, the "Rah, Rah" was changed to "Rock Chalk," and finally in the enthusiasm of the early football days, the long roll twice repeated was substituted for the first part of the slogan. And so the yell "that sounds o'er land and sea" was introduced into K. U.

By Professor Edgar Henry Summerfield Bailey, Ph.D.
Kansas Professor of Science 1881–1931
Written for the 1917 Jayhawker *Yearbook*

Uncle Jimmy Green

Uncle Jimmy Green, the best friend of the students in the University of Kansas, has passed away. He was our friend because he was loyal to us. We were his friends because, from the nature of things, Uncle Jimmy was just one of us. His spirit never could grow old—and it can never die.—The University Daily Kansan, November 4, 1919.

"GREEN, James Woods, lawyer," Who's Who catalogued him.

"James W. Green, A. M., Dean of the School of Law," he was listed in the University catalog.

But neither was correct. Had their information been gathered from the students of the University of Kansas, his name would have appeared as simply "Uncle Jimmy." For so was he known among the thousands who passed through the University during his forty-one years of service on the Hill.

And had in addition sobriquets been asked, the students could have given many. From "The Prince of Sports," the title he bore for a long time while on the Athletic Board, to the more formal "Judge Green" of maturer years, and finally to "The Grand Old Man of K. U.," all Uncle Jimmy's names reflect the love and affection the students bore him.

Uncle Jimmy was nearly 78 years of age at his death, on November 4, 1919. He was born April 4, 1842, at Cambridge, Washington County, New York, of Scotch-Irish parents. His early education was in the district schools, and from Phillips Academy he entered Williams College in 1862. He received an A. B. degree in 1866, and several years later was given an A. M. degree by the same institution.

After leaving school, the youthful jurist read law in an office at Elmira. In June, 1869, he was admitted to the bar by the Supreme Court of New York, and early the next year he came to Kansas, where he entered the law office of Thatcher & Banks at Lawrence. He left soon after for Olathe and there formed a law partnership with S. A. Devenny. In 1875 he was elected county attorney of Johnson county on the Democratic ticket, and served one term.

While holding this office, he returned to Lawrence and married Miss May Stephens, on December 7, 1875. Mrs. Green was a daughter of Judge Nelson T. Stephens, whose idea it first was to place a Department of Law in the University of Kansas. Cyrus S. Crane, 1 '87, at the memorial exercises in Kansas City, November 15, 1919, stated that Judge Stephens "more than anyone else is entitled to the credit for the department, and it seems eminently fitting that his daughter should have been the wife of our friend."

"Jim" Green was his name in those days. As to what sort of an attorney he was, we have the word of a colleague: "He was a lawyer. He did not have the forensic ability that some of his brothers at that time had, but he was always prepared with the law. He was—and he wanted to be—just a plain, every-day lawyer."

In 1877 he established a permanent home in Lawrence and in 1878 was elected county attorney of Douglas county. In the latter year the Board of Regents decided to establish a department of law at the University, and the young county attorney was asked to take charge of it.

Law classes in those days were held early in the morning, after which the faculty of two and the student body of eighteen left the Hill for downtown offices. There the instructors plied their profession and the students read law, for there was then no law library.

Uncle Jimmy received a new appellation in 1879, of which he told as follows at the dedication of Green Hall: "I find by the catalog of that year that the head of the department was given the title of Dean, although it was long after this date that I ascertained the fact."

The state made no appropriation for the department and the faculty took for their compensation what fees were collected of the students." These fees were $25 a year, and the requirement for a degree was attendance at two annual terms of seven months each.

Uncle Jimmy's interest in football commenced in 1891, when the game was first introduced to K. U. He was long prominent on the Athletic Board, and a banquet in honor of the football team was held at his home yearly until the health of Mrs. Green made this impossible. It was in 1906 that Dean Green began to make his forecasts of football victories, and after that no football rally was complete without him, nor did he ever miss a game up to the season of 1919. His nickname of "The Dean of Football" well expresses his deep interest in the game.

The Uncle Jimmy of the early nineties loved to drive about Lawrence with his wife, behind their fine team of horses. The Greens were recognized social leaders, but all their friends of whatever social rank were always welcome at the Green home.

The Law Building was dedicated November 3, 1905, and named Green Hall in honor of the Dean. Here, fourteen years and a day before his death, Uncle Jimmy made a prophecy which he lived to see fulfill times without number. He said:

"In this quiet and beautiful retreat, dedicated by the state to a most noble purpose, the young men and women of the state will gather for years to come to hear the laws of their state and of the Union expounded, and they will go forth from its halls broader, wiser and more useful citizens; better able to take up the battle of life and better fitted to make and uphold the laws of their country."

Mrs. Green died April 16, 1916, and this together with the death of a brother soon after, saddened Uncle Jimmy's declining years. He had no children of his own; so he became the "uncle" and friend of every student. A former K. U. man, paying tribute to Uncle Jimmy after his death, said of this element in his character: "I have often thought that because Uncle Jimmy's affections were not centralized or focused on children of his own, his great heart went out to us and we had more of him ourselves than if that had not been true."

The "Uncle Jimmy Day" banquets were yearly events in the School of Law. They were always held on the Thursday nearest Uncle Jimmy's birthday, April 4, so that the students might have a holiday next day in his honor. The banquet held April 3, 1919, served to celebrate the fiftieth anniversary of Uncle Jimmy's admission to the bar as well as his seventy-seventh birthday. In addition to the yearly celebration of "Uncle Jimmy Day," there were annual banquets held by the Kansas City alumni. Students of law are keeping the custom of "Uncle Jimmy Day" banquets. One was held April 8, 1920.

Kidney and heart trouble were the immediate cause of Uncle Jimmy's death, but up to a few weeks previous he had attended to his duties regularly. Hundreds of students and friends attended the funeral. It was held at the Episcopal Church, of which Uncle Jimmy was long a member. The Reverend Evan Edwards conducted the services, and faculty members and alumni acted as pall bearers.

His quiet, droll humor, his gentle, intimate interest in all that concerned University students, his tolerance and his greatness of heart, made spontaneous tributes come to him from all sides during his life, a statement which can be made of few men. How often Uncle Jimmy saved repentant young men from the results of their folly in conflicts with the civil authorities as well as with the University, no one will ever know. How often in his administrative duties he erred on the side of justice or logic in order to allow mercy to prevail cannot be calculated.

In the words of W. H. H. Piatt, LL. B. '96, at the memorial exercises: "He was a lawyer untinctured by pettifoggery; a teacher unalloyed with pedantry; a citizen loyal and patriotic. He was a sincere and consistent Christian. He was an affectionate and exemplary husband and an ever dependable, faithful friend."

Written for the 1919 Jayhawker *Yearbook*

THE JAYHAWKER AND THE SAVITAR

JAYHAWKER 1911 – BORDER WAR 1910

In the final game of the season against the Tigers in Kansas City, Kansas crossed her opponent's goal line and suffered her own being crossed. The result was a 5 to 5 tie.

SAVITAR 1911 – BORDER WAR 1910

The team went to Kansas City expecting to win. The rooters who accompanied them expected them to win. And they virtually did win. Every one knows how the Tigers were kept from winning by the robbery of one of the officials-not once, but many times-when victory was almost within their grasp. With fate and Thompson against them, the Tigers succeeded in [tying] the Jayhawkers, however, which is greatly to their credit.

JAYHAWKER 1912 – BORDER WAR 1911

[There is no description of the game. Game tied 0-0.]

SAVITAR 1912 – BORDER WAR 1911

For the first time since Missouri began to play football with Kansas, the game was played in Columbia, and it was the second game played away from Kansas City since 1890. Both teams were confident and the day was ideal, but the field was soft. The Jayhawkers had been encamped at Moberly since Monday, while

the Tigers had rested from Wednesday until Saturday on George Evans' farm near Columbia. The desire to win this game had brought Deatherage, Klein, Curtis, Miller, Ristine, Kirk, and Burress – all famous Tigers of former years – back to assist Coach Brewer. Old students and [graduates] began to assemble at Columbia the middle of the week, and on Friday night the biggest mass meeting ever held at M. U. took place in the auditorium. A few Kansas rooters appeared Saturday morning, but the streets were swarming with Tiger supporters. The Missouri bleachers began to fill up at one o'clock, and by the time the game started every seat was taken. The crowd numbered about nine thousand. Kansas sent only one hundred and fifty rooters. The Tigers arrived on the field first and the rooters gave them a glorious welcome. Every player was in good shape, and Hall punted the ball seventy yards in practice. This looked might good to us.

When the first whistle blew, "Dobbie" kicked the ball out of bounds. On the second trial he booted it to the ten-yard line. Kansas could not gain and had to punt. Neither team was able to make consistent gains, and both sides punted frequently. Kansas had the ball in Missouri territory most of the first quarter. Hiel was [out-punting] Mills, and this gave the visitors an advantage. Both teams played extra good football. The Tackling was exceptionally good. LeMire, Knoble, and Mills were gaining the ground for the Tigers. The first half ended 0-0. It was a hard fought half, with neither team gaining an advantage. Captain Shuck was playing the game of this life. He went down on the punts with lightning speed, and his tackles were sure. Missouri spirit was at its best, and yells filled the air. The few Jayhawker rooters made themselves heard occasionally by their ancient "Rock-Chalk."

No changes were made in the line-up for the second half. Both teams started off strong, but it was not long until Missouri rooters were quivering. Kansas had the ball on our two-yard line, and had three downs to carry it over. The Tiger line braced, as it had in previous games, and after three trials, the ball was on our four-yard line. Captain Ammons had made two unsuccessful attempts to penetrate the Tiger line. The bleachers went wild as Mills punted out from behind the goal. Delaney was sent in to kick for Kansas. He soon dropped one over from the twenty-five-yard line, for the first score of the game. The third quarter ended with a score of 3-0.

The Tigers began the fourth quarter with an increased fighting spirit. Hall went in for Mills and on an exchange of punts with the ball was in Kansas territory. Blees began to use open play and two successful passes put the ball on the visitors' twenty-yard line. Dexter hit the line for six yards, then Shuck dropped back for a kick. The ball was near the side-line, and the kick looked impossible for our captain. But "Jimmie" was as cool as if he were only practicing. Wilson made a perfect pass, and the ball sailed directly between the posts for three points. Such cheering was never before seen at Missouri. "Jimmie" was the hero. Play was resumed and Captain Ammons broke through our line, headed directly toward the goal, with no one but "Billy" to stop him. Blees made the play of his life, when he threw the 175 pound [79 kilogram] Jayhawk to the ground. "Billy" was carried off the field as a result of the collision, and Woodward took his place. The final whistle soon blew with the ball in the middle of the field.

SAVITAR 1913 – BORDER WAR 1912

The twenty-second annual battle between Kansas and Missouri was the first in the history of the great contests to be played in the home of the Jayhawker, but like thirteen of the other games, it was a defeat for the Tigers. Missouri has gained four victories out of the twenty-two games with Kansas, while four have been ties.

A fine bright day dawned on that November 23. A slight wind increased in the afternoon but scarcely harmed the game, although it chilled the rooters. Missouri had sent a record crowd – at least a thousand strong – to cheer for Old Missouri. The great god "Spirit" was there in greater glory than ever before and his worshippers, the "Old Guard," were the last to leave the field where the Tigers had lost. The rooters stayed with the team to the last second.

The first quarter ended, Missouri 3, Kansas 0. It was essentially a Missouri period in every department of the game that far. The optimists thought the game was won. Shepard's kick from the 50-yard line seemed to give the impression of an eleven of invincible Tigers which the Jayhawkers could not touch.

But the spirit never to be subdued which has so often characterized Jayhawker teams showed itself in the second quarter and Weidline of Kansas made a place kick from the 35-yard line, tying the score. Then the Crimson and Blue lads began to perfect their Minnesota shift play and found the whole of the Tiger line to be as vulnerable as Achilles' heel. That one play was the mystification and humiliation of the glorious Tiger. Every man of the team fought and worked for all that was in him, but it was child's play against a might wind. The Minnesota shift, somewhat akin to the Nebraska shift which had been so thoroughly destroyed on Rollins Field in Columbia, was unsolvable, apparently to the Missouri lads. When they regained consciousness from a period of stupefaction, Kansas had added another scalp measuring 12 to 3, to its belt.

A touchdown followed soon after the score was tied and on failure to kick goal, the score stood: Kansas 9, Missouri 3. Coach Brewer untwisted the cruel kinks in the tail of his feline pet between the halves and taught them some points in blocking the terrible shift – enough, at least, to deflect any more Kansas scores on touchdowns. But one more field goal was tallied before the referee's whistle tolled the knell of the visitor's departure in defeat.

It was a fine game and a clean game. Both teams played [sportsman's-like] football and put up a sight most pleasing from the point of view of the spectators. It was estimated that 18,000 people saw it. How or why it happened, no one yet knows, but everyone was satisfied that the Jayhawkers never had won a harder battle on a gridiron.

By Thomas S. Hudson
Missouri Alumnus 1915

JAYHAWKER 1914 – BORDER WAR 1913

The Jayhawker lost her final feather when she met the Missouri Tiger at Columbia, November 22. Mud was the predominating feature of the closing game, though the players on each side put up a beautiful fight. It might be true that the Missouri team outplayed the Crimson and Blue, but they did not outdo them in scrappiness and spirit.

In the first quarter the Jayhawks seemed to have the "edge" on the Tiger eleven. Wilson continually outpunted Shepard, while Steuwe, Tudor and bishop hit the line for short gains that seemed sure to score. But the tigers took a brace and the score failed to materialize. In the second quarter the Missourians came back strong, and played most of the remainder of the game in Kansas territory. In the latter part of the third quarter the Tigers carried the ball to the Kansas fifteen-yard line, but were unable to advance farther. On the fourth down Captain Wilson dropped back and with a neatly timed kick placed the ball squarely between the Jayhawkers' bars. It was a beautiful kick and marked down the only score of the game. Twice during the third and fourth quarters the Tigers seemed sure of a touchdown, but each time the Kansas line strengthened and held. In the third quarter, also, the Kansans advanced the ball close enough towards the Tiger goal for Weidlein to try a place kick, but the field was too heavy and it fell short. One minute before tie was called on the last quarter the Kansans placed the ball on Missouri's forty-yard line, and Weidlein, taking a last desperate chance to tie the score, dropped back for a place kick. He sent the ball straight for the Tiger goal, but it fell short five yards and the game was lost.

Hundreds of true Missourians grumbled at the weather the morning of the annual Missouri-Kansas football game. That night, which had been promisingly clear, became a thunderstorm early in the morning and the athletic field became soaked from the torrents. Every lover of sport knew that the Tigers would be at their best on a dry field where fast and open playing could be effective. Every Missourian knew that the beef of Kansas was at a better advantage in the mud than the slightly lighter weight of Missouri men was.

In spite of the dreary morning and the rain which fell until about 9 o'clock, the Missouri students began their "Big Peerade." This was the second time that the Kansans had visited Columbia to see the annual game between Missouri and Kansas on Rollins Field. The older students remembered the mud battle of three years before. The two teams had fought to a standstill until Delaney of Kansas kicked a field goal. Then, in the last few minutes of play when every rooter was breathless Glen Shuck saved the day by kicking goal from a difficult angle. This year the students knew that Missouri had the better team on the dry field, but they also remembered the Minnesota shift used by Kansas the year before at Lawrence.

But the parade was begun in spite of the wet streets. And the parade was a sight that thrilled every true Missourian. Alumni with their class banners, the cadets in uniform, the students by classes, the floats representing various schools and departments made the gala day one to be remembered in student history of the University of Missouri. Governor Major visited Columbia and saw the campus thronged with people who witnessed the celebration of the home-coming day. And best of all to the first year men, freshmen caps were consigned to the fire. But by noon this crowd became silent. The contest between the two institutions was to begin within the next few hours. This game meant more to the Missouri team than any game which could be played at Columbia or anywhere else. It was the old spirit of border days which will demonstrate itself on the gridiron when the two teams – jayhawkers and Tigers – are fighting the final fight of the season, and that always between each other.

The ominous silence lasted until the bleachers began to fill at 2 o'clock. Then came that real thrill of college life where youths and men lose themselves and shout at their greatest lung capacity the yells of their universities. The yelling was spontaneous. The critical time of the day was near at hand. And the thunderstorm of yells burst forth as the band played "Dixie" and the Tigers trotted on the field.

Yet Missouri fear was great. The gridiron was almost a morass and the Tiger attack was dependable upon speed and trickery. The field meant a calamity to every Missourian when they measured with their eyes the largeness of the Kansas warriors and compared with this the smallness of the Tigers. The whistles down town went riot. Ten thousand persons looked down on Rollins Field

and were absolutely dead as far as the outside world concerned them. At this moment the official blew the little whistle.

The Game

Right on the jump the tigers began the game with a trick. McWilliams gathered himself and with his short steps sped toward the ball as if he would on the kickoff drive it over the bar – but stop! The ball went almost straight in the air and dropped about ten yards away. Was it a bad kick by McWilliams? But the tall Shepard, the Missouri halfback, had caught this short kickoff and had charged the Kansas ranks. This play worried the visitors as they saw that in spite of the pools on the field Missouri would resort to trick playing.

Then began the real battle which will go down in history as the year of a certain hero, Harvey Lee McWilliams, the diminutive quarterback for the Gold and Black who won the game. But this first quarter was without event. It was a struggle in the mud in which the Tigers and Jayhawkers were fairly evenly matched in pushing and slipping and sliding. Kansas did have a slight advantage when the period was up as the visitors had made the ball on two downs and Missouri on one. Shepard, the Tiger punter, was off form that day because of a bad leg and was slightly outpunted.

The first quarter was a period for punting. Many short gains were made but consistent rushing was lacking on both teams. This necessitated a punting duel. In this period, however, Wilson of Kansas made the longest gain which was 20 yards through the Tiger line. This quarter was more a time for the teams to test out the strength of each other. But late in the period Kansas tried a forward pass. Then came Strother's punt which drove the ball deep in Missouri territory. The Tigers punted back. The quarter ended scoreless with the ball on the Missouri 45-yard line and in the possession of Kansas.

The Kick

In the second quarter the history of the game was made. The Missouri Tiers began the period with a fierce attack and gradually drove the heavy Jayhawkers back. McWilliams had begun this work. He had received a Kansas punt and had returned it 20 yards before he was downed. More and Shepard were then sent against the heavy Jayhawker defense and with fair success. On the Kansas 25-yard line the defense was stronger. McWilliams sent two mass plays through center for a total of 10 yards. McWilliams then made 1 yard. On the next two lays the Tigers were held to 2 yards. And it was just at this pint that McWilliams staked the result of the game on the accuracy of his toe.

A touchdown was almost in sight, but the heavy Kansans had resisted successfully three attacks. Seven yards were necessary in one gain for the Tigers to keep the ball. McWiliams called the signals for a place kick. There was a sudden hush in the bleachers when it was evident that McWilliams would attempt a goal from the field. The question in every rooter's heart, whether he was a Missourian or Kansan was, could the deed be done? McWilliams dropped back five yards behind his regular position and deliberately wiped the mud off his foot. The ball was snapped, caught and placed on the ground for the Tiger quarterback. With clock-like precision McWilliams kicked the ball and scored a field goal from placement, the only three points of the game.

After this feat of the Tiger quarterback the Missouri men played their best ball of the game. They "opened up and threatened the Kansas goal. The Jayhawkers saw their pet shift go to smash on the heavy Gallagher who ploughed through and spoiled the whole thing or on Jake Speelman who sped around the ends and nabbed the runner before the play was under way. These heavy Kansans would hold a consultation of war on the field and try to scheme a new attack. But all the consultation would not work. And it was at this stage of the game that Herbert K. Thatcher, track captain, was sent in form the sidelines.

It was the work of Thatcher that came near making him a hero on the gridiron but which fell short a yard or two because of a technicality. Thatcher was the surprise that Brewer and Schulte had for Kansas. It is known that Thatcher's forward pass tossing surpassed that of any Tiger football man. Thatcher had an accurate whip of 40 yards. The Tigers were within scoring distance when this Thatcher play was attempted. The tall Missourian who had just gone in received the ball. The Kansans rushed at him on both sides. They had circled the defending ends and were almost upon Thatcher. But right at this point of the play Thatcher surprised everybody by his coolness in slowly dodging the charging opponents and by running to one side. This gave Speelman a chance to get behind the Jayhawker goal; then came the pretty play of the season, that of Thatcher throwing the ball directly into the hands of Speelman. The bleachers went riot. It seemed that the cleverest play of the day had given the Tigers a touchdown against the Jayhawkers. But a sudden hush came when the referee brought the ball back to the scrimmage field and gave it to the Kansans. Speelman had been just outside the ten yard limit zone behind the goal line when he caught the ball. The touchdown did not count.

The remainder of the game was a battle which gave a little advantage to Missouri at times. Twice the heavy Jayhawkers tried a field goal in an attempt to stave off defeat, and twice they failed. McWilliams also failed on a field goal. Late in the fourth period the Thatcher play was tried again. The tall Missourian was sent in when the Tigers were threatening the west goal. The minute that Thatcher went in the defending team was on the alert for one of these dangerous forward passes. And here was where the blot on Missouri playing came. Through a mistake somewhere from the sidelines to the scrimmage spot Thatcher tried three forward passes when he had little chance of completing them. It was the one flagrant shortcoming in the Tiger tactics. But even with this Missouri had a defense that made good that day and which was better than Kansas ever had met here. The Missouri team had held Kansas scoreless and had won. And great was the celebration over the famous team of 1913.

JAYHAWKER 1915 – BORDER WAR 1914

The last game of the season was the big disappointment. Missouri beat us 10 to 7. Kansas was doped to have the advantage by all who had seen the two teams play and from comparative scores for the season. The game started with Kansas playing a whirlwind game. After a series of plays Wood, the little Kansas quarterback, got away for a run and was downed on the Missouri 4-yard line. Here the ball was carried to the 1-yard line and "Bonnie" Reber went over for a touchdown. During this time the Jayhawkers had completely outplayed the Tigers and it looked like a sure Kansas victory. However in the second quarter the tide turned and Missouri scored a touchdown, making three yards on a fourth down to do it. The half ended 7 to 7. In the third quarter both sides fought desperately and neither side scored. In the last quarter Missouri got possession of the ball deep down in Kansas territory, executed a successful place-kick, and the score stood 10 to 7 with Missouri on the long end. The rest of the game, though very short, was a fight on the part of Kansas in a vain effort to score, and on the part of Missouri to hold the Jayhawkers in check.

SAVITAR 1915 – BORDER WAR 1914

The Kansas eleven rushed the football to the Missouri goal line in the first ten minutes of play, - score, Missouri 0, Kansas 7. But before the last whistle blew the Tigers had turned the tables, - score, Missouri 10, Kansas 7.

The day was wonderfully adapted to the occasion, both for spectator and player. For the former, the air was cool, but comfortable; for the latter, the atmosphere was brisk and invigorating. Sunshine lighted the scene of the Tiger triumph. It was the sixth enjoyment of victory for Missouri in twenty-four years of gridiron battle.

Since 1909, the great "Roper Year," rations have bee short in the Crimson and Blue quarters. Missouri won in 1909, tied in 1910 and 1911; won in 1913 and in 1914. The age of triumph is upon the Tiger colors; history is about to adjust her reckonings.

The Tigers did not open up the rush. They waited to see what the Jayhawkers were going to do. The Tigers were expected to use open style of play, but when Kansas stayed with the old game, the Missourians carried the ball over the gridiron lines by the might and main of a terrific charging line and the headwork of the pony backs. Each eleven tried only one forward pass, and each toss was intercepted by the enemy. The Tigers beat their ancient enemy at their own game. Here is a paragraph by C. E. McBride on the game:

"The Missouri eleven, coming from behind a 7 to 0 count, simply tore the weightier K. U. line to shreds. The light-haired Lake, the dark-haired Shepard, the   speedy Dunckel,

and the flashy Miller, - these were the boys who were shooting like human catapults through the Kansas forwards. But listen, - Lake and Shepard and Dunckel and Miller and Graves simply were the lads who carried the ball. Lansing, Graham, Drumm, Van Dyne, Groves, Speelman, and Captain Clay, they were the boys of the line, the wickedly charging demons who played their heavier opponents off their feet, opening up the holes that put the names of Lake and Shepard and Dunckel and Miller and Graves in the mouths of the mob."

Reber of Kansas made the touchdown for Crimson and Blue, in the first period of the game. In the next quarter, Captain Clay's men began their most brilliant and most consistent attack. Five times the Old Gold and Black scored first downs and then the diminutive Mister Woody made the score of six points, and to thoroughly cinch the job, he kicked goal himself, [tying] the score. :Toby" Graves missed one goal from placement from the 20-yard line in the third period, but a few moments later sent the ball soaring from under the steady fingers of Quarterback Clinton Collins, squatting on the 24-yard line, over the bar. The game was won, Missouri 10, Kansas 7.

Ten thousand tooters saw the jayhawkers go down before the victorious Tigers.

By Thomas S. Hudson
Missouri Alumnus 1915

JAYHAWKER 1916 – BORDER WAR 1915

The Tiger game was another disappointment to us, but J. Pluvius, not Missouri, was the cause. Rain began with the kickoff and by the end of the first quarter there was not a square foot of the field above water, and the rain kept it up all during the game. It was not a question of Missouri stopping us, but how far we could go without getting stuck in the mud. Missouri made one first down on a pass. Their lone touchdown was the result of a fumble close to our goal line, while the most of the game we had them backed up against their own goal line. On a dry field the game would have compared favorable with the Washburn game for us.

By Darl Anthony "Tony" James
Kansas Football Captain 1914
Kansas Alumnus 1915

SAVITAR 1916 – BORDER WAR 1915

Before passing to the Kansas affair, it may be said that the Tigers attempted little new "stuff" during the season's routine. Constant effort by Schulte to develop a kicker good for at least three points a game met without success. Perhaps the men were too new at the game to be given much instruction in fancy formations or bewildering passes.

It should be said, though, that Schulte did have a rattling good football team on the field before a downpour greeted the rival elevens from Missouri and Kansas. The men had steadily improved during the season; they had learned more about the game and gained new confidence. More than one Missouri rooter thought that the Tiger would down his feathered foe on that memorable Thanksgiving [Day]. And more than one will tell you now and forever that it was a sea of mud, not a superior team, that brought defeat to the Tiger lair.

The day of the Kansas game dawned bright and cheery. Ten minutes before the game started the stands were crowded to their capacity with a maelstrom of jostling humanity, colors fluttered, mums were in evidence everywhere, women came gaily bedecked with all shades of festive attire.

It was such a scene as this that received the wrath of the heavens but a few minutes after the twenty-two football warriors had been sent springing at each other like human catapults.

A safety, counting two points, was the only thing that prevented Missouri from getting a tie. The first quarter was well under way when Lindsey, the Jayhawk kicking demon, failed to toe the oval over the bar from the 15-yard line. None the less credit for Mr. Lindsey, for this gentleman later proved the worth of his boot by counting six points — two field goals — for his Jayhawk team-mates.

But after his first failure, the ball went to Missouri on her own 20-yard line. It was up to Missouri to kick. The center pushed the pigskin, which looked more like a mudball, to Pittam, who stood ready to receive it. It went a little wild. The element, the condition of the field – everything – was against the chances of the Tiger back to capture it and get away with a decent kick. The ball struck the ground, bounding back of the goal line, where Pittam fell on it, registering two points for Kansas.

With these two points as a starter the visitors added six more by two miraculous field goals, negotiated by Lindsey. Just how he manipulated those two kicks, everything considered no one knows. But they counted six pints and no one denies Mr. Lindsey the credit.

Not until the third quarter did Schulte's Bengals threaten the Kansas lead. When Lindsey fumbled a poor pass, Captain Jake Speelman, playing his last gridiron game for Missouri, snatched the ball off the surface of the water and sprinted forty yards for a touchdown and Missouri's only score.

The rest of the game is the story of one team, light, fast and scrappy, but unable to show its worth on account of a disgruntled weather man, battling against a heavier, more experienced eleven men, better equipped as mud-horses.

The game ended – a drenched, silent crowd stalked out of Rollins Field – and Kansas had downed Missouri for the second time in seven years.

By Ralph H. "Scoop" Turner
Missouri Alumnus 1916

SAVITAR 1917 – BORDER WAR 1916

It was the usual with Kansas. The Jayhawkers had beaten Nebraska, the first Conference defeat for the Cornhuskers since 1910, and there was no great deal of sorrow along the Valley of the Kaw. The Lawrence natives were offering 2 to 1 odds, so the stories in Columbia had it, and many a Missouri householder pawned the family plate to get capital for an investment upon which he believed he could realize 100 per cent profit. Around the Eldridge house, however, it was the same old Kansas, confidence but with not much to back it.

The game, after the teams had settled down in the first quarter, until the next to the last play, when Stankowski let the Kansans return a kickoff and recover it on Missouri's 20-yard line, was Missouri all the way. A little crossbuck of 1900 vintage proved the undoing of the great team coached by the former Yale star.

The "Illinois spread" spread with no results, the Tiger ends were secure and the line impregnable. Stankowski watched the Jayhawker tackles playing a mile wide and sent his plays between them. The tackles never drew in – and Collins, Rider and McMillan never stopped the march via the simple split play which baffled the Rock Chalk. For five, six and even ten yards at a time, until the ball was in striking distance of the goal line, did they plunge. Three trials for goal by the kicking route went wild, but Collins and Stankowski each went over for the six-point counters. The score was the largest Missouri has ever registered against the common enemy, and it was some victory, nevertheless and notwithstanding what my friend "Mac" [C. E. McBride, Sports Editor] of the Kansas City Star had to say.

By Frank H. King
Missouri Alumnus 1917

JAYHAWKER 1917 – BORDER WAR 1916

But the Thanksgiving Day game with Missouri on McCook Field was the really bad part of the season for the Kansas team. After playing a brilliant game of ball against Nebraska the Jayhawkers were picked for winners against Missouri. The confidence spirit entered the Kansas camp while the same fight which won for Kansas against Nebraska was tried by Missouri against Kansas and the result was 13 to 0 for the Tigers. Collins, Rider and Pittam plugged the Kansas line in the same holes time after time but the Kansas line could not hold. Substitutes proved of no avail and on straight line plunges, delayed plays and few open plays Missouri marched down the field for two touchdowns on straight football. Kansas was unable to take advantage of any near chances to score.

JAYHAWKER 1918 – BORDER WAR 1917

This was Kansas' year to even up with her old rival for several past defeats – from all reports she did. The light Tigers were unable to stop the drives of the heavy Kansas backs. Captain Nielsen and Pringle, especially, gave their Missou opponents trouble. Missouri's attempt to use the forward pass in the last few minutes of play proved futile. When Captain Nielsen made his touchdown in the fourth quarter, he scored his last for Kansas and for the season of 1917.

SAVITAR 1918 – BORDER WAR 1917

The Tiger team had proved a loser. The Kansas game on Thanksgiving, if won, would have offset all the other defeats of the season. But the "Old Gold and Black" went down to defeat for the second time in five years against the Jayhawkers. After all tho, what is one little victory or defeat? The best men of "Old Missouri" were out fighting in that greater cause; we numbered our gridiron stars by the number of stars on our service flag, rather than by the number of men who trotted out on the field on Homecoming Day. When the last whistle blew, Kansas emerged the victor 27 to 3.

JAYHAWKER 1919 – BORDER WAR 1918

[There was no game this year due to the War of Nations and an influenza quarantine in Missouri.]

SAVITAR 1919 – BORDER WAR 1918

[There was no game this year due to the War of Nations and an influenza quarantine in Missouri.]

JAYHAWKER 1920 – BORDER WAR 1919

[There is no description of the game. MU won 13-6.]

SAVITAR 1920 – BORDER WAR 1919

Missouri is glad and sad over the result of that Kansas Day battle. The lamentable fact is that Kansas thought she had a football team equal to that of the "Tiger" state. Never in the history of the Missouri-Kansas struggles has there been registered a [cleaner] cut victory, never before has the chief executive of the State of Missouri been better readied for his journey to Mount Oread than was Governor Gardner after that 13-6 victory over Kansas Thanksgiving Day.

It is common knowledge that the 13 to 6 score did not begin to tell of the strength of the Tigers. Lewis had three more touchdowns that should have been chalked up. Peterson made one, but by an unfortunate turn of fate he was called back while the sport writers were flashing another touchdown for Missouri. The fact that Kansas was fighting against a terrible offense was evident to the thousands in the bleaches after the first whistle blew. Those who wore the crimson and blue saw their All-Valley ends, Laslett and Lonberg, swept aside as Collins circled Laslett and Lewis dashed past the futilely struggling Longberg in a march that ended only when the goal line was crossed. Lewis and Ruth in a spectacular forward passing combination put over the other score when Ruth leaped high and fell with the magic spheroid just over the line.

It was a great day for a great end of a perfect football season. Bleak, raw and lowering the cold November afternoon drew to

a close, while Missouri's warriors, their two outstanding stars, Lewis and Travis, battling as they never had before, surged back and forth on a field that was flecked with small patches of ice. With the coming of night Missouri's band, it notes ringing clear over the historic old battleground, sounded "taps." It was the end of the high ambitions of the haughty Jayhawkers. And there was written on the pages of history, along with the names of Lewis and Travis and the others, a Missouri Valley Football championship for "Old Mizzou."

By Duke N. Parry
Missouri Alumnus 1920

Cartoon from the 1912 Jayhawker *Yearbook*

The passing of the Volstead Act combined with an economic boom, resulting from the post-war victory in Europe, caused the "Roaring Twenties" to initiate. Prohibition saw the emergence of illegal and clandestine locations called a "speakeasy," where patrons were still able to inebriate themselves. Jazz and a new style of music, "swing," were being played at many of these speakeasies and the communist ideology was firmly in place in Russia and other member states of the Union of Soviet Socialist Republics, which had come into existence during the Great War. Former brewers, such as Anheuser-Busch in Saint Louis, Missouri, were either forced to close or sell products without alcohol and, nearing the end of the decade, a pilot named Charles Lindberg flew, without stopping, across the Atlantic Ocean in an airplane named the "Spirit of St. Louis."

In 1920, famed basketball coach Forrest Clare "Phog" Allen, took control of the Jayhawk football team for one season. Although scoring the first points of the game, the Tiger attack ended the game in Missouri's favour 16-7. Earlier in the season, in a game played against Nebraska at Kansas' McCook Field, Allen coached his team from a 20-0 deficit in the first half to tie the game. The incident inspired Allen to replace Kansas' old field with wood bleachers into something more monolithic. Soon after the game, $200,000 was pledged to create a modern, concrete stadium and construction began immediately. The stadium was opened on October 29, 1921 and named Kansas University Memorial Stadium to honour those that had died in the Great War.

The same year of Kansas building its new stadium, Missouri began fundraising to build its own Memorial Stadium, which was not begun construction until December, 1925 and not completed until October 2, 1926. During the time that it took to raise the funds to build the new stadium, Missouri had one of its most trying seasons in 1922. The coach hired for that year was Thomas Kelley, who had previously served the team as a line coach for the 1919 team. Apparently, Kelley's treatment of the team was quite poor, whose antics included cursing at members of the team for losing games and it was reported that he kicked a player in anger. His actions were brought to the attention of Missouri University President John Carlton Jones. Jones forced Kelley's resignation with two

Tom Kelley

games left before the end of the season, leaving the team in a leadership vacuum. Although an event such as this might have spelled doom for the remainder of the season, the team became united under the leadership of, assistant turned head coach, Henry "Hank" Garrity. Garrity, in turn, was supported by freshman coach Bill Dunckell and a highly respected former Missouri team captain, Charles L. "Chuck" Lewis.

The team responded immediately to the leadership change, which showed the talents of a sports prodigy named Allen George Lincoln. Upon his graduation from Webster Groves High School in Missouri, "Linc" had already been declared the best athlete produced in the Saint Louis area in a decade. Amongst his numerous high school athletic accomplishments, Linc was able to score at least half of his team's points in every sport and game in which he played; football, basketball, and track. As a junior high school quarterback in 1917, Lincoln scored 46 of his team's 76 points in a high school Thanksgiving Day game rivalry, which at that time was the highest individual single-game scoring record for that year in the nation and possibly the highest single-game scoring record at that time.

In the 1922 Missouri-Kansas Thanksgiving Day game, before 20,000 fans, which among them included Bill Roper from Princeton, Al Lincoln shined in a game drenched in rain and mud. Lincoln's six-point touchdown in the second quar-

Al Lincoln in 1922

ter was soon overshadowed by the 49 yard field goal that he kicked from the 45-yard line squarely between the posts. Although Kansas was able to score a touchdown and earn the extra point, the game was won by Missouri. For his play in this last game of his college career, Lincoln was awarded a football medal by his team with the inscription "MU 9 – KU 7," engraved on it.

Lincoln was such an exceptional athlete that it was expected for him to become a professional in the National Football League. However, due to the influence of this father, who had always desired his son join a "gentlemanly" profession, Lincoln did not. He returned to Missouri the next year as the freshman football coach and stayed there for a few years before embarking on adventures that would parallel those of Ernest Hemingway.

...GRAND MEMORIALS AND THE BIG SIX

In 1923, Gwinn Henry started the first year of his eight-year tenure as the head coach of Missouri football. Despite his 37-21-9 record at Missouri and his winning of three Missouri Valley Intercollegiate Athletic Association Championship titles, Kansas always seemed to deny him a win when it came to the Border War Game. Against Kansas, Gwinn's teams only won three of eight contests, one of the games ending in a tie. In his nine years of coaching at Missouri, Gwinn had only three losing seasons at Missouri; his first and last two years. Despite Missouri having a 7-1 record and Kansas a record of 1-5-2 in 1924, Kansas thwarted an expected victory by tying Missouri in the Border War Game, setting the stage for the 1925 game.

Future Missouri head coach, Chauncey Simpson, was a Missouri player from 1922-1924

The 1925 game was played before 30,000 fans at the Kansas Memorial Stadium between a 6-1-1 Missouri team and a 2-5-1 Kansas team. Missouri scored in the first few minutes of the game on a 25-yard pass from Sam Whiteman to Bert Clark, to which Kansas responded in the second quarter by a 63-yard pass from Harold Zuber to Wilbur Starr to the goal line, after which Gene Hart carried the ball over the line from the first scrimmage. In the second half of the game, Missouri neared the Kansas 10-yard line twice, coming close to scoring on another drive that reached the 1-yard line. With sparse time remaining on the clock, Missouri's first All-American, Ed Lindenmeyer, kicked the ball into the wind to the Missouri 35-yard line, only to be penalized an additional 15 yards, placing the ball on the 20-yard line. Three plays later on the 16-yard line, Kansas' Captain, Babe Smith, called a timeout and into the game came a replacement player named Stoney Wall. Wall kicked the game winning field goal, resulting in crazed Kansas fans carrying Wall and

Charles "Stoney" Wall in 1925

Missouri breaks ground for its stadium in December 1925

the goalposts from the field with the good fortune that this year a cat had not been found and crucified, as was done to the chicken in the 1909 game.

In 1928, the Missouri Valley Intercollegiate Athletic Association was larger and more disparate than when it had begun and included both private and public land-grant schools. The member schools in 1927 were; Drake University, Grinnell College, Iowa State University, University of Kansas, Kansas State University, University of Missouri, University of Nebraska, University of Oklahoma, Oklahoma A&M University and Washington University. The larger schools wanted the conference to reflect their characteristics, so the six largest split the conference and formally retained the conference name, although they were more commonly known as the Big Six Conference; whose membership in 1928 was Kansas, Kansas State, Iowa State, Missouri, Nebraska, and Oklahoma. Missouri added to its list of notable distinctions of being the last school to win the Missouri Valley Intercollegiate Athletic Association football championship title in the last year of the conference before it split. The remaining schools, Drake, Grinnell, Oklahoma A&M, later to change names to Oklahoma State, and Washington University remained in a separate conference, whose name became and remains in 2008, the Missouri Valley Conference.

Missouri Footbal (7-1) - Head Coach John F. Miller
Row 1: Lincoln, Springgate, Hill, Captain Chuck Lewis, Blumer, Packwood, Williams. Row 2: Shannon, Ruth, Fulbright, Humes, Vilkas, Hardin. Row 3: Coach Miller, Goepel, Bunker, Athletic Directore Clevenger, Andrews, Travis, Coach Phelan.

MU Football Captain
Charles L. Lewis

Kansas Football (5-2-1) - Head Coach Forrest Clare Allen
Row 1: Reed, Wilson. Row 2: Lamb, Allison, Bunn, Bross, Johnson, Seifert, Dunkley, King, Welch, Harrison, Higgins, Loftus. Row 3: Saunders, Simon, Lonborg, McDonald, Nettels, Laslett, Godlove, Mandeville, Jones, Woody, Davison. Row 4: Sproud, Farrell, Stelter, Kane, Bell, Cox, McAdams, Little, Ivy, Hale, Jackson, Ford, Wulf, Pringle, Harris, Hart, Arthur, Spurgeon, Morrison, Meeker, Fraker, Lawellin, Endacott.

KU Football Captain
George E. Nettels

Missouri Football (6-2) - Head Coach James Michael Phelan

Row 1: Knight, Lawrance, Bond, Captain Herb Blumer, Hamilton, Bunker, Packwood.
Row 2: Forrester, Williams, Pruitt, Saville, Sinz, Maxwell, Scott. Row 3: Roberts, Browning, O'Reilly, C. Keller, Hill, R. Keller, Al Lincoln.

MU Football Captain
Herbert Blumer

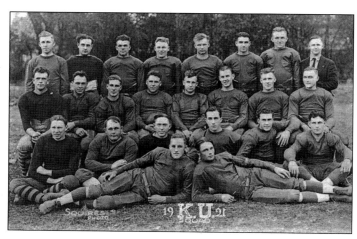

Kansas Football (4-3) - Head Coach George M. Clark

(Unordered, Incomplete) Jones, Higgins, McAdams, Wilson, Saunders, Spurgeon, Reedy, Black, Krueger, Griffin, Boone, Davidson, Weidlein, Freeze, McDonald.

KU Football Captain
Paul R. Jones

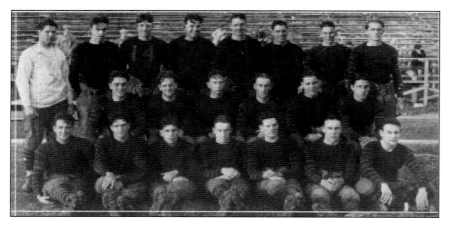

MU Football Captain
Herbert Bunker

Missouri Football (5-3) - Head Coach Henry Garrity
Row 1: Walsh, Bond, Palermo, Smith, Scannell, Mack, Bundschu. Row 2: Lewis, Adams,
Ferguson, Hays, Wertz, Etter. Row 3: Lincoln, Knight, Fowler, Dunn, Van Dyne, Bunker,
Keller, Hill.

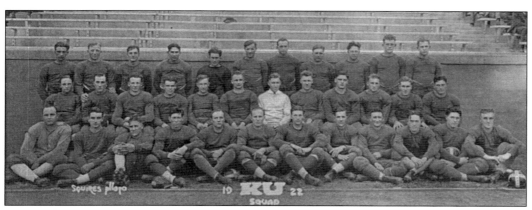

KU Football Captain
Severt E. Higgins

Kansas Football (3-4-1) - Head Coach George M. Clark
Row 1: Harris, McDonald, Hodges, Shannon, Graham, Thompson, Theis, Baldwin, Stover, Pierson,
Norton, Lonborg. Row 2: Wilson, McLean, Ivy, Davidson, Coach Clark, Captain Higgins, Coach
Schlademen, Weidlein, Cave, Black, McAdams, Spurgeon. Row 3: Anderson, Boone, Burt, Haley,
Griffin, Woodruff, Mosby, Calvert, Hoderman, Edwards, Krueger.

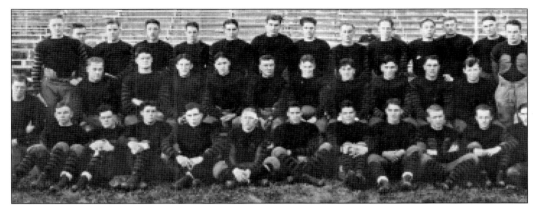

MU Football Captain
Clyde Smith

Missouri Football (2-3-3) - Head Coach Gwinn Henry

(Unordered) Captain Clyde Smith, Art Bond, Frank McAnaw, Ralph Keller, Charles Van Dyne, Jerry Lewis, Jim Palermo, Tom Etter, Nig Wagner, Sam Writeman, Don Faurot, Maurice Moulder, Doss Richerson, Joe Hennessey, Nig Stafford.

KU Football Captain
Charles Terence Black

Kansas Football (5-0-3) - Head Coach George M. Clark

MU Football Captain
Arthur D. Bond

Missouri Football (7-2) - Head Coach Gwinn Henry
Missouri Valley Champion - Los Angeles Christmas Festival Bowl Invitation
(Unordered) Captain Arthur Bond, Maurice Moulder, Clyde Smith, Sam Whiteman, Charles Van Dyne, Jerry Lewis, Jimmy Palermo, John Walsh, Don Faurot, Fred Stafford, Doss Richerson, Pete Jackson, Lloyd Thomas, Edgar Lindenmeyer, Ted O'Sullivan, Charely Tuttle, Emmet Stuber, Chauncey Simpson, Ralph Fergason, Ray Walker, Thomas Etter.

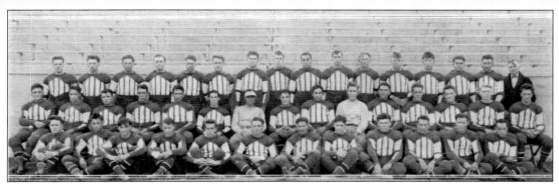

Kansas Football (2-5-1) - Head Coach George M. Clark
Row 1: Hodges, J. Anderson, Endacott, Walters, Lindley, Isett, B. Baker, Starr, P. Snyder, Powers, Crawford, H. Smith. Row 2: Russell, Smith, W. Anderson, Halpin, Davidson, Testerman, Wellman, Coach Clark, Burt, Haley, Coach Schladerman, Hardy, Reginald, Smith, Mullins, Sinborn, Hart. Row 3: Millman, Voight, Baker, Taylor, Williamson, Swope, Zuber, Patterson, Franks, Brown, Cloud, N. Snyder, Mandeveille, Pingry, Pierce, Trainer Kelly.

KU Football Captain
Harold Allen Burt

Missouri Football (6-1-1) - Head Coach Gwinn Henry
Missouri Valley Champion

(Unordered) Captain Sam Whiteman, Maurice Moulder, Pete Jackson, Ralph Studebaker, Ray Walker, Clifford Morgan, Glenn Smith, Emmett Stuber, James Tarr, Wynne Casteel, William Bigson, George Flamane, Edgar Lindenmeyer, Arthur Coglizer, Doss Richerson, Carl Bacchus, Teddy O'Sullivan, Bert Clark, Joe Milligan, Jack Nicolds, Charles Grantello, Victor Hicks, Lloyd Thomas, Ralph Ferguson, Nig Stafford, Bob Miller.

MU Football Captain
Samuel Whiteman

KU Football Captain
Reginald Smith

Kansas Football (2-5-1) - Head Coach George M. Clark

Row 1: Perry, Kullman, Isett, Hodges, Lindsey, E. Coulter, Rooney, Leifer, D. Mullins, Halpin, Anderson, Hart. Row 2: Zuber, Hamilton, Powers, Lattin, W. Mullins, Cramer, L. Davidson, Smith, Burton, Schmidt, Mackie. Row 3: Sabo, Schlademan, Wall, Starr, Wellman, H. Baker, J. Coulter, Taylor, Sanborn, Clud, Voights, Testerman, Myers, Davidson, Clark. Row 4: R. Baker, Lebewk, Snyder, Brown, Blackburn, Freese, Hawkins, Keller, Ropp.

Missouri Football (5-1-2) - Head Coach Gwinn Henry

(Unordered) Captain Carl Bacchus, George Flamank, Edgar Lindenmeyer, Bert Clark, Cliff Morgan, Glenn Smith, Emmett Stuber, James Tarr, Charles Tuttle, Ted O'Sullivan, R. J. Studebaker, Miller Brown, Charles Gann, Robert Miller, Francis Lucas, Charles Wecott, Robert Byars, Sam Gorman, Ray Walker, Earl Deimund, Henry Rosenheim, William Smith, Hilary Lee, Carl Lyons, Enoch Drumm.

MU Football Captain
Carl Bacchus

Kansas Football (2-6) - Head Coach Franklin C. Cappon

(Unordered, Incomplete) Zuber, Hamilton, Wall, Baker, Cloud, Anderson, Lattin, Starr, Voights, Davidson, Wellman, Burton, MacKie, Taylor, Kullman, Meyers, Shannon, Cramer, McMillen, Hauser, Raup, Fritts, Shenk.

KU Football Captain
Harold Zuber

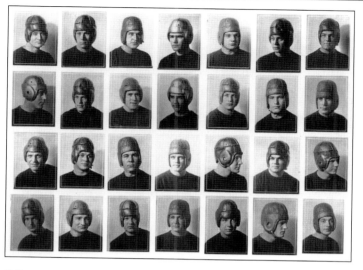

MU Football Captain
George Flamank

Missouri Football (6-3) - Head Coach Gwinn Henry
Missouri Valley Champion

(Left-Right, Top-Bottom) Row 1: Tarr, Deimund, Miller, Morgan, Waldorf, Hursley, Howze. Row 2: Tuttle, Mehrle, Rosenheim, Clark, Swofford, Willner, Hawkins. Row 3: Lucas, Huff, Smith, Drum, Lyons, Schaff, Maschoff. Row 4: Smith, Gibson, Wescott, Brown, Kennedy, Byars, Gorman.

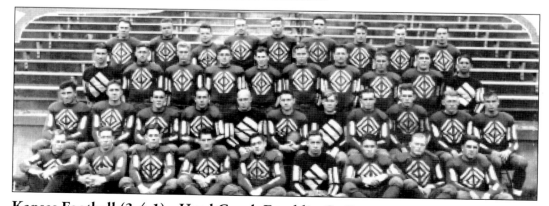

Kansas Football (3-4-1) - Head Coach Franklin C. Cappon

(Unordered, Incomplete) Hamilton, Hauser, Myers, Cramer, Lyman, Shenk, Logan, Cooper, Olson, Fritts, McMillan, Lawrence, Douglass, Ash, Shannon, Schmidt, Cochran, Sherwood, Kullman, Burton, Hadley, Schopplin, Akers, Profernick.

KU Football Captain
Barrett Hamilton

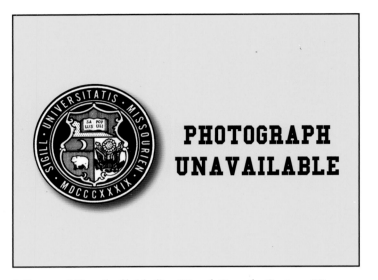

PHOTOGRAPH UNAVAILABLE

MU Football Captain
Miller Brown

Missouri Football (4-4) - Head Coach Gwinn Henry

KU Football Captain
Harold Hauser

Kansas Football (2-4-2) - Head Coach Homer Woodson Hargiss

Row 1: Wallace Lumb, Roy Klass, Bert Itoga, Howard Said, Tom Cox, Don Cooper, Art Lawrence, Russell Broshous, Don Loudon, Roland Logan. Row 2: Dr. J. M. Mott, Edgar Schmidt, Andy Olson, Jack Schopflin, Floyd Ramsey, Coach Lynn O. Waldorf, Captain Harold "Dutch" Hauser, Coach H. W. "Bill" Hargiss, Edwin Bramlage, Herman Schroeder, John Shannon, Property Man Julian Ralston. Row 3: George McCormick, Leland Perdew, Bob Gump, Paul Fisher, Fred Moseley, Willis Ward, Nelson Sorem, Art Schroeder, Dick Mullins, Charles Smoot, Russell Cooper, Forrest Cox. Row 4: Ed Ash, Jake Lieberman, Dean Briggs, William Knipe, Leon Bauman, Vergil Paden, Coach John W. Bunn, Mort White, Allen Cochran, Bob Maney, Foster Payne.

MU Football Captain
John Waldorf

Missouri Football (5-2-1) - Head Coach Gwinn Henry
Row 1: Morgan, Gladden, Hursley, Nash, Lindenmeyer, McGirl, Buchholz, Hartman, Kerby, Marvin. Row 2: Yeckel, Garner, Robbins, Derry, Captain Waldorf, Kennedy, McCauley, Poole, Buell, Bockmeier, Hudgens. Row 3: Hupert, Kimes, Garrison, Baker, Cotham, Smith, Schaff, Armstrong, Edmiston, Hudgens. Row 4: Coach Rosenheim, Eschen, Reece, Bittner, Gallais, Huhn, Packard, Peck, Wood, Johanningmeier, Gallaway, Coach Lansing. Row 5: Coach Crangle, DeVoe, Kilgroe, Erckson, Niblo, Austin, Dills, Coach Henry, Oldham, Cox, Brayton, Cambell, Van Dyne, Coach Gorman.

KU Football Captain
Steward Lyman

Kansas Football (4-4) - Head Coach Homer Woodson Hargiss
Row 1: Smay, Logan, Paden, Smoot, Madison, Reitz, Mullins, Ash. Row 2: Coach Bunn, Dr. Mott, Lawrence, Payne, Cox, Coach Hargiss, Captain Lyman, Coach Getto, Bausch, Ramsey, Sorem, Dr. Allen, Coach Hinshaw. Row 3: Carlson, Allen, Schopflin, Foy, Kruse, Sorem, Sanders, Bausch, Atkeson, Bramlage, Schmidt, Fisher. Row 4: Itoga, Bowdish, Geist, Cochran, Kennedy, Adams, Rost, Miller, Ehly, Fetty, Black.

HOW TO KNOW THE K'S

FOOTBALL

BASKETBALL

BASEBALL

TRACK

CROSS COUNTRY

TENNIS

More than 1,000 K sweaters have been awarded by the University since 1898, when the custom was inaugurated. They were apportioned approximately as follows: football 250, baseball 200, track 200, basket ball 150, tennis 150, and others for minor sports. The letters are awarded by the Athletic Board on recommendation of the coach. There are usually from six to eight competitors for every K to be given. In 1919-20, 53 letters were awarded, as follows: Football 18, baseball 14, track 12, basket ball 9.

ALLEN GEORGE LINCOLN

My grandfather, Allen George Lincoln, was born on September 15th of the year 1900 in the Webster Groves area of St. Louis, the only son of Albert Gere Lincoln, editor at that time of the St. Louis Post-Dispatch. During his years at Missouri University, my grandfather, because of his "sterling athletic character" became what many reporters agreed was "the most feared fullback in the Missouri Valley."

During his early life in Webster Groves, my great-grandfather, the quintessential Victorian gentleman, painstakingly tutored my rough-and-tumble grandfather with daily readings from "The Man Who Wins" section of the Post-Dispatch. These articles and others emphasized important traits of a successful gentleman. Evidently, there was real power in those articles as my grandfather proved to be not only a leader and gentleman, but a true athletic wonder.

"Al," who we affectionately called him at his request, spent several summers at a lumber camp in Wisconsin, building a brawny six-foot, 200-pound [180 cm, 90 kg] build few could rival at that time. A mainstay and team captain for unequaled basketball and track teams at Webster Groves High School, football was his true passion. In a historic 1917 game against the Kirkwood Pioneers, Al ran, threw and kicked the ball totaling nearly 400 yards, six touchdowns and making good on 10 of 11 extra-point kicks, earning 46 of the 76 points scored in the shutout of Kirkwood.

Al's years at Missouri University continued to prove good his father's training in leadership and success. A member of Beta Theta Pi fraternity and the Mystical Seven, Al was a force to be reckoned with for Tiger athletic opponents. He scored the first touchdown ever for the Tigers against the St. Louis University Billikens in October of 1920, winning the starting position as fullback after that 44-0 win, but suffered injuries that plagued him for several games. By late November, he was back in condition and the "hero of the battle" against Kansas, reeling off first down after first down in the 16-7 win and earning a place on the All-Valley conference and on the All-American football team.

In the summer of 1921, Al spent several weeks in Parker Memorial Hospital recuperating from knee surgery but proved to be a scoring star for the Tigers again the following season, raking up two touchdowns against the Iowa Aggies, three against St. Louis and claimed "invincible" in the backfield against the Ames Cyclones in a 17-14 win, though not personally scoring. Injuries to his knee in the 5-7 loss to the Kansas Aggies and to his ribs in the 24-14 win over the Oklahoma Sooners prevented more scoring late in the year but he was still named to the second team All-Valley.

Al's last year at Missouri saw a short stint alternating field general and half-back duties as the team struggled to find their way. Coach Thomas Kelly exited mid-season after a stomping from Nebraska where Al suffered an injured shoulder. However, in the final football match-up of his life, Al departed in a "blaze of glory" by scoring the Tiger's only touchdown late in the second quarter and at the beginning of the third period his "trusty toe" sent a record-breaking long goal through the Kansas Jayhawker's goal posts from a muddy, rain-drenched 49-yard mark in front of 13,000 spectators for a final of 9-7. That year, he again made the first team All-Valley.

In 1923, after a stellar track season for Ol' Mizzou, Al continued his affiliation with the football program by helping with the Tiger team. Within a few months, however, his adventurous spirit drew him south to the Everglades in Florida where he spent the next few years as foreman working with natives to clear swampland in preparation for development and construction of the City of Clewiston. During his travels, Al fell in love with a piece of land south of Nashville in Tullahoma, Tennessee. He purchased the farm and settled there, raising his two sons with the former Virginia Whetton, his wife of over 60 years. For nine years, he served on the staff of University of the South in Sewanee, Tennessee as head coach of track and basketball and assistant coach of football.

At that time, Al determined to join the war efforts but was refused by the U.S. military due to football injuries to his back and knees. He ultimately honorably served his country in western Africa and on the German front in France as Field Director for the American Red Cross during the Second World War. Later, he represented Metropolitan Life Insurance Company and worked his beautiful farm. Enjoying a long life with the love and respect of his family and friends in Tullahoma, Al passed from this life on September 17, 1987.

By Lori Lincoln Grizzell
Granddaughter
Written Tuesday, August 26, 2008

DESTROY IT AND THEY WILL COME

By onset of the Roaring Twenties, the popularity of Kansas' outdoor athletic teams had outgrown the seating capacity of McCook Field, their first permanent home. This makeshift stadium was more than 30 years old, and its bleachers and grandstands had seriously deteriorated. The time had come for its replacement with a larger and more modern facility.

On May 10, 1921, in an event dubbed "Stadium Day," more than 4,000 students and faculty members turned out to tear down McCook Field. It took them only an hour and 18 minutes to destroy the venue that had seen 32 Kansas football teams struggle, with varying success, against their peers from regional schools like Nebraska, Oklahoma, and Missouri. Afterward, students and faculty members enjoyed a barbecue at the University's expense. Undoubtedly, the moment was not without a few wistful remembrances of Kansas' early athletic contests played on a field that had come into existence through the unexpected beneficence of a stranger.

The origins of McCook Field can be traced to December, 1889, when a coalition of students and faculty members formed  the University Athletic Board. Their aim was to coordinate Kansas' rather haphazardly organized sports teams and events. In its efforts to direct and encourage competitive sports at the University, the Athletic Board formed the "triangular league" by arranging intercollegiate games of football, baseball, and tennis with Baker University

John James McCook

and Washburn College. From its inception, the Athletic Board sought to develop both an athletic field and a gymnasium. Raising the necessary funds, however, proved problematic for the board until it found, in the words of the 1893 Quivira, "an unexpected benefactor in Colonel McCook, of New York."

According to the self-reported Who's Who in America, John James McCook had left Kenyon College to join the Union Army during the Civil War. Wounded in the Wilderness Campaign of May, 1864, the young officer was brevetted to the rank of Colonel. His father, eight brothers, and five cousins also served as Union Army officers in the Civil War and were called the "fighting McCooks of Ohio," a title the *University*

Review claimed was known "wherever the history of the nation is known."

In 1866, the year he turned 21, McCook graduated from Kenyon College. Three years later he received a law degree from Harvard University and entered the employ of Alexander and Green, one of the oldest and most prestigious law firms in New York. McCook appears to have enjoyed a successful practice and a respectable career. He was reportedly offered a cabinet position by United States President William McKinley, and became a member of the board of directors of the Atchison, Topeka & Santa Fe Railroad.

In this latter position, McCook met Charles S. Gleed, who sat on the University of Kansas Board of Regents. Gleed invited McCook to be Kansas' 1890 commencement speaker, and the New York lawyer delivered a rousing speech in which he attempted to link a classical education to the "material progress"

of Kansas. McCook was apparently taken with Kansas and decided to bestow a gift upon the University. After witnessing the Senior-Faculty baseball game on the Massachusetts Street sports grounds south of the University, he resolved to donate $1,500 to the Athletic Board for the creation of a more suitable field. He later added another $1,000.

Following McCook's unexpected contribution, the Athletic Board began to debate the future location of the field. Two possibilities presented themselves, the Massachusetts Street field already in use, or a 12-acre gully northwest of campus owned by former Kansas Governor Charles Robinson, who was willing to donate half of the property to the University and accept payment for the other half at below-market value.

A vigorous dispute between proponents of each site lasted for nearly a year. Supporters of the Massachusetts Street location begged the board not to adopt a "pennywise policy" that would place the field in an unsuitable "ravine, gulch, or hollow." Those who called for buying Robinson's land pointed to the much higher cost of acquiring the Massachusetts Street property and argued that the northern grounds were "nearer the actual

center of [the] student population." Ultimately the Athletic Board decided to buy the land from Robinson, even though it involved the cost of grading the gullies.

In the spring of 1892, the grading of the grounds began, and by September of that year a high-board fence was being erected around the new field. On October 27, 1892, the Jayhawk football team defeated Illinois 27-4 in the first game played on McCook Field. The gridiron ran east-west, or crosswise to the layout of present-day Memorial Stadium.

Initially, McCook only had a covered 800-seat grandstand in the northwest corner of the field. The University gradually added to this seating until by 1911, bleachers that could accommodate 10,000 people surrounded the field on three sides. Outside the fence were trees in which young children could climb to watch the games, as well as two small brooks, one of which originated in Potter Lake, while the other trickled down from a spring in Marvin Grove. At the confluence of the two

creeks stood Hamilton Hall, which acted as the dressing room for the Jayhawks and their opponents.

During the 1910s, the bleachers and buildings of McCook Field began to decay. In October, 1915, the *University Daily*

Former Chancellor Strong and current Chancellor Lindley on Stadium Day

Kansan reported that one of the bleachers' planks had broken at a game and resulted in a minor injury. For the remainder of the decade, repairs followed every year. This maintenance could only accomplish so much and, in 1920, the University declared that the grandstands were "a menace to those who thronged them." As the campus had grown considerably since 1892 and since football had risen in popularity, the school decided to replace McCook Field with a stadium that was to be dedicated to the memory of the 130 Kansas students who had lost their lives during World War I.

The new sports ground was constructed quickly following the demolition of McCook Field. On October 29, 1921, Kansas officially dedicated the partially completed Memorial Stadium in a game against Kansas State. Although McCook Field has disappeared into the University's past, the donor who made possible the school's first on-campus athletic facility has not been forgotten entirely. The road that provides access to the Memorial Stadium parking lot bears McCook's name eighty years after his field's last day.

By Mark D. Hersey, Ph.D.
Kansas Alumnus 2006
Written for This Day in KU History
www.KUHistory.com

H. W. "BILL" HARGISS

Emerson said, "All history is but the lengthened shadow of a great man." If so, the history of Kansas sports finds few men who cast longer shadows than my grandfather, H. W. "Bill" Hargiss. My grandfather came on the scene of Kansas athletics in the early days of the 20th century. He was an excellent athlete in his own right, but on top of that he had the ability to promote athletic ability in others. His long and rich life, in its entirety, was spent in the world of athletics.

Homer Woodson Hargiss was born on September 1, 1887 on a farm in Cherokee County in southeastern Kansas. He gave himself the name of "Bill" when he became a schoolboy and was forceful enough to make it stick. "No one ever called me Homer Woodson. It just didn't fit." The only person who continued to call him "Homer" was his mother. My grandfather grew up tall, strong and athletic as the middle of five competitive brothers.

Beulah, a small town seven miles west of Pittsburg, Kansas, had a high school team that was the scourge of the Cherokee Neutral Lands of the early 1900s. The football team played just three legitimate students including my grandfather and his brother. At that time it was not thought important that all players attend school. Other players including the coach were ex-college players. My grandfather was a three-sport standout at Beulah High School and led the football team as a fullback to an undefeated season.

He attended college at Kansas State Normal 1905-1909, known today as Emporia State University. There he played football, basketball, was active in track and was the regular first baseman in baseball when a game did not coincide with a track meet. He played fullback on the football team, center on the basketball team, first base in baseball and could double in most of the track events. He also participated in gymnastics and boxing and was named a team captain five times and earned 16 college athletic letters while working his way through school.

After graduation in 1909, he coached at Marion High School, Kansas for one year, the College of Emporia for three years, Kansas State Normal for three years, Oregon Agricultural College for two years, Kansas State Normal again for seven years and at the University of Kansas for 15 years, beginning in 1928. He helped coach a professional football team in 1942, went overseas during World War II as an armed services sports director, served as executive director of the Kansas Athletic Commission from 1952-1962 and coached the Air Force Olympic team in 1960.

At College of Emporia in 1910, my grandfather produced its first winning football season going on to a 17-6-1 record over

three years. There he coached a talented quarterback, Arthur Schabinger, a Kansas Hall of Famer. As a football innovator, my grandfather utilized Shabinger's athletic prowess to implement the forward pass as a regular offensive play in 1910, at a time when the rules permitted its use but was a feature unused by nearly all coaches until Knute Rockne and Gus Dorais at Notre Dame were credited for using it in 1913. In 1910, he introduced the pass option play, pulled linemen to run interference for the ball carrier possibly for the first time, and he prototyped for the first time a lightweight football shoe by modifying a baseball shoe, which was introduced by Spalding in 1911 after their inspection of it was complete.

My grandfather was director of physical education and a coach of athletics at Kansas State Normal during the periods of 1914-1917 and 1920-1927. His achievements as a coach include state track championships in 1915, 1916, 1917, 1922, 1923, 1925, and 1926, and conference football titles in 1915, 1916 and 1926 and tied for top honors in 1927. The gridiron teams he fielded won 61 games, lost only 23 and tied 12, having the highest win percentage in Emporia State University history. Three of his teams went undefeated, one was undefeated and untied and one never had its goal line crossed. The 1926 team was one of his greatest. It won the Kansas Conference championship, was undefeated and untied, its goal line was never crossed and it scored 144 points to the opponents' three. The team placed six men on the All-Conference team and two on the All-State eleven.

At Kansas State Normal, my grandfather introduced the defensive huddle there in 1923. He coached John Kuck, who won collegiate titles in the shot put and javelin throw and Olympic gold in the shot put in 1928, Earl McKown who was a two-time national collegiate champion in the pole vault, Lige Williams who held the intercollegiate record for 220-yard dash on the curve, and Fran Welch who played football and became a Kansas Hall of Fame coach.

Between his periods at Kansas State Normal, my grandfather was the head football, track and basketball coach at Oregon Agricultural College, now known as Oregon State University, in Corvallis, Oregon, from 1918-1919. There he coached Harry Cole of the Oregon Aggies, who set the intercollegiate indoor discus throw record at 140 feet 9 inches [42.90 metres]. In 1918, he introduced the offensive huddle to football. Before that time, all signals were barked out by the quarterback to team members in their regular positions. In order to eliminate confusion that was caused by crowd noise, he one day tried having his linemen just turn around and face the quarterback, forming a wide cup around him as the signals were called. From this he developed the close huddle, some distance back of the line of scrimmage, which accomplished the purpose much better. He later experimented with it at Oregon State, "Other coaches criticized it because they said it cost time, but I put a stop-watch on it and it often was faster than the signal calling system."

He brought the huddle to Kansas in 1920 and soon Bob Zuppke of Illinois began employing it.

In 1928, Missouri claimed that Kansas had violated the anti-scouting rule and produced evidence to show that persons not connected with the Kansas staff had acted as volunteer scouts at previous Missouri games and had provided Coach Cappon with charts of the Tiger plays that enabled him to improvise a method of stopping Clark and Flamank, Missouri ball carriers, in their devastating cut-back plays. The upshot of the affair was Cappon's resignation, causing Kansas to engage my grandfather in 1928, who was already enjoying a long and successful career as head coach of the Emporia Teachers. He went on to Kansas as head football coach in 1928, serving as such until the 1932 season. He had some pretty fair clubs at Kansas and he had one great one in 1930. Those were the days of "Jarring Jim" Bausch, his brother Pete, Ormand Beach, Arch Stuck, and a bunch of other mighty good boys.

There had been a complaint around Mount Oread that KU teams had been too colorless so, among other things, my grandfather instituted a revolving huddle that brought his players wheeling into position like a couple of squads of cavalry. It wasn't as fancy as Chick Meehan's military march performed by his Violent Violets of New York University, but it looked good to Jayhawk alumni who were football hungry for a winner. In fact, Kansas was too hungry, the rest of the Big Six schools declaring that my grandfather and his boys had to answer charges of professionalism. His 1930 team went 6-2 to win a rare Big Six league title and he compiled an overall 18-16-2 record as Kansas' head football coach.

On October 8, 1932 the Oklahomans came to Kansas. They gave Kansas a sound drubbing, going home with a 21 to 6 victory. The athletic board got their heads together as a result and decided Assistant Coach Adrian Lindsey should replace my grandfather to head the varsity coaching staff. My grandfather was surprised and hurt, but didn't protest. He gave up the head coach's job but

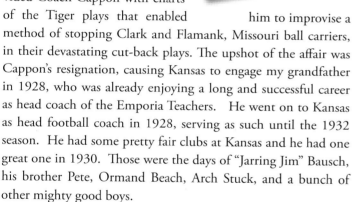

continued to serve Kansas as a scout, a freshman coach and as head track coach until 1943.

At Kansas in track, my grandfather coached National Collegiate Athletic Association champions Glenn Cunningham, 1932 and 1933 mile, Elwyn Dees, 1935 shot put, and Clyde Coffman, 1935 American Athletic Union pentathlon. He also coached Olympians Jim Bausch, 1932 decathlon gold medalist, Glenn Cunningham, 1932 1,500 meters fourth place, 1936 1,500 meters silver medalist and Clyde Coffman, 1932 decathlon seventh place.

My grandfather retired in 1962 at the age of 72 and honors continued to come his way during the next 16 years of his retirement. The qualities that made him one of the greatest athletes and coaches Kansas ever produced were evident in the interesting life he made for himself in retirement. He was a sought after public speaker, painted in oils, worked in wood with power tools, played golf, looked after his yard and grew tea roses, traveled, and was an educated spectator at football games and other athletic events. He passed away on October 15, 1978 at 91 years of age in Lawrence, Kansas and is interred in Emporia.

My grandfather is honored in the Kansas Sports Hall of Fame as a charter member, the National Association of Intercollegiate Athletics Hall of Fame, the University of Kansas Hall of Fame with his portrait hanging in Allen Fieldhouse, the Emporia State University Hall of Fame as a charter member and as one of their top 25 football players over the last century, and as an Emporia State Distinguished Alumnus. In 1970, over 200 persons, comprising his former athletes, came to Emporia from across the country to pay tribute in a celebration for him with the Mayor declaring a Bill Hargiss Day for Emporia.

While he received many honors and awards during his long and busy athletic career, the most rewarding to him was the help he provided for those who sat at his feet. Few people have influenced for good the lives of as many people as has my grandfather. The men and women who fell under his spell lived and enjoyed a better life because of him.

By G. Clarke Oberheide
Grandson
Written Wednesday, August 13, 2008

NEITHER BEAST, FISH NOR FOWL

The "Jayhawk" is a myth. It has no historical use. It is neither beast, fish nor fowl. The myth had its rise in the characters of two birds that frequent the Missouri Valley, namely the blue jay, a noisy quarrelsome robber that takes delight in pouncing upon small birds and robbing their nests of eggs and young birds, and the sparrow hawk, a genteel killer of birds, rats, mice and rabbits, and when necessary a courageous and cautious fighter. Just when, where and by whom the names of the two birds were joined in "Jayhawk" and applied to human beings, no one knows. However it is known that the term "jayhawk" originated in the home territory of these birds somewhere between Texas and Nebraska. It is known that it was applied to an overland company of gold-seekers on their way through Nebraska to California. It was applied to Jennison's band of free-booters, to Montgomery's rangers, to Missouri guerrilla bands of border ruffians, and finally in a general way to the free-soilers of Kansas.

In the early days of uncertainty of government, life and property, whenever bands were organized requiring purpose, courage, boldness and reckless daring, they were always candidates for the name either through choice or through the derision and hatred of enemies. It is significant also that "jayhawking" become a general term to express marauding or plundering.

It is not known how the name gradually became applied to all residents of Kansas. Perhaps it was because Kansas was nationally known as the center of disturbance and jayhawk became a nationally known byword. Probably Jennison's band of fighters and freebooters, followed historically by Jennison's "Jayhawk regiment" in the Civil War had something to do with causing the name to adhere to Kansas. But Kansas accepted the totemic appellation with good grace and every loyal Kansan is proud to be a member of the Clan-Kansas that now stands for nobler things than "jayhawking." The "Jayhawk" myth has become a spirit of progress and power. Gone has the spirit of robber birds; gone the reckless spirit of the law and disorder bands of the stress and storm period. Only the spirit of comradeship and the courageous fighting qualities to make and keep Kansas free, remain. The spirit of the modern Jayhawk is to make Kansas great and strong and noble in good deeds. It is a benevolent spirit.

Kansas University seized the word as a shibboleth and attached it to the earth with "rock chalk" and brought out the K.U. yell, the greatest lung developer of all times. It is the voice of the clan. It is a call to courage and the fighting spirit; but more it is a call to comradeship, truth, learning and righteousness.

The artists have tried to express the mythical bird in clever totemic designs, which range all the way from a "dicky-bird" with a huge bill, wearing boots to a disconsolate crow and to a fierce looking fighting bird. All very well as a totem of the clan can express unity and loyalty, but the spirit of the Jayhawk refuses to be photographed.

But no matter about the origin of this mythical creature, about its uncertain history, about its early use by people whose actions were sometimes questionable; today "Jayhawk" embodies the Kansas spirit, the University spirit of unity, loyalty, honesty and right living. Rock Chalk, Jay Hawk K.U.

By Frank Wilson Blackmar, Ph.D.
University of Kansas
Professor and Dean of the Graduate School 1889 – 1930
Published in the Annual KU Radio Nite Program,
December, 1926

"...KANSAS MUST HAVE A STADIUM!"

Though it may not be immediately obvious to the casual observer, Kansas' imposing athletic stadium was the University's first major war memorial, built in the years following the First World War to commemorate the 130 students and alumni who died making "the world safe for democracy."

Thus, fittingly, on the four-year anniversary of when the guns fell silent in Europe, nearly 18,000 people packed the Kansas Memorial Stadium on Armistice Day, November 11, 1922, and fell silent themselves, if only briefly, to witness the stadium's formal dedication and the University's salute to the honored dead. The proud feelings and positive energy that pervaded that day were not enough, sadly, to rally the Jayhawks to victory in the game that followed. In what by then had become, and indeed remains, an almost routine occurrence, Kansas fell to Nebraska, 28-0.

After four years of human and material devastation unparalleled to that point in world history, there was no question of whether a World War I memorial was to be built on campus, but rather what kind and how soon? That Kansas could claim 130 of the fallen as its own, including America's first officer killed-in-action, Lt. Dr. William T. Fitzsimons, 1912 alumnus, made the University's desire to pay its proper respects all the more pressing. What resulted was a plan to launch the ambitious Million Dollar Drive, officially begun in the fall of 1920.

There was, however, no immediate consensus as to what form the memorial should take; among the many suggestions, according to Kansas historian Robert Taft, were "an auditorium, a health building, a student loan fund, and a tower and chimes." The two leading contenders were a new stadium and student union, though admittedly, this was due more to the University's perceived need of such structures, rather than to their intrinsic memorial value.

Even before the actual inception of the Million Dollar Drive, there were many on campus urging that a new athletic stadium be the centerpiece of any war memorial effort. Incidentally, this concept of building utilitarian structures and affixing the adjective "memorial" to them was indeed quite popular at universities nationwide in these years, and would remain so after the Second World War as well. A new stadium at Kansas, however, would be more than a mere luxury. Considering the dilapidated state of McCook Field, the University's original outdoor athletic grounds, it was something approaching a necessity, as Civil Engineering Professor Clement C. Williams pointed out on March 23, 1920, in the Oread Magazine.

McCook's 25-year-old wooden bleachers had served the University well enough, allowed Williams, during "the days

of small beginnings," but time and increased attendance now made them wholly inadequate. "The present bleachers are not only unsightly and hazardous as to fire and decay, but they are exceedingly uncomfortable." Williams also claimed he had "witnessed several instances when women have been compelled to leave the game because of the cold, and many cases of illness attributable to this exposure have been reported."

These conditions, coupled with a steady rise of alumni and student interest in Kansas football, made construction of a new, permanent stadium a top priority and if it also served a commemorative function, then so much the better. Additionally, as Professor Williams pointed out, such leading universities as Princeton, Harvard, Yale and Michigan, had all recently built giant stadiums, so there were a number of different facilities Kansas could emulate.

The man running point in the early stages of the stadium construction project was Dr. Forrest C. "Phog" Allen, the University's Director of Athletics. In 1920, he recommended that Kansas' new stadium be modeled after Princeton's after returning from an inspection tour of eastern universities. The dual-purpose football and track facility would sport a U-shaped design and have a maximum capacity of around 32,000.

Although Allen's recommendation was eventually followed by the stadium's designers, Kansas architecture professor LaForce Bailey and the aforementioned Clement Williams, one exhortation was not: Allen had originally lobbied to have the stadium named after the late Kansas football and basketball great Tommy Johnson, the University's first All-American, but that idea was vetoed in favor of memorializing the University's war dead.

World War I affected and changed the world in countless ways and, according to Kansas Chancellor Ernest H. Lindley, "One result of the great war is a nationwide recognition of the commanding importance of physical education." Even before opening the University's Million Dollar Drive, Lindley was reminding potential donors that "all authorities agree that the best form of physical education … is to be found in the outdoor sports," and "this calls for large grounds and ample equipment." Moreover, a new stadium would truly be "a wonderful agency in the development of unity and spirit," for it would "bring together all the sons and daughters of the University" not only for athletic contests, "but for many other University functions" as well.

In a very detailed and attractive brochure, dated September 1920, the University addressed the question "Why we need a stadium" by reiterating the inadequacies of McCook Field and the advantages and long-term economy of building a permanent reinforced concrete structure. Not only would it be "much less an eyesore than the average, dingy, rickety wooden bleachers," but will "have an attractiveness and dignity" that will "justify on our part an attitude of pride." It was important to realize as well that "other schools throughout the country are rapidly swinging into line," and thus imperative that Kansas students, faculty, friends and alumni not allow their University to be "a laggard."

Perhaps the most impressive part of the promotional brochure was a six-page section of comments from prominent citizens and University people on why Kansas should have a new stadium and, more specifically, why one should make a generous donation to the Million Dollar Fund. "Yale is famous for its bowl, Harvard for its stadium. Why not K.U. too?" asked C. E. McBride, sporting editor for the *Kansas City Star*. Basketball inventor and Kansas legend, Dr. James Naismith, told alumni that they "must act at once by backing the stadium project with their financial as well as moral support."

"Rome had her Coliseum. Kansas must have a stadium!" cried "Phog" Allen. The final page contained an "In Memoriam," in which Kansas structural engineering professor H. A. Rice first mourned the death of the McCook bleachers, then heralded the birth of Memorial Stadium. "Nobly they served their purpose, and now death has overtaken them, may they rest in peace. Rising from their ashes will be the great Stadium – a giant replacing a pigmy – beautiful, commodious, a monument to the past and an inspiration to the future."

After months of hyping and organizing the Million Dollar Drive, the University finally opened its campaign on November 18, 1920, which was, fortuitously as it turned out, just a few days after the big homecoming football game between Kansas and the heavily-favored Cornhuskers of Nebraska. The outcome was an astonishing 20-20 tie! So miraculous apparently was this non-loss, that it galvanized the student body and all others connected with the University to do their utmost in support of the University's fundraising plans for a new stadium and student union. "How vital was that deadlock … on old McCook Field?" asked Lawrence Journal-World columnist Bill Mayer. "It created Memorial Stadium – that's how important it was."

The "real victory," claimed the Graduate Magazine, belonged to Kansas, for within two weeks, students and faculty had pledged nearly $225,000 and a "new spirit" had enveloped the campus. According to the *University Daily Kansan*, not losing to Nebraska was just the first sign that the University had entered "a new era of growth" that would end with Kansas becoming "the biggest and best in the Middle West." They would accomplish this "by every single student in the school boosting all the time, doing every thing he can to increase fellowship,

to promote loyalty, to develop a sense of responsibility among students, to encourage wholesome reaction, to raise scholastic standards, and to create fair, worth-while student activities and class spirit."

Indeed, the early results of this new spirit were most impressive, especially in terms of how much money students themselves pledged to the Million Dollar Drive. Out of a total enrollment for 1920-21 of 4,226, the students pledged more than $190,000, an average of around $45 each, a remarkable amount of money, really, from students of any decade. Posters adorned campus with slogans such as "Every Student a Giver," "The Alumni Are Watching Us Now" and "Another Way to Beat Missouri."

Faculty members compounded this magnificent expression of school spirit and generosity by pledging $35,000 of their own, leading everyone to believe that nothing could slow the Million Dollar Drive's momentum. Indeed, as Kansas historian Clifford Griffin has noted, once the Lawrence community, the state of Kansas, and alumni nationwide had been canvassed, pledge totals were rocketing towards the magic million-dollar figure. "By May, 1921, total pledges had reached $550,000; by October they had passed $600,000; by the late fall of 1922 they were over $850,000."

Kansas never actually received $1 million worth of pledges; it fell $35,000 short when the Million Dollar Drive came to an end in 1925. However, this was the least of the University's problems. Pledges, after all, are not payments, and to the consternation of the Memorial Corporation, set up to direct the fundraising efforts, only $655,000 of the pledged $965,000 was ever actually received and it took until September 1931 to collect even this amount. It seems that the intense flurry of enthusiasm that followed the Nebraska game led many to promise more than they were willing or able to deliver. Also, although most agreed to fulfill their pledge through semi-annual payments over a period of up to four years, time and distance naturally wore down many people's generosity. All this meant that the stadium would take much longer to build, let alone finance, it not being fully paid off until 1947.

"Yet in the spring of 1921," wrote Griffin, "with over $500,000 pledged and hopes of payment high, construction of the new stadium began with the destruction of the old." Just as Proffesor Rice had spiritedly, if melodramatically, foretold the year before; death was indeed about to overtake the bleachers of McCook Field. In order to perform the ritual, Chancellor Lindley declared May 10, 1921, to be Stadium Day and turned loose hundreds of male students and faculty who proceeded to physically tear down the bleachers in only 78 minutes. It was "one of the greatest events in the history of the school," according to the

University Daily Kansan, "a grand and howling success." Some 4,000 people participated in the destruction, which was followed by lunch, speeches, and games. The festivities were then capped by the unforgettable sight of the University's chancellor, "clad in overalls," plowing a "straight furrow" across the former McCook Field, the intended site of Memorial Stadium.

Actual construction of the new stadium, estimated to cost a half-million dollars upon completion, began on July 16, 1921. But with only a quarter-million in the bank, the Memorial Corporation could only pay for the east and west sides; rounding off the U would not be possible until 1927, when full capacity reached 38,000, and only then after raising ticket prices and floating hundreds of thousands of dollars worth of bonds. None of this really mattered to Kansas football fans, though, as more than 5,000 crammed into the incomplete, yet sturdy Memorial Stadium for the first time on October 29 to cheer on the Jayhawks as they defeated their arch-rivals from Manhattan 21-7. A month later, at the annual Thanksgiving Day game with Missouri, Kansas scored another victory before a whopping 15,480 fans.

It was another year, however, before the stadium was officially dedicated. The ceremonies of November 11, 1922, served a two-fold purpose, being both a recognition of Armistice Day and an opportunity to honor the 130 Kansas men and women killed in World War I in whose memory the stadium was built. The day began with a parade led by the Kansas Department of the American Legion, followed by a rifle salute and the playing of taps. After addresses by Kansas Governor Henry J. Allen and Chancellor Lindley, the assembled sang a memorial hymn:

"Within the light on Oread's hill
Above the valley's golden beauty,
Our comrades' spirit hovers still
The mem'ry of their faith in duty
They died that we might have the peace
For which mankind has ever striven.
Their call to us will never cease:
'Give ye always as we have given.'"

Of course, there was a football game against Nebraska again, no less, yet this time the Jayhawks could not even manage a tie.

In the decades that followed, perhaps the most memorable of the stadium's millions of visitors were the World War II veterans who lived under it, in the makeshift dormitories of what became known as McCook Hall. Faced in the fall of 1946 with an overwhelming 9,100 students, 5,600 of whom were male veterans, the University struggled to find any and all possible places to house them. One of these was the area beneath the stadium, which proved room enough for 64 students during the late 1940s until more appropriate, and more spacious, residence halls could be constructed.

Since 1921, Memorial Stadium, which, incidentally, is the seventh oldest in Division I athletics, has indeed undergone a number of serious renovations and additions, from press boxes and luxury suites, new seating tiers and artificial turf, to giant video and scoreboards. Its current capacity is 50,250, that is, according to Lawrence Journal-World columnist Mayer, "if you use crowbars, shoe horns and Vaseline to cram everyone in." Something like that happened on October 13, 1973 when 51,574 fans, the all-time attendance record, watched Kansas roll over Kansas State, 25-18.

Yet for all its additions and expansions, Memorial Stadium has lost an intangible quality that was once considered quite precious, even essential; its "memorial" aspect. As one archival source notes, "memories are short. 'Memorial' was, in the late '40s, officially deleted from the [Kansas] Union, and is seldom used in connection with the Stadium."

Moreover, in 1946, as the University was debating whether to build a "memorial" field house to honor the 276 Kansas men and women who died in World War II, Chancellor Deane W. Malott vigorously protested: "The Stadium was built as a World War I memorial. [Yet] no one thinks as he sits in it about the sacrifice of several score of young men of this institution who lost their lives in that struggle. We have been determined this time that we would have a memorial that would be truly a memorial, and not merely use that as an excuse to fill a need at the University."

True to his pledge, Malott and his allies succeeded in building the Memorial Carillon and Campanile, a structure which, although serving no utilitarian purpose, nonetheless reminds students hourly of the sacrifices of those Jayhawks who came before them, so that they might live free.

By John H. McCool
Kansas Alumnus 2002
Written for This Week in KU History
www.KUHistory.com

THE JAYHAWKER AND THE SAVITAR

JAYHAWKER 1921 – BORDER WAR 1920

By Edward B. Smith
Missouri Alumnus 1921

A TURKEY DAY FEED FOR THE TIGER

Yes, we lost to Missouri, too. It was the hardest game for the rooters to lose and proved to be too hard for the team to win. But it isn't a blot on the season's history, despite the 16 to 7 score, for the Tigers had a great team, full of individual stars, all welded together with the intent and purpose of plucking the Jayhawk bird. And Al Lincoln, Jack Fulbright and Chuck Lewis were not to be denied, though Kansas through the great work of Lonborg "showed" Missouri a few things.

A valiant fight, the gamest kind of a game, was staged by the Jayhawkers at Columbia, but the Kansas line could not hold Missouri line-plunges. And again the passing game was unsuccessful, as it had been at Oklahoma. The great aerial display failed to score in every instance, except once in the early part of the game, when a toss to Lonborg, via Bunn, netted a touchdown.

Missouri came right back and scored two touchdowns. Lewis flipped to Fulbright over the goal line for the first one, and Al Lincoln got the other after a series of plunges. Then Captain Lewis drop-kicked very neatly from the 22-yard line after the Lincoln lad had carried the ball from mid-field.

Lonborg clinched his All-Valley quarterback position by his great playing in his last game. Mandy, Reid and Nettels all put up a good brand of football, too, but this was Missouri's year.

SAVITAR 1921 – BORDER WAR 1920

And now for the Jayhawker. Although a championship had been lost, consolation was in store If Kansas could be given a drubbing.

Nearly 12,000 persons, the largest crowd ever on Rollins Field, saw the Jayhawk fall in humiliation on that Homecoming Day. And every one of them will say that the 16 to 7 score does not tell the story. The Jayhawk, taking Captain "Chuck" and his men by surprise, registered the first score. Mandeville fled across the line with the ball and kicked goal, ending the quarter with a 7 to 0 score. But the Tiger was out for blood, and with the light of victory in his eye he fought with a new fire. The Lewis – to – Fulbright pass gave Missouri a touchdown. The score was tied. Then Missouri started to break through the Kansas line, and another touchdown was inevitable. Fulbright scored in the third period on an end run and Captain Lewis scored a filed goal in the last quarter. The game was won, 16 to 7.

It was a day of atonement for all our suffering. True, we had lost a championship, but in the annals of Valley history another Tiger victory over Kansas was recorded, and to sons of "Old Mizzou" that is as good as a championship.

JAYHAWKER 1922 – BORDER WAR 1921

DEDICATING THE STADIUM
WITH TIGER MEAT

Lewis draws first blood The Jayhawkers, playing against greater odds and superior weight in the thirtieth annual football classic, defeated their rivals, the Missouri Tigers, in the new stadium. Thanksgiving Day, before a crowd of 22,000 persons, by a score of 15 to 9. It was the first time in five years that Kansas had won on the home field. The game was one of the most exciting and closely contested in recent years. Early in the first quarter Missouri crashed through the Jayhawker line for substantial gains which brought the ball to the Kansas five-yard line. After being held for three downs, "Chuck" Lewis dropped back and sent a dropkick over for the first score of the game. The three points against them put the fight in instead of taking it out, and Spurgeon carried the ball through center and around the ends for gain after gain. Krueger also proved his worth as a backfield star and spread his husky frame through many a Tiger defense. Krueger replaced Wilson at the passing end of the game, and Wilson, Spurgeon and McAdams each figured on the receiving end of some successful passes. Ten minutes after Missouri had drawn first blood, and on the fourth down, Wilson passed 20 yards to Krueger over the goal line for the first touchdown of the game.

The second Kansas touchdown came as a result of straight football, Spurgeon going over for the score. The Tigers attempted a rally, using the air, with Lewis playing fifteen yards behind the line. And it was here that Max Krueger won his way into the Kansas Hall of Fame, when Krueger intercepts he intercepted a Lewis pass and ran for sixty-five yards before being forced out of bounds on the Missouri five-yard line. But Kansas found a stiffened Missouri line and lost the ball on downs. Starting the second half with nearly perfect interference for Lewis in his end runs, the Missourians scored a touchdown in the first few minutes of play. It was their last consistent effort. Krueger intercepted another Lewis pass and Kansas started the ball down the field, only to be stopped on the Missouri five-yard line again, losing the ball on downs. Lewis dropped back to punt out of danger, standing behind his own goal line. On a bad pass from center he fumbled and managed to regain possession of the ball, but was downed back of the line for a safety. In the last quarter Missouri carried the ball to the Kansas twenty-yard line several times, but always when a completed pass meant a touchdown, Kansas produced the fight and ability to break it up. Never have two teams fought with such determination before on McCook field, and never have two teams fought so cleanly to win. The results of the game were in doubt until the final whistle blew with Kansas in possession of the ball on their own twelve-yard line.

SAVITAR 1922 – BORDER WAR 1921

When the last whistle of the gridiron season blew and 5,000 loyal Tigers uncovered and sang "Old Missouri," the newly dedicated K. U. stadium witnessed a grand sight – one that displayed that famous Missouri spirit, one that brought to life that popular line:

"You can defeat the Tigers, but you can't beat 'em."

But the game –

Missouri traveled to Lawrence that twenty-fourth of November all ready to feast on Jayhawk meat. Although Missouri was first to score when Lewis' toe netted three points, K. U. soon took the lead and held it throughout the game. The score at the end of the first half was 13 to 3.

The third quarter belonged to the Bengals, and the game could have been won in this period, but fate decided in favor of the Kansans. A touchdown by Lewis was the only other score the Tigers could make.

Although every regular played a whirlwind game that day, the subs who filled the empty spots played a great game, namely, Simpson, Schwimmer and Bailey.

JAYHAWKER 1923 – BORDER WAR 1922

The Missouri Game on Thanksgiving Day

Kansas met an unexpected 9 to 7 defeat at the claws of the Missouri Tiger on Turkey Day at Columbia.

Consistent with the other big Kansas games this season, it was played in a drizzling rain which made handling the ball a difficult matter. The Missouri touchdown came in the second quarter after the Tiger had marched down the field to the 16-yard line and a Kansas penalty put the ball at the edge of the chalk mark. Lincoln, Missouri's full back, smashed through the line for the necessary inches for the first touchdown of the game. Later in the same period he booted a 48-yard kick which gave Missouri the victory.

In the fourth quarter Spurgeon grabbed a pass from Wilson on the 25-yard line and broke away for Kansas' lone touchdown. Wilson kicked goal. This ended the scoring for the game, but both teams fought desperately to the final whistle.

SAVITAR 1923 – BORDER WAR 1922

In a drizzle of rain, 20,000 loyal Missourians packed the bleachers on Rollins Field to witness the Annual Valley Classic between the Tiger and Jayhawk.

The story reads like fiction. It was the old story of the team that came back; a fitting sequel of the M. U. – K. U. game of 1909. Recent years have not witnessed a harder fought game on Rollins Field. It was a battle. The rain was forgotten, and umbrellas were thrown aside as the Tigers plowed their way through the Jayhawk line toward the coveted goal. Forgotten were the other defeats of the season. Forgotten was the "dope" of a K. U. Victory as Tiger player and rooter united in a fight for victory.

Lincoln's touchdown in the second quarter gave M. U. a six-point lead. In the third quarter, after several unsuccessful attempts, "Link" booted the ball from the 45-yard line squarely between the posts. The Kansans forced over one touchdown and kicked goal. The final whistle found Lincoln completing a 40-yard run around end and the Tigers on their way for more score.

The Jayhawk backfield worked perfectly but their line would not hold. The Tiger line and backfield worked like a machine. The game was a fitting climax to the season and 20,000 voices sang "Old Missouri" as it had never been sung before.

SAVITAR 1924 – BORDER WAR 1923

[Missouri lost to Washington University the previous week, which was an assumed victory.]

But the Tiger tightened the belt that encircled an empty stomach, set his jaw, and, smiling grimly, faced Jayhawkward. Coach Henry housed the squad together – it talked nothing but football. The practices were light. Missouri's chances were staked upon grim fight. The dope sheets gave Kansas heavy odds.

Special trains carried a great part of the student body to Lawrence with the team and the snow fell on as much Old Gold and Black as Crimson and Blue in the Kansas stadium on Thanksgiving Day. The white flakes fell steadily and the kick-off was delayed half an hour while the field was dragged and swept. The two squads face the movie men – Kansas the overwhelming favorite.

Missouri had the advantage of the north wind as Kansas kicked off. The ball was fumbled and Kansas recovered on Missouri's 27 yard line. Two plays gained 20 yards for the Jayhawker. Then the Tiger defense set and refused to yield an inch. Captain Black of K. U. dropped back and kicked an easy field goal from 20 yards. An exchange of punts after the next kick-off gave Missouri a 25-yard advantage and first down on the Kansas 35-yard line. Seven plays carried the ball to the 12-yard line and Whiteman dropped back to kick   as the quarter

ended. The change of goals put the wind against the Missouri halfback and the try missed by a yard. With the score 3 to 0, the Tigers opened the second half with a pounding offensive, of which Bond was the star. In three straight first downs, Bond and Faurot took the ball to the 6-yard line. With the 3-yard line to go for the first down, Bond missed by a fraction of an inch and Kansas took the ball, punting out. But back came the Bengal's line and backfield smashing the 'Hawk to the 20-yard line. Then John Walsh, called back from end, kicked a perfect goal from the 33-yard line. The wind advantage returning to Kansas in the last quarter, but a skillful, hard-fighting defense staved off all scoring. Three Jayhawk place-kicks failed and the 3 to 3 tie stood.

Thus the Missouri team rose again to the great occasion and saved the season,. Only the statistics are needed to stage the superiority of the "Bengal beasts whose tail was due for a twisting."

First downs – earned, Missouri 6, Kansas 2; on penalties, Missouri 2, Kansas 1. Yards penalized – Kansas 10, Missouri 12. Yards gained in scrimmage – Missouri 122, Kansas 78. Kicks returned – Missouri 48 yards, Kansas 10 yards. Average of punts – Missouri 28 yards, Kansas 34 yards. Forward passes – Kansas completed 1, was allowed 1 on a penalty, 1 intercepted, Missouri 0.

By Tilghman R. Cloud
Missouri Alumnus 1924

JAYHAWKER 1925 – BORDER WAR 1924

The Turkey Day Defeat, 0-14

The Missouri line outcharged that of Kansas Thanksgiving Day and the annual game ended with a Tiger victory, 14-0. The Tiger linemen consistently broke through the Red and Blue defense to throw the Kansas backs for losses.

Captain Bond, Faurot, and Whiteman found almost impossible looking holes in the Kansas line and charged through for gains. The Kansas team was going good but lacked the necessary punch to carry the ball over for a score. Several times the ball was carried, by strategic plays, to the twenty-yard line, only to be lost on downs.

The first half was almost even. The Kansas team threatened to score in the first quarter when runs by Burt and Starr, coupled with a Tiger fumble, brought the ball to the two-yard line, where it was lost on a fumble. In the third quarter a Missouri half went through center for 21 yards and a touchdown. Another followed in short order. The Missouri team used the "huddle" play successfully. Smith and Haley did the best in the Kansas line, and Zuber showed up well at punting and passing.

SAVITAR 1925 – BORDER WAR 1924

And then came Kansas to topple before Rollins Field's greatest crowd, bowing before the Tigers, 14 to 0, in a game which gave Missouri the conference championship. Trips to California and victories over Big Ten champions pale before the Kansas game, and that battle of Thanksgiving Day, 1924, stands out above them all. Never was there a more beautiful football game, and never did a Jayhawker go home so decisively squelched. Through two desperate quarters the teams battled, each putting its all into the game, but unable to score. The Tigers had the advantage everywhere except on the score board. Then early in the third quarter Kansas tried a pass deep in her own territory. It was good, but the receiver fumbled and the Tigers recovered. Faurot smashed the line twice and then Whiteman jumped through center for 20 yards and six points, afterwards adding a seventh with a twelve-yard place kick.

Back came the Tigers from the kickoff with a series of smashes by Bond and then a whirlwind dash by Jackson down the sideline for 60 yards, putting the ball on the Jayhawker five-yard line. But the Jayhawkers stiffened and the Tigers lost the ball on a pass across the goal. Again Kansas passed in her own territory, and up went Faurot after the ball. He and Bond carried the pigskin back to the Kansas five-yard line and Jackson drove through center for the second touchdown. Again Whiteman kicked the extra point.

Missouri had won from Kansas and in so doing hoisted over the Tiger camp the Championship of 1924.

By John Phillip Hamel
Missouri Junior 1915

JAYHAWKER 1926 – BORDER WAR 1925

Then came the fateful Homecoming game and Stony Wall's memorable kick which sent the champion Tigers back to Columbia overwhelmed by the desperate Crimson and Blue heroes. With all of the injured men back in the line-up and 10,000 loyal Jayhawkers screaming for victory, the Bengals never had a chance to win. They started out rather suspiciously by scoring from a mid-field pass. Their success was short-lived, however, for Twink Starr took a pass from the mighty Zuber, ran to the 3-yard line, and gave it to Hart, who plunged through the Tiger line for six points. Wall tied the score with a perfect place kick.

Then began the desperate attempts of the brilliant Missouri team to score, but their efforts were without avail, and after a 75-yard kick by Zuber and with 15 seconds to play, Wall's kick was good for the most glorious victory over the ancient enemy from Mizzou that the Jayhawks have ever won. The entire Kansas section surged out on the field amid a barrage of cushions, while the Missouri side stood spell-bound and soon trickled silently out of the stadium and back to Tiger land.

SAVITAR 1926 – BORDER WAR 1925

Perfect would be the story if it ended here, but Kansas in 1925 managed to avenge all the ignominy of the previous five years and all the insults that have been heaped upon her since [Quantrill] sacked Lawrence in the fifties. The Jayhawks won the annual classic 10 to 7 before 31,000 persons and the governors of the two states.

A strong north wind swept through the Mt. Oread stadium the afternoon of the fateful day, and all the scoring was with the wind. Missouri scored in the first quarter when Whiteman passed twenty-five yards to Clark for a touchdown. Kansas scored in the second quarter when a 30-yard pass put the ball on the six-inch line and Hart dived over.

With the gale at their backs again in the third quarter the Tigers staged a drive that was stopped only within the Kansas one-yard mark. In the last period the Bengals could not threaten. They were badly outkicked and could not pass far enough in the teeth of the wind to get the ball behind the Jayhawk backs. The game remained a deadlock until the final play, when an event such as old-timers tell credulous listeners and spindle-chested freshmen dream about, occurred.

Kansas had the ball on Missouri's 35-yard line with time for but one play. The Jayhawk captain called time out and looked inquiringly to the sidelines. One Wall, a substitute place-kicker, was sent in to do the Casey-at-the-bat act. He fared a great deal better than the Casey of song, however, for he sent the ball squarely between the posts. The timekeeper fired his gun; victory-crazed Kansas swarmed over the field, tore down the goal posts and carried off the players.

By Tom Mahoney
Missouri Alumnus 1927

JAYHAWKER 1927 – BORDER WAR 1926

Playing in the new Missouri stadium before a crowd estimated to have been 35,000 persons, the Jayhawkers were forced to take a 15 to defeat. The game was played in a continuous downfall of snow which grew heavier as the game went on and which hampered the playing of both teams and slowed up the game.

SAVITAR 1927 – BORDER WAR 1926

A record crowd of 30,000 Homecomers sat through a swirling snowstorm to watch the Tigers defeat Kansas in the thirty-fifth annual classic, the Saturday before Thanksgiving. Kansas failed to prove as formidable as in recent years and the Gold and Black triumphed 15-0.

Tuttle scored the first touchdown in the second quarter after a 30-yard pass, Stuber to Clark, had placed the ball on the Jayhawk 10-yard line. The Safety came in the last quarter when Captain Bacchus blocked Captain Zuber's punt on the goal line and Tarr recovered the ball after it had rolled beyond the end zone.

Stuber intercepted a Kansas pass near the end of the game; ran to the 6-yard line; and on the next play O'Sullivan passed left-handed to Bacchus for the final touchdown. Stuber's kick was successful after the first touchdown.

Missouri made eight first downs to the Kansans' two, and gained a total yardage of 201 to the Jayhawk 36.

JAYHAWKER 1928 – BORDER WAR 1927

What could be sweeter? Here's Kansas with a mediocre record and Missouri claiming the Valley championship even before the end of the season. 27,000 students and old grads were in the stadium to witness the "battle of the century," a touchdown made by the Tigers in the first minute of play, and then an explosive Kansas offense that scored two touch-downs and ripped through the Missouri line. That clawing, fighting Jayhawk slipped two long passes over the Missouri team and the Tigers were taking time out to wonder where the ball was going and where it was going to stop. What could be sweeter? Every man on the Kansas team played his best game of the whole season. It was a Kansas Day!

SAVITAR 1928 – BORDER WAR 1927

Memorial Stadium, Lawrence, Kan., Nov. 19. – Kansas upset predictions today and defeated Missouri, 14-7, in the 36th annual football clash.

After taking advantage of a fumble by Kansas early in the first quarter of the classic game to make a touchdown two minutes after the whistle had started the contest, the Missouri Tigers were humbled, 14-7, by their traditional rivals and enemies, the Jayhawks. The team from Mount Oread, playing before a homecoming crowd of 30,000, demonstrated some superb football in the biggest upset of the Missouri Valley for the year. No alibis are needed. The tiger was unable to cope with the Jayhawk attack. Kansas did not win on the breaks of the game. Clean-cut football was used by the 'Hawkers to outplay the Missourians in every department of the game. The Kansans stopped the heretofore formidable passing combination, Flamank to Clark, and countered with their own deadly aerial game, which the Tigers were unable to stop or solve. The Jayhawkers were the underdogs in the Valley all year. But against their bitterest enemies, the Tigers, Kansas came into her own and spin-played the Tiger till he grew fairly dizzy in trying to watch the ball. Only three Tiger passes were completed. 'Twas a gloomy crowd that invaded the Tiger's lair that Saturday night…

JAYHAWKER 1929 – BORDER WAR 1928

Since 1917, K. U. has been the loser in the famous Jayhawk-Tiger duels by a slight margin. Missouri has won six times to Kansas' four. This year William Hargiss joined the illustrious line of Kansas coaches to do or die against the traditional Tiger enemy.

SAVITAR 1929 – BORDER WAR 1928

Thirty-six years of football tradition and 26,000 yelling football fans looked down on Memorial Stadium for the Homecoming game with the Jayhawks. Bands from both universities played tunes and Alma Maters while the battle songs of Kansas and Missouri rang out to the crowd. Homecomers came from far and near on trains, busses and automobiles. Everybody was happy and pulling for a Tiger victory. A special train and several airplanes added to the mob of old-timers. It was a perfect football game from the standpoint of everyone except the Kansas team and fans. A warm November sun and invigorating breeze made the setting ideal. Smarting under defeats by Nebraska and New York, the determined Tigers came back with a vengeance – and how? The first quarter ended 0-0. In the second quarter, Waldorf plunged over for a touchdown and the first Tiger score. The stands went wild. Gold and Black balloons hied skyward. Hats flew far and wide. Voices old and voices young mingled in the uproar. Not satisfied with one tally. Waldorf went over for his second touchdown; and Brown's try for the extra point was successful. Hence the score was Missouri 13, Kansas 0, as the half ended! In the first half Missouri made 14 first downs to 5 for Kansas. Kennedy, Mehrle, Byars, and Waldorf smashed their way to the Jayhawk 4-yard line from where Mehrle went over for the third touchdown. Kansas stiffened and pushed over the lone score when Lyman went through center for three yards to a touchdown. In the middle of the fourth quarter, Russell Dills, a substitute back, caught a Kansas kickoff on Missouri's goal line and aided by perfect Tiger interference, raced the length of the field, 100 yards for a touchdown. It topped a great Tiger win with the most sensational and longest run ever made in Memorial Stadium. The classic of the Middlewest ended 25-6 for Missouri. More feathers than fur flew on Memorial Stadium as the largest crowd ever to witness a Missouri-Kansas football game looked on, amazed at the fury of the enraged Tiger. What a game! It was the most decisive score ever made against a Jayhawk eleven by a Missouri team.

By Charles L. "Chick" Nathan
Missouri Alumnus 1930

JAYHAWKER 1930 – BORDER WAR 1929

The Kansas-Missouri game was a colorful spectacle with a record homecoming crowd of 32,000 packing the stadium, but the result was saddening to hopeful alumni and friends. Though the Jayhawk outgained and outdowned the Tiger, the traditional gridiron enemy of Kansas went back to its lair with a few scars but with a 7 to 0 victory in its grasp.

It was early in the first period when Derry, the Tiger yardage-maker, broke away for a 33-yard dash to Kansas' 23-yard line. Speed Atkeson succeeded in nabbing him. Then, after three thrusts at the line had failed, Captain Waldorf hurled a pass to the elusive Dills and the lone touchdown was scored. Catching the Jayhawkers off their guard, Dills raced around right end for the extra point.

The second half found renewed hope for the Kansans. Lawrence thrilled the crowd with a 40-yard dash. His well-timed and accurate passes kept the Tiger goal line constantly in danger. Kansas fans went wild when Jim Bausch warmed up to enter the game, but he stayed on the bench. They groaned when Kansas lost the ball ten yards from the goal line; they sighted with relief when the Tigers were stopped eight yards from another touchdown. Hopes rose and fell, but – for the Jayhawkers – the bottom dropped out when the final whistle sounded.

SAVITAR 1930 – BORDER WAR 1929

The next conference game found the Tigers full of grim determination. Kansas, long the traditional rival of Missouri, is the one team the Tigers would rather defeat than any other. A football, or basket ball, season is a success if the Jayhawk is humbled in the dust before the banner of the haughty Tiger. Therefore the team journeyed to Lawrence with the taste of defeat still smarting on their lips, but with the glint of victory in their eyes.

The stage was set for a Kansas victory since it was their Homecoming, and they too, were out for Tiger blood. The first quarter started with the teams fighting on an even basis and turned into a punting duel with Missouri having the better of the bargain. Campbell was outkicking his opponent consistently. The second quarter started with a march down the field by Missouri which ultimately ended in a touchdown. Waldorf plunged across the line on the fourth down and the score was 6-0

One of the features of the game followed, when the diminutive Dills dropped back for a place kick, caught the ball and ran around the end to add the extra point to the score.

The third and fourth quarters were rather uninteresting, because neither team threatened to any extent. Naturally the Tigers derived supreme satisfaction from plucking the plume of the Jayhawk and they traveled back to Missouri triumphant.

A great number of students went to Lawrence to see the game, and those who could not find it convenient to make the journey satisfied themselves with the radios that were to be found around Columbia. Kansas had a powerful team and it was a distinction for any school to claim a victory over them.

By Marion L. Plessner
Missouri Alumnus 1931

THE 1930s

In the early part of 1930 the economy in America was fine, but it quickly made a drastic downturn from which it would take an entire decade and a half and a second world war for it to recover. The Great Depression in America affected the entire world and likewise became a world depression. Radio became the dominant mass media during this decade and a new animated character, Mickey Mouse, made his debut in cinemas. By 1939, another theatrical milestone would be reached when The Wizard of Oz would become the first widely distributed movie to use colour.

The decade of the 1930s began in promising fashion for the University of Kansas with an All-Big Six fullback, James Aloysius Bernard "Jarring Jim" Bausch, who would later win a gold medal at the 1932 Los Angeles Olympics in the decathlon. Although Kansas won the Big Six Conference Championship and beat Missouri handily 32-0 that year in November in the Border War Game, a shock was heard around the conference prior to the game on October 24 when faculty representatives of the conference met in Columbia and left their meeting with the announcement that the five schools would no longer schedule any future contests with the University of Kansas due to violations regarding athlete recruitment and subsidization. The charges were lodged against Kansas regarding Jim Bausch by Missouri's faculty representative, Professor William A. Tarr. Bausch arrived at the University of Kansas in 1929 after playing for Fairmount College for a year, now Wichita State University, as a freshman. His coach at the time, Bill Hargiss was quoted by Bob Hentzen in 1974 at the Capital-Journal in Topeka as saying, "I spent a lot of time trying to get him to go to Emporia," where Hargiss was coaching between 1920 and 1927. "When he graduated from Wichita Cathedral High, he planned to go to Fairmount for a year and then transfer to KU." Fortunately for Hargiss, Kansas made him head coach in 1928 and he was there when Bausch arrived in 1929 at the age of 23. However, Bausch took a job from Kansas booster

"Jarring Jim" Bausch in 1929

Red Lupton to sell insurance. As Bob Hentzen further quoted Hargiss, "The less said about that the better, but the accusations weren't true. They were unfair and uncalled for. He was making $60 a month and sold $120,000 worth of insurance." With the prospect of Kansas being suspended or removed from the Big Six Conference, Bausch rescinded his eligibility in December by announcing his intention to play in the East-West Shrine Game, which was a post-season bowl game played by the nation's best football players. With Bausch's rescission, the matter became resolved with the rest of the Big Six Conference and future contests with Kansas were scheduled including the Border War Game.

The calamitous affairs affecting the country during the Depression also lead Missouri's football program to one of its lowest points, which was only accentuated by comparison to its teams of the 1920s. Missouri was still paying on the bonds from the creation of Memorial Stadium, whose financial commitments were exacerbated by the economic hardships of that time. Also, in 1931, an injury to Gwinn Henry's leg in August caused him chronic pain to his sciatic nerve, causing him to miss most of the season. In the Border War Game, Kansas was a 4-5 team and had not crossed a conference goal line all season. In the Border War Game's fortieth anniversary meeting, Kansas ended its season by scoring on Missouri twice, finishing the game 14-0. Likely due to posting his first two losing seasons since his introductory season as head coach, the financial commitments facing the athletic department and the instability

Gwinn Henry, the only man to have been head coach at Missouri and Kansas

caused by his health problem, Missouri announced that Henry had retired as he began practice for the 1932 season.

Chester Brewer worked quickly to find a suitable successor, but a Joplin, Missouri lawyer named Mercer Arnold, who was on Missouri's Board of Curators, orchestrated a plan to bring a "big name" coach to Missouri. The man that he brought was a 23-year-old, twice elected All-American quarterback from Knute Rockne's fabled last two undefeated Notre Dame teams. Often described in his first two years at Missouri as arrogant, Frank

Frank Carideo

F. Carideo led Missouri to a three-year record of 2-23-2, only humbling himself for his third season as Missouri head coach. It is presumed that Carideo might have been released after his first year, had Missouri chosen to break its gentlemen's agreement to keep him for three years. Carideo, unfortunately for Missouri, relied too heavily on the "Notre Dame shift," which, as the 1933 Savitar notes, "the limited material he had could not master the intricacies so dominant in the Notre Dame system – notably the precise blocking."

In his first Border War Game, Carideo's 1-6-1 season seemed destined to add another scoreless tie to his team's record until, with four minutes left to play, Kansas' Carnie Smith ran 48 yards and then made a long pass deep into Missouri territory to Elmer Schaake, culminating in them getting the game winning touchdown. This sequence of events was especially disappointing to Missouri because Kansas did not gain one yard from the line of scrimmage for the entire first quarter and, in the second half, Missouri's Woodrow Hatfield took a kick-off behind Missouri's own goal line, ran the ball back 50 yards before being tackled by the last Kansas player standing between him and the Kansas goal line.

The 1933 season was again so dismal for Missouri that the Savitar yearbook mentions that "the success of the Missouri Tigers of 1933 must be judged from the spirit and fight shown by a squad which was completely outclassed from the standpoint of experience by [every one] of its opponents." At the end of the 1934 Border War Game, Frank Carideo tendered his resignation to Chester Brewer, who was also relieved of his position as athletic director prior to the 1935 season.

Missouri chose as its next football head coach, a man who would have its field named for him, Donald Burrowes Faurot. Don Faurot was born in Mountain Grove, Missouri and graduated from the University of Missouri in 1925. As a testament to his natural athleticism, Faurot never played an organized game of football until arriving at the University of Missouri. Once at Missouri, he earned letters in three sports, football, basketball, and baseball, playing fullback his senior year in 1924, being coached by Gwinn Henry. In 1925, Faurot became the freshman football coach at Missouri and the next year, began a successful coaching career at Kirksville State Teachers College, which

Don Faurot in 1922

would later change names several times to variations of Northeast Missouri State University and finally, in 1996, to Truman State University, where he amassed a 63-13-3 record, also beating Frank Carideo's Tigers in 1933, 26-6.

With the excited homecoming of Don Faurot to the University of Missouri, whose reputation from his service at Kirksville also preceded him, alumni in Kansas City of both the University of Missouri and the University of Kansas, decided to introduce to their rivalry an award for the game, purchasing an aboriginal "war drum" from a local pawnshop. Since its official introduction at the game in 1937, the "Indian War Drum" has passed to the victor of the Border War Game, with three total drums being used from 1935 to 2007. There are two stories that mainly circulate about the originations of the drum, the foremost being that the Niukansa (Osage) Nation built the drum for the series, but it seems likelier that the drum was in fact purchased at a pawn shop and that the "creation" of the drum was in fact a fabrication to create a better story for its introduction and connection to the game in 1937. The first drum had a Tiger and Jayhawk painted on either end of the drum and the team captain of the winning team was supposed to autograph the head of their respective school's head at the conclusion of the game. The original drum now resides at the National Football Foundation's Collegiate Football Hall of Fame in South Bend, Indiana. Two other drums were put into use for the game, the latest being the Bass Drum, introduced in 2003.

In his first year as head coach of Missouri, Don Faurot's Tigers posted a 3-3-3 season and tied the Border War Game with Kansas, 0-0. Given the record of the previous three years and having not won the Border War Game since 1929, this seemed a vast improvement to the Missouri fans. Don Faurot's Missouri Tigers steadily increased season records and the Border War Game once again became competitive affairs, Missouri carrying a 4-0-1 record against Kansas since Faurot's arrival. A crucial ingredient to Missouri's success was the addition of "Pitchin' Paul" Christman and the 1939 game reintroduced Missouri's old coach, Gwinn Henry, as the new head coach of the Jayhawks. As the Great Depression began to wane, a new horrible spectre began to loom in its place, which might once again affect the football programs at Missouri and Kansas.

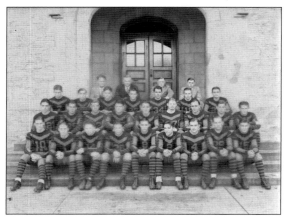

Missouri Footbal (2-5-2) - Head Coach Gwinn Henry

Kansas Football (6-2) - Head Coach Homer Woodson Hargiss
Big Six Champion
(Top to Bottom) Row 1: Coach Murphy, Coach Hargiss, Coach Getto, Athletic Director Allen. Row 2: Coach Hinshaw, J. Bausch, Madison, Beach, N. Sorem, Foy, P. Bausch, Paden, Cecil Smay, Schaake, Dr. Mott. Row 3: Smith, Stuck, Aikeson, Davis, Burcham, Hanson, Gridley, Lathrom, Black, Shroyer. Row 4: M. Sorem, Smoot, Fisher, Page, Rost, McCall, Zvolanek, Cox, Kite, Ch. Smay, Brazil.

Missouri Football (2-8) - Head Coach Gwinn Henry

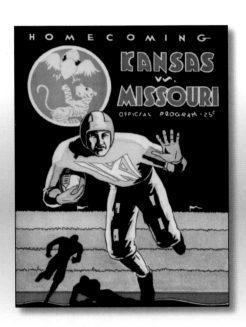

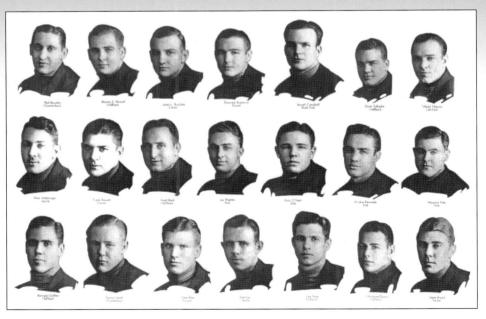

Kansas Football (5-5) - Head Coach Homer Woodson Hargiss (Top to Bottom) Row 1: Borello, Plaskett, Burcham, Kvaternik, Campbell, Schaake, Hanson. Row 2: Mehringer, F. Bausch, Black, Plumley, O'Neil, Kennedy, Kite. Row 3: Gridley, Smith, Rost, Foy, Page, Dumm, Brazil.

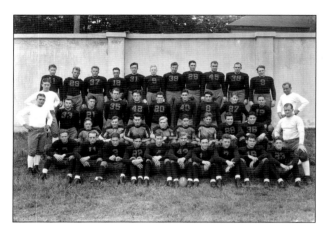

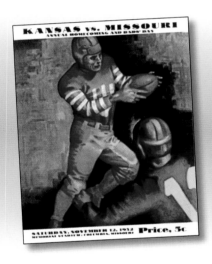

Missouri Football (1-7-1) - Head Coach Frank F. Carideo

Kansas Football (3-4-1) - Head Coach Adrian Hobart Lindsey

Missouri Football (1-8) - Head Coach Frank F. Carideo

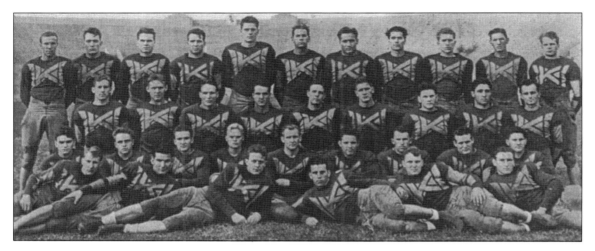

Kansas Football (5-4-1) - Head Coach Adrian Hobart Lindsey

Missouri Football (0-8-1) - Head Coach Frank F. Carideo

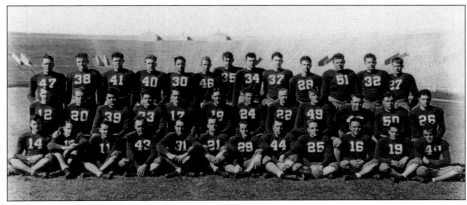

Kansas Football (3-4-3) - Head Coach Adrian Hobart Lindsey

Row 1: Lindley, Kincaid, Decker, Guiese, Kell, Laub, Humphrey, Ferris, Phelps, Hapgood, Giannangelg, Layman. Row 2: Harris, White, McCall, Sklar, Denny, O. Nesmith, Stukey, Landes, D. Nesmith, Clawson, Dees, Smith. Row 3: Hayes, Mitchell, Minter, Watkins, Antonió, Pitts, Siegle, Wells, Lutton, Goff, Moore, Peterson, Lemster.

Missouri Football (3-3-3) - Head Coach Donald Burrowes Faurot

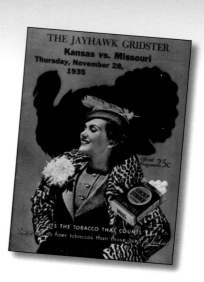

Kansas Football (4-4-1) - Head Coach Adrian Hobart Lindsey
Row 1: Laub, Harris, Hardacre, Card, Moreland, Hapgood, Decker, Giannangelo, Phelps, Denney, Robinson, Nichol. Row 2: Guntert, Green, Smith, Loughmiller, Trombold, Sklar, McCall, Humphry, Hayes, Burnett, Stukey, Winslow, Shaffer, Kvaternik. Row 3: Bruening, Vogel, Kruse, Weinicke, Douglass, Harrington, Peterson, Siegle, Lutton, Barcus, Hormuth, Hanson, Stapleton, Nesmith.

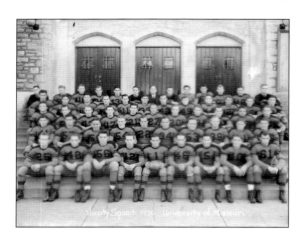

Missouri Football (6-2-1) - Head Coach Donald Burrowes Faurot
Row 1: Betty, English, Heidel, Murray, Londe, Frye, Mahley, Kirk, Nelson. Row 2: Gasparac, Kinnison, Hogan, Pieper, Ewing, Begers, Mondala, Bogash, Dunard, Rau. Row 3: Moss, Perkins, Seward, Pettyjohn, White, Davite, Horton, Doerr, Hamann, Thomas, Snyder. Row 4: Henderson, Duncan, Kolb, Dickenson, Boain, Gordon, Waechter, Hawthorne, Benizio, Sneed, Mason, Simon. Row 5: Coach Faurot, Caste, Moore, Kubler, Bearce, Manager Caulkins, Trainer De Victor, Coach Orr, Eskridge, Everly, Czarcinski, Lower, Coach Bengston.

Kansas Football (1-6-1) - Head Coach Adrian Hobart Lindsey
(Top to Bottom) Row 1: Vogel, Ward, Divens, Wallace, Nelson, Bosilevac, Stapleton. Row 2: Gearhart, Loughmiller, Green, Shirk, Hall, Wienecke, Giannangelo. Row 3: Richardson, Masoner, Cannady, Harrington, Hardacre, Moreland, Burnett, Replogle, Lutton, Anderson. Row 4: Seigle, Eichen, Hanson, Hapgood, Boardman, Paronto, Douglass.

126

Missouri Football (3-6-1) - Head Coach Donald Burrowes Faurot

Row 1: Heidel, Simon, Murray, Boain, Betty, Kirk, Mason, Moss, Duncan, Mahley, Rau. Row 2: Johnson, Amelung, Everly, Pieper, Hogan, Dickenson, Ewing, Kinnison, Pettyjohn, Bearce, Buchner, Hydron, Waldorf. Row 3: Rob. Orf, Whalen, Dullard, Czarcinski, Pickett, Benizio, Robb, Christenson, Ettinger, Kolb, Gibson, Moser, Cooper, Morrison. Row 4: Hawthorne, Bailey, Camfield, Rol. Orf, Horton, Hamann, Doerr, Wetzel, House, Gurley, White, Klinck, Wakeman, Wager, Jones. Row 5: Coach Faurot, Trainer DeVictor, R. Faurot, Sneid, O'Byrne, Hulse, Currence, Warden, Evans, Gordon, Shires, Moore, Haas, Leach, Hans, Bryant, Coach Bunker, Coach Bengston, Coach Simpson.

Kansas Football (3-4-1) - Head Coach Adrian Hobart Lindsey

(Top to Bottom) Row 1: Meier, Connody, Richardson, Douglass, Rhule, Amerine, Huff, Wilson. Row 2: Ebling, Schelonick, Weineke, Massoner, Moreland, Warren, Turner, Burnett. Row 3: Stapleton, Sullivant, Chitwood, Hole, Gearhardt, Shirk, Ward, Bosilevac. Row 4: Hardcore, Divens, Replogle, Anderson, Turner, Coldwell.

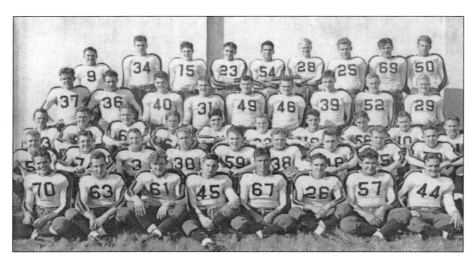

Missouri Football (6-3) - Head Coach Donald Burrowes Faurot

Row 1: Moss, Ewing, Rouse, Waldrof, Kinnison, Moser, Haas, Dickenson. Row 2: Czarcinski, Rau, Jones, Amelung, Wakeman, Hydrow, Wetzel, Hans, Hogan. Row 3: Hamann, Wallach, Gudzin, Schultz, Ducheck, Leech, Wager, Slaybaugh, Gale, Cooper. Row 4: Whalen, Ellis, Pickett, Amelung, Hawthorne, Starmer, Currence, Christman, Rol. Orf. Row 5: Pettyjohn, Council, Faurot, Siedel, Notowitz, Rob. Orf, Robb, Hirsch, Krebs.

Kansas Football (3-6) - Head Coach Adrian Hobart Lindsey

(Top to Bottom) Row 1: Gihbens, Renko, Bukaty, Sihlanick, Burge, Wenstrand, Meier, Lenhart, Cadwalader. Row 2: Massare, Bumen, Masoner, Arnold, Pint, Sullivant, Replogle, Turner, Bosilevac. Row 3: Shirk, Wilson, Rhule, Miller, Naramore, Caldwell, Divens, Anderson. Row 4: Amerine, Merkel, Crowell, Warren, Chitwood, Jenkins, Andrews, Hall.

**Missouri Football (8-2) - Head Coach Donald Burrowes Faurot
Big Six Champion - Orange Bowl Participant**

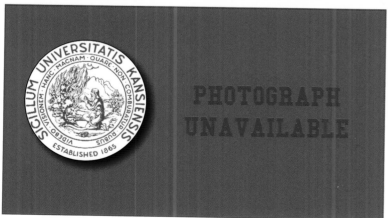

Kansas Football (2-6) - Head Coach Gwinn Henry

CAPTAINCY AND THE GREAT BORDER WAR GAME

From their earliest start, sports usually had a team captain. Football in America was no exception, but a team captain had greater meaning in the early years. As the game advanced and the rules became more complicated, it was important that a team had a man on the field that was designated to make decisions on the field during play. The team captain had many responsibilities, including: Reading signals from the coach, organizing the players on the field, calling plays, make decisions for various penalties, and, in effect, do the best job of running the team on the field for the coach. This was particularly important when, in its earliest years, football did not allow substitution changes. Therefore, the coaches were greatly prohibited in communicating to the players what he wanted to have happen on the field.

As the game of gridiron football developed and the rules changed, coaches were able to influence more of what was happening on the field through player exchanges. From the year 1930, until some time after 1940, the role of "captain" became one described as a "honorary" title than one of a specific job function.

As player substitutions became more frequent, more than one team captain was needed for the game. In its earliest years, players played both offense and defense and seldom left the field in the middle of a game. Rule changes allowed for two team units to play as offense and defense, so that at least 22 players were needed to properly execute a competitive team and, likewise, this increased the need for two captains; one for offense and one for defense.

In time, the game allowed for many more substitutions

FOOTBALL

Football Schedule and Record

Kansas	11	Normal	
Kansas	24	St. Mary's	0
Kansas	12	Aggies	0
Kansas	11	Oklahoma	0
Kansas	10	Washington	0
Kansas	23	Washburn	5
Kansas	20	Nebraska	5
Kansas	10	Iowa	4
Kansas	10	Missouri	20
Kansas	131	Opponents	
	267		

and began to utilize special positions, such as punters, long-snap centers, kick-off teams, and kick-off return teams. With these many new specialized positions and player changes, the role of captain was extended even further so that there might be three or more captains for any particular game.

Sometimes, different team captains were selected for each game in the season and then a final team vote occurred to select the year-end team captain or captains; sometimes, the captains were voted entirely by the team and sometimes, only the coaches picked the captains.

Through the years, although sometimes difficult to ascertain, a captain has been a part of every game and every season. This book tracks only those until 1930 and it is regretful that it does not track more.

By Shawn Buchanan Greene
Kansas Alumnus 1991
Written Friday, September 26, 2008

THE DRUM

The "Indian War Drum" or "tom-tom" was introduced to the game by Missouri and Kansas alumni in Kansas City, most notably; George "Dumpy" Bowles, the author of "I'm a Jayhawk," and Lyle Kendig of Missouri. The drum was purchased from a pawn shop in 1935 and each head was painted with a Jayhawk and a Tiger. It was officially introduced to the game in 1937, with the intent that the captain of the winning team was to autograph the drum head of his respective school. The drum was held and traded by the Missouri and Kansas National Honorary Society chapters of Omicron Theta Kappa.

The tradition of exchanging the tom-tom was briefly forgotten during World War II but it was resumed in 1947. The original "tom-tom" was again forgotten and lost during the 1980s, so a second drum was created, this time by the Tiwa (Taos) Nation of Taos, New Mexico. That drum had the Hal Sandy Jayhawk on it, the first drum having the 1923 version. Eventually, the original tom-tom was found buried beneath some boxes in the basement of Read Hall at the University of Missouri and donated to the Collegiate Football Hall of Fame in South Bend, Indiana.

In 1999, the second tom-tom was replaced with a marching band bass drum. The second tom-tom now resides at the Missouri Alumni Association in Columbia, Missouri.

By Shawn Buchanan Greene
Kansas Alumnus 1991
Written Friday, November 7, 2008

(Clockwise) The 1937 introduction of the "tom-tom," the Jayhawk and Missouri heads of the original tom-tom, the heads of the second drum, the Mizzou head of the bass drum in 2007.

THE RETURN OF "JARRING JIM"

On February 20, 1939, a traveling auditor for the Internal Revenue Service returned to the town of his alma mater on business. Nine years earlier he had been the best football player at Kansas, as well as a star center for the University's basketball team and a conference champion in three track-and-field events. His athletic dominance, especially in football, had elicited the attention of universities throughout the Midwest and after claiming the decathlon gold medal in the 1932 Olympics in Los Angeles, sportswriters across the country had plunged into a lively debate over whether or not he had surpassed the immortal Jim Thorpe as the greatest athlete in America's history. However, glory had proven short-lived for Kansas' James Aloysius Bernard "Jarring Jim" Bausch. By 1939, he had all but faded from the national consciousness. To his credit, he did not seem to mind its passing.

Upon hearing that the former Kansas football, basketball and track star was in town, Bill Hargiss, Kansas' track coach, invited Bausch to attend a practice. The 1932 Olympic decathlon champion donned his track togs for the first time in nearly six years and took a lap around the track before spotting some shot putters working in a remote corner of the field. "To their delight," the *University Daily Kansan* reported, "he offered his assistance." His "work with the putters" so occupied him, the student paper continued, "that he almost forgot a dinner engagement" and left the field with only 20 minutes to shower and dress for his appointment. It was not the first time Bausch had made a rather quick exit from Kansas in the interest of propriety.

"Jarring Jim" Bausch in 1929

Ten years earlier, Bausch was a 23-year-old sophomore who had just transferred to Kansas from Wichita University, now Wichita State University. He starred on the football team during his first semester, earning All-Big Six Conference honors for his performance as a fullback and the nickname "Jarring Jim" for the ferocious intensity with which he played.

Not all of his nicknames were so complimentary. In 1929, newspaper reporters from Manhattan, Kansas criticized the 6-foot 2-inch, 200-pound [188 cm, 91 kg] back as an "all-star yellow-belly" after Kansas' cross-state rival upended the Jayhawks 6-0 in Memorial Stadium that year. Bausch did not forget this slight. In the opening kickoff of the following year's game in Manhattan, he returned the opening kickoff for a touchdown and kicked the extra point. Later in the game, he ran an interception back for a score and again kicked the extra point. He was the only player on either team to score in a contest that ended 14-0 in the Jayhawks' favor.

This achievement was not, however, an unmitigated triumph. It also raised a number of suspicious, and perhaps envious, eyebrows within the Big Six Conference. When the other schools in the conference discovered that a Kansas booster from Topeka had provided Bausch with a job at his insurance company as an enticement to transfer from Wichita, they began an investigation into Kansas' football program.

Contrary to what one might expect, the other schools were not upset that Bausch had a job. It was considered quite proper for a college athlete to be employed, so long as he actually worked for the money. Rather, Kansas' adversaries charged that Kansas had actively recruited Bausch and thus had violated conference rules, for it was considered improper at the time for a coach, administrator or booster to seek to influence a player's choice of school. Adding to the charge of illegal recruitment, Kansas' conference rivals pointed out that there existed some doubt as to whether or not Bausch had actually sold any insurance at all for the Topeka company. Even if he had, the $75 stipend that he received each month seemed quite excessive to the other schools, so they accused him of "professionalism."

Kansas Athletic Director Forrest C. "Phog" Allen, Kansas Chancellor E. H. Lindley and the majority of Kansas newspapers joined together in denying the existence of any impropriety whatsoever. They attributed the investigation to Conference opponents' jealousy of the Kansas team, which was well on its way to the league's championship. As the accusations and denials increased in their intensity, Bausch spoke out in his own defense, charging that representatives of Missouri's athletic department, which was one of the chief instigators of the investigation, had offered him money to lure him away from Kansas during his first season in Lawrence. His allegation muddled the investigation but did not hinder the fervor of Kansas' adversaries. This was not the first time that alleged rules violations had tarnished the Kansas football program. In 1910 the Missouri Valley Conference, to which Kansas belonged, very nearly decided to abandon football altogether as a consequence of the pervasive cheating of its schools that characterized the sport. Kansas, it should be noted, was hardly innocent in this regard.

When it became apparent that Kansas had no intention of declaring its star player ineligible, the other conference schools turned to their trump card. On October 24, 1930, four of the five schools in the conference voted to refuse to schedule games against Kansas the following year. Of the Big Six schools, only Kansas State, Kansas' intra-state rival, had abstained from the vote. The balloting amounted to an ouster of Kansas from the Conference. By December, faced with the unappealing possibility of being left without a conference in 1931, the University of Kansas decided that it would be in its best interest to declare Bausch ineligible. Before that happened, however, the Jayhawk star announced that he would be giving up his eligibility to play in the East-West Shrine game, a post-season bowl game in which the nation's best players competed against each other.

After leaving Kansas, Bausch remained in Lawrence throughout 1931 and continued to train with Kansas track coach, Brutus Hamilton. Although he had attracted attention primarily as a football player at Kansas, Bausch had starred in basketball and track as well. As a sophomore, he had won the Conference title in the shot put, discus, and pole vault, and had carved out quite a niche as an all-around athlete. Competing for the Kansas City Athletic Club at the Kansas Relays on April 17, 1931, Bausch participated in his first decathlon and, despite a wet field, set a new Relays record. In fact, he very nearly beat the American record for the event. He won another decathlon two months later and in September of that year set a new American record in the pentathlon.

In June 1932, having established a reputation as one of the nation's best decathletes, he tried out for the United States Olympic team. He was not the only competitor from Lawrence to vie for a spot on the team. Clyde Coffman, a Kansas junior, and Wilson Charles, the defending Amateur Athletic Union champion and former Haskell Institute star, also sought a chance to head to Los Angeles for the Tenth Olympiad.

As fate would have it, the three men with Lawrence connections swept the decathlon trials and so constituted the entire decathlon team for the United States. All told that year, Kansas sent four students to the Olympic Games: Bausch and Coffman for the decathlon, Glenn Cunningham for the 1,500-meter run, and Peter J. Mehringer as the nation's 191.5-pound [87 kg] freestyle wrestler. With Charles also competing, Lawrence could claim five Olympians, an impressive total for a town its size, as local papers pointed out at the time.

In winning the trials, Bausch set a new American record and gained some personal momentum. However, neither he

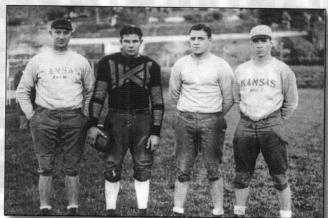

(Left-Right) Coach Hargiss, Jim Bausch,
Coach Getto, Coach Murphy

nor his Sunflower State teammates were favored in the Olympic event. That honor went to Finland's Akilles Jarvinen who, at his nation's trials, had set a new world record of 8,255 points. His teammate, Paavo Yrola, who had won the gold medal four years earlier, was also expected to be a contender.

On August 5, 1932 the decathlon competition began. After the first day of the two-day competition, Charles led the field while Bausch held onto fifth place. The former Jayhawk star had reason for optimism, as his best events were to come in day two. However, sportswriters pointed out, he had cause for concern as well since Jarvinen sat in third place with his best events also awaiting him the following day. Never lacking in confidence, Bausch promised his fellow athletes in the Olympic village that night that he "would not only win the decathlon ... but break the world's record, too."

Despite placing sixth in the first event of day two, the 110-meter high hurdles, Bausch moved into third place while Jarvinen took over second. Bausch went on to win the next three events, the discus, pole vault and javelin, in dramatic fashion. In the discus, an event for which Bausch was the favorite and had very nearly qualified as an individual competitor, he easily claimed victory with a toss of 146 feet 3¼ inches [44.58 m]. In the pole vault, Bausch waited until everyone else had vaulted at least once, and some had already finished, before taking his initial vault. He and Coffman tied for first in the event with an impressive height of 13 feet 1½ inches [4.00 m]. It was, as Francis W. Schruben later wrote for Kanhistique, "a tremendous feat with the old stiff poles for a man his size." He managed his greatest coup, however, when he defeated Jarvinen in the javelin throw, the Finn's best event, by nearly two feet [61 cm], establishing a new Olympic decathlon record for the event in the process.

Following Bausch's three consecutive victories, the decathlon's final competition, the 1,500-meter run, proved anticlimactic. Bausch had already racked up 7,900 points; all he needed to do to secure the gold medal was finish the race. He ran the "metric mile" in 5:17, a time so slow that reporters mistook his "plodding around the track" as a sign of fatigue. In fact, though he finished second to last, he set a new personal best in the event. The 500 points he received for the decathlon's last race boosted his score to 8,462.23 points. His total not only shattered Jarvinen's mark, it eclipsed the unofficial world record of 4,412 that had been set in 1912 by Jim Thorpe. Track and field officials had invalidated Thorpe's score when they found him guilty of "professionalism" for playing semi-pro baseball as a student at Carlisle Indian Industrial School. In 1982, the International Olympic Committee returned the gold medal for the event to his family.

Having made good on his previous night's boast, the brash gold medalist deflected praise from his accomplishment by declaring that he would have broken 8,600 points had his knee not bothered him. Hearing the decathlon champ's remarks, the United States Olympic coach Lawson Robertson reputedly asked Bausch, "Jim, did you ever get a group picture taken of yourself." Indeed, many believed the former Jayhawk's ego to be enormous, though some, like Glenn Cunningham, reasoned that "what most people thought was boastful was in reality just a statement of fact. [Bausch] would talk about what he was going to do, and then he would do it." That he might be forgiven some excessive pride was, perhaps, not too much to ask. An Olympic gold medal and world record in what was then the signature event of the Olympic Games certainly provided reason for both confidence and celebration.

Following his victory, sportswriters, coaches, and fans launched a debate over whether or not Bausch had surpassed Jim Thorpe as the greatest athlete in American history. Ed Pollock, in an article for the Philadelphia Public Ledger, asserted that the "big 'I' man from Kansas [a reference to his position as a running back, not his ego], decathlon champion and world's record-holder, is crowding the Indian [Thorpe] for the honors, and in the opinion of many has displaced Thorpe." Pollock cited Robinson, the Olympic coach, Hamilton, Bausch's college coach, and Amos Alonzo Stagg, the Hall of Fame football coach, who had seen Thorpe in the 1912 Olympics, as notable personalities who believed the former Jayhawk to be the greatest American athlete of all time.

Others, such as Dr. Leroy Mercer of the University of Pennsylvania, who had been Thorpe's teammate in 1912, maintained that if dominance in other sports were taken into account then Thorpe surpassed the Kansan. A comparison of their decathlon performances did little to solve the argument, since each had bested the other in five events. Prudently, neither Bausch nor Thorpe entered the fray on their own behalf.

Even as the debate began, Lawrence scrambled to make plans to welcome home its five Olympic athletes, who included not just one, but two gold medal winners, as Kansas' Pete Mehringer had taken home a gold medal in wrestling. The city invited suggestions from the community at large of ways in which it might honor the Olympians. The University considered naming a building after Bausch and the city contemplated doing the same thing for a street. No mention was made, however, of bestowing a similar honor on Mehringer. In fact, by the 1950s, regional papers had forgotten the wrestling gold medalist entirely. When Kansas' Al Oerter claimed a gold medal for the discus in the 1956 Olympic Games, local publications asserted that it was the second such honor awarded to a Kansas athlete and cited Bausch as the first.

For a few brief years following his record-breaking performance, Bausch enjoyed the life of a minor celebrity. In late 1932, for example, newspaper gossip columns reported his supposed engagements to Mildred Harris Chaplin, Charlie Chaplin's first wife, and actress Minna Gombell. In January 1933, 600 sports reporters voted to award the former Kansas star the 1932 Sullivan Memorial Medal. The Sullivan award was annually presented to the athlete who "by his performance and by his example and influence as an amateur and as a man, has done most during the past year to advance the cause of sportsmanship." Among the reasons the journalists offered to justify their selection of Bausch was that he had "worked his way through school and turned down professional offers for two years" to play football for Kansas. Thus the honor was perhaps a shade ironic in light of both his brazenness and the charges that had been brought against him while at Kansas.

As the national media had taken notice of the former Jayhawk only after his victory in Los Angeles, Kansas columnists seized the opportunity to lambaste the East Coast papers and draw attention to their region. They pointed to Bausch's career at the University in criticizing their colleagues to the east for claiming that "he never came into prominence until the Olympics." Similar charges of an East Coast, journalistic bias against Bausch echoed not only from Kansas, but from throughout the Midwest.

Although he played professional football and basketball briefly, Bausch's real passion, apparently, did not lie in the world of athletic achievement. As his true talent did lie there, perhaps it is not surprising that his renown dissipated quickly after he gave up sports entirely in the mid-1930s. Four months after winning his medal, he took a job as a singer for a jazz orchestra. So serious was he about developing a career as a "crooner," reputed to sound like Bing Crosby, that he skipped the Association of American Universities championship meet in 1933 in order to sing with his band. When his attempt to establish a singing career fell by the wayside and the glory of his Olympic victory faded into the past, he took a job with the IRS. It was this job that brought him back to Lawrence in 1939, a year after an apartment fire had destroyed his gold medal, or so Clyde

Coffman later remembered. He went on to a number of other occupations including, ironically enough, one as an insurance salesman. Later in his life he battled alcoholism, though he apparently "scored his greatest triumph" by overcoming it shortly before his death in 1974.

Bausch was not entirely forgotten following his brief moment in the sun. Four months after he visited his alma mater in 1939, the *University Daily Kansan* released the results of a poll concerning the greatest athlete in the university's history. Bausch topped the list, with Cunningham, Tommy Johnson, Charlie Black, and Ray Ebling rounding out the top five. Fifteen years later, at halftime of a game against Oklahoma in Memorial Stadium, his former gridiron teammates stood beside him to cheer as the executive secretary of the Big Seven Conference presented him with a plaque commemorating his induction into the National Football Hall of Fame, now the College Football Hall of Fame.
In 1979, the National Track Hall of Fame added to that honor by making him one of only a handful of people who have been enshrined in the halls of fame of multiple sports. Even so, for an athlete once compared to Jim Thorpe, his standing certainly pales by comparison. In a nation with a what-have-you-done-for-me-lately sports mentality, it is not surprising that in 1999 when Sports Illustrated listed the greatest athletes of the century, Bausch did not even rank among the top 10 Kansas had produced.

Mark D. Hersey, Ph.D.
Kansas Alumnus 2006
Written for This Week in Kansas History
www.KansasHistory.com

DON FAUROT

His parents and the values of the small town of Mt. Grove, Missouri strongly influenced the character of my father, Don Faurot. He was as famous for his honesty, loyalty, integrity, and enormous energy as he was for football exploits. My father was the second of eight children who grew up on a state experimental fruit farm. My horticulturist grandfather somehow built a cinder track with hurdles and a tennis court and there was room for all sports for the Faurots and their friends. All four boys went on to play football and other sports at Missouri University, even though Mt. Grove High School had no football team.

My mother, Mary Davidson Faurot, also strongly influenced my father. Besides being almost totally in charge of the three Faurot girls, Jane, Aileen, and Julie, on game days she entertained the family, friends, boosters, and often the press doing all the cooking before the days of caterers. She attended practice every day and really suffered through the games, even long after my dad retired.

We three girls adored our father, though often absent he was great fun when he was home. Each Sunday night he would cook us pancakes. He let me, his eldest, sit in the corner during coaches' meetings, where I watched with fascination as the 35 mm camera would run the film forward, then backward over and over. Coach John Hi Simmons would give his colorful scouting reports. How times have changed. Dad never had more than four or five assistants and they all fit nicely in our tiny dining room.

In 1943 my dad's brother Bob, a halfback at M.U. and a fighter pilot in the New Guinea area was killed in action. My dad, despite being in his mid-forties and missing two fingers and having three children, joined his other brothers in the Navy. We all moved to Iowa City, Iowa where dad coached the Iowa Pre-Flight team, number 2 in wartime America. He was so taken with the Navy he taught us all the lingo, and insisted we call the floor the deck, toilet the head, and so on. The next few years we moved every six months to another team as dad tried to get a combat assignment. He finally was assigned to the aircraft carrier, the FDR, but the war ended during its maiden voyage. We returned to Missouri in time for the 1946 season.

Most family vacations, with the exception of a week at the Lake of the Ozarks, involved football. There were bowl games; the North-South game in Miami, the East-West in San Francisco, and coaching clinics in various parts of the nation. We always managed much sightseeing on these trips. We were well traveled children in an age when that was unusual. They finally settled on a long term relationship with the Blue-Gray game in Montgomery, Alabama and both looked forward to seeing their many Alabama friends each Christmas. Dad coached and picked the Blue Squad.

Dad studied agriculture at Missouri and earned a masters degree in horticulture while playing basketball (4 years), baseball (4 years), football (2 years) and one year of track. He also coached the freshman football team one year and on graduation was made head football coach at Kirksville State Teachers' College, now Truman State University. He turned his love for horticulture into a large vegetable garden and lovely flowers in the yard. Aileen and I weeded, picked vegetables, stemmed green beans, shelled peas and managed to learn nothing. Our sister Julie soaked up knowledge and has always had a lovely yard with lots of effort.

One of Don Faurot's chief characteristics was his love for the state of Missouri and its University. He had many lucrative offers from bigger schools, but couldn't bring himself to leave Missouri. He was quite insistent that we girls attend Missouri. My mother thought we should go away to school, but dad said we would marry in some far state and he'd never see us. We all graduated from Missouri, married hometown men, and never lived within 500 miles [800 kilometres] of Missouri until my husband and I returned to Columbia when he retired. The best laid plans....

To conclude, my father, despite being a very busy football coach and athletic director had a very fruitful and interesting family and private life. He and mother were very popular in the community and had a robust social life. Some of their best friends were a group who all moved to Columbia in 1935 and became lifelong friends. Dad played golf, hunted, and loved float trips on the Current River. In later years he very much enjoyed his eight grandchildren on our annual two week visit at their Lake of the Ozarks cottage.

He was very well known and handled with great humility the adoration of his many fans including his family.

By Jane Faurot Hazell
Missouri Alumna 1955
Written Monday, November 10, 2008

RAY MOSS

Our dad's heart for Missouri grew out of the heart of the state. Ray Woodson Moss was born the third of four children and raised in Hallsville, Missouri in 1914. His maternal grandparents and other extended family all lived in Boonville, Missouri and the surrounding area. He grew up a central Missouri farm boy during the Great Depression and his favorite foods included pieces of bread broken into a glass of milk for a snack and corn meal hoecakes on the griddle.

While Hallsville is only 10 or 15 miles from Columbia and the university, it might as well have been clear across the country as far as the poor, rural Moss family was concerned. Our Dad had no hopes of a higher education until he accompanied a friend to Moberly to visit with the track coach at the Junior College. The coach noticed that this strong, lean, young companion might also be an asset to his track team. Along with the track scholarship was the opportunity to play football, followed by the great fortune to play football as an end at Mizzou for Don Faurot. Dad's quiet leadership qualities soon lead to serving as co-captain with All-American Paul Christman and to membership in the Mystical Seven at the University of Missouri.

Dad's loyalties remained in Missouri as he went on to teach math and coach in Monett, Missouri for a year. He then married Jean Stoerger, an elementary education major he had met at Mizzou and they moved to Webster Groves, a suburb of St. Louis, making it their home for more than forty years.

When World War II broke out, our Dad's loyalty to his country caused him to seek enlistment in the armed services, but his plans were stymied by the fact that he was colorblind and his one leg was slightly shorter than the other, which always gave him a distinctive stride.

During the "Moss years" at Webster Groves High School, our parents attended Mizzou football games in Columbia whenever his coaching schedule allowed. It's quite likely he influenced a number of young men, like Jack Frier and Hank Kuhlman to attend Mizzou. All of the four children in the family attended Mizzou for all or a portion of their education. Another "evidence" of our parents' enduring loyalty to Mizzou, is that they preserved Dad's letter sweater and his MU football blanket from 1938-1939. (Both the sweater and the blanket have been known to show up at Colorado – Mizzou football games when worn by one of the Moss daughters, all residents of northern Colorado.)

Our father's teaching and coaching career was focused on instilling the highest of values in young people. Discipline, hard work, teamwork, kindness and respect for others, truthfulness, and a positive attitude were always important to him. The re-spect he gained at Webster earned him a "Favorite Teacher" title in a contest held in 1960 by a local newspaper for the combined Webster-Kirkwood area. Dad and Mom were awarded the "trip of their lifetime" to Aruba.

After a thirty-five year career at Webster, where he spent decades of summer growing seasons tending to the grass and moving sprinkler hoses twice a day, the former Memorial Field was renamed Moss Field in his honor. In 1982, a mere five years after receiving this honor, our Dad succumbed to cancer at the age of 67.

While the family has moved away, our roots are long and deep on the rich soil of the Missouri heartland.

By Gentry Moss Moellenhoff
Daughter
Written Monday, October 6, 2008

Raymond Woodson Moss, 1937

SAVITAR 1931 – BORDER WAR 1930

Missouri was enjoying the largest and most glamorous Homecoming in her history until 2 o'clock on the afternoon of November 22, but from then on things dimmed quite noticeably in the Tiger camp.

Beginning at that time the Kansas Jayhawks, set on handing the Tigers no uncertain defeat, opened up a passing and line attack which the Missouri aggregation was unable to stop, and when the final gun was fired the Tigers had been smothered under an avalanche of five touchdowns and two extra points.

Led by "Jarring Jim" Bausch, the Kansans opened up with an attack that was too much for the Tigers. The Jayhawks seemed to have everything in their hands, and were encountering little opposition from the Tigers. There were bright spots in the Tiger defense, for they held once or twice when it seemed inevitable that Kansas would score, but the versatility and quick changes in the Jayhawk attack bewildered Missouri, and the Kansas scores were made on sensational passes and long runs.

The powerful Kansas defense smothered all attempts of the Tiger offense, plays were not clicking, and it was hopeless to try and gain anything through the Jayhawk forward wall. It was simply a question of giving all they had on defense and waiting for the final gun to take them out of a game which they could not hope to win.

By Orville H. Read
Missouri Alumnus 1933

SAVITAR 1932 – BORDER WAR 1931

Kansas, whose eleven had not crossed a Conference goal line all season, sent her heavy quarterback, Carney smith, over twice to win the 40th annual engagement between the two teams, 14-0. The victory put the Jayhawks in 4th place in the Big Six and left Missouri sharing the cellar with Oklahoma.

Smith scored his first touchdown in the last minutes of the first quarter. A passing attack, Stuber to Collings, threatened to even matters up, but collapsed before the goal line was reached, and Smith then added his other touchdown to clinch the game. Lee Page booted both goals for Kansas.

The Tiger line could not stop the smashes of Schaake and Smith. After Gill left the game in the first few minutes of play with a broken foot, the weakened secondary was torn to shreds time after time as the Jayhawks drove through for a total of 221 yards from scrimmage to the Tigers' 23 yards.

Schiele played a strong game defensively, but was far off his pass receiving. The Tigers hooked up only 11 passes out of 35 attempts.

JAYHAWKER 1933 – BORDER WAR 1932

Although the final [tally] was 24 to 6, it was a moral victory for the Jayhawkers. After an inspiring Hobo day the Jayhawkers handed a rejuvenated Tiger team the small end of a 7 to 0 score in one of the hardest fought games ever played between the two schools.

SAVITAR 1933 – BORDER WAR 1932

In the last four minutes of play Kansas converted an almost certain scoreless tie in to victory, after a 48-hyard run by Smith and a long pass deep into Missouri territory from Smith to Schaake.

In the first quarter Kansas did not gain one yard from the line of scrimmage. Only once during that time was the ball out of Kansas territory. The second half started spectacularly when Hatfield, taking the kick-off behind his own goal line, ran the ball back for Missouri fifty yards before Mehringer, the last Kansan between him and the goal line, downed him. Up until half the final quarter was over each team had made two first downs, and neither had made a serious scoring threat. Then came Smith's long run and pass.

SAVITAR 1934 – BORDER WAR 1933

[There is no description of the game. KU won 27-0.]

JAYHAWKER 1935 – BORDER WAR 1934

[There is no description of the game. KU won 20-0.]

1930S

SAVITAR 1935 – BORDER WAR 1934

Before a large Homecoming crowd which braved a drizzle that later turned into a downpour, the Missouri eleven closed another disastrous season against their traditional rivals, the Kansas Jayhawkers. The rain handicapped the pass combination of Lochiner to Bourne, which had been Missouri's main chance for a victory. The game was a duel of the lines, with Kansas having a decided weight advantage. The Tiger backfield could do little against the massive Jayhawk tackles. Hapgood of Kansas was the outstanding ball-carrier for the day. Fight hard though they did, the Tigers finally had to succumb to the superior play of the Kansas eleven.

SAVITAR 1936 – BORDER WAR 1935

[There is no description of the game. Game was tied 0-0.]

JAYHAWKER 1937 – BORDER WAR 1936

The game with Missouri, the game which the team had been concentrating on, was played Thanksgiving Day at Columbia. On the first scrimmage play of the game a Missouri back fumbled and Kansas recovered on the Tigers' 19-yard line. Three plays gained only three yards so a place kick was called for. With the crowd holding its breath Douglass, junior fullback, swung his foot into the ball back on the 25-yard line and the ball sailed squarely between the goal posts. This surprising turn of events so heartened the Jayhawkers that they stymied every thrust made by the aroused Tigers in the first half. Missouri drove furiously but the fighting Kansans repulsed them every time they got inside the 10-yard line. On one occasion Kansas took the ball on downs on its 6-inch line. Not only did the Jayhawk defense show power but the Kansas offense also got moving. At one point in the first half three first downs in a row were manufactured by the Jayhawkers with Replogle doing most of the ground gaining. In the second half Cannady, subbing for Douglass, got away for two runs of more than 10 yards. The second half, however, found the Jayhawk defense finally being overpowered. A penalty which gave Missouri the ball on the Kansas 31 -yard line was followed b y a march to a touchdown with Missouri, unable to score through the line, tallying on a pass from the 2-yard line. A 55-yard drive by Missouri accounted for its second touch- down and a beautiful 60-yard sprint by Mahley ended the day's scoring. 19-3 was the final score and it marked the first game since 1929 that Missouri had scored on Kansas.

SAVITAR 1937 – BORDER WAR 1936

Thanksgiving Day marked the culmination of a football season which convinced the football public that once more Missouri is a member of the Big Six.

Of course, the Tigers' decisive 19-3 victory over the Kansas Jayhawk was sufficient excuse for calling Missouri's 1936 season successful, but the fact that the Tigers finished second in the Big Six caused the most skeptical to concede that Don Faurot had in two short years whipped Missouri's football machinery into smooth operation.

By Francis X. Zuzulo
Missouri Alumnus 1937

JAYHAWKER 1938 – BORDER WAR 1937

A homecoming crowd of 24,000 the largest in two years was on hand to watch the Jayhawkers make their final bid for the conference title against Missouri. Should Kansas defeat Missouri and K State win from Nebraska on the following Saturday, KU would tie with Oklahoma for first place. But that was not to be.

Kansas passed up two glorious opportunities to score early in first half, when the Jayhawkers recovered the opening kick-off on the Tiger 36 and a fumbled Tiger punt a bit later. Neither team displayed much superiority in the first half though Kansas outgained Missouri, and at times showed she could go places. Jayhawker drives, unfortunately, started in their own territory, but by the time they reached mid-field, bogged down.

The game produced few thrills until late in the fourth quarter. Douglass, who played a whale of a game both offensively and defensively, almost undid his good work when he fumbled a low pass from center on the KU 10. Missouri recovered and drove to the five where Mondala tried a field goal that was wide. KU was offside on the kick and the five yard penalty put the ball on the two-foot line. Missouri rooters, however, soon quieted down; for Mondala's drive off the Jayhawker right tackle was stopped cold.

SAVITAR 1938 – BORDER WAR 1937

"Gone with the wind" went Kansas' mathematical chance for the conference championship when the Jayhawk found the Tigers too formidable as they battled to a scoreless tie in the annual blue-ribbon classic and in the final analysis, the Sunflower Staters were fortunate to escape with a draw.

The Jayhawks held the upper hand for three quarters, but it is doubtful that they ever spent a longer fifteen minutes than they did in the final period, at which occasion Missouri threatened times immeasurable to salt away the verdict.

In one series of downs, for example, a short pass from Murray went way wide of its target – Ray Moss, who was alone in the end zone, Stan Mondala's field goal try missed the uprights by a whisker and after K. U. penalty had nullified that Tiger failure and had given them another chance, a fourth-down plunge from the one-yard line was stopped cold.

Tigers have to fight for it

Although by this time the Kansas forces were small in number, they were high in spirits and determined to give the up-and-coming Missourians the battle of their lives. Fortunately, there were no lives taken by either side, and the Bengals, after a hot contest, satisfied themselves by walking off with the few remaining tailfeathers in the old Bird's tail.

"Pitchin' Paul" Christman, the Tigers' sensational sophomore performer, and Jimmy Starmer (drat the luck another Kansas boy), pass-snagging half-back, were the principal flies in the ointment. The former once trotted eighty yards to pay dirt on a fake lateral that the locals had practiced all week to stop, and then later threw a thirty yard touchdown pass to Starmer for the second counter. The Jayhawkers had previously scored after a long march through the Tiger line conducted by Bill Bunsen, Milt Sullivant, and Divens, who had returned to the lineup for this last game.

SAVITAR 1939 – BORDER WAR 1938

Missouri counts any season a victorious one if the Kansas Jayhawk is beaten, Kansas, playing over its head, was unable to stop the Tiger.

In review the year was both successful and promising. Such a strong sophomore aggregation will always bear watching, and when it includes such a combination as Christman – Starmer success is almost certain.

SAVITAR 1940 – BORDER WAR 1939

Missouri's Tigers brought their first Big Six Conference football title to the Missouri lair by plucking the tail of an indignant Kansas Jayhawk 20-0 here today. A Kansas homecoming crowd of 20,000 witnessed the expected defeat.

Traditional rivals of Missouri, the Jayhawks played inspired football in the first quarter, but a penalty moving the ball from the Tiger 32 to K. U.'s 34 broke Kansas' resistance. In three plays Missouri had its first touchdown, King scoring on a reverse from Gale.

The rest of the afternoon was devoted to Missouri as the Tigers counted once in the third quarter on Christman's plunge and again in the fourth when Dan Wager threw a pass to Bud Orf.

The game completed the Tigers' most successful season, and Missouri waited confidently for the bowl bid expected.

Cartoon from the 1933 Jayhawk Gridster *Game Program*

THE 1940s

Unresolved affairs left from the Great War, combined with connected events from the Great Depression, caused another devastating world war to erupt. While swing music became ever more popular, so did the sounds of "big band" music. By the end of the decade, another form of music called "rhythm & blues" was introduced. The decade of the 1940s is best described in its first half as the most destructive decade in world history, while its second half may be viewed as one of the more prosperous as the world rebuilt itself.

World war had already threatened the football programs at both schools and had caused Missouri to not play in the Border War Game of 1918. Many students at both schools left on sabbatical to join the war effort. In 1943, Don Faurot would do the same, but not before creating one of football's greatest innovations in 25 years, the Split-T formation. After the 1940 season, Paul Christman graduated and left for the war. Christman was Missouri's starting quarterback for three years and was an incredible performer for Missouri, being elected as an All-American player twice and being Missouri's all-time leading passer until 1976, when he was surpassed by Steve Pisar-

kiewicz. In his senior year, 1940, Christman was also the nation's leader in touchdown passes. Faurot, realizing that Christman's departure would leave his remaining, young team exposed to teams with more experienced players, devised a variation of the T-formation, in which players stood further apart on the line of scrimmage, causing the defensive players to correspond and create wider holes through which offensive players could run. Additionally, backs running around to the sides of ends would force defensemen into a two-on-one situation, causing them to have to commit to defending against a player, not knowing who would have the ball. Faurot's Split-T was enormously effective, causing the Tigers to go 8-2, losing only their first game of the season and their end of the season Sugar Bowl game, which the latter's loss being attributed to the rain causing the Split-T to be ineffective.

In the 1940s, Missouri beat Kansas seven games to three, outscoring them 287-132. Gwinn Henry never brought Kansas a winning season in four years and was released after the 1942 season as a result. Don Faurot joined the United States Navy in 1943, which placed his longtime assistant Chauncey G. Simpson in charge of the Tigers. After two losing seasons, Simpson was finally able to have a winning season and he was able to win a Big Six Championship and take the Tigers to the Cotton Bowl. In the Border War Game, Simpson was able to beat Kansas two of three games and fortunately, for both schools, the game was never cancelled during the wartime years. Before the 1944 Border War Game,

Paul Christman

Jim Kekeris

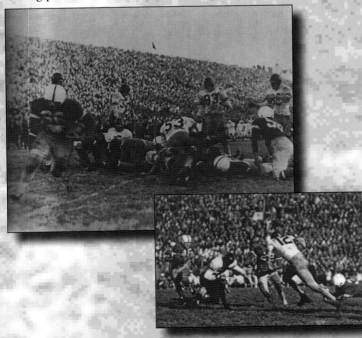

The 1946 Border War Game (top and right photographs)

Simpson devised a "secret weapon" for the game, turning 134 kilogram tackle Jim Kekeris into a fullback. Unusually quick for his size Kekeris battered himself through the Kansas defense that was unable to stop him.

Chauncey Simpson

After the war, Faurot returned to the Tigers in 1946 with Simpson resuming his role as assistant coach. There were many expectations for the Tigers, coming off a 6-2 season, a Cotton Bowl appearance and the return of Faurot and Missouri's other returning gridiron greats who had gone to war. However, war changed the returning war veterans and it was up to Faurot to pull a team together comprised of people who had not had him as a coach and those who would no longer submit so willingly to his control. At Kansas, a wartime Lieutenant Colonel, George Sauer, returned from war to lead the football squad. In two years, he would amass a 15-3-3 record, beating Missouri twice with narrow margins in the Border War Game.

In the 1947 game, Kansas was led by All-American Ray Evans and was unbeaten, with two ties. The crowd at Kansas' Memorial Stadium was a record-breaking 40,000, who witnessed a thriller ending to an assumed Kansas victory. In the game, on a fourth down on the Kansas 6-yard line, Missouri seemed poised to spoil Kansas' undefeated season as they were leading 14-13. On the fourth down, Nick Carras ran around the right side and was downed on the 4-yard line by the outreached hand of Kansas' Forrest Griffith, who tripped Carras. With only a few minutes left on the clock, Ray Evans drove the Jayhawks 95 yards down the field to score from the 1-yard line, leaving 63 seconds on the clock and eventually winning the game 20-14. With the win, Kansas was able to share in

Ray Evans

the Conference Championship and was invited to the Orange Bowl, losing that game.

Equal to the thriller of the 1947 game was the one played in 1949 to end the decade's series. Missouri was the favourite in that game, but nearly lost after a myriad of mistakes, which included turning over the ball seven times on fumbles and having a punt blocked. Kansas scored first when they recovered a fumble caused when Missouri's quarterback, Phil Klein, aligned himself behind the guard, Gene Pepper, instead of the center, Bob Fuchs. Missouri then proceeded to score four touchdowns to lead the game at the half 27-7. At the start of the third quarter, Kansas returned the favour to Missouri scored the next three touchdowns, leading Missouri 28-27. The game seemed a win for Kansas when Forrest Griffith fumbled a punt and Missouri's Bob Ebinger recovered it at the Kansas 37-yard line. Seven plays later, Missouri's Johnny Glorioso took a pitchout to the right and passed to Dick Braznell who scored from the 15-yard line to lead Kansas 34-28. The victory was assured when a replacement defensive back for Missouri, Jack Frier, intercepted a pass at the Missouri 12-yard line.

Kansas' Coach Cooper at the 1948 game

The Jayhawk mascot at the 1948 game

Missouri Football (6-3) - Head Coach Donald Burrowes Faurot

Row 1: Everly, Landers, Ellis, Duchek, Crocker, Cunningham, Wakeman, Chase, Notowitz, Counsil. Row 2: Starmer, Jeff Davis, Schultz, Jackson, Wallach, Hemmel, Greenwood, Jeffries, Otten, Hirsch, Liebig. Row 3: Jerry Davis, Ice, Horton, Beattie, Sischka, Carter, Aussieker, Phelps, Komen, Fitzgerald, Eckdahl, Metzinger. Row 4: Trainer DeVictor, Christman, Steuber, Seidel, Lightfoot, Brenton, Creed, Adams, Calovich, McMillan, Reece, Jenkins. Row 5: Coach Faurot, Coach Simpson, Coach Betty, Smith, Amelung, Meyers, Sweeney, Shelton, Lister, Ekern, Coach Bunker.

Kansas Football (2-7) - Head Coach Gwinn Henry

Missouri Football (8-2) - Head Coach Donald Burrowes Faurot
Big 6 Champion - Sugar Bowl Invitation

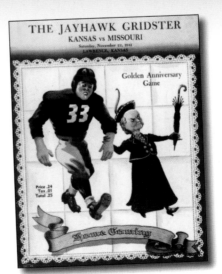

Kansas Football (3-6) - Head Coach Gwinn Henry

Missouri Football (8-3-1) - Head Coach Donald Burrowes Faurot
Big 6 Champion

Row 1: Wade, Fitzgerald, Keith, Davis, Ekern, Steuber, Captain Reece, Adams, Carter, Lister, Pitts, Morton. Row 2: Darr, Sweeney, Pepper, Carpenter, Milla, Bowen, Shurnas, Hodges, Bouldin, Tarpoff, Abrams, Callahan, Ghrist. Row 3: Ekern, Van Dyne, Gerker, Shepherd, Klaus, Hughes, Wren, Morrow, Austin, Schultz, Reginato, O'Hara, Broeg, Brauss. Row 4: Becker, Ihm, Enteminger, Parker, Archer, Fritz, Rogers, Volz, Smiley, Wood, Moore, Wyatt, Bockhorst, Quick. Row 5: Coach Simpson, Coach Faurot, Trainer Da Victor, Vlcek, Parente, Downing, Weis, Kling, Wade, Nevins, Coach Bunker, Coach Smith, Coach Simmons.

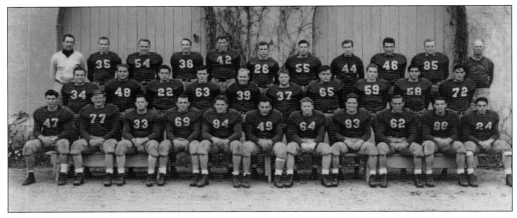

Kansas Football (2-8) - Head Coach Gwinn Henry

Missouri Football (3-5) - Head Coach Chauncey G. Simpson

Row 1: Henderson, Ihm, Anderson, Morton, Captain Reece, Ekern, Stewart, Collins, Dellastatious. Row 2: Brady, Jones, Sheppard, Tuchness, Pinfold, Green, England, Arbeitman, Bussell, Edwards. Row 3: Harris, Wimmers, Brown, Bear, Wright, Block, Knault, Reilly, Sigelberger, Hicks. Row 4: Shinkle, Watzig, Watson, Trippe, Stone, Wheeler, Gibbs, Dawdy, Kekeris, Versen. Row 5: Coach Simpson, Trainer De Victor, Evans, Clevenger, Dawson, Farris, B. West, Bragg, Gardner, Smith, Coach Bunker.

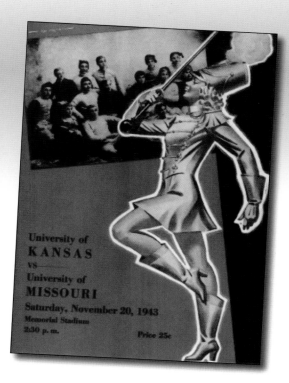

University of
KANSAS
vs
University of
MISSOURI
Saturday, November 20, 1943
Memorial Stadium
2:30 p.m.

Price 25¢

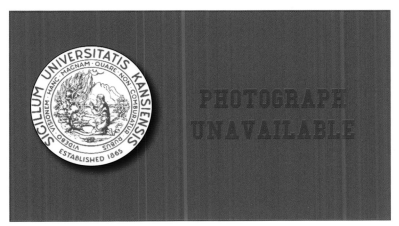

PHOTOGRAPH
UNAVAILABLE

Kansas Football (4-5-1) - Head Coach Henry A. Shenk

Missouri Football (3-5-2) - Head Coach Chauncey G. Simpson

Row 1: Cliffe, Grosse, Janson, Kekeris, Dellastatious, Collins, Exler, Eigelberger, Erlinger, Stone. Row 2: Riddle, Johnston, Clevenger, Brown, Croak, Whitaker, Gibbs, Bridgett, Hopkins, Daniels, Meier, Beck, Riley, McGrane, Mickelson, Campbell, Ewing, O'Connell. Row 3: Katzman, Tuckness, Walsh, Kesterson, Keane, Williams, Owens, Halls, Quirk, Henderson, Murphy. Row 4: Houston, Hearne, Radison, Stephens, Johnson, Pirtle, Weier, Harrison, Sandback, Tieman, Dailey, Knappenberger. Row 5: Moffatt, Hale, Coach Simpson, Coach Bunker, Coach Botts.

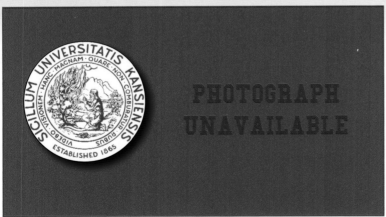

Kansas Football (3-6-1) - Head Coach Henry A. Shenk

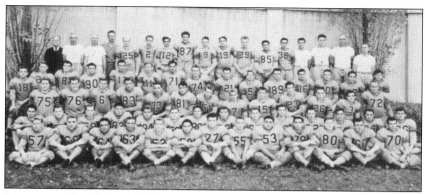

Missouri Football (6-4) - Head Coach Chauncey G. Simpson
Big 6 Champion - Cotton Bowl Invitation
Row 1: Ihm, Riddle, Cliffe, Whitaker, Dellastatious, Brown, O'Connell, Eigelberger, Kekeris, Stewart, Croak, Henderson, Hopkins.
Row 2: Chase, Nichols, Mills, Burk, Glauser, Cox, McHenry, Bonnett, Clodfelter, Lindley, Oakes, Kaiser, Vosevich, C. Howard. Row 3: McHugh, Terry, Whitacre, Baum, Thrasher, McDaniels, Mais, Howard, Rudolph, Grinnen, Marsh, Harrison, Parsley. Row 4: Williams, Olvis, Stevens, Bender, Day, Smith, Duke, Mehrens, Bush, Dickey, Huss, Broaders, Wheeler, Grennin, Thompson. Row 5: Trainer De Victor, Coach Botts, Coach Simpson, Student Manager Hale, Hearne, Anderson, Scavuzzo, Stokes, Hittner, Lamothe, Pascal, Gatts, Bales, Eckdahl, Coach Pickett, Coach Bunker, Coach Betty.

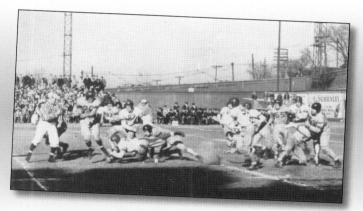

Kansas Football (4-5-1) - Head Coach Henry A. Shenk

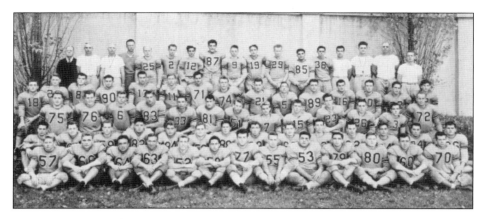

Missouri Football (5-4-1) - Head Coach Donald Burrowes Faurot

Kansas Football (7-2-1) - Head Coach George H. Sauer
Big 6 Co-Champion

Missouri Football (6-4) - Head Coach Donald Burrowes Faurot

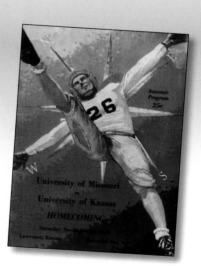

Kansas Football (8-1-2) - Head Coach George H. Sauer
Big 6 Co-Champions - Orange Bowl Invitation

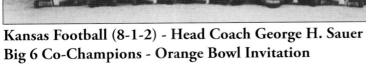

151

Missouri Football (8-3) - Head Coach Donald Burrowes Faurot
Gator Bowl Invitation

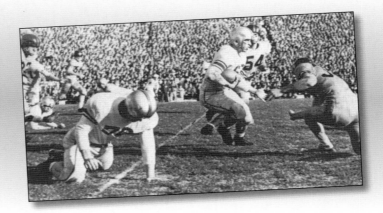

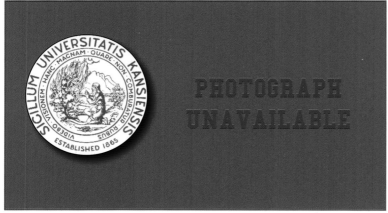

Kansas Football (7-3) - Head Coach Jules Verne Sikes

Missouri Football (7-4) - Head Coach Donald Burrowes Faurot
Gator Bowl Invitation

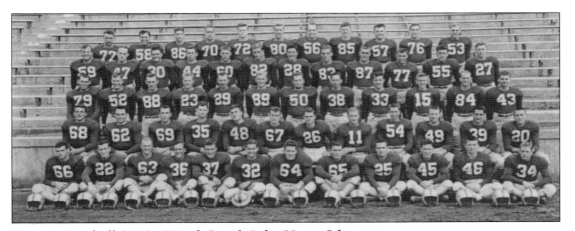

Kansas Football (5-5) - Head Coach Jules Verne Sikes

MR. MAGOO EYES

Growing up with Paul Christman was quite a gift and an adventure, I have to say. Paul Christman was my dad and quite a great father, at that. I can think of a million things to tell you about him, but I'll try to narrow it to a few favorites.

First, my dad was an athlete and a good one. Once, he told me and my two older brothers, "Here's the deal, I'm going to teach you every sport I can. It's not optional or negotiable. Once you learn it and get good at it, then you can decide if you ever want to do it again." As a result, I'm good at many things and I love that great gift he gave to me. Second, and most important for me, is my dad's courage, which has gotten me through many things throughout my life.

He had a great way with people and was quite a selfless man, always trying to help the other person, especially the underdog. He greatly loved my mother and between playing pro-football and then, in the 1960s, broadcasting for NBC, he was a "Manufacturer's Representative" for RB Tools. It's funny for me to write it because every time someone would ask me as a child, "What does your dad do?," I would tell them he was a "Manufacturer's Representative," even though I had no idea what that meant and I prayed no one would ask me. They never did, ever. As long as he was alive, I had no idea what he really did, besides knowing of his football past and until he became a broadcaster, thank God!

After he passed, my mom took over his business and when I admitted to her that I didn't know what he did, she admitted to me, neither did she and she was his wife! All we knew is that he'd go work and then come home. He had a great plan for after work to deal with his exhaustion. He built, in the 1960s, one of those hanging, whicker chairs and he also created for it a fancy stereo system, way ahead of its time. Then, when he'd come home, he'd plop in his swing, put his head phones on and listen to music until he was de-stressed. Then he'd come hug my Mom, turn on some music and dance around with her. It was a delightful time in my life.

He had a great sense of humor and he loved the small things in life. He had a dog named "Beckett" and oh, how he loved that dog. Also, he had a "frog-crossing" out in the back yard, by the forest. He and my mom would sit out on the patio at sunset and laugh and chat. That was their favorite time of day. After he passed on, my mom wrote the loveliest poem, "I Miss You Most at Twilight Time."

One last thing that I've shared with many people is that I lost my dad at 22 years old, when he was 51, I believe. Everyone loses loved ones, but I always try to remind people to celebrate their lives, rather than focus on the sadness. I share with my dad the same tiny, "Mr. Magoo" eyes, so I nicknamed him "Magoo" long ago and even call him that now. I hope everyone has someone in their life that they love as much as I did my dad. I'm sure he's smiling with me, right now, with a twinkle in those tiny, "Magoo" eyes.

Victoria Lee Christman
Daughter
Written Friday, September 5, 2008

THE "DUZE" AS A FATHER

"The Duze," as he was sometimes known, related best to my brother and me through sports. It didn't matter if it was a 40-yard pass laid right in my hands, smacking a cork ball in the middle of Lincoln Avenue in Park Ridge, Illinois, or a soft touch jump shot while playing "horse," X-man the All-American from Missouri, the Chicago Cardinal and Green Bay Packer, was the all-time sports dad.

He was a natural at those pursuits involving hand/eye coordination. While I could swim well, I had little talent at football, baseball and golf, three pursuits at which he was like Lance Armstrong on a bike. Pro sports treasures from his off-season job at Wilson's Sporting Goods were always bonuses. He got me the New York Yankee's Billy Martin's cast-off mitt and I sometimes wore Pitchin' Paul's All-Star jersey and one of his giant bowl rings.

When I was a freshman at 5'10-1/2" and 148 pounds [178 cm, 67 kg] I went out for the high school football team. It's too bad I didn't wait a year, because during those 12 months I grew to 6'2" and 192 pounds [188 cm, 87 kg]. As a freshman I was ungainly, had no speed and little chance of starting at defensive end. Yet in the distance on the road beside the practice field, I saw my father peering through the side window of his Nash Rambler as it idled nearby our workouts and tackling gantlets.

He liked kidding all three of us kids and while I was the butt of many a zinger, my brother Dave and sister Tory often were compared to those celebrities with exaggerated characteristics. If you dropped a pass, he'd say, "Too bad, got you in a bad place; the hands." If you moved too slowly, he might call you "Joe Pants." Brother Dave and I often relegated younger sister Tory to minor sports roles and Dad might say to her, "What's the matter, ragamuffin?"

It wasn't that he spent a lot of time with his three kids; it was more that the time he did spend was quality time, and we laughed our way through many an outdoor sporting contest we all knew he would win.

By Paul J. Christman, Junior
Son
Written Wednesday, September 10, 2008

GIVE HIM TIME...

If Gwinn Henry ever decides to quit coaching football, he will have no trouble locating a job. Tomorrow morning he could walk into the office of any telephone executive or booking agent in the country and be hired on the spot as a trouble shooter or a magician. From the time Henry started coaching hack in '11 until he was brought to Mt. Oread to put some oomph in Jayhawker athletics and later the athletes themselves, the mastermind of the gridiron has been continually patching up broken-down systems or, to coin a phrase, pulling rabbits out of hats.

When the Kansas athletic department was in the process of reorganization in 1937, those in charge hunted a long time to locate a man whom they thought capable of building up a sports program of which the students and the alumni of the University could be proud. Henry was finally chosen and he immediately began to put the department on a sound footing.

Last winter when it was decided to make a change in the football coaching staff Henry seemed to be the logical choice. But before the task could be placed on the capable shoulders of this man, two things had to be accomplished. First, Henry himself had to be persuaded to come out of his self-imposed shell of retirement from active coaching, and second, the Board of Regents had to be induced to rescind its ruling that the director of athletics at the University could not coach. Sentiment was so overwhelmingly in favor of Mr. Henry that both obstacles were soon removed.

The new Jayhawker mentor fell heir to the remnants of a club that finished in the cellar of the Big Six conference last year. Only a few sophomores possessing varsity potentialities are lending a hand in the process of reconstruction. The toughest opponents in the league have improved considerably over last season. Yet Henry has set himself to the task with a right good will and is fashioning a football machine that is catching the fancy of the fans. It is a team capable of reeling off long and thrilling touchdown maneuvers from any spot on the field.

All Henry lacked in winning his first contest as a Kansas coach was a pass that slipped through the fingers of a lone figure standing in the end zone. Then came his first home game and his first Big Six start at K.U. His Crimson and Blue club did itself proud in smashing over two quick touchdowns against Iowa State and otherwise outplaying the Cyclones throughout the game. But before saying more about Henry's doings on Mt. Oread, let us gaze back over the past and consider some of the things that have led sports writers and observers to tag him as one of the craftiest mentors in the business.

Gwinn started his coaching career in 1911 at Oklahoma Baptist University and after staying there two years returned to his alma mater, Howard Payne college, to coach during 1913-14-15. The school year of 1916-17 found Henry at the Georgia Military

school as track coach, then he returned to Howard Payne to finish work on his degree.

This set the stage for his first step up the ladder of coaching greatness. College of Emporia brought him to this sector in 1918 and from the very start he began producing sensational teams. In five years at Emporia, his Presbyterian elevens dropped only three games. C. of E., during the Henry administration, was one of the most feared of all the smaller colleges.

This marvelous record gave Gwinn Henry his chance in the big time coaching racket when Missouri lured him to Columbia in 1923 to begin tutoring its sons of the gridiron. After a mediocre season in which he built foundations for great teams, Henry got his Tigers rolling in high gear. In 1924 and the next three years Missouri stacked up 25 victories, lost only 6 games, and tied 3. The Bengals won the Big Six championship three times out of four in this span and outside the loop chalked up triumphs over Northwestern, Chicago, and West Virginia, among others, in addition to tying Tulane and Southern Methodist

Nebraska's scarlet horde had been the bane of the Tigers ' existence before Henry went to Columbia, but he ended that in a hurry. In his first year at M.U. the Tigers tied the Huskers and three of the next four seasons found them winning from the Lincoln lads. The Cornhuskers thumped the Notre Dame team that boasted the famous "Four Horsemen" and they downed Illinois when "Red" Grange was on the loose, but they could not beat Henry's Missouri teams.

After winning the conference title in 1927, the Tigers tied for second with Oklahoma in 1928 and took undisputed runnerup honors in 1929. During the following two seasons Henry was struck down with illness and could be with his teams only a part of the time. Missouri lost as many games during those two years as it had in the previous seven campaigns under Henry. In 1931 the Tigers dropped eight out of ten and that brought an end to the nine-year Gwinn Henry regime at Missouri.

For two years Henry was out of the game regaining his health, but in the fall of 1933 he donned the moleskins again to take over the head coaching duties for the St. Louis Gunners, an independent professional outfit. The Gunners were given no consideration at all in pre-season dope, but Henry put his football magic to work and the Gunners astounded everyone by roaring through a 16-game schedule with only two defeats. They topped off the season by tying the Chicago Bears, national professional champions.

After a year at St. Louis Henry returned to the Southwest, the great open spaces where he spent his youth. He went to the University of New Mexico as director of athletics and head football coach. In his three years there before coming to Kansas, Henry met with much success, winning the Border conference championship his first season at Albuquerque.

Not only can Henry teach other men to excel in athletics, he was a champion himself. During his undergraduate days at Howard Payne Gwinn was an all-star end on the football team and a crack baseball player, but on the track he fairly scintillated. He ran the 100-yard dash in 9.6 seconds, the 220 in 21.2, threw the discus 145 feet, and put the shot 42 feet, all of these performances being Texas records.

In 1910 and 1911 Henry ran for the Irish-American athletic club of New York, where he set a world record for the 125-yard dash at 12.2 seconds and equalled the world records of 10.8 for the 110-yard dash and 7.4 for 75 yards indoors. He was selected on the All-American track squad in the 100-yard dash by Lawson Robertson and James E. Sullivan. After winning every race he entered during 1911, Henry was picked for the 1912 Olympic team without competition, but was unable to run because of illness.

Girding himself for the difficult task of lifting the Jayhawkers' football fortunes out of the mire of the Big Six conference, Henry picked a pair of capable assistants who had served him well in years gone by. Vic Hurt, line coach, was a star center at College of Emporia in 1918-19 when Henry piloted the Presbys through two consecutive undefeated campaigns. Gwinn's head scout and analyst is Harry Lansing, who served in this same capacity when his boss was at Mizzou.

As these three men united together so did the varsity gridmen. A bunch of Kansas football players that had in times past operated as disgruntled individuals suddenly became a smooth-functioning unit with one purpose in mind that being to play the best brand of football possible.

This squad does not possess the manpower and experience of some of the other schools in the conference. A team in this condition must make up for such deficiency with willingness to train hard, finesse on attack, and an inconquerable spirit. This outfit has these requirements, but it has so much difference to make up that one can't expect it to do better than spring an upset or two.

Henry has a wealth of good backfield material that works nicely into his system. He has Bill Bunsen and Ed Hall for heavy duty work. There is Dick Amerine and Jake Fry, a pair of elusive, swivel-hipped ball carriers, for broken field running. In Ralph Miller, Frank Bukaty, and Eldreth Cadwalader Henry has triple threat talent to waste. Milt Sullivant is as sweet a blocker and field general as any coach would want. Then there is Ed Suagee, Kenneth Caldwell, the Gibbens boys, and others just waiting for a chance to do their bit.

The backfield is well and good, but the forward wall is spotted rather than sprinkled with linemen who are good enough to play in the Big Six conference. There are some who know what

it is all about, but are handicapped by lack of size. Others have plenty of heft, but when weighed in the balances are found wanting in experience, ability, or both. There are too few rough and ready gridders in the Kansas camp who relish the milling and are big enough to do something about it.

A football team, like a chain, is no stronger than its weakest link. On days when the Kansas line plays inspired ball like it did against K-State last fall then the Jayhawkers will be a hard bunch to handle. On other days they will be a team capable of pulling a long run or two, but not a team capable of causing too much damage.

But remember what the gridiron's mastermind did when he got his start in the Big Six. He spent his first year at Missouri laying the groundwork for championship teams in the future. Then he cut loose and won two loop titles in a row. Perhaps history will repeat itself. The bulk of this year's starting lineup will be back for another crack at the Big Six. Several promising freshmen are slated to move up. They will all have had a year getting used to the "Henry System." And football players and students alike are of the opinion that it is not a bad thing to get used to.

By Jay Simon
Kansas Alumnus 1940
Written for the 1940 Jayhawker *Yearbook*

1939 Kansas coaches: Vic Hurt, Harry Lansing, and Gwinn Henry

THANKS, DICK!

I was fortunate to grow up in Webster Groves, Missouri, where I played high school football with a friend of mine named Dick Gilman. Dick had moved to Webster Groves in high school from Arkansas because his dad was in the military. I was the starting quarterback and team co-captain my senior year, but whooping-cough had me sidelined much of that season.

My high school coach was a great man name Ray Moss, who had been a stand-out football player at the University of Missouri. I went to go play for them and played under his same coach Don Faurot, who is one of the nicest gentlemen that I ever met. I was fortunate to have played football for two coaches that would later have fields named for them; Moss Field, in Webster Groves; and Faurot Field in Columbia. Actually, I was fortunate to play for five coaches in various sports who had high school or college fields named for them: Ray Moss, Froebel Gaines, Don Faurot, Tyke Yates, and John "Hi" Simmons.

My buddy Dick Gilman went to play for Kansas and did pretty well there. He was an All-Big Seven halfback his junior year and he had netted 744 yards in passing when I got to meet him again in Lawrence, Kansas for the annual game.

I was a reserve player until the Oklahoma game but, because Mike Ghnouly got injured, I became the new starting safety. I had a pretty good game against Oklahoma batting down a pass in the end zone and making a bunch of tackles. In the game against Kansas, I was up against my old friend Dick. It was a close game all the way to the end in the fourth quarter, when Kansas pushed its way to inside the 30-yard line. On a fourth-down play, Dick lined up as a fullback, forcing me to possibly have to cover him.

On the play, Dick counted three after the snap and then ran straight down the middle without coverage. The goal posts were the old "H" type and you had to be careful not to run into them in the end zone. A pass was made to Dick, which rolled off his fingers ending the play, but, in his defense, he had that goalpost to avoid.

I was so relieved that he didn't score a touchdown on that play and show me up. There was a huge yell from the Missouri fans and, as I ran past Dick to go to the sideline, I had to smile and say, "Thanks, Dick!"

I loved my schools and from my former coach at Webster Groves, I recruited the best backfield in the State of Missouri in 1954 to play for the Tigers. Maybe you've heard of them; Hank Kuhlmann, Glenn St. Pierre, Charlie James, and Joe Heimlicher, "The Four Horsemen." I have only missed two home Missouri football games since 1947 because of heart valve surgery in 1993 and I gave a football to the athletic department that all Missouri football coaches had signed since Don Faurot.

Dick was a great athlete and I competed with him and against him for eight years on some great football and baseball teams. After high school, Dick joined the Marines and I served in the Coast Guard just after the end of the war. We both went to college after we had served our country and we remain good friends to this day. Thanks, Dick!

John Frier, Junior
Missouri Alumnus 1950
Written Thursday, October 22, 2009

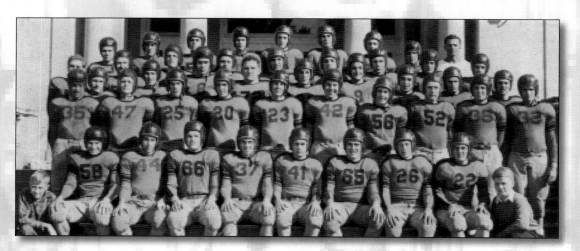

1944 Webster Groves Football - (First Row) Jack Frier #41, Don Keller #65, and Dick Gilman #26. Former Missouri 1938 team co-captain, Ray Moss, is in the back row, right, wearing a white shirt.

YOU'RE WELCOME, JACK.

My father was commanding officer of Company A, 137th Infantry in Atchison, Kansas, from 1925 until the unit was called into active service in 1941. Our family accompanied him to Little Rock, Arkansas, the site of Camp Robinson. In 1942, at the end of the first semester of my ninth grade year, he was transferred to Jefferson Barracks, Missouri, where we lived on the post and attended school in Webster Groves. My older sister, Mary Ruth, graduated from Webster Groves High School in 1943 and I graduated in the class of 1945. Immediately after graduation I enlisted in the Marine Corps and shortly afterwards my father returned to civilian status and moved the family back to Kansas before I left the Marines. I have never been back to Webster Groves.

By the time I was nine years old I had no other career interest other than being a high school coach, so with that interest in mind, I played every sport available to me. At Webster Groves I played football, basketball and baseball under the tutelage of Coach Ray Moss, a former All-Big Six end at Missouri and Coach Walton Smith. For the record, let me say here, a few years too late, I am afraid, that my experience in playing for those two fine men only heightened my desire to follow in their footsteps.

1948 Jayhawks: Bertuzzi, Gilman, and Amberg

At Webster Groves, one of my team-mates in all three sports was Jack Frier who later attended the University of Missouri where he played both football and baseball as I did at the University of Kansas. While we competed against each other several times in what was always a heated rivalry, it had not yet escalated into the fever pitch rivalry now known as "The Border War." The 1949 Missouri-Kansas game was contested on the Memorial Stadium field before a crowd of perhaps 40,000 in Lawrence. Jack was playing safety for the Tigers and another former Webster team-mate, Don Keller, was also playing at tackle for them. Don, a 236 pound [107 kilogram] bear of a man, was a two-time Missouri State heavyweight wrestling champion and a real handful on the gridiron. I was playing fullback for the Jayhawks.

The game was close all the way and the issue was far from being decided as we played into the fourth quarter. We drove into Missouri territory but reached a point where we faced a fourth down situation inside the thirty. The play call was a pass and my job was to sift through the line and run a route straight down the middle. Defensive linemen and linebackers are schooled to prevent such a route by any means possible but on this particular occasion, I found myself running free into the end zone directly under the goalpost with no defenders in the area. Our quarterback, Jerry Bogue, threw a perfect pass into my hands near the line and I dropped it. The ball simply rebounded off my hand and fell to the ground. The pro-Kansas crowd sat in stunned silence while the Tiger rooters began to breathe again. There was nothing to do but get back into my defensive position as the Missouri defense ran off the field. Jack ran past me on his way to the bench and said, "Thanks, Dick."

Was the play disappointing? Was it embarrassing... even humiliating? It was all three, in spades! But, I believe it made me a more compassionate and understanding teacher and coach. After all, it's just a game played to teach young men to deal with life. It's just a game, isn't it?

Joseph Richard Gilman, Junior
Kansas Alumnus 1950
Written Tuesday, August 5, 2008

JAYHAWKER 1941 – BORDER WAR 1940

In their forty-ninth annual grid battle, it was Missouri nearly all the way. While over 17,000 people looked on, the Tiger team began to roll just nine minutes after the game had begun. The Tigers took the ball on their own 20-yard stripe and advanced it to the Kansas 4-yard line, where Christman carried it over. Cunningham kicked the extra point.

Kansas went right back to the Missouri 12-yard line but passes into the end zone stopped that drive. In the second quarter, a lateral from Chase to Harry Ice was good for another Tiger score. After K. U. drove again futilely, Christman passed to Starmer for the third Tiger score. The Tigers led at the half, 20 to 0.

Just after the second half started, Christman threw a 35-yard pass to Crocker, who went to the Kansas 10-yard strip. Another pass to Starmer tallied. Then Kansas came to life and a pass from Hall to D. Gibbens found K. U. on the 5-yard line. A line drive by Ed Hall scored the touchdown. Hall kicked the point.

Almost immediately Missouri's Chase carried the ball over from the K. U. 10-yard line. And as the final quarter started, Missouri again took the ball deep into Kansas territory, only to have Christman dive across for another tally. With the ball changing hands three times in a row, Hall tossed a line pass to Gibbens, who skipped the other eight yards to a score.

Then the Tigers retaliated with a long pass from Christman to Starmer who ran out on the 1-yard line so that a teammate, Myron Council, could make the score. On

the second down, Council plunged over for the tally. In the last minutes of play, Irving Hayden tossed a 25-yard pass to Gregory Studer, who was standing in the tiers end-zone.

SAVITAR 1941 – BORDER WAR 1940

MEMORIAL STADIUM, Nov. 21-Missouri piled touchdown on touchdown this afternoon as the graduating seniors of the 1940 Tiger team bade farewell in their last game by smothering Kansas, 45-20. Showing a capacity homecoming throng a powerful offense, protected by an almost impregnable defense, the colorful game saw the Tigers score eight times.

After receiving the opening kickoff, Kansas was forced to kick out. The Tigers then displayed an eight-yard touchdown drive climaxed by Paul Christman's plunge over the 4-yard line behind potent blocking. Ice counted once on a run in the first half and Starmer caught a Christman pass for the other first half touchdown.

The Jayhawks struck back with a sustained drive in the second half, and with the help of two long passes, ran their count up to twenty points. The Tigers roared right back at them to score four more touchdowns overshadowing the K. U. assault. Sportsmanlike gestures by Starmer and Christman enabled graduating seniors Notowitz, blocking back, and Counsil, senior fullback, to score their first intercollegiate touchdowns.

Missouri's sophomore contingent played a powerful brand of ball throughout the game, and the efforts of Ice and Jenkins aided the Tiger cause.

SAVITAR 1942 – BORDER WAR 1941

Rain, snow, sleet, and the Kansas University Jayhawks were not able to stop the Tigers from becoming the 1941 Big Six champions as Missouri crushed Kansas 45-6 in the traditional Turkey Day game, November 22. The victory was the eighth straight for the Bengals and it shoved them into a position for a choice post-season game in one of the bowls.

A heavy, cold rain was pouring down from dark clouds as the game got under way, but on the second play from scrimmage Harry Ice took a lateral from Adams and scampered 5 yards before lateraling to tackle Bob Brenton, who scored for the first touchdown. Steuber's kick was good and the score stood 7 to 0. Later in the same period Steuber dashed 46 yards to the K. U. 3, and two plays later he carried it over to make the score 13 to 0. His kick was wide.

The score was still 13 to 0 at the half-time, when sleet and large flakes of snow began to fall. On the second play of the third period Ice skirted his right end for 57 yards and the third touchdown for the game. Steuber's kick was good and the score

was 20 to 0. A few plays later Steuber circled left end for 55 yards and the fourth counter. His kick was good.

Ralph Miller, Jayhawk star passer, swiped a Missouri lateral on the Tiger 35 late in the period and scored the only Kansas touchdown.

On the first play of the fourth quarter Red Wade dashed 23 yards for the fifth Missouri score. A few plays later Ice broke loose on the K. U. 36 and then lateraled to Chase, who was stopped on the 5. Three plays later Chase went over. Lister's kick was blocked. Flavin passed from the midfield stripe to Morton for the seventh and last Tiger touchdown.

The Bengals charged across the sodden turf to roll up 449 yards from scrimmage. The game was the last conference tilt for Harry Ice, Wallach, Brenton, Chase, Jeffries, and Jenkins.

JAYHAWKER 1943 – BORDER WAR 1942

In the fifty-first annual football meeting between Missouri and Kansas, the Jayhawks came out on the short end of a 42 to 13 score. It was a game in which lateral and forward passes were thrown with wild and reckless abandon. The Jayhawkers were hopelessly outmanned, but they never gave up the fight.

SAVITAR 1943 – BORDER WAR 1942

The Tigers retaliated [losing to Fordham University] with a 42 to 7 Homecoming win over Kansas.

SAVITAR 1944 – BORDER WAR 1943

Lawrence, Kansas, November 20, 1943.

Yes, it really happened. For the first time since 1934, a homecoming crowd saw the outgained Jayhawkers hang one on the Missouri Tigers by the thinest of margins, 7 to 6. The Tigers charged, recharged, huffed, and puffed, but in that almighty important department of points after touchdowns they fell short. The Tigers scored first, when midway in the second quarter, Ekern took a lateral from Collins on the Kansas 40 yard line, and scampered on to pay dirt. Ihm's attempted placement went wide, and with it went the game. In the third quarter George, Jayhawker halfback, smashed over right tackle from the Missouri 11 and scored. Bill Chestnut, drop kick expert, cleared the bar with a beautiful exhibition of his art, and sewed up the old game. The Tigers came back beautifully, and were within scratching distance of the coveted double stripe for the remainder of the game, but fumbles and a stouthearted defense by the Jayhawkers kept the end zone unmarred for the remainder of the period. Final score, Kansas 7, Missouri 6.

SAVITAR 1945 – BORDER WAR 1944

In the 53rd traditional meeting between M. U. and K. U. the Tigers completed a successful season. Successful, in as much as they over-powered their arch rivals, Kansas, 28-0.

The brunt of the Missouri attack was borne by 273 pound [124 kg] Jim Kekeris, a converted fullback. He ripped the K. U. line to shreds and averaged 5.5 yards per try on 16 thrusts at the line. He scored two touchdowns and four conversions.

The other Missouri touchdowns came on scores by Captain Paul Collins, playing his last game for the Tigers; and Van Robinson.

The game was a fitting climax to the season for a fighting M. U. team.

JAYHAWKER 1946 – BORDER WAR 1945

For the final gridiron tiff the Jayhawks went to Kansas City, this time to fight the Missouri Tiger. The final defeat was received – not with a battle – as the conference champions won, 33-12. Twenty-one thousand spectators finished their Thanksgiving dinner early to see the traditional battle which helped Missouri get a Cotton Bowl invitation. Schmidt and Pumphrey accounted for the two Kansas touchdowns.

SAVITAR 1946 – BORDER WAR 1945

Kansas City, MO.-Nov. 24-The University of Missouri remained undefeated in 1945 Big Six Conference play and brought the big Six crown to Columbia for the first time since 1942 by defeating Kansas University here at Ruppert Stadium today, 33-13.

A sustained 75-yard drive climaxed by Loyd Brinkman's plunge over the goal line gave Missouri the first score early in the opening period. kekeris' kick for pint was not good. The first play of the next quarter had the Jayhawks tying the Tigers 6-6 but just before the half Bill Dellastatious hit Bengal End Oakes with a 65-yard pass good for a second touchdown.

The high pint of the day came on a faked lateral that saw Jim Kekeris, 285-pound [130 kg] lineman, rumbling 6-yards to a score. Howard Bonnet netted Missouri another tally later after a 75-yard jaunt downfield by the Tigers.

Kansas scored once again in the final period and Missouri's Hopkins tallied once more to end the game.

JAYHAWKER 1947 – BORDER WAR 1946

Defeated Missouri for the first time since 1934 at Columbia. Broke the spell of the Tiger's Don Faurot who had never lost to a Kansas team since taking over the Missouri helm in 1935. Here is the way the scoreboard looked after KU outlasted Missouri on Thanksgiving Day to deadlock the title at four victories and a single loss.

SAVITAR 1947 – BORDER WAR 1946

Columbia, MO., Nov. 28-Ray Evans waved his magic wand over the Missouri Tigers here today before 29,000 Homecoming fans and controlled the Bengals in every way to lead Kansas to a thrilling 20-19 victory in a battle that gave the Jayhawkers a share of the 1946 Big Six title with Oklahoma.

Both teams were gripped with shaky hands and kept bouncing the ball back between each other with fumbles. A Kansas fumble on their own 17 set up Missouri's first touchdown. A lateral play from Brinkman to Bowman from five yards out accounted for the game's first tally. Kekeris missed the extra point.

Kansas came back in the very opening minute of the second period. A 63-yard pass play from Evans to Small was good for a touchdown. Fambrough added the extra point.

After a brief exchange of fumbles and punts, Missouri found itself and started rolling on a power drive from their own 49, Dutch Wyatt adroitly mixed the Missouri attack which eventually found Kekeris bulling over on a fourth down plunge from the two yard line. Again the extra point was missed, but Missouri held a 12-7 lead.

Then it came, the play which undoubtedly decided the ball game. With two seconds remaining in the first half, Evans faded to pass but could find no receiver; he then ran toward the sidelines, changed course diagonally across the field and shot past a trio of Missouri tacklers and did not stop until he zoomed over the two striper 54 yards away. The extra point was missed but Kansas held a 13-12 halftime lead.

Kansas, for safety's sake added another touchdown in the third period after Hopkins' fumble had been recovered on the Missouri 46. After three smacks at the Missouri line, Ray Evans was again called in the battle to power his way across from the two. This time Fambrough added the extra point for a 20-12 lead.

Missouri also wound up its scoring in the third period on a brilliant pass play from Entsminger to Bounds. This play carried 73 yards. Bounds took Entsminger's toss on the Missouri 45 and outran the Kansas safety men for the score. Bill Day kicked the extra point.

JAYHAWKER 1948 – BORDER WAR 1947

The climax of the Kansas pigskin season came one week later before 40,043 shouting spectators in Memorial stadium as the Jayhawkers smashed their way to a 20 to 14 win over a tough crew of Missouri Tigers. The record-breaking homecoming crowd saw the Crimson and Blue team grind out a 94-yard scoring drive in the last six minutes of the game to bring the second conference co-championship to Lawrence in the last two years. Ray Evans for the second straight year proved the Tiger nemesis

as he scored one touchdown, passed to halfback Bud French for another and played sensationally on defense. The winning Kansas score came when fullback Forrest Griffith took the ball for the fourth consecutive time and scored from the 1-yard line, one minute remaining in the game.

SAVITAR 1948 – BORDER WAR 1947
TIGERS DROP THRILLER

Missouri's Tigers dropped to third place as they lost their final contest to Kansas, 20-14, at Lawrence before a record Homecoming crowd of 40,000, in a game full of spills and breakaway runs. Afterwards, 206-pound [94 kilograms] tackle Chester Fritz was elected Bengal captain for next year's team.

All-American Ray Evans capitalized on a blocked Tiger punt and passed to Bud French in the end zone for the first TD. The possible one-pointer was blocked. The Tigers struck back four minutes later when Dick Braznell threw from the KU 38 to Kenny Bounds in the end zone. Bob Dawson converted. Evans rebounded in the second quarter by returning a Tiger punt to the MU 45, and on the next play breaking into the open for a touchdown. The one-pointer was good. The Bengals again went on the march, featuring Nick Carras inside and outside the right tackle down to the Jayhawk goal line where Carras spurted over. Dawson again converted.

In the last quarter, the Jayhawkers clinched the game as they drove 93 yards, and Forrest Griffith went over from the one.

JAYHAWKER 1949 – BORDER WAR 1948

Playing on Thanksgiving Day in Columbia, the Kansas eleven closed out the season by going down before the M.U. Tigers 7 to 21. 32,000 fans, the largest crowd ever to see a grid contest at Missouri, turned out to see the 57th annual game between the two schools.

The Tigers hadn't beaten the Jayhawkers since 1945 and they were eager to avenge the two narrow defeats they had suffered at the hands of Kansas since then. Rated three touchdowns better than K.U., the Missourians seemed certain not only to beat the Hawkers, but to humiliate them as M.U. led 21 to 0 at the half. Beat them they did, but they did not humiliate the Crimson warriors.

Although pushed around badly the first two periods, the Kansans dominated play in the second half. Holding the Tigers to a standstill, Kansas proceeded to score seven points before the final gun and prove to fans that they wouldn't be beaten without a fight. The K.U. touchdown was made by halfback Bertuzzi on a 1-yard lunge early in the fourth quarter climaxing a drive from the M.U. 36.

M.U. touchdowns were set up by a pass interception and two fumbles in Kansas territory during the first half which is not to say Missouri won on breaks. The Tigers outgained K.U. on the ground 237 yards to 199 and in the air 47 to 0, Kansas failing to complete even one aerial in eight tries.

SAVITAR 1949 – BORDER WAR 1948

Missouri . . . . 21 - Kansas 7

Columbia, Nov. 25.-Over 32,000 spectators watched the Missouri Tigers take second place in the Big Seven conference today, as the Bengals downed the Kansas Jayhawks, 21-7. It was the fifty-seventh meeting of the two rivals.

Twelve minutes of the first quarter had elapsed before the Tigers had scored their first touchdown. Runs by Carras, Braznell, and a 13-yard pass from Entsminger to Braznell put the Tigers in scoring position. Entsminger went over from the 2 to give the Tigers a lead which they never relinquished.

The Tigers struck again two and one-half minutes later after Carras returned a pass interception to the K. U. 14. Braznell, with perfect blocking, went over from the 10. The final Tiger TD came midway in the third period after Win Carter had recovered a Jayhawk fumble on the 23. Sheehan speared a pass from Entsminger on the 18, and was stopped on the Jayhawk 10. Carras picked up four more yards before Entsminger took the ball over. Bob Dawson kicked his third conversion of the day to give the Tigers a 21-0 lead.

After a scoreless third period, Kansas managed to pick up a fourth quarter score. Bud French recovered an M. U. fumble on the Tiger 37. Runs by Griffith, Moffat and Bertuzzi gave the Kansans their only score of the day. Ken Sperry converted.

The Jayhawks continually threatened the Tiger goal line in the last half, but were unable to penetrate Missouri's forward wall. Following the game, the Tigers elected Bob Fuchs captain for the 1949 season.

SAVITAR 1950 – BORDER WAR 1949

MU 34, KANSAS 27

MISSOURI:	14 - 13 - 0 - 7 -- 34
KANSAS:	7 - 0 - 14 - 7 -- 28

Lawrence, Kas., Nov. 19-Missouri University's Tigers played a dual role of good samaritan and villain this afternoon, as they fumbled away a 13-point lead in the third period and then turned around in the fourth stanza to edge the Kansas Jayhawks 34-28.

After Kansas drew first blood early in the opening quarter, the Bengals erupted for four touchdowns in the next 25 minutes.

But with the beginning of the second half, the Tigers turned tame, and before they took up their warring ways again, the Jays had caught and passed them, and were nursing a slim but reassuring 28-27 [lead].

Then the Missourians went to work. Grinding their way from their own 39 to the KU 35, they then switched to the ozone

for the play destined to become the game-winner. Glorioso flipped a spot pass to Braxnell on the 25, and the brilliant MU half sprinted and feinted his way for the remaining 25 yards and the touchdown.

The Tiger victory was especially sweet for Don Faurot's gridmen. Only one week ago, his charges absorbed a beating at the hands of Oklahoma U., and this win restored their national prestige and may mean a bowl bid for them.

Missouri offensive power was brought to the fore in the first half, when drives of 81, 75, 78 and 60 yards were used in scoring. These drives were highlighted by accurate, telling passes by quarterback Phil Klein, and some razzle-dazzle, wide-open football on the part of Klein, Harold Carter and Win Carter that featured complex reverses and baffling lateral plays.

In the aftermath of World War II, America found itself in a geopolitical, ideological, and economic "Cold War" with the Soviet Union. As the Korean War raged in Asia and the fear of nuclear weapons grew as a silent spectre, teenagers began to shake their hips to a new music style known as "rock 'n' roll." Rock 'n' roll had its beginning with a local Saint Louis musician named Chuck Berry, who armed with a guitar and his "duck walk," performed such songs as "Roll Over Beethoven" and "Johnny B. Goode." Television, which had been released after the end of World War II, was now a common home device and many people were now moving from urban centers of living to the suburbs. By the end of the decade, racial segregation would end as schools across the country would be legally required to integrate.

As is the case with many heated rivalries, team records are irrelevant when the two teams meet on the field and so has been the case for many Thanksgiving Days between Missouri and Kansas. On Thanksgiving Day 1950, Don Faurot's 3-4-1 Tigers met Jules Sikes' 6-3 Jayhawks at Rollins Field, but not before the temperature plunged the evening before to sub-freezing temperatures. Unfortunately for the Jayhawks, the team came to Columbia without long underwear, stockings, and gloves. As a result, Kansas fumbled the ball eight times while a well equipped Missouri team won the game 20-6, with two-way player Ed Stephens, of Joplin, Missouri, scoring two touchdowns and rushing for 122 yards.

In 1951 freshmen were made available to both teams because of the outbreak of the Korean War and Kansas won the game as expected, 41-28. Also, in 1951, the game between Missouri and Kansas moved permanently to Saturday, instead of Thanksgiving Day. In previous years, the game had been held on Saturday for various reasons, but in the 1940s, the game was always held on Saturday when the game was played at Missouri, so that the school could execute a homecoming celebration. Holding the game on Thanksgiving Day greatly minimized attendance because many families wanted to stay home; and so it was that the oldest Thanksgiving Day game west of the Mississippi River ended.

In 1953, Jules Sikes ended his six year career at Kansas, after a 2-8 season and a 32-25 overall record. For his series against Missouri, however, he only had one victory. Taking charge of the Jayhawks was a high school football coach named Charles V. "Chuck" Mather. Although his first year of coaching high school football in 1937 he posted a 0-7 record, his last 13 years before taking the Kansas job his record was 57-3 with six consecutive high school state football championships in Ohio. With his installation as head coach, Mather changed the red Kansas jerseys to blue and the players wore yellow helmets so that receivers could

be easier spotted and also the Kansas bench was moved to the west side of Memorial Stadium with a television being installed on the sidelines to give an aerial view of the game to the Kansas coaches. The most sensational change, however, seemed to be the use of corporate giant International Business Machines (IBM) Corporation to grade player efficiency on a per play basis, which seemed quite extraordinary at that time. The player grading was so extensive that the coaching staff reviewed movies of the game after its conclusion and gave grades to each player for each play in which he participated based, for example, on stance, moving with the ball, approach to a block, and blocking down field.

Two years after Mather joined Kansas, Don Faurot's career as head coach of the Missouri Tigers ended due to pressure concerning his policy of recruiting mostly Missouri players. The policy, while sound during the depression and post-war years, was now outdated as America was becoming a more mobile society and many felt that Missouri needed to commit itself better to recruiting talent beyond its borders for football as a result. Faurot would not leave the University, however, as he was to be elevated to the role of athletic director, where he would serve for the next nine years. The last game of his career, before a homecoming crowd of 28,000 at Rollins Field, seemed destined to end his career with a 13-13 tie against Kansas until the final minutes of the game. With just over a minute left, Kansas lost 16 yards on an attempted pass play by Wally Strauch. Despite the lost yardage, there seemed no way for the team to score with Kansas in possession of the ball. Kansas' coach, Chuck Mather, mistook the distance and thought his team was on the 9-yard line instead of the 4-yard line. As a result, Mather called for a reverse play from Strauch to Bobby Robinson, which he would never had done that close to the goal line had he not mistook the distance. Missouri's left tackle, Chuck Mehrer, read the play, barrelled through the line, tackling Robinson in the end zone for a 2-point safety and winning the game for Missouri and Coach Don Faurot. The Tigers carried Faurot and the goalposts from the field amidst a standing ovation.

Ed Harvey

The first black player to play on either team and in the Border War Game was Ed Harvey, who played for Kansas in the 1893 game. Harvey's parents were born enslaved and were living in Lawrence, Kansas during Quantrill's raid. It took another 62 years for another black player to join the Jayhawks. In 1955, Homer Floyd joined the team, starting in all of his games from 1955-

YOUR TURKEY DAY AND EAT IT, TOO.

Homer Floyd

1958. Floyd came to Kansas at the urging of his former high school coach at Massillon High School in Ohio; Chuck Mather. At Massillon, Floyd was a prolific player. He led the Jayhawks in rushing in 1956, 1957, and 1958 and was team captain in 1958.

A year after the Brown versus Topeka Board of Education case was decided by the Supreme Court; Missouri had its first two black athletes join the team on scholarship who were recruited by Frank Broyles, who had come to the Tigers from the Georgia Institute of Technology (Georgia Tech), where he was an assistant coach. The players, Norris Stevenson, from Saint Louis, and Mel West, of Jefferson City, joined the team with little controversy from players, faculty, and fans alike, according to former Missouri player and assistant coach Hank Kuhlmann. Although Frank Broyles recruited Stevenson and West, he did not have an opportunity to coach them as Broyles left Missouri three weeks after the 1957 Border War Game ended in a 9-7 victory for Kansas. Broyles left Missouri to coach for the University of Arkansas, where he enjoyed a long and successful career, causing Don Faurot to hire a coach that he had previously considered for the position but did not hire because he still had a year remaining on his contract; Dan Devine. In Kansas, Chuck Mather, despite all of the innovations that he introduced, was unable to produce enough wins to keep his job and was released on Thanksgiving Day, 1957, with a record of 11-26-3. Replacing Chuck Mather was Jack Mitchell, who was a former All-American quarterback with Oklahoma University and was coaching at Arkansas where his three-year record there was 17-12-1.

Missouri's new coach, Dan Devine was born December 22, 1924 in Augusta, Wisconsin. In his thirteen seasons with the University of Missouri, he became the winningest football coach in that school's history. His first season coaching the Tigers produced the same season record as Boyles team had the previous year, 5-4-1, and the Border War Game ended in a 13-13 tie. However, by his second year as head coach, Devine brought the

Tigers a 6-5 record and a 13-9 victory over Kansas. The game that year was a wonderful exhibition as future professional star quarterback, Kansas' John Hadl, playing at halfback, brought the football to Missouri's 1-yard line on a fourth down, with Missouri ahead in the game 13-7. With four minutes left to play and with the football on its 1-yard line, Missouri ran through three plays before assistant coach Harry Smith suggested to Devine that they give Kansas a 2-point safety to secure their lead. On the fourth down the Missouri punter stepped behind the end zone giving Kansas the 2-point safety. The punt from Missouri went to Kansas' Hadl, who was able to run seven yards to the Kansas 41-yard line. Kansas was able to advance the ball to the Missouri 34-yard line before having the ball stripped with only 71 seconds left to play. The 13-9 Missouri victory gave them a bid to the Orange Bowl, losing that game. However, the team was destined to return to the Orange Bowl the next year after the most controversial game in the history of football between Missouri and Kansas.

Norris Stevenson (left) and Mel West (right)

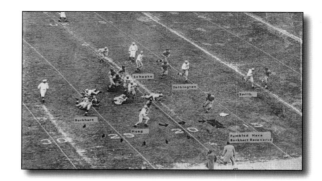

Missouri Football (4-5-1) - Head Coach Donald Burrowes Faurot

Kansas Football (6-4) - Head Coach Jules Verne Sikes

(Unordered) Rodgers, Smith, Murphy, Stroud, Steanson, Lamping, Tice, Roberts, Schaben, Wenger, Unruh, Rinehart, Winter, Mayer, Piss, Hannel, Schaake, Abel, Clement, Laughlan, Cox, Austin, Unruh, Hoag, Garnett, Spencer, McMullen, Frasier, Simons, Linville, Talkington, White, Luschen, Wells, Rengel, Co-captain McCormack, Mace, Sandefur, Nelson, Co-captain Amberg, Pierson, Huber, Stinson, Correll, Kennard.

Missouri Football (3-7) - Head Coach Donald Burrowes Faurot

Kansas Football (8-2) - Head Coach Jules Verne Sikes

Missouri Football (5-5) - Head Coach Donald Burrowes Faurot
Row 1: Fitzgerald, Fessler, Burkhart, Lordo, Hook, Merrifield, Follin, Willson, Borgschulte, Fuchs, Schoonmaker, Wilkening. Row 2: Rowekamp, Udell, Scardino, Stein, Rutter, Phillips, Bull, Carras, Androlewicz, Rose, Piskulich, Goodwin, Brown. Row 3: Buhr, Ekern, Martin, McMichael, Gellman, Gillham, Makin, Aaron, Ard, Hurley, Swetnam, Jennings. Row 4: Coach Faurot, Brase, Hennessey, Heyl, Tanner, Roberts, Bauman, Ekern, Eaton, Wilinson, Fox, Burson, Stefanides, Hanners.

Kansas Football (7-3) - Head Coach Jules Verne Sikes

Missouri Football (2-8) - Head Coach Donald Burrowes Faurot

Row 1: Jennings, Bull, Bauman, Hanners, Rose, Phillips, McMichael, Follin, Roberts, Eaton, Stefanides, Corpeny. Row 2: Tanner, Kroenke, Scardino, Hurley, Piskulich, Thomeczek, Brown, Schoonmaker, Stein, Boyd, Merrifield, Willson. Row 3: Salmons, Gentry, Swetnam, Schoonmaker, Gillham, Douglass, Shively, Brase, Fox, Makin, Ekern, Burson. Row 4: Smith, Fischer, Milne, Pirch.

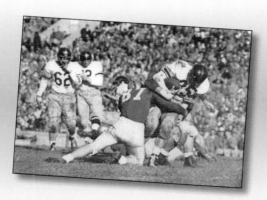

Kansas Football (6-4) - Head Coach Jules Verne Sikes

95

Missouri Football (4-5-1) - Head Coach Donald Burrowes Faurot

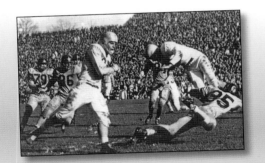

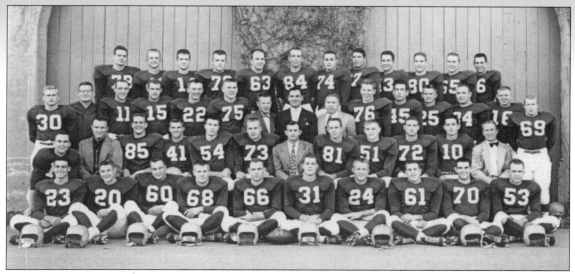

Kansas Football (0-10) - Head Coach Charles V. Mather

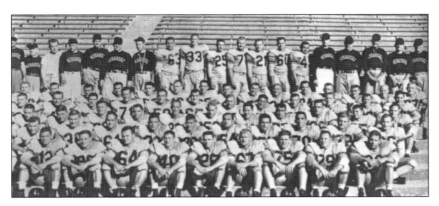

Missouri Football (1-9) - Head Coach Donald Burrowes Faurot

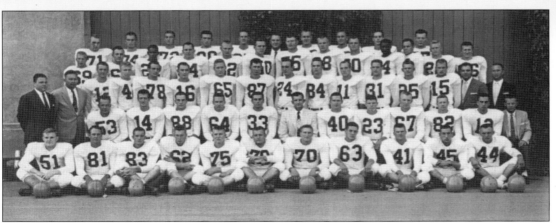

Kansas Football (3-6-1) - Head Coach Charles V. Mather

Missouri Football (4-5-1) - Head Coach Donald Burrowes Faurot

Row 1: Schulz, Mehrer, Stringer, Rice, Roll, Hunter, Doane, Martin, Curtwright, Stuber, Wynn, Browning, Barrickman, Lee, Plumb. Row 2: Lineberry, Cramer, Pidcock, Galamba, St. Pierre, James, Kuhlmann, Clemenson, Griep, McKinney, Craig, Hopkins, Osterlob, Czapla, Worstell. Row 3: Wright, C. Steinmetz, L. Steinmetz, Hammer, Fisher, Toney, Sharp, C. Johnson, Stout, Loudon, Anderson, Rash, L. Hall, Isset. Row 4: Chadwick, M. Johnson, Alburtis, Morrell, Jensen, Kramer, Tlapek, Boucher, Hessing, Bucke, C. Hall, Lathrop, Turner, Mason. Row 5: Sweeny, Slaughter, Field, Sweeny, Brown, Stoner, Hansen, Kelly, Wilkinson, Poorman, Henger, Hicks, Mahiger. Row 6: Trainer De Victor, Coach Cooper, Coach Schlosser, Manager Beagler, Manager Mercer, Coach Jennings, Coach Simmons, Coach Beatty, Coach Kadlec, Coach Smith, Trainer Wappel, Coach Faurot.

Kansas Football (3-6-1) - Head Coach Charles V. Mather

Missouri Football (5-4-1) - Head Coach John Franklin Broyles

Row 1: McKinney, Fischer, Alburtis, Plumb, Lee, Johnson, Clemensen, Hopkins, Worstell, Griep, Cramer, Jensen, Anderson. Row 2: Hessing, Curtright, Kuhlmann, St. Pierre, Kramer, Haas, Pidcock, Henger, Loudon, Stoner, Slaughter, Rash, Boucher. Row 3: Snowden, Chadwick, Starr, Cook, McCoy, Mucke, Swaney, Feind, Kirkpatrick, Mackey, Sloan, Kelley, Rice, Meyers. Row 4: Grossman, Whetstine, Mahiger, Brinkman, Holland, James, Shaffer, Cameron, Vanderlinde, Jordan, Rya, Rittman, Magac, Mason. Row 5: Beadles, Comfort, Hodge, Stock, Poorman, Taylor, Kohler, Murray, McGinnis, Humphrey.

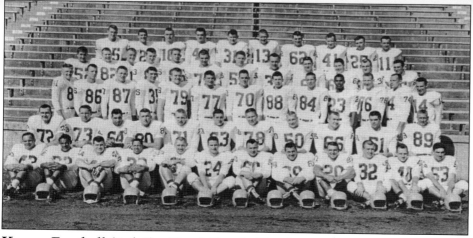

Kansas Football (5-4-1) - Head Coach Charles V. Mather

Missouri Football (5-4-1) - Head Coach Daniel John Devine

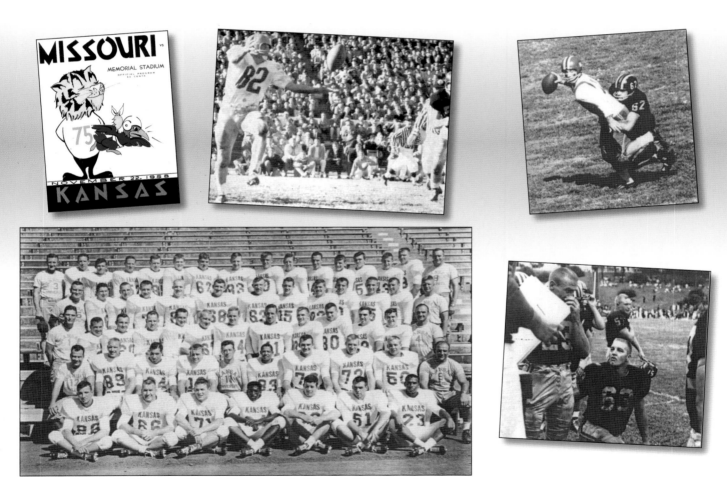

Kansas Football (4-5-1) - Head Coach Jack Churchill Mitchell

Missouri Football (6-5) - Head Coach Daniel John Devine
Orange Bowl Invitation

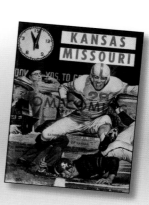

Kansas Football (5-5) - Head Coach Jack Churchill Mitchell

ROCK CHALK, JAYHAWK, KU

In the fall of 1891, Kansas University fielded its first football team. This new sport was enthusiastically received by the students, but the cheering which rang from the south stands of the field was highly unorganized. KU did have a yell though. It was the Rock Chalk yell which some members of the Biology Club had devised five years earlier. The form of the Rock Chalk was kicked around a lot in the '90's varying from a staccato "Rah, Rah, Jayhawk, KSU," to an elaborate:

> "Mush and milk and sunflower seed,
> That's the stuff on which we feed.
> We're the hot stuff of creation,
> We're the Kansas aggregation.
> Jack take a bit.
> Jill take a chew.
> Rock Chalk, Jayhawk, KSU."

By 1909, KU cheerleaders had appeared on the scene and were directing the efforts of the "thundering thousand" at Mc-Cook Field.

Although the cheerleaders are the most spectacular part of the pep organizations, their history is obscure. A Ralph Spotts is mentioned in 1910 newspapers as being the cheerleader. Probably he was chosen shortly before this time. A good guess would be that he was elected at a pep assembly of the students either during or a year after the all-victorious 1908 football season. It was Spotts who coined the phrase, "thundering thousand," which was used for many years to characterize the KU fans. He also led a booster's club among the students. However, this club died after Spotts was graduated.

1956 Kansas cheerleaders

The next step in the evolution of the pep organization took place in 1919. That year two students, C. C. Carl and Bob Rowland by name, put on a medicine show as a pep rally before the Missouri game, the second Homecoming. "Doc Yak," their medicine man, stayed on the

1956 Kansas Jay Janes

campus only a few years, but another idea of these two has been a lasting one.

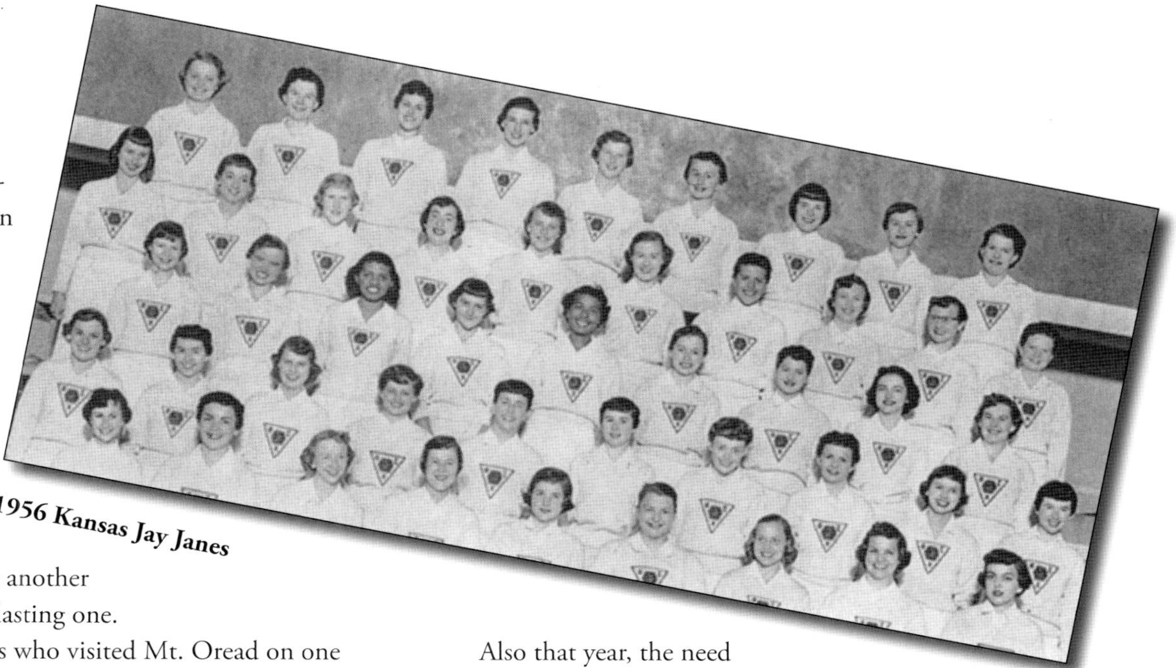

With the Oklahoma fans who visited Mt. Oread on one October Saturday, a few weeks before the Missouri tilt, was a pep club known as the "Razzers." Carl and Roland were impressed by this organization and decided that Kansas should have a similar one. They spread their idea so well that one hundred men met a few days before homecoming to organize a pep club and prepare some half-time stunts for the game. When the game started, the members of this newly formed Ku Ku Klan were very noticeable in their white shirts, red sashes, and blue turbans. However, they had chosen a name too similar to the Ku Klux Klan. No matter how many stunts they put on at the games or how much time they spent selling concessions to provide fruit for the team, they were at first classified as trouble-makers.

The name of the group had been shortened to Ku Ku's by 1923 when it became the first chapter of a national honorary fraternity of pep clubs, Pi Epsilon Pi.

Also that year, the need for a women's cheering organization was fulfilled. A few students met in the basement of the Theta house in November of 1923 to found the Jay Janes. The club made its first appearance on the Wednesday night before the Homecoming game with Missouri. On that evening the fifty-two character members of the Jay Janes took part in a torchlight parade while wearing a costume similar to their present one. Then, as now, they took part in many campus service projects in addition to their enthusiastic support of the school teams. The Jay Janes helped found a national organization similar to that to which the Ku Ku's belong. They were among the charter members when Phi Sigma Chi was begun in 1933.

The cheering sections of these two clubs were combined in 1925. The Rock Chalk yell had been developed into its present chanting Form by this time, but other suitable cheers were scarce. The Jay Janes sponsored a contest among the KU students in 1927 to correct this situation. The three best cheers submitted to the contest were selected for use at games.

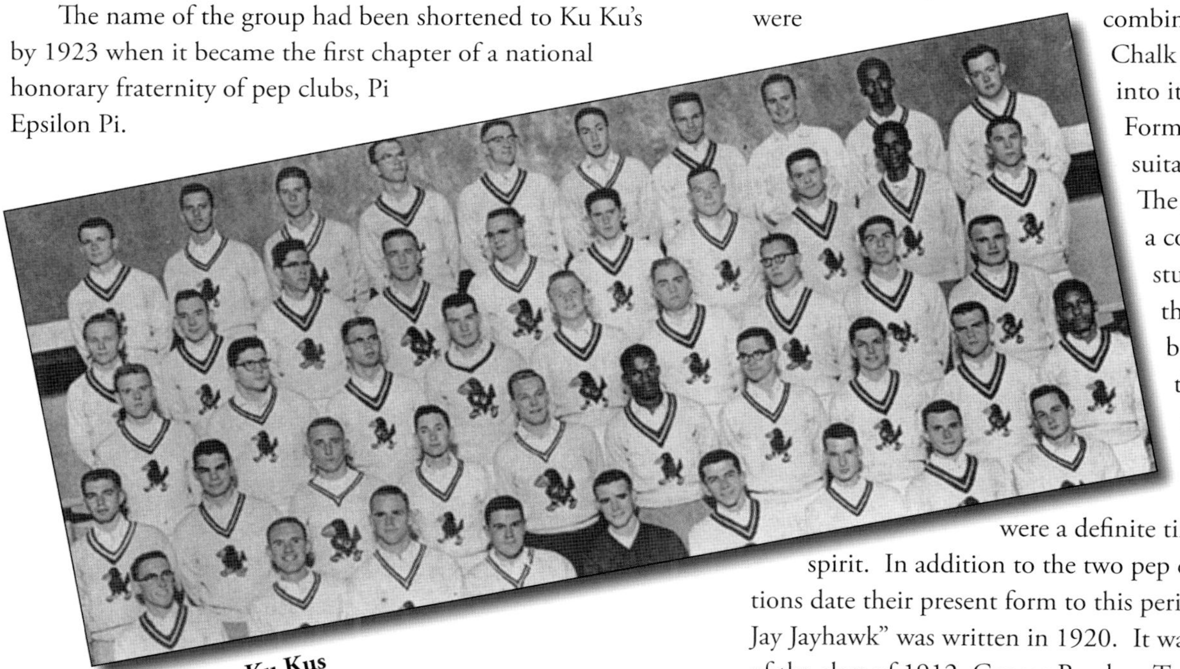

These first few years of the twenties were a definite time of re-birth of school spirit. In addition to the two pep clubs, a couple of traditions date their present form to this period. The fight song "Jay Jay Jayhawk" was written in 1920. It was written by a graduate of the class of 1912, George Bowles. Two years later, a couple of

1956 Kansas Ku Kus

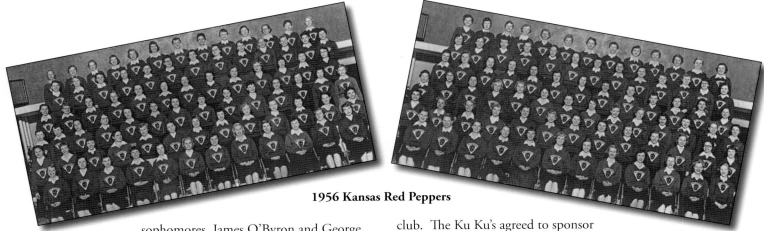

1956 Kansas Red Peppers

sophomores, James O'Byron and George Hollingbery, designed the ancestor of the present-day Jayhawk.

KU had acquired the name Jayhawk from the free-soil border fighters of the 1850s and 1860s. A series of legends about he mythical bird, terming it "half jay and half hawk," had been begun. It was supposed to be invisible except for special occasions such as Coronado's visit to Kansas or the game with the Missouri Tigers. However, no one was certain what its true appearance was when it was visible. The bird had changed shape as fast as artists were graduated from KU. When the Nebraska game approached in 1922, the students planned a caravan of cars to carry them to Lincoln. "Show them you're Jayhawks, even if you have to pain it on your windshields," one cheerleader exhorted. This is just what O'Byron and Hollingbery did. They designed a figure which was not as comical as its predecessors had been and which displayed the confidence and power that the creators envisioned the school symbol. Since the time that these two painted Jayhawks on windshields, the Jayhawk has undergone several refinements, non of which were so drastic as the one in 1922. For the next twenty years no great change took place in the organization or activities of the KU pep clubs. In 1947, pressure arose for a freshman men's pep club. The Ku Ku's agreed to sponsor such an organization. A freshman cap, one red and one blue sock, and either a red or a blue sweater were the early attire of a Froshawk member.

With the Missouri game approaching again in November of 1949, the Jay Janes undertook to organize the freshmen women into their own pep club. The freshmen had previously been allowed a small representation in the Jay Janes, but there were far more freshmen than the Jay Janes could take within their club. By Homecoming, the Red Peppers were ready to make their appearance in the cheering section. Red sweaters and blue skirts have been standard dress for them from the first.

Throughout the history of Kansas University athletics, other organizations have helped create school spirit. For instance, Sachem has charge of the tom-tom which symbolizes victory in the KU-MU tilt. This society kept the gilded football before the tom-tom and was instrumental in building the Rock Chalk Cairn. However, these four clubs, Ku Ku's, Jay Janes, Froshawks, and Red Peppers, have served under the leadership of the ever-present cheerleaders as a nucleus for KU rallies and cheering.

By Park McGee
Kansas Alumnus 1956
Written for the 1956 Jayhawker Yearbook

1956 Kansas Froshawks

THE COACH BOWS OUT

Head Kansas football coach Jules Verne Sikes resigned that post November 21 just after the KU-MU Homecoming football game.

Sikes, coach here since 1948, announced his departure in the dressing room shortly after the final game of the season, and said, "This is a fine University. I have made many friends in my stay here and have enjoyed the six years."

The day before the resignation was made public, Sikes was given a new automobile and a $500 check by fathers, sponsors, and friends of the football players "in appreciation for his efforts in six years at KU."

To newsmen gathered in the coaches' private dressing room, Sikes handed a typewritten statement which said:

"I have written Dr. Franklin Murphy, chancellor of the University, resigning my position as head football coach, University of Kansas.

"I would like to take this opportunity to thank the members of the University staff, the faculty, the student body the alumni, and friends of the University for their splendid cooperation and their many contributions to the success of our football program here. I urge all our friends to continue their support of the University of Kansas.

"I am especially grateful to the boys on this year's squad. They have given their best under very trying circumstances. I am proud to have been their coach.

"We have had many splendid victories here, and of course, some disappointing defeats, but on the whole our life here has been a happy one. Evelyn (Mrs. Sikes) and I will be sorry to leave the many friends we have made during our stay in Kansas."

In reply, Chancellor Murphy said:

"In accepting the resignation of Mr. Sikes, we are grateful for the six years of untiring service which he has given to the University of Kansas. He leaves KU with the best wishes of the University family and with our feeling of appreciation for his technical skill as manifested by the over-all record of his teams."

Sikes, 48, coached the Jayhawkers to 35 victories and 25 defeats. The contract he had signed in 1951 was to expire March 1, 1954.

By Stan Hamilton
Kansas Alumnus 1955
Written for the 1954 Jayhawker *Yearbook*

REFLECTIONS FROM A PLAYER, GRADUATE ASSISTANT, AND COACH

I was an eye-witness to the Missouri-Kansas football rivalry for 16 out of 17 seasons, from 1955-1971, as either a player, graduate assistant, or coach. I grew up in the St. Louis area, so as a young player at Mizzou I didn't realize how intense the rivalry was for the people living in the Kansas City area, because of constant interaction between the Missouri and Kansas alumni for bragging rights.

My high school coach was Ray Moss, the captain of the 1938 Missouri football team. He was a great influence on my going into football coaching because of his approach to the game and his sportsmanship. My high school team was

Football Greats, Past and Present - Al Lincoln (left), legendary Webster Groves and Missouri footballer, hands Hank Kuhlmann (right), also of both schools, the Charles A. Roberts Memorial Award as the year's outstanding high school athlete in 1955.

undefeated in 1954 and the four backfield players on that team, Glenn St. Pierre, Joe Heimlicher, Charley James, and me, went to Missouri on football scholarships. Our high school team captain, Olin Lippincott, also played freshman football with us at Missouri. We were recruited to play at Missouri by another Webster Groves High School and 1940s Missouri football player, Jack Frier.

By my senior year I was fully aware of the rivalry between Missouri and Kansas and as a coach I knew it was a necessity to beat Kansas. As a freshman coach, I watched Tom Fletcher, the varsity backfield coach, break down film of all the Kansas games

of the current season. Usually, only the previous three games of the opponent were studied, impressing on me the need to beat Kansas especially. In those years, the game against Kansas was always the last game of the season and one of the most important.

Some of the memorable games during my time at Missouri were; late in the game in 1956, Chuck Mehrer tackled a Kansas back in the end zone for a safety resulting in a Mizzou win 15-13. This was Don Faurot's last year of coaching and a fitting end to his career. In 1960, Missouri was ranked #1 in the nation going into the Kansas game. Mizzou lost 23-7 and, of course, lost the #1 ranking. I was in the service at Ft. Leonard Wood that year, and this was the only game I was able to attend that season. What a heart breaker! In the first quarter of 1963, Kansas was on the 2-yard line and Ken Coleman, back, fumbled the ball in the end zone to our defensive back, Vince Turner. Vince ran 103 yards for a Mizzou touchdown. The extra point was missed, but Missouri won 9-7 on a 22 yard field goal by Bill Leistritz in the last quarter. In 1969, Mizzou was victorious in Lawrence, 69-21, with 651 yards total offense. Our first seven possessions were scores.

As a coach I was more aware of how important beating Kansas was to the alumni. Losing to Kansas very often could cost a coach his job. Fortunately, I served as an assistant under Dan Devine, the winningest coach in Missouri's history.

By Henry N. Kuhlmann, Junior
Missouri Alumnus 1959
Missouri Assistant Coach 1966-1970
Written Wednesday, August 13, 2008

Hank Kuhlmann (23) running from Jayhawk pursuers in 1956

MATHER MOVES IN

Charles V. Mather assumed his first coaching position at Brilliant, Ohio, in 1937, where the high school grid squad presented him with a 0-won 7-lost season's record. In his next 13 years of prep coaching, at three other Ohio schools, Chuck Mather won 111, dropped 11, and tied 5. His past 6 years have been spent at Washington high in Massillon, where Mather's record reads 57-won, 3-lost, and six consecutive state championships.

When football coach Charles V. "Chuck" Mather took over last spring, most people expected a great many changes in KU football. These people have not been disappointed. Although the season has produced no victories so far this year, Coach Mather has initiated many new policies. The "Big Red" team sported new blue jerseys with yellow helmets to provide for better spotting of pass receivers. The players' bench was moved to the west side of Memorial stadium. A television was installed on the sidelines to give an aerial view of the game to the coaching staff. Players on the bench wore Frank Buck sun helmets to combat the heat. The list seems endless. However, the most famous innovation Mather has started is the use of IBM for the grading of with his I.B.M. paraphernalia player efficiency. This system appears very complicated, but at a closer look, it is revealed as merely a simple method of figuring statistics. After each game, movies of the game are studied by the coaching staff, and each player is given a grade for every play in which he participates. For example, on downfield blocking, players are graded on stance, moving with the ball, approach to the block, position of the block, and follow through. Thus, only one-fifth of the rating depends on the opposition.

The players' scores on each play are fed into the IBM, and averages are computed. With these averages, Mather and his assistants can determine the most effective players in each phase of the game.

A common problem of college football today is the feeling that the team is playing not for the students, but for the administration and the alumni of the University. To combat this, Coach Mather has instituted a student "quarterback club" which meets every Tuesday night in the Student Union ballroom. Mather shows the movies of the previous week's game and comments on the pictures. At the end of each session there is a question-and-answer period when students are invited to ask about any phase of the team or its coaching staff.

Coach Mather has impressed many persons with the thoroughness of his coaching technique. The coaching staff leaves no stone unturned in their effort to achieve perfection. The attitude of Mather and his staff can be well summed by the motto found on the wall of the football office, which reads, "It takes work to be good, and if we are not good, we have no one to blame but ourselves."

By Betty Lou Watson and Dick K. Walt
Kansas Alumna 1957 and Kansas Alumnus 1955
Written for the 1955 Jayhawker *Yearbook*

THE JAYHAWKER AND THE SAVITAR

JAYHAWKER 1951 – BORDER WAR 1950

The Jayhawkers, who had gone two complete games without fumbling, suddenly developed a violent aversion to the football in the Columbia, Mo., cold and eight times gave the ice-plated pigskin over to Missouri.

Considering that the Jayhawkers only had the ball 13 times, this put a terrific crimp in their scoring power, and they lost, 6 to 20. The Thanksgiving day debacle closed the K. U. season with a record of six victories and four defeats. It was Kansas' third straight loss to Missouri.

During the year the Jayhawkers broke three school offensive marks for a single season-total yards, yards rushing, and first downs.

When Kansas had the ball, it had no great difficulty in ripping through the Tiger line for short gains,. The Jayhawkers averaged only a fraction less yardage than Missouri for each play. Charlie Hoag and Wade Stinson each gained 102 yards rushing, but each fumbled the frigid football over to Missouri three times. Jack Luschen and Dean Wells also fumbled the ball to the Tigers.

The Tigers, much warmer than the 17-degree weather, drove 65 yards to score after receiving the opening kickoff. Ed Stephens scored on a 10-yard run around end. It was only the beginning of a great day for Stephens. He gained 122 yards, scored two touchdowns, and recovered four fumbles.

Kansas then drove to the Missouri 12-yard line where Hoag fumbled and a Tiger recovered. ON the firs M. U. play, Phil Klein's pitchout was wild and Aubrey Linville recovered for Kansas on the three-yard line. It was the first of only two Missouri fumbles. Stinson knifed through tackle on first downs to score his 14th touchdown of the season-a new K. U. record. Fox Cashell missed the extra point attempt and Kansas trailed, 6 to 7.

The rest of the game was a nightmare for the Jayhawkers. They fumbled on the M. U. 12, M. U. 7, M. U. 23, K. U. 10, K. U. 12 (Missouri scored), M. U. 30 (Missouri scored), M. U. 3, and M. U. 45.

Midway in the second quarter, the Kansas line put on a great defensive display. It held the Tigers for downs on the K. U. seven. Hoag then fumbled on the first play, but K. U. again held for downs. The ball was stolen from Hoag two plays later, and Missouri finally was able to punch across to score. In this span, Missouri had 11 cracks at the K. U. line from inside the 15-yard line before scoring.

Bill Houston scored the second-quarter Tiger touchdown to give his team a 13 to 6 halftime lead. Stephens scored the final touchdown from two yards out.

SAVITAR 1951 – BORDER WAR 1950

Missouri 7 6 7 0 – 20
Kansas   6 0 0 0 – 6

PRESS CLIPPINGS WENT UNHEEDED when the Missouri Tigers smacked favored Kansas, 20-6, before the Homecoming crowd, to "make" the season. The Tigers played a furious defensive game, forcing the Jayhawkers to fumble 9 times and recovering 8 of these! Blocking and tackling were as crisp as the 14-degree weather.

MIZZOU OUTPLAYED K.U. in all departments to take third place in the Conference. Ed Stephens led Mizzou's offense and recovered four Kansas fumbles to take individual honors.

SAVITAR 1952 – BORDER WAR 1951

The outlook was even less bright when the Tigers left for Lawrence and Kansas' mighty Jayhawks. Scardino and Eaton were out and Cox was not to finish the first half.

Kansas recovered two Bengal fumbles and scored twice before Missouri made their first move. Cox brought the Tigers to the Kansas 21 before leaving the field. Hook, for the first time, went into the deep position in the "spread."

1950S

His second toss went to Fessler in the end zone and each team scored again before the half. Trailing 28-14, Missouri matched Kansas score for score in a wild final period. Hook had a hand in both Tiger touchdowns to cap a fine performance. The final: Kansas 41, Missouri 28.

JAYHAWKER 1953 – BORDER WAR 1952

In their final game and their final bid for high honors in the Big Seven for the season the Jayhawks lost a heartbreaker to Missouri 20-19.

Kansas scored first on a beautifully executed play beginning with a pass from Robertson to Reich who then lateraled off to Brandeberry for the tally. Mizzou countered with an 82 yard run by Bill Rowekamp and led 7 to 6. Another second period score gave them a 14-6 halftime advantage.

In the second half Robertson put his shoulder to the grindstone and guided the Hawks to two touchdowns. One he carried across himself on a sneak, and for the other he passed 52 yards to Jerry Taylor to register the points. Reich was able to convert only once. Kansas held this 19-14 lead until the fourth quarter when a deflected KU aerial fell into unfriendly hands and resulted in the winning score.

In those final moments the Jayhawks fought back and drove deep into Missouri territory, but they were unable to gain those needed points.

SAVITAR 1953 – BORDER WAR 1952

COLUMBIA, Nov. 22, 1952–Missouri, the team that was picked for no better than fifth place in the 1952 Big Seven conference race, today nailed down the league's No. 2 spot with a hair-raising 20-119 win over arch-rival Kansas.

Oklahoma, as per usual, won the title, its fifth in a row, by swamping Nebraska, 34-13, at Norman.

Missouri fought from behind twice during the course of the game. K. U. broke on top 6-0 early in the game on Bob Brandeberry's score, but late in the second quarter Mizzou had forged a 14-6 lead on the strength of Bill Rowekamp's 82-yard scamper and Nick Carras' off-tackle smash late in the same quarter. Paul Fuchs added the vital P.A.T.'s.

Kansas roared back into the lead with two third-quarter scores, the first on Jerry Robertson's one-yard quarterback sneak and the second on a 53-yard pass play, Robertson to Jerry Taylor.

But Coach Don Faurot's gritty Tigers wrapped up this finest win of 1952 on Tony Scardino's one-yard swing around right end late in the game.

JAYHAWKER 1954 – BORDER WAR 1953

After the many setbacks and disappointments of the year, one might have expected the Jayhawkers to fold completely in their Homecoming game with Missouri, but the Kansans did far from that.

In fact, they played probably their finest game, even though heavily outmanned by an improved Tiger squad. A lat-minute Jayhawker touchdown followed by a wild free-for-all slugging match in the middle of the field brought an exciting climax to the year, if not a successful one.

The Tigers pushed over a second quarter touchdown, added the conversion, and tallied a fourth period field goal from the KU 11, while KU scored with 21 seconds left on a 52-yard pass.

SAVITAR 1954 – BORDER WAR 1953

LAWRENCE, Nov. 21 – Ol' Mizzou surged past ancient rival Kansas, 10-6, here this afternoon to nail a share of second place in the final Big Seven standings. Two senior backfielders, halfbacks Bob Schoonmaker and "Skimp" Merrifield, led Coach Don Faurot's club to victory in another link of the oldest collegiate rivalry west of the Mississippi. Schoony completed two passes, both to Jack Fox, to carry the pigskin to the K. U. two from Mizzou's 47. The Lebanon senior plowed over from there for M. U.'s first touchdown in the second period. Merrifield booted the extra point. The Tigers added their final three points on Merrifield's field goal in the fourth period. With the game in its final 25 seconds, the Jayhawks scored their lone touchdown on a long pass, but with the play came a skirmish on the Kansas side of the field which developed into a free-for-all. After the brawl the clubs played out the clock. The loss left Kansas 2-8 for the year and the victory gave Missouri a 6-4 mark, its best record since 1949.

JAYHAWKER 1955 – BORDER WAR 1954

[There was no mention of the game. Missouri won 41-18.]

SAVITAR 1955 – BORDER WAR 1954

Missouri romped easily to their highest score of the season with a 41-18 triumph over a winless Kansas team, thereby balancing the long-standing rivalry at 28 games apiece. Even with the 21 points the Tigers rolled up in the first half, the majority of the play before a Homecoming crowd was a slow-moving and haphazard. In the second half, however the tempo increased when both teams resorted to frenzied offense to score three times each. Three quick Kansas tallies closed the Tiger advantage to 34-18 and Coach Don Faurot was forced to send his regulars back into action. They took the situation in hand, adding the final marker on a 10-yard pass from Vic Eaton to Jim Hunter. The one-sided contest went into the record books as Missouri's best performance to date in the 1954 season. The Tigers racked up 485 total yards, 312 of them on the ground. Eaton retained his Big 7 passing leadership, adding 100 yards, and Harold Burnine kept his receiving record alive with three grabs for 114 yards.

The Kansas trouncing put a happy ending on the week-long festivities of Homecoming, and optimism ran high for the Tigers who were to face staunch competition the following Thursday at Maryland. The Missouri eleven coasted to a 34-0 third quarter lead before the Jayhawks showed any signs of evening the count. John Anderson led a bruising attack for the Kansas comeback, but despite three straight touchdowns, Missouri seemed undisturbed by the uprising. The Bengal fist string returned to set the hapless visitors fat into the background. The win threw the Tigers into a two-way tie with Colorado for third place in the Big Seven race.

JAYHAWKER 1956 – BORDER WAR 1955

UNCLE CHUCK BAGS HIMSELF A TIGER

THE JAYHAWKS delighted a homecoming crowd of 30,000 by containing Missouri's offense and out-charging the vaunted Tiger line to pick up a 13-7 victory in the final game of the season. Again it was reserve quarterback Dave Preston who sparked the Jayhawk victory, as he connected with end Lynn McCarthy for the winning touchdown late in the third quarter. Kansas took the opening kickoff and marched 85 yards for a touchdown, with a pass from Wally Strauch to John Francisco covering the final 15 yards. Handley booted the extra point. The drive was featured by the running of Dick Reich and the pass receiving of end Paul Smith. The Tigers retaliated in the second quarter with quarterback Jim Hunter, progably the outstanding player ont he field, sneaking over from the one. After KU bounced back to take the lead in the third quarte, the Jayhawk defense stopped two Missouri drives inside the KU 20 in the last quarter.

SAVITAR 1956 – BORDER WAR 1955

It was just one of those seasons

For the first time in twenty years, Missouri has ended up in last place. Kansas University, arch enemy of the Tigers, kicked them down into the cellar with a 13 to 7 victory. Coach Don Faurot summed up his worst season in twenty-six years of coaching football by saying "Our boys tried hard all season, but we couldn't click in the clutches." It was a disappointing season, both for the team and the fans, as far as the scoreboard was concerned. It was not disappointing as an athletic contest. Each game was worth watching, and when we made the long walk to Memorial Stadium on Saturday afternoon, we saw the Tigers go against some of the nation's top teams. And we were confident that the team never stopped playing until the final whistle.

JAYHAWKER 1957 – BORDER WAR 1956

kansas 13 - missouri 15

MISSOURI TACKLE Chuck Mehrer smeared KU halfback Bobby Robinson in the KU end zone with 39 seconds left in the game to give Missouri coach Don Faurot a 15-13 win in his last game as coach of the Tigers. KU's Wally Strauch threw touchdown passes to Charlie McCue and Jim Letcavits to give the Jayhawkers a pair of leads-6-0 and 13-7-but the Tigers kept battling back. Missouri finally tied the score with 3:12 left in the game on a 11-yard pass from Dave Doane to Larry Plumb. KU appeared to have the tie clinched with a first down on its own 20 with a little over a minute left to play, but Strauch lost 16 yards attempting to pass, and Mehrer caught Robinson in the end zone on the next play. Seven KU players saw the alst action of their careers in this game. They were Jon Drake, Frank Black, Don Pfutzenreuter, Ted Rohde, Don Martin, Galen Wahlmeier, and Bill Bell.

SAVITAR 1957 – BORDER WAR 1956

The Homecoming game of 1956 will never be forgotten by Missouri football fans. This was Don Faurot's last game as head coach of the Missouri football team. This was the last game for Hunter, Doane, Rice Stringer, Morrell, Stuber, Roll, Craig, Mehrer, Osterloh, Shulz, Martin, Barrickman, Browning, McMichael, and Hammer. This was the game in which 225-pound [102 kilograms] Chuck Meherer, with 39 seconds remaining, grabbed a Kansas back and wrestled him to the ground in the Jayhawk's end zone for a safety that won the game. As the gun sounded ending the game fans poured out on the field and surrounded the Tiger squad. Faurot and Mehrer were lifted onto the shoulders of the other players and carried across the field where the Kansas coach congratulated them on their victory. The victory for the Black and Gold evened the Kansas-Missouri grid series and provided a climactic touch to Don Faurot's coaching career at Missouri.

SAVITAR 1958 – BORDER WAR 1957

Ray Barnes, a 27-year-old sophomore halfback from Tacoma, Wash., placekicked a 14-yard field goal with 48 seconds left to give Kansas a 9-7 victory over the Tigers at Lawrence. This ended a determined Jayhawk drive against the clock. First it appeared that the Tigers just about had the game seed up. Heavy-duty Hank Kuhlmann scored late in the first quarter after halfback George Cramer had returned a punt 49 yards. Charlie Rash added the extra point–his twentieth of the season. The Jayhawks had scored swiftly in the game's first five minutes when Homer Floyd, junior halfback, broke off right tackle, cut to the nearby right sideline and hurried 72 yards to a touchdown. With quarterback Phil Snowden's passing arm injured and no passing or outside running threat to complement Kuhlmann's hard-hitting fullback plunges, the offensively cautious Tigers could not offer a varied attack. Missouri drove from their own 18 to the Kansas 15 only to fumble in the late stages of the game. Kansas then drove

77 yards in 13 plays. Here, senior tackle Merv Johnson and his fellow linemen seemed to rise to a goal-line stand, but Barnes booted the fatal field goal as the Jayhawkers gave Coach Mather a going-away present and once again took the lead in the 66-game rivalry between Missouri and Kansas.

SAVITAR 1959 – BORDER WAR 1958

MISSOURI 13 – KANSAS 13. The terribly trite adage of "the game's not over till the gun sounds" was terribly true in the case of the Missouri-Kansas Homecoming clash. Trailing 13-7, with less than a minute to go in the game, the Jayhawks received a final chance to win when Charlie Rash's attempted field goal went astray. On the first play from scrimmage, Homer Floyd, the Birds scooting halfback, picked off a pass from his quarterback and ripped off down the field 80 yards to tie the score. With little or no time left in the game, it looked as though the Tiger Homecoming game would go into the books as a loss. But Dale Pidcock crashed through to block the attempted conversion and save the Benals with a tie score. The tie left the local squad in undisputed possession of second place in the Big Eight standings and with a 5-4-1 seasonal mark. The tie seemed to mar whatever glory the Tigers might have had, since the Devine men led all the way and gave the appearance that they would turn the game into a rout. But each time, the Jayhawks from Lawrence held on vainly and stopped the Missouri drives. The big troublemaker for Mizzou throughout the entire contest was Floyd, whose number 33 was all over the field. On several occasions, the Tigers were saved from disaster when Floyd appeared to be on his way to long touchdown runs. But the senior scant back saved his run for the final 20 seconds. Despite the tie, the Tigers dropped the curtain on the season in elegant fashion with the crowning of the Homecoming Queen and all the bright homecoming festivities.

SAVITAR 1960 – BORDER WAR 1959

Mighty Missouri won a 1500 mile trip to the Orange Bowl–by one foot! 40,000 fans watched as the Tigers defeated the Kansas Jayhawks at Lawrence 13-9. The Tigers were leading 13-7 with three minutes left in the fourth quarter when Kansas halfback John Hadl received a screen pass from Duane Morris and almost went over for the t.d. But a second team fullback, Ron Toman, broke through a mass of blockers to stop him on the one foot line and the Tigers came back from a one point defeat by Colorado three weeks ago to climax their best season since 1953, and knock Kansas into third place.

Quarterback Phil Snowden called the plays in the second quarter that sent the Bengals from their 42 to the Jayhawk 30. Then he pitched a 14-yard pass to end Gordon Smith and followed by hitting Donnie Smith for the first touchdown. In the fourth quarter, Bob Haas returned a K.U. punt to the Missouri 49 and Snowden then directed a drive to the Kansas 27. After two incompleted passes, and a one yard run, the Tigers found it fourth down and nine. Kansas then assisted with an illegal substitution that made it fourth and five and Snowden hit Russ Sloan for 17 yards. Jim Miles scored the second touchdown two plays later.

Kansas pressed hard during the game, leading Missouri on the ground 253 yards to 148. But Mike Magac, who won a second team berth on the NEA All-American football squad, led a Missouri defense that hit hard enough to recover 5 costly Kansas fumbles. Fullback Doyle Schick blasted 30 yards in the third quarter for the lone Jayhawks TD.

And so, when the dust finally settled, the Missouri Tigers found themselves proudly sitting on the Kansas Jayhawks-gazing south.

JAYHAWKER 1960 – BORDER WAR 1959

A chance tackle by a third team quarterback stopped K.U. eight inches from paydirt and a New Year's Day vacation in Miami. Ron Toman sent the Tigers to the Orange Bowl when he downed John Hadl in the closing minutes of the Homecoming game.

Viewing an all-out effort from both teams, the 40,000 fans had much to cheer about.

Kansas fought back after the half to tie an earlier Bengal score, then the Missourians countered again. The score was 7-13 when Toman nipped Hadl.

Coach Dan Devine had his squad give the Jayhawks two points on an intentional safety which enabled M.U. to punt from its 20.

Fumbles gave the Tigers the ball five times, and they took advantage of their breaks.

THE 1960s..

"The Swinging Sixties" began with a dashing, fictional English spy named, "Bond, James Bond" and ended with a three-day music festival in upstate Woodstock, New York. "Counterculture" quickly became the mantra of the decade as "hippies" began to stage Vietnam War protests across the nation. Despite the influx of British music resulting from The Beatles performing on the Ed Sullivan Show, a local Saint Louis married couple, Ike and Tina Turner also received national attention and Eastman Kodak would introduce a new home film format known as "Super 8," which would allow for the easy and affordable filming of 10 minute per reel home movies.

Not since 1930 has there been, and to this day still, so much controversy regarding the Border War Game than in 1960. The controversy is so pronounced that the game is counted as a "win" by both schools with no resolution in sight. At the center of the issue is the illegal recruitment of star halfback, Bert Coan, from Texas Christian University. After Kansas acquired Coan, the National Collegiate Athletic Association investigated Kansas and found them guilty of several "recruiting irregularities," which resulted in Kansas being placed on probation and excluded from any post-season football games. Bert Coan was the major issue in the finding, with a couple of other minor infractions also being

Bert Coan

cited. However, the decision allowed for Coan to continue playing for Kansas during the entire regular season, which he would have done had he not sustained a shoulder injury. Coan was made healthy in time to play for Kansas' last two games of the regular season against Colorado and Missouri. Kansas was already undefeated in the Big 8 and had lost only twice in close games to teams both ranked number one in the country when they played Kansas; Syracuse and Iowa. With Coan's return, Kansas beat Colorado and prepared to play an undefeated Missouri team who that week was ranked number one in the country, a distinction for Kansas being that it played three number one ranked teams in one season. Prior to the game, informal polling among the member schools of the Big 8 concerning the eligibility of Coan indicated that he would not be ruled ineligible because of a seventy-five percent voting rule in the Big 8 Conference, which meant that for the measure to pass, six of the eight schools would have to

approve the measure. Missouri could not garner the necessary votes that it wanted to disqualify him because Kansas, Kansas State, and Oklahoma State continued to oppose his disqualification. In the Border War Game, Kansas stopped Missouri the entire first half from getting a first down and held them to only 61 yards rushing and 53 yards passing the entire game. Coan, however, scored Kansas' first touchdown on a 19-yard pass from All-American quarterback John Hadl. Another Kansas player of note in the backfield in that game was Pro-Bowl player Curtis McClinton. Kansas left Columbia that day

Curtis McClinton

handing Missouri its first loss of the season and taking the Big 8 Conference Championship with it. Because they were prohibited from post-season play, they were denied the ability of going to the Orange Bowl, to which Missouri accepted the invitation, however, in addition to blemishing their undefeated and untied record, their mood was further soured by the fact that with the loss to Kansas they lost the ability to play in the National Championship game.

Three weeks after the Border War Game was played, on December 8, faculty representatives of the Big 8 met in Kansas City and, as part of the meeting, formally voted on the matter of Bert Coan. Before the vote on Bert Coan occurred, however, a vote was taken and passed to remove the seventy-five percent voting rule, replacing it with a simple majority. The rule was changed and as a result Bert Coan was subsequently proclaimed ineligible by the Conference, forcing Kansas to forfeit its two last games in which he played and the Conference title. Missouri then played and beat Air Force in the Orange Bowl, winning its trophy with an undefeated and untied season and the Big 8 Championship. Bert Coan was ruled by the Big 8 to be ineligible for the first five games of the 1961 season, which became a moot issue because he broke his leg prior to the start of the season and, after his leg healed, joined the American Football League.

Until 1963, the past six years of the Border War Game were epic battles in which neither team had won by more than 12 points. It also happened that whichever team that was favoured to win the game, was the team to lose it in that six-year stretch. As another odd coincidence, whichever team was hosting the game also happened to be the team that lost the game within the

THE GAME THAT IS WON BY BOTH

past five-year stretch. The 1963 game was influenced strongly by these factors, but also by the postponement of the game for a week because of the assassination of President John F. Kennedy in Dallas, Texas on November 22. In the 1963 game, hosted by Kansas, Missouri was unable to move past its 47-yard line in the entire first half. Kansas was demonstrating its clear offensive superiority when Ken Coleman and All-American Gale Sayers maintained a drive on five first downs and 16 plays which brought them to the Missouri 2-yard line. Unexpectedly, as Coleman crossed over the goal line, he fumbled the ball into the hands of Missouri's Vince Turner.

Gale Sayers

Turner then ran 101 yards to score against Kansas. By the half, Kansas was leading Missouri 7-6, but the game would not be decided until, with six minutes left in the game, Missouri was able to kick a field goal and earn an upset victory against Kansas, 9-7.

In 1964 the Conference officially changed its name to the Big 8 Conference. From 1962 to 1966, despite having two-time

1964 Border War Game

All-American Gale Sayers, Jack Mitchell seemed unable to do anything significant with Kansas, earning him detractors. After Sayers had left the team, Kansas posted records of 2-8 and 2-7-1, causing him to resign in December, 1966. As a result, Kansas hired the reserve quarterback and place-kicker of Georgia Tech's 1952 National Championship team, Franklin C. "Pepper" Rodgers. After a 5-5 season in 1967, Rodgers won the Big 8 Conference Championship in 1968 and, for the second year of its long tradition of the Big 8 sending its best team to the Orange Bowl, Kansas went to the game, unfortunately losing by one point to Pennsylvania State University.

At Missouri, Dan Devine continued to build winning teams, winning five of seven Border War Games against Jack Mitchell in the 1960s. Against Pepper Rodgers' 1967 Jayhawks, Devine's 7-2 Tigers lost to Pepper's 4-5 team and then again in 1968. How-

ever, in 1969, Devine had his revenge. Although, at its time, the 1969 game's point differential stood as the largest in Border War Game history, it is now tied for that title with the games held in 1978, 1979, and 1986, at 48 points. Despite the current four-way tie, Missouri's scoring of 69 points still stands as the most points scored by either team in the contest. After the game, Dan Devine had to endure what many coaches must do at some point in their career, defend themselves against the charge of "running up" the score. As any coach will tell you, it is difficult to tell players, especially reserve players, to withhold scoring or to allow the other team to score uncontested. In situations such as this, one team is able to play seemingly unhindered, while the other succumbs to physical and, most importantly, mental exhaustion. In his defense, in the post-game locker-room interview, Devine stated that he had come to the game with 47 players and had played 47 players, providing clear evidence that he had done what he could to give balance to the game without blatantly instructing his players to give the other team points. The victory against Kansas secured the Big 8 Championship for Missouri, taking the team again to the Orange Bowl, where they unfortunately lost.

Missouri Football (10-1)* - Head Coach Daniel John Devine
Big 8 Champion* - Orange Bowl Champion

Row 1: Calhoun, Moyer, Snyder, Stevenson, Carpenter, G. Smith, D. Smith, Mehrer, Langan, West, Miles, Brossart, LaRose. Row 2: Taylor, Beal, Garvis, Watkins, Reinhold, Curtright, McCartney, Tobin, Johnson, Raines, Hertz, Hesselroth, Ston. Row 3: Nichols, Magnusson, Dobbs, Bukowsky, Fisher, Palmer, Schueler, Siekierski, Hitchler, Vermillion, O'Dowd, Blaine Hunter. Row 4: Manager Bechtold, Goodwin, Brown, Russell, Walsworth, Hinkley, Geiger, Lockett, McAllister, Crawford, Krugman, Leslie, Wallach, T. Smith, Manager Kimes. Row 5: Manager Vereb, Henley, Estes, Lavender, Thomas, Underhill, Phillips, Gorman, Musgrave, Wainwright, Pickett, Walaskay, Hilto, Fowler. Row 6: Coach Cooper, Coach Johnson, Coach Rash, Coach Fletcher, Coach Devine, Coach Onofrio Coach Smith, Trainer Chambers, Trainer Wappel.

* Kansas won the Border War Game and Big 8 Championship upon conclusion of the game but a 5-3 Big 8 Conference vote taken after the game forced Kansas to forfeit the game and the Big 8 Conference Championship. The team records do not reflect the forfeiture.

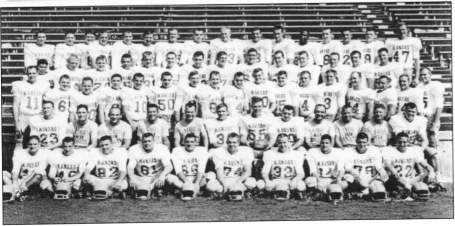

Kansas Football (7-2-1)* - Head Coach Jack Churchill Mitchell

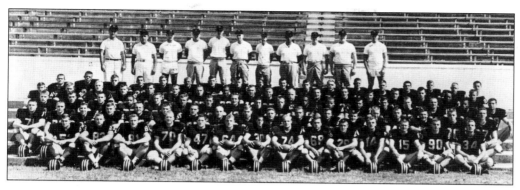

Missouri Football (7-2-1) - Head Coach Daniel John Devine

Kansas Football (7-3-1) - Head Coach Jack Churchill Mitchell
Bluebonnet Bowl Champion

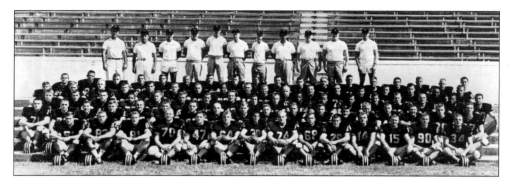

Missouri Football (8-1-2) - Head Coach Daniel John Devine
Bluebonnet Bowl Champion

Row 1: Vermillion, Hitchler, Wainwright, Siekierski, Tobin, Hertz, Russell, Wallach, Phillips, Crawford, Johnson, Lavender, Palmer, Otto. Row 2: Gill, Ritter, Lockett, Medford, Gilchrist, Underhill, Maples, Krugman, Muellerleile, Lurie, Thomas, Oliver, Turner, Jones, Hinkley, Kubinski, Sevcik, Crumpler. Row 3: Morrow, Caughey, Lane, Brown, Mills, Jansen, Harvey, Weber, Buerkle, Eldridge, Stevenson, Seals, Matthews, Kuhn, Taylor, Wyrostek, Villars, Lynn. Row 4: Berkley, Snyder, Cooksey, Powell, Overstreet, Tatum, Kuba, Roland, Kirby, Cummins, Meadows, Widenhofer, Leistritz, West, Schultz, Comfort, Griffin, Waller. Row 5: Reece, Darnaby, Sevcik, Heddell, Heisler, Hofsinger, Eisele, Thimmesch, DeLassus, Rich, Eader, Forcelledo, Jones, Howard, Tobin, McHarg, Dennis, Manager Dyer. Row 6: Trainer Thomas, Trainer Wappel, Coach Garvis, Coach Fletcher, Coach Mackey, Coach Cooper, Coach Devine, Coach Onofrio, Coach Dotsch, Coach Smith, Coach Kuhlmann.

Kansas Football (6-3-1) - Head Coach Jack Churchill Mitchell

Missouri Football (7-3) - Head Coach Daniel John Devine

Row 1: Jansen, Harvey, Gilchrist, Hinkley, Seals, Turner, Underhill, Oliver, Lurie, Kubinski, Gill, Sevcik, Sevcik, Krugman, Wyrostek. Row 2: Berkely, Lynn, Buerkle, Brown, Jones, Ritter, Matthews, Leistritz, Lane, Stevenson, Crumpler, Kuhn, Allison, Otto, Murphy. Row 3: Cooksey, Snyder, Darnaby, Thimmesch, Valentik, Waller, Phelps, Reese, Kuba, Chester, Caughey, Tobin, Jones, Young, Obermark, Comfort, Davis. Row 4: Stelmach, Jenkins, Myers, Jones, Hall, Alton, Boston, Tatum, Kistner, Van Dyke, Abell, Murphy, Rich, Meadows, LeMone, Holsinger. Row 5: Robben, West, Jenkins, Howard, Delassus, Lionberger, Powell, Eader, Stanfield, Creekmore, Jeffries, Widenhoger, Whalen, Lytle, Fitzgerald, Parson. Row 6: Coach Fletcher, Coach Mackey, Coach Dotsch, Coach Kuhlmann, Coach Smith, Coach Devine, Coach Cooper, Coach Onofrio, Coach Geiger, Manager, Dyer, Trainer Thomas, Trainer Wappel.

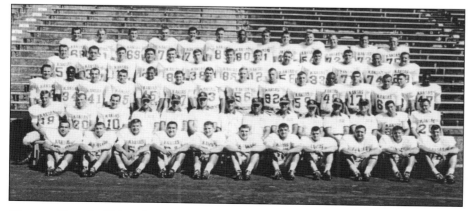

Kansas Football (5-5) - Head Coach Jack Churchill Mitchell

Missouri Football (6-3-1) - Head Coach Daniel John Devine

Row 1: Leistritz, Abell, Buerkle, Ritter, Wyrostck, Captain Otto, Tobin, Brown, Jansen, Bilchrist, Crumpler. Row 2: Caughey, Comfort, Thimmesch, Darnaby, Lane, Saussele, Holsinger, Roland, Allison, Van Dyke, Waller, Snyder. Row 3: Bates, McIntyre, Chettle, Whalen, Chester, Jones, Fitzgerald, Kistner, Nelson, Powell, Carr, Denny. Row 4: Valentik, Howard, Cooksey, Weber, Veech, Schuppan, Wetmore, Wienert, Peeper, Jost, Brown, West, Bernsen. Row 5: Widenhofer, Peay, Cadell, Ziegler, Clark, Whitaker, Hottle, Grana, Bidnick, Mungal, Grossnickle, Hall, Boston. Row 6: Kornbrink, Thorpe, Jenkins, Tatum, Gold, Reese, Lynn, Eader, Alton, Creekmore. Row 7: Jones, Kirby, Hyland, Coach Dotsch, Coach Mackey, Coach Smith, Coach Cooper, Coach Devine, Coach Onofrio, Coach Fletcher, Coach Kuhlmann, Assistant Trainer Belman, Trainer Wappel.

Kansas Football (6-4) - Head Coach Jack Churchill Mitchell

(Top-Bottom, Left-Right) Row 1: Harvey, Walters, Pilch, Catlin. Row 2: Garber, Crandall, Micek, Skahan, Robben, Hornung, Kampschroeder. Row 3: Fairchild, Oelschlager, Becker, Schweda, Gerhards, Wohlford, Johnson, Thompson, Elias. Row 4: Perry, Stokes, Duff, Roth, Elder, Shanks, Marsh.

192

Missouri Football (8-2-1) - Head Coach Daniel John Devine
Sugar Bowl Champion

Row 1: West, Peay, Boston, Darnaby, Lynn, Co-captain Roland, Co-captain Reese, Co-captain Van Dyke, Eader, Lane, Snyder, Allison, Waller. Row 2: Kombrink, Powell, Brown, Berg, Kistner, Whitaker, Denny, Schuppan, Phelps, Bates, Nelson, Bernsen, Valentik. Row 3: Washington, Graham, Lang, Griffin, Wetmore, Carr, Grossnickle, Alton, Whalen, Fitch, Grana, Wienert, Short. Row 4: Fitzgerald, Scott, Thorpe, Jeffries, Ziegler, Jost, Hall, Pepper, Young, Chester, Deneault, Chettle, Mungai. Row 5: Saeger, Willsey, Lischner, Juras, Snadon, Wempe, Frieders, Meyer, Hiles, Powell, Bailey, Garber. Row 6: Albin, Dye, Ewing, Kelemen, Goggin, Cox, Weber, Veech, Weber, Kahl, Lewis, York, Barnett, Keiser. Row 7: Coach Kirby, Manager Walker, Smith, Boyd, Collins, Lynn, Wilson, Tinsley, Murphy, Noskay, Barnes, Coach Wade, Manager McCraith. Row 8: Trainer Wappel, Trainer Belman, Coach Kuhlmann, Coach Smith, Coach Devine, Coach Cooper, Coach Onofrio, Coach Fletcher, Coach Dotsch, Coach Mackey.

Kansas Football (2-8) - Head Coach Jack Churchill Mitchell

Row 1: Skahan, Johnson, Abernethy, Miller, Coleman, Perry, Sweatman, Bouda. Row 2: Hudspeth, Peloquin, Stokes, Bacon, Shinn, Waxse, Peterson, Elias, Montgomery.

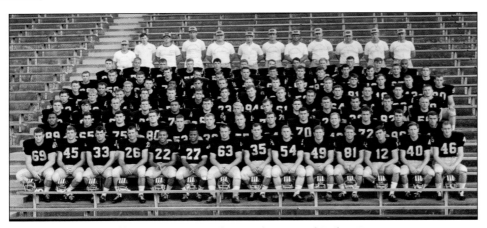

Missouri Football (6-3-1) - Head Coach Daniel John Devine

Row 1: Powell, Denny, Murphy, Valentik, Brown, Thorpe, Nelson, Bernsen, Kintner, Whitaker, Schuppan, Alton, Grosstickle, Bates. Row 2: Washington, Pepper, Short, Ziegler, Powell, Chettle, Garber, Wempe, Ewing, Frieders, Juras, Deneault. Row 3: Scott, Benhardt, Brewer, Kemperman, Jones, Butler, Kembrink, Weber, Jost, Cook, Grana, Bailey, Lercy. Row 4: Kahl, Lewis, Hiles, Douglas, Rees, York, Wehrli, Collins, Albin, Dischner, Doak, Kayzak, Keith, Mitchell. Row 5: Adams, Schmitz, Weber, Stoeckel, White, Griffin, Moss, Elzea, Thomas, Barnett, Mayer, Stevens, Sharp, Tinsley, Smith. Row 6: Veech, Barnes, Willsey, Parker, Kurtz, Tietjen, Mungai, Boyd, Schmitt, Jonaitis, Wiley, Danilke, Hebik, Sloan. Row 7: Hall, Anderson, Judd, Melten, Spengel, Vereecken, Fitzgerald, Sangster, Long, Hauptman, Moore, Phelps. Row 8: Trainer Wappel, Manager McCraith, Trainer Nauert, Coach Lynn, Coach Smith, Coach Devine, Coach Weber, Coach Onofrio, Coach Kuhlmann, Coach Kadlec, Coach Cooper, Coach Frale.

Kansas Football (2-7-1) - Head Coach Jack Churchill Mitchell

(Left to Right) Shanklin, Greene, Dahl, White, Skahan, Wohlford, Riggins, Bouda, Peterson, Christensen, Zook, DiBiase, Douglass, Kreutzer, Sweatman, Dercher, Greene, Turgeon, Butler, Wertzberger, Heck, Shawger, Hawlings, Ball, Johnson, Anderson, Doyle, Jackson, Lynch, Buda, Hixon, Abernethy, Hunt, Kampschroeder, Perry, Elias, Waxse, Montgomery.

Missouri Football (7-3) - Head Coach Daniel John Devine

KANSAS vs MISSOURI

SATURDAY, NOVEMBER 25, 1967

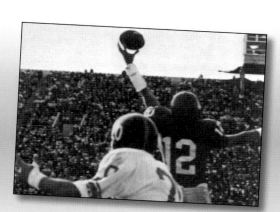

Kansas Football (5-5) - Head Coach Franklin C. Rodgers

(Left to Right) Perkins, Anderson, Lukert, Fortier, Carmichael, McDaniel, Wertzberger, Weir, Bell, Hixon, Kreutzer, Munkres, Medford, Aikens, Montgomery, Christensen, Mosier, Sweatmean, Zook, Dercher, Hicks, Greene, Kissell, Jackson, Shanklin.

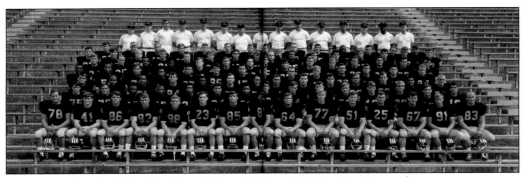

Missouri Football (8-3) - Head Coach Daniel John Devine
Gator Bowl Champion
Row 1: Hobik, Moore, Juras, Judd, Weber, Wehrli, Benhardt, Schmitt, Garber, Anderson, Rees, Cook, Boyd, Barnett, Brewer. Row 2: Sangster, Angle, Bray, Hunter, Glosson, Brown, Staggers, Boyd, Hauptman, Adams, Shryock, Davis, Poppe, Kenemore, McMillan. Row 3: Stevens, Phelps, Clark, Colclasure, McBride, Stoeckel, Kuhlman, Lundholm, Wallace, Crnko, Carroll, Hertz, Cox, Lowder. Row 4: Walls, Sparks, Haynes, Fountain, Taylor, Tegerdine, Weaver, Kelley, Sloan, Smith, Esther, Wilson, Keith, Melton, Row 5: Smith, Maloney, Moore, Harrison, Coan, Mizer, Henley, Gardocki, Weisenfels, McDonnell, Farmer, Luther, Rudanovich, Dobbs, Swaney. Row 6: Kelley, Schwab, Pundmann, Brinkman, Woods, Bennett, McCarthy, Blackstun, Stiles, Vital, Hamilton, Captuo, Lappin, Pirotte, Oswalt, Burns. Row 7: Dawson, Moore, Bush, King, Schindler, Green, Stephenson, Bohnsack, Kephart, Hager, Jackson, Obermark, Bunton, Snyder. Row 8: Trainer Wappel, Trainer Bigos, Manager Vaughn, Coach Frala, Coach Weber, Coach Tobin, Coach Dissinger, Coach Calhoun, Coach Devine, Coach Kuhlmann, Coach Kadlec, Coach Onofrio, Coach Rapp, Coach Gautt, Coach Cooper.

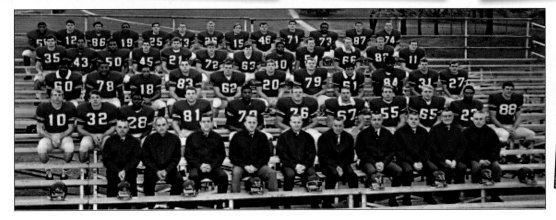

Kansas Football (9-2) - Head Coach Franklin C. Rodgers
Big 8 Champion - Orange Bowl Invitation

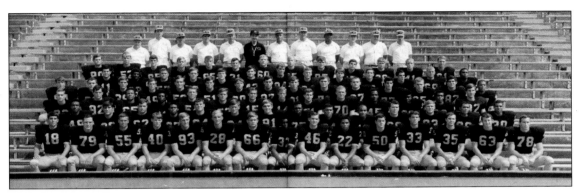
Missouri Football (9-2) - Head Coach Daniel John Devine
Big 8 Co-Champion - Orange Bowl Invitation

Row 1: McMillan, Kuhlmann, Lundholm, Davis, Shryock, Poppe, Carroll, McBride, Kenemore, Staggers, Crnko, Boyd, Stockel, Adams, Sloan. Row 2: Walls, Weisenfels, Ketley, Fountain, Colclasure, Hauptmann, Bennett, Jackson, Brown, Phelps, Wallace, Smith, Taylor, Britts. Row 3: Borgard, Kelley, Vital, Gray, Luther, Wilson, Brinkman, Farmer, Stephenson, Lowder, Moore, Harrison, Slosson, Weaver. Row 4: Manda, Buha, McClean, Hamilton, Gillespie, Dawson, Henley, Dobbs, Sewat, Burns, Kephart, Caputo, Mauser, Schmitt, Brinkley. Row 5: Stotler, Brown, Marshall, Brown, Cowan, Bardocki, Oswald, Gibson, Dudney, Brattie, Bell, Barnes, Doak. Row 6: Moore, Kanatzer, Smith, Wardell, McKee, Baker, Kamradt, Frieze, Venturi, Shawn, Fink, Gebhard. Row 7: Coach Wappel, Coach Lewis, Coach Dissinger, Coach Tobin, Coach Cooper, Coach Devine, Coach Onofrio, Coach Kuhlmann, Coach Gautt, Coach Rapp, Coach Kadlec, Coach Cowdrey.

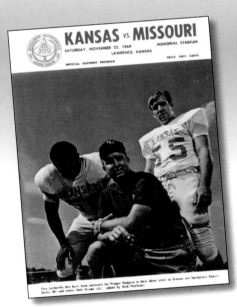

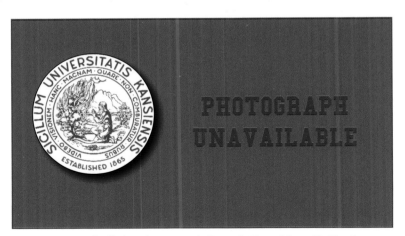

Kansas Football (1-9) - Head Coach Franklin C. Rodgers

JACK MITCHELL

FRANK "PEPPER" RODGERS

Jack Mitchell was Kansas' 28th football coach and, with the exception of Dr. A. R. Kennedy who was 52-9-4 from 1904 to 1910, was the winningest mentor. Mitchell succeeded Chuck Mather on Thanksgiving Day of 1957. With a 44-42-5 record, he remained as head coach for nine seasons--longer than any other football coach in Jayhawk history. For his 14 years of college coaching, Mitchell wound up 74-59-7. While at KU, he sent several players to the professional ranks: Curtis McClinton, Fred Hageman, Bert Coan, Mike Johnson, Brian Schweda and All-Americans John Hadl and Gale Sayers.

Mitchell is a native of Arkansas City where he was a prep star in football, basketball, and tennis. Following graduation, he attended Arkansas City Junior College and Texas University before entering the military service in World War II. After the war, Mitchell attended Oklahoma University where he was an All-America n quarterback. Graduating in 1949 with a psychology major, Mitchell then assumed his first coaching post at Blackwell (Oklahoma) High School. In 1950 he became an assistant at Tulsa University for one year and then moved to Texas Tech for two years, also as an assistant.

Mitchell first became a college head coach at Wichita in 1953 and 1954, compiling a 13-5-1 record. His next post was at Arkansas in 1955-57 where he was 17-12-1. Taking over the reins at Kansas in 1958, Mitchell had two so-so seasons (4-5-1 and 5-5). Then in 1960, he coached the Jayhawks to a 9-0-1 record and their first clear-cut conference championship since 1950. Later, two of these games were forfeited because of an eligibility ruling. In 1961, the Hawks were 7-3-1 and subdued Rice in the Bluebonnet Bowl 35-7 for the first KU bowl victory. In 1962-64, in spite of the presence of the great Gale Sayers, Mitchell had seasons of 6-3-1, 5-5, and 6-4. Because of the poor showing of KU teams in these years, KU fans became disenchanted with Mitchell. With opposition to him growing, Mitchell's teams slumped to 2-8 and 2-7-1 seasons in 1964 and 1965, and his resignation was announced this December.

Written for the 1967 Jayhawker *Yearbook*

On December 16, Frank "Pepper" Rodgers was named as Kansas' new head football coach, his first such assignment. Throughout his football career, the 35 year old Rodgers has been associated with nothing but winners.

A former Georgia Tech quarterback and an advocate of wide-open offensive football, Rodgers gained a reputation for developing imaginative attacks during his nine years as backfield coach for Tommy Prothro at UCLA, Ray Graves at Florida, and Ben Martin at the Air Force Academy. Among the top names he helped develop are Heisman Trophy winner Steve Spurrier of Florida, Larry DuPree of Florida, Rich Mayo of Air Force, and both Gary Beban and Mel Farr of UCLA—all of them All-American selections. During his last two years at UCLA, the Bruins won seventeen games while losing only three and tying one. Rodgers has participated in seven bowl games, three times as a player and four as a coach. Of the seven games, his team has won six and tied one. Pepper played under Bobby Dodd at Georgia Tech from 1951-53 when the Yellow Jackets amassed a 30-2-1 record, including three bowl victories. In his final game as a player, Rodgers was voted the most outstanding player in the Sugar Bowl. He threw three touchdown passes and kicked four extra points and a field goal in routing West Virginia 42-19.

Coach Rodgers selected for his coaching staff Jack Green, former Army All-American guard and head coach at Vanderbilt, defensive ends and linebackers; John Cooper, another former Prothro assistant, defensive backs; Dave McClain, former assistant at Cornell and Miami of Ohio, defensive interior linemen; Don Fambrough, a KU assistant for 15 years, offensive tackles and tight ends; Larry Travis, former All-Conference guard and assistant at Florida, offensive guards and centers; Charlie Mc-Cullers, former assistant at Tampa, Wichita, and Parsons (Iowa) College, offensive backs; Dick Tomey, former Davidson assistant, fresh-man coach and varsity aid; Floyd Temple, also KU's baseball coach, varsity aid; and John Hadl, former KU All-American and starting quarterback for San Diego in the AFL, recruiter and coach for passers and receivers in the spring drills.

Written for the 1967 Jayhawker *Yearbook*

WHO WOULD HAVE EVER THOUGHT?

Missouri and Kansas have been rivals since the Civil War. The intensity of that rivalry has been evidenced on the football field during the season ending games between the University of Missouri and the University of Kansas. This was particularly true during the decade of the 1960s. Mizzou started off that decade ranked number one in the nation and undefeated. My introduction to the Missouri-Kansas rivalry was listening to the 1960 game on the radio which was played in Lawrence. I was listening to that game in the St. Louis suburb of Webster Groves and was disappointed by the 23-7 Kansas win. Kansas led by John Hadl, Curtis McClinton, Bert Coan, and Doyle Schick spoiled Missouri's No. 1 ranking and even an Orange Bowl victory over Navy, led by Heisman Trophy winner, Joe Bellino, could not ease the pain of Missouri fans over the Kansas loss. That game set the tone for the Border War rivalry of the Sixties.

I started attending Missouri games in 1962 the same year as a young Missouri half-back from Corpus Christi, Texas famed Johnny Roland burst onto the Tiger's team. One particular game in the rivalry stands out: In 1964, the Tigers and Jayhawks met in Columbia featuring two of the great halfbacks in college football history, Gale Sayers for Kansas and Johnny Roland for Missouri. Although Johnny Roland had been switched to defense, he was called in on offense once the Tigers reached its opponents 20-yard line. Kansas, in an apparent attempt to confuse the Tiger's defense, played Gale Sayers at flanker rather than as a halfback in the backfield. The deception did not work, Sayers was contained, Johnny Roland was not, and the Tigers won handily, 34-14.

Johnny Roland

My participation in the Missouri-Kansas rivalry switched from spectator to player when I entered Mizzou on a football scholarship in 1967. When he recruited my class of freshman at Mizzou, Head Coach Dan Devine told recruits that he was recruiting the team that would play Notre Dame in Columbia during their senior season. "Do you want to be on that team or not?" Devine challenged us. Devine's challenge worked, because my class included Mizzou stars Joe Moore, Larron Jackson, Jim Harrison, John Henley, Mike Bennett, John Cowan, and we were joined as sophomores by Mel Gray and Tyrone Walls from Fort Scott Junior College. Devine's coaching staff had coaches who had experienced the Border War rivalry not only as coaches but as players. Clay Cooper, John Kadlec, Hank Kuhlmann, and Vince Tobin had all played football at Mizzou. Although he did not play at Mizzou, defensive coordinator Al Onofrio had experienced nine Border War games by the time we arrived.

Football teams of our era were made up primarily of high school fullbacks. Some became lineman, others halfbacks, and still others linebackers and defensive players. Although I played both fullback and linebacker in high school, I became a linebacker without even stepping on Mizzou's practice field for the first time. When the freshman assembled for our first team meeting, I saw a huge man standing at one side of the meeting room who looked as if he was in his mid-20s and stood 6 feet, 4 inches tall and weighed 240 pounds [109 centimetres, 109 kilograms]. I assumed that it was Johnny Roland, who Coach Devine had brought back to inspire the freshman. Since my mother had taught me my manners, I promptly went up to "Johnny" and introduced myself. To my surprise he said he was not Johnny Roland, but was a fellow freshman from San Antonio, Texas named Jim Harrison. After recovering from my initial shock, I asked Big Jim what position he played. "Fullback," he said, "and what about you?" I did not hesitate for a second as I responded "I am a linebacker."

Jim Harrison

As freshmen, we had a separate football schedule and did not practice with the varsity. The freshman played four games, against Nebraska, Kansas State, Iowa State, and Kansas. Our team was 2-1 going into the Kansas game. Our loss came at the hands of Nebraska. We did not know much about the Kansas freshmen, but Mizzou's seniors made sure we understood the importance of the rivalry. As it turned out, among the Kansas freshmen was future Hall of Fame fullback John Riggins. Riggins was from the small Kansas town of Centralia. Legend had it that the 6 foot, 2 inch, 230 pound [188 centimetres, 104 kilograms] Riggins single-handedly won the state high school track meet for Centralia, including a victory in the 100-yard dash in a time of 9.8 seconds.

One of the things our team learned early about Riggins was that we needed to gang tackle him. He had great balance and he always kept his legs pumping. If you were the first to hit him, you needed to get help or he would run over you. We were fortunate to beat Kansas' freshmen that game but our Tiger teams battles with Kansas were just beginning.

In 1968, my first season on the varsity, I played linebacker. Kansas and Missouri both had successful seasons going into the final game. Missouri was 7-2 and 5-1 in the Big 8 Conference. Kansas was 8-1 and 5-1 in the Big 8. Missouri lost the season opener at Kentucky and to Oklahoma, in Norman. Kansas' lone loss was also to Oklahoma. The stakes were high. The winner of the game would share a portion of the Big 8 Conference title and go to the Orange Bowl. Kansas traveled to Columbia for the season finale with a team that included Bobby Douglas at quarterback, John Riggins at fullback, Junior Riggins at halfback, John Zook at defensive end, Emory Hicks and Mickey Doyle at linebacker. The game was hard fought with Kansas taking an early 14-0 lead after a Terry McMillan pass was intercepted and returned for a touchdown. The Tigers did not quit. Our defense, which included Bill Schmidt and Benny Benhardt at defensive ends, Carl Garber, Roger Boyd and Rocky Wallace as defensive lineman, and Roger Wehrli, Butch Davis and Denny Poppe in the secondary, stopped Kansas and gave our offense a chance to get us back in the game. Led by a punishing ground game, the Tigers fought back to try to tie the game in the late minutes of the game. Because Missouri missed an extra point, the Tigers had to go for a two-point conversion in the fourth quarter. Terry McMillan ran a quarterback option that appeared to be successful when, at the last second, Emory Hicks hit McMillan at the goal line and the officials ruled the two-point conversion failed. Kansas got the ball with a 21-19 lead and three minutes left to play. The Tigers

Bobby Douglas

successfully stopped the Jayhawks for the first two plays of the possession. On third down and 12 to go for a first down, Bobby Douglass rolled out to his left on a run/ pass option. I rolled with Douglass from my linebacker position and saw the tight end running toward the flat, but Douglass was breaking into the clear. I was faced with the choice of trying to contain Douglass to force the pass but leave the tight end open or cover the tight end and run the risk of Douglass running for the first down. I chose to contain Douglass who threw the ball to his tight end just as I hit him. The pass was complete for a first down and with no time-outs remaining, we watched helplessly as Kansas ran-out the clock.

What happened next made a lasting impression on me about Missouri football fans: As was the case in all games under Coach Devine, the team immediately ran off the field at the conclusion of the game after a brief post-game huddle with Devine. As we ran off the field after the game, all of Mizzou's fans gave us a standing ovation. I realized what great fans Mizzou football fans are and how much they appreciated the effort our team made that day. As a result of its victory, Kansas went to the Orange Bowl and Missouri went to the Gator Bowl.

College football celebrated its 100th Anniversary in 1969. Missouri was coming off a great 35-10 victory over Alabama in the Gator Bowl. Kansas was coming off a heartbreaking 15-14 loss to Penn State in the Orange Bowl. The Bowl game results would end-up foreshadowing each team's performance in 1969. Missouri had returning from its 1968 squad, Terry McMillan at quarterback, most of its offensive line, Joe Moore, Mel Gray, and much of its defensive unit. Kansas, on the other hand, lost Bobby Douglass, Junior Riggins, much of its offensive line, and its defensive front. As a result, Missouri came into the 1969 finale with Kansas with an 8-1 record. Kansas on the other hand was 1-8. Despite the disparity in our records, Coach Devine and his staff emphasized that this was the Missouri-Kansas game and records could be thrown out.

The game was played on a beautiful, fall day in Lawrence, Kansas. Missouri's offense started fast and by half-time Missouri was leading by a score of 28-7. The game really got out of hand in the second half and ended with Mizzou scoring 10 touchdowns pounding Kansas by a score of 64-21. Coach Devine ordered our place kicker, Oleary Brown to miss the last extra point because he thought that "70" might sound like Missouri was running the score up. However, as the score indicated, the outcome of this game was never much in doubt. What made the game interesting was some of the things that happened on the field.

Kansas still had a great running threat in fullback, John Riggins. Although Riggins was a tremendous competitor, he was not the sort of guy to let the score of a football game get him down. During the third quarter, with the game out of hand, Riggins carried the ball on a fullback sweep. I, with the help of several of my teammates, tackled Riggins. While we were in the pile of players, Riggins says to me "Nip, what are you doing after the game? Big party at my place." Although it was one of the most tempting invitations I have ever received, I thought it best to decline, since Coach Devine probably would not understand my reason for not riding home on the team bus.

The 1969 game also spawned the story of the "peace sign" incident. After the game, in his post game comments, the Kansas coach, Pepper Rodgers, when asked what he had done to try to keep the score down, said that he had given Coach Devine the peace sign, but Coach Devine gave him half of it back. Coach Devine denied the incident, but the story is often retold when people talk about the intensity of the Border War rivalry. After Missouri's victory over Kansas, and completing a 9-1 season, Missouri was selected to go to the Orange Bowl. Mizzou, like Kansas the year before, faced Penn State. Missouri endured a disappointing 10-3 loss.

Missouri's 1970 squad had high expectations. Although Terry McMillan was gone at quarterback, Mizzou returned a veteran team which included Joe Moore, Lamar Jackson, Mel Gray, Tyrone Walls, Rocky Wallace, and Mike Bennett. Joe Moore and I were co-captains of the team. Our quarterbacks, Chuck Roper and Mike Farmer were both capable of leading our team to the success which the preseason pollsters had predicted. However, injuries intervened and kept us from reaching that promise. During that season, Mizzou had all 22 starters injured at one point or another. Joe Moore was lost for the season after the Nebraska

Joe Moore

game, our fourth of the season. I was injured after the second game and had to have knee surgery, usually a season ending injury in those days. Both quarterbacks sustained injuries as did several of our defensive players. I managed to be able to return after missing four weeks. My comeback was accelerated by Coach Devine who visited me in the hospital after knee surgery and suggested that "…our team needs a captain." Although our team continued to fight through the injuries, Missouri was a disappointing 4-6, going into the Kansas game.

On the other hand, Kansas had better success in 1970 than in 1969 but did not have the success of the 1968 team. The 1970 version of the Jayhawks relied primarily on the run featuring now senior John Riggins. Kansas entered the game with a 5-5 record.

The 1970 Border War game was in Columbia in what turned out to be Dan Devine's last game as Missouri's coach. Although the game had little significance for either team's post season hopes, it was Missouri-Kansas and it meant a lot to the players and our fans. The game went back and forth most of the afternoon. Our defense had difficulty stopping Riggins and Kansas was ahead late in the game. Kansas had just scored to take a 17-14 lead. Coach Devine then did an unusual thing. On the kick-off return after the Kansas score, he put Mel Gray back deep. Mel had not returned a kick since his sophomore year. However, he took this kick at the goal line and proceeded to run what seemed like a 9 second flat, 100-yard dash to the end zone. Mel found a little crease in the first wave of tackles that he burst through and then flashed past everyone else. No one wanted to chase him because it seemed like everyone but Mel was standing still. That gave Mizzou the lead for good on the way to a 28-17 victory. We finished the season with a 5-6 record which was Coach Devine's first and only losing season, but we beat Kansas

Mel Gray

which helped salve the wounds of an otherwise difficult year.

The traditions of the Border War games and the intensity of the rivalry make the game great for the fans. For the players, the rivalry creates great memories. It also creates some unexpected events. In 1997, almost 30 years after we competed as rivals, I found myself playing in a golf tournament in Columbia, Missouri held by then Coach Larry Smith, in which two of my partners were Bobby Douglass and Mickey Doyle. Bobby's son, Ryan, was a back-up quarterback and Mickey's son, Sean, was a starting linebacker for the Tigers. Who would have ever thought when we were playing in 1968 that their sons would wind up playing football for Mizzou?

By John R. "Nip" Weisenfels, J.D.
Missouri Alumnus 1971
Written Thursday, October 2, 2008

SAYERS SOARS

Kansas football fans knew that they had a star in the making in sophomore running back Gale Sayers. As freshman were forbidden to play for the varsity team, the Omaha, Nebraska native did not get a chance to prove himself against top-notch competition until opening day of the 1962 football season.

In his first game for the varsity squad, Sayers rushed for 114 yards in a loss to Texas Christian University. Two weeks later, he again rushed for more than one hundred yards, this time against the University of Colorado. Nonetheless, no one expected him to have the sort of game he would have against the Oklahoma State Cowboys at that school's Lewis Field on the last Saturday of October, 1962.

A headline in the Friday, October 26, edition of the *University Daily Kansan* noted that the "Limping Jayhawks Must Beat 'Pokes," and the game was, indeed, a critical match-up for both teams. It was especially so for Kansas, which had been riding high after winning its first-ever bowl game the preceding January.

After losing their season-opener to Texas Christian University, the Jayhawks had reeled off three consecutive victories. But the Kansas team had fallen to the University of Oklahoma in Lawrence's Memorial Stadium the week before it was to play the Sooners' cross-state rival. Thus Kansas' record stood at 3-2 with Kansas State, Nebraska, California, and Missouri still on the schedule. A loss to Oklahoma State University would jeopardize the prospects of a winning season.

Despite a rash of injuries that had led Coach Jack Mitchell to comment that Kansas was in "the worst physical shape [it had been] in all year long," the odds-makers in Las Vegas favored Kansas by two touchdowns.

A disastrous first half for the Jayhawks on October 27, however, sent the team to the locker room at halftime trailing 17-7. According to the *University Daily Kansan*, Mitchell told his football team that there was no way he or the other coaches could make the students play with desire. "If you want it, go get it," he said, before he and the other coaches stormed out.

"What happened in the Jayhawk dressing room [following the coaches' exit]," noted the *University Daily Kansan*, "remains a mystery," but apparently after some finger pointing and scuffling, quarterback Rodger McFarland gave a speech that fired up the players.

The Kansas team took the opening kickoff of the second half and, twelve plays later, punched the ball into the end zone. After a two-point conversion, they had cut the Cowboys' lead to 17-15. With forty-three seconds remaining in the third quarter, Kansas scored again to take a 22-17 lead into the fourth quarter. The Jayhawks added two more touchdowns in the final stanza of the game to make the final score 36-17.

The story of the game, however, was not Kansas' come-from-behind victory, though Mitchell ranked it as the best such victory he had ever witnessed. It was instead the "fleet-footed Omaha, Nebraska sophomore."

Admittedly, Oklahoma State's defense, to quote its coach, Cliff Seegle, "didn't exactly set the world on fire with [its] tackling." Seegle's team allowed Kansas to grind out a total of 499 rushing yards, a number that still stands as one of the five greatest games Kansas has enjoyed in terms of racking up rushing yardage.

Nonetheless, Sayers' outstanding game drew praise from Kansas and Oklahoma State University fans alike. His 283 yards on the ground on only 22 carries, an average of 12.9 yards per carry, was made more remarkable by the fact that part way through the fourth quarter, Mitchell had pulled him from the game.

Following a play in which Oklahoma State's Don Derrick tackled Sayers well after the Kansas back had run out of bounds, "Sayers' temper flared and he sent a right to Derrick's rib cage." A melee between the teams ensued, and although the referees did not inform Mitchell that they had officially ejected his star tailback, the Kansas coach removed Sayers from the game so as to avoid "the chance of him getting hurt."

When his coach removed him, the sophomore running back had already accumulated 268 rushing yards, including one play in which he had broken loose for a 96-yard touchdown. Upon hearing that radio commentators were noting how close their star sophomore was to the Big 8 single-game rushing record of 270 yards that had been set by Iowa State's Dave Hoppman the previous year, some of Sayers' teammates pleaded with their coach to put Sayers' back in. Mitchell capitulated to their request.

On his first play back in the game, Sayers took a handoff and squirted through a hole for 15 yards. Afterwards, however, the officials called a dead-ball penalty on Kansas for using Sayers whom the officials claimed they had ejected. Mitchell objected because he had not received any notification of his tailback's official removal from the game, but the penalty stood.

Nonetheless, because yardage gained during plays in which a dead-ball penalty was called was credited to the offense, it had to be credited to a player as well. Thus the 15 yards counted towards Sayers' total, and he left the game having eclipsed the previous rushing record by 13 yards.

The game served as a harbinger of greater things to come for the tailback from Omaha, soon nicknamed the "Kansas Comet." He led the team in rushing, touchdowns, and kickoff returns in 1962, as he became only the second back from Kansas to rush for more than 1,000 yards in a single season.

His junior and senior seasons he again led the team in the categories he had as a sophomore but added to them punt returns and receiving. Not surprisingly, in both years he earned a selection as an All-American. As a junior he set a NCAA record for the longest rush from the line of scrimmage by scampering 99 yards for a touchdown against Nebraska. He closed out his collegiate career having averaged 6.5 yards per carry and having amassed 3,917 all-purpose yards.

The Chicago Bears and the Kansas City Chiefs selected Sayers in the first round of the NFL and AFL drafts respectively. While at his first training camp as a Bear, he met Brian Piccolo, a less-heralded white running back from Wake Forest, who became one of his closest friends. The Bears assigned the two to room together on road trips, making them the first racially mixed roommates in the history of the franchise.

After cancer brought Piccolo's life to an untimely end, Sayers wrote a book documenting their friendship titled *I Am Third* that became the basis for the TV-movie Brian's Song. The film, which starred Billy Dee Williams and James Caan, won the 1972 Golden Globe Award as the Best Film Made for Television.

It also spawned a rash of disease-of-the-week television-movies, as well as a cult following that has persisted for almost three decades. The recently released DVD version of the film includes an interview with Sayers in which he reminisces about the film and his career. Disney and ABC-TV released a new version starring Mekhi Phifer and Sean Maher in 2001.

At the risk of understatement, Sayers put together an outstanding, albeit short, career in the National Football League. In 1966, his second year in the NFL, he led it in rushing and set an NFL record by amassing 2,440 total yards, including kick returns and receiving yards. Three years later, after two injury plagued

seasons, he led the league in rushing again. So dominant was he that when the Associated Press announced an All-Time NFL team in 1969, it listed the former Jayhawk as the greatest running back in the NFL history.

During his seventh season in Chicago, Sayers suffered a career-ending knee injury. He retired from the sport in 1972, and for the next four years served as Assistant Athletic Director at Kansas. While back on Mount Oread, Sayers completed a Bachelor of Arts in Physical Education, and earned a Master of Arts in Educational Administration. In 1977, at age 34, Sayers became the youngest person and the first Jayhawk ever inducted into the Pro Football Hall of Fame.

By Mark D. Hersey, Ph.D.
Kansas Alumnus 2006
Written for This Week in KU History
www.KUHistory.com

THE JAYHAWKER AND THE SAVITAR

SAVITAR 1961 – BORDER WAR 1960

Missouri was rudely awakened from a dream of a happy Homecoming with dismal contest against Kansas. With the eyes of tiger fandom and the nation riveted on the Tigers' attempt to complete their first undefeated season, and assure themselves of a mythical national championship, traditional enemy Kansas upset the Bengals 23-7 before a disappointed overflow crowd of 43,000.

After a scoreless first half of rugged action which featured fumbles and a brilliant goal line stand by the hard-pressed Tigers, K.U. scored in the third period on the toe of Roger Hill who boomed a 46 yard field goal.

Another counter came on a 19 yard pass from talented John Hadl to halfback Bert Coan following a Tiger fumble. John Suder converted to bring the third quarter score to 10-0.

The Jayhawks' Coan brought the Tigers more misery in the final quarter by leading a 69 yard foray which he climaxed with a two yard scoring smash. Suder again converted.

Mel West returned the kickoff 54 yards to the K.U. 36 and six plays later Mizzou got its only score on a 17 yard pass from Ron Taylor to West. Bill Tobin cut the deficit to 17-7 with his 22nd consecutive PAT effort.

Kansas got another break when an intercepted pass gave it the ball on the Tiger 26. Roger McGarland passed two yards

to an end Sam Simpson six plays later for the final touchdown. Suder's conversion completed the heartbreaking game.

After the game was completed, it was announced that the Tigers had accepted a bid to play Navy in the Orange Bowl.

SAVITAR 1962 – BORDER WAR 1961
Tiger Defense Holds K.U. As Dogs Defend Goalposts

The University of Missouri Tigers produced one of the most rewarding triumphs in recent years by taking everything Kansas could dish out and more than matching it for a brilliant 10 to 7 conquest. The win halted a six-game K.U. victory string and the two teams tied for the runnerup spot in the Big 8 Conference behind Colorado with 5-2 records. Coach Dan Devine's team finished the 1961 season with a 7-2-1 record and was again one of the country's finest grid squads.

The game between the two mighty midwest teams was predicted to be a battle between Mizzou's standout defense and K.U.'s strong offense. The Black and Gold held the losers to 150 yards on the ground while pounding out 174 themselves, but it was the passing of Ron Taylor, the fine Bengal quarterback, that gave the Tigers the well-balanced attack to defeat the Kansans.

JAYHAWKER 1963 – BORDER WAR 1962

Kansas pulled the season and league records out of the fire by tying a highly favored Missouri team 3-3 on a fourth quarter 2-yard field goal by Gary Duff. Duff's score, following the Missouri tally booted by the Tigers' Leistritz, was little indication of the actual work done by the fired-up Jayhawkers.

Battling against one of the top defensive teams in the nation, the Hawks ground out 191 yards rushing while holding the traditional rivals to 137. Brian Palmer came off the bench to toss two passes good for 17 yards to complete the Kansas gain total. The Missourians gained but 19 via the air to place Kansas clearly atop the statistical charts.

In another statistical comparison, Hawk rookie standout Gale Sayers outrushed his conference archrival Johnny Roland to the tune of 72 yards to 34. The gain by Sayers pushed his total to 1,125 yards gained for the season, and left him just 4 yards shy of the Kansas school record. His rushing total established him firmly on top of the Big 8 rushing race in addition to a third place spot in the National rankings.

Attitude after the team's "surprise" finish verged on disappointment with the players thankful for the tie, but feeling that they should have won.

1960S

Possibly the highlight of the game was the Kansas line play. Battling against one of the toughest end-to-end combos in the nation, the young Kansas units did their share and more of the pushing. Tackle Marvin Clothier furthered his establishment as an All Big 8 tackle, and led teammates Pete Quatrochi, Ken Tiger, and Mick Walker in slowing the Tiger rushing thrust.

Although Sayers was handed the biggest offensive chores of the day, it was the inside power running of fullback Armand Baughman and the early slotback thrusts by Tony Leiker and David Crandall that kept the defense from stacking for Sayers' wide attack. Baughman contributed 32 yards on 9 endeavors and Leiker provided the longest run of the day with a 31-yard jaunt in the second quarter.

Biggest thorn in the Jayhawker's side was the running of Tiger quarterback Jim Johnson. The lanky field general ran both inside and wide for 59 yards on 14 carries.

Kansas owed some of its disappointment to bad breaks. Starting slotbacker and ace punter Tony Leiker succumbed to an ankle injury in the second quarter and was out for the rest of the game. In a game nearly free from mistakes and penalties, the Hawks dropped an expensive five of their ten yards in penalties when a shift formation near the Tiger goal line set them back and forced the field goal that tied the game.

The season in retrospect revealed a 6-3-1 showing far above what had been predicted for the rebuilding team. The Missouri game could have given Coach Jack Mitchell his best season for the duration, but the comeback as the season faded was enough to keep spirits from drooping, and left a young team ready to start it over next year.

SAVITAR 1963 – BORDER WAR 1962

A record breaking crowd of 46,000 saw the Tigers battle the Jayhawkers to a 3-3 tie in the 71st playing of the nation's fifth oldest rivalry.

Defense dominated the game for both sides with the stout Tiger line holding Kansas without a touchdown for the first time in 46 games. Neither team scored until the 4th quarter when a 14 yard roll out by Tiger quarterback Jim Johnson set up sophomore Bill Leistritz for a 11 yard field goal.

Missouri ended its conference season with a 5-1-1 record finishing 2nd in the Big 8 and a bid to the Bluebonnet Bowl in Houston, Texas.

SAVITAR 1964 – BORDER WAR 1963

In a game that seemed almost anti-climactic, Missouri squeaked by arch-rival Kansas, 9-7, in a well-played game at Lawrence. The game had been postponed a week due to the assassination of President Kennedy.

It was only fitting that the hero of the game should be unheralded defensive ace Vice Turner who was playing in his last college game after completing a brilliant career.

Turner grabbed a fumble by Kansas' Ken Coleman in midair and ran 102 yards for a touchdown after it appeared that the Jayhawks were on the way to their second touchdown.

Steve Renko, the Jayhawks' three sport star, sneaked over from the one for a Kansas touchdown and the conversion was good, giving them a 7-0 lead.

Bill Leistritz missed the point-after-touchdown attempt following Turner's run but made amends later by booting a game-winning field goal.

JAYHAWKER 1965 – BORDER WAR 1964

Being favored once again proved disastrous in the annual KU-MU battle as the Tigers put together their biggest scoring punch of the year in a 34-14 romp over the Jayhawks. With Oklahoma's upset over Nebraska the same day, a Kansas victory would have meant a share of the league crown and a possible bowl bid. But they were no match for the much-improved Tiger squad, who continually blasted over and around KU's defense. The game marked the first time in the Mitchell-Devine series that either team had won on their home field, and dropped the Hawks to a 6-4 overall record.

In the first half, neither team had much luck until George Hornung pounced on a fumble on the Tiger 34, setting up the first KU score. Gale Sayers then sprinted around right end for the TD. Gary Duff's extra point tied the school record in that category at 49. The Bengals then drove 45 yards following the kickoff to the 19 but failed in an attempted field goal. Early in the second quarter MU took over on the Hawks' 25 after a blocked punt, but lost the ball when Gus Otto fumbled and Duff recovered. Another partially blocked punt set up Missouri's TD, a pass from Lane to Waller. The extra point attempt was no good, and the Jayhawks carried a 7-6 lead into the half.

The second half was a different story, however, as the Tigers drove 83 yards in 11 plays to take the lead. KU picked up their only other tally on the ensuing kickoff when quarterback Bob Skahan hit end Sandy Buda on a 65-yard pass play. Skahan took it over from the one for the touchdown, and Duff added the point after. From then on it was all Mizzou, with their line blasting big gaps in KU's defensive line. The Tigers had one scoring drive of 68 yards in 11 plays and another of 57 yards in 9 plays, with sophomore Charlie Brown doing most of the work. As if that weren't enough, they then blocked a Skahan pass and recovered it on the KU 11. Waller took another pass from Lane for his second TD of the day, but the extra point again failed.

Sayers, the Jayhawks' All-American back ended his career in frustration, picking up only 19 yards in 8 carries, an all-time career low. Mike Johnson led Kansas in that department with a 4.3-yard average, ahead of Sayers. Defensive standouts were Duff and Greg Roth.

SAVITAR 1965 – BORDER WAR 1964

The Tigers, on the bright side, eliminated Oklahoma and Kansas from title contention in the last two weeks of the season. Missouri tied the Sooners, 14-14, at Norman before concluding the campaign by stomping Kansas, 34-14.

SAVITAR 1966 – BORDER WAR 1965

One of the most unpredictable rivalries in college football comes at the close of each season between Missouri and Kansas.

Last season's contest was no exception as the underdog but spirited Jayhawks threatened to upset the Tigers with two early touchdowns.

Before a regional television audience and thousands of visiting Missourians, Kansas blocked a punt on M.U.'s 10-yard line and took a 7-0 lead several plays later.

After the Tigers had tied the game, Johnny Roland tipped a long pass into the hands of Kansas receiver Halley Kampschroeder, who gave the hosting team a 13-7 margin on the 51-yard play.

This was the Jayhawks final threat of the game, however, as the Tigers pulled themselves together to rack up an eventual 44-20 victory.

SAVITAR 1967 – BORDER WAR 1966

Closing the season at home, a 54-yard pass from Kombrink to Earl Denny gave Missouri a 7-0 victory and a 4-3-1 Big 8 record.

SAVITAR 1968 – BORDER WAR 1967

In the final battle of the season, the Tigers outgained Kansas in passing and rushing, but fell to the Jayhawks, 17-6. Kansas scored on two long touchdown passes and an intercepted Kombrink aerial from the eight-yard line.

JAYHAWKER 1969 – BORDER WAR 1968

In the season's final game the Orange Bowl bound Jayhawks met the Missouri Tigers on Nov. 23 in Columbia. Before the largest Missouri crowd ever to watch a sporting event the Big Blue turned back the Gator Bowl bound Tigers 21-19 for the Hawk's 9th victory against one loss.

The Hawks were led to a great defensive showing by Dave Morgan, senior safety. Morgan recovered a fumble and intercepted two passes returning one 33 yards for KU's first touchdown, and he picked off his second one late in the game to stop a Tiger drive, and to kill Mizzou's hopes for victory. For his play Morgan was named as Sports Illustrated's back of the week.

Bobby Douglass once again showed his All-American form as he hit George McGowan on a 33 yard pass play, and ran in another late in the game.

Thus the Missouri Tigers became the ninth victims for the Big Blue from Kansas. In this the "Year of the Hawks" one mythical game remained in a sort of mythical place-off to the Orange Bowl in Miami, Florida.

By Joseph R. Childs
Kansas Alumnus 1971

SAVITAR 1969 – BORDER WAR 1968

Two bowl-bound teams, Kansas and Missouri, battled for the Big 8 title. Although the Tigers won in first downs (20-15), passing yardage (233-143) and total yardage (398-326), the Jayhawks scored two more points and won the game, 21-19. Kansas scored two quick touchdowns in the first quarter. Staggers put Mizzou on the scoreboard with a 5-yard run in the second quarter, but the PAT [point after touchdown] was blocked. In the fourth quarter, Kansas scored after a Tiger fumble. Then suddenly the Bengals struck twice as Staggers blasted through for six points, followed by a ten yard aerial tally. The point after made the final score 21-19.

SAVITAR 1970 – BORDER WAR 1969

Border-rival KU still doesn't know how Missouri beat them, 69-21.

AMADEE

Who is the embodiment of "Missouri Spirit?" The man is no other than the artist who decorated the covers of the Missouri football program for nearly 30 years, Amadee Wohlschlaeger.

Amadee, who preferred to be known only by his given name, was not only an avid Mizzou fan, but he was an artist, illustrator, cartoonist, and caricaturist during his career. He lives in Saint Louis, Missouri and for almost 50 years was the illustrator of the "Weatherbird" for the *St. Louis Post-Dispatch*. The Weatherbird is Amadee's most recognized work and the bird not only commented on the weather in the morning paper but also depicted history in the making: The attack on Pearl Harbor, the Civil Rights Movement, the assassination of President Kennedy, and Neil Armstrong being the first to walk on the Moon.

Even Kansas fans enjoy the humour of Amadee's illustrations of the Missouri Tiger preparing for a Thanksgiving Day feast of Jayhawk, which he drew from 1960 until 1992. For 32 years, the Missouri Tiger, drawn by the fanciful hand of Amadee, has been seen feasting, chasing, and intimidating rival team mascots with his jagged teeth and sharpened claws.

Besides being a living legend of Missouri fandom, his cartoons oftenly were the feature of *The Sporting News* magazine covers. The bronze statue of Stan "The Man" Musial by Harry Weber in front of the Missouri Sports Hall of Fame was taken from an image drawn by Amadee in 1963 - known as "The Boy and The Man."

Amadee is well known around the Saint Louis metropolitan area, not only for his cartoons and humour, but for his involvement to make the area a better place to live. Amadee was Vice Chairman of the original Sunset Hills City Zoning and Planning Commission and he was the yearly caricature artist of the Catfish Awards Roast for the Saint Louis Press Club. In 2002, he received the Sportsman of the Year Award from the Saint Louis Ambassadors and he was inducted in 2006 to the Saint Louis Media Hall of Fame. Thank you, Amadee, for making it so much fun to hate a Tiger!

By Shawn Buchanan Greene
Kansas Alumnus 1991
Written Wednesday, September 30, 2009

THE 1970s......

The decade of the 1970s was an unsettled decade from previous decades since the 1940s. The United States withdrew its troops from Vietnam unceremoniously and President Richard Nixon would resign from office due to the developing story of the Democratic National Headquarters burglary at the Watergate Hotel. The country experienced its first serious economic recession since the 1930s and an oil crisis caused hour-long waits in line at the gas station. By 1975 a new filming format known as "Video Home System," commonly known by its acronym "VHS," was introduced that would later revolutionize the making of home movies. Many factors of style became exaggerated and eccentric as shirt collars became longer, as well as hair, which often appeared disheveled in photographs. A movie named Saturday Night Fever, made an icon of a young actor named John Travolta for a new style of music and lifestyle known as "disco." By the end of the decade, disco was quickly reviled and replaced by another youth lifestyle and musical type known as "punk rock."

After ending 1968 and 1969 with a Conference Championship and an Orange Bowl appearance for each school, Dan Devine and Pepper Rodgers started the new decade each posting a 5-6 record. In the Border War Game that year, Devine's 4-6 Tigers were able give Kansas the loss, leaving both with losing season records. Dan Devine, having his first losing season since taking control of the Tigers in 1958, took a job the next season with the Green Bay Packers of the National Football League. Pepper Rodgers, likewise, also left Kansas for a job as head coach of the University of California – Los Angeles Bruins.

Taking control of both teams were longtime assistant coaches for both teams, Albert Joseph "Al" Onofrio for Missouri and Don Preston Fambrough for Kansas. Both coaches were considered beyond reproach in their ethics and faithfulness to their schools. Al Onofrio came to Missouri with Dan Devine from Tempe, Arizona and Don Fambrough came to Kansas as part of the Servicemen's Readjustment Act of 1944, also known as the G. I. Bill, as a player and then served as an assistant coach under several head coaching changes at Kansas. The first game that the two played against each other in 1971 was scoreless until the third quarter when Kansas quarterback David Jaynes completed a 35-yard pass to Marvin Foster in the end zone to lead the game 7-0. In the fourth quarter with two minutes left in the game and after running three plays and being penalized for delay of game, Kansas found itself on their own 8-yard line with the possibility of kicking a punt that might give Missouri the field position to score a touchdown. Instead of punting, Don Fambrough talked to punter Marc Harris and told him to run around the end zone and under no circumstances to exit the end zone or fumble the football. Harris was able to run for 12 seconds in the end zone until he was tackled, safely punting the ball from the 20-yard line to Missouri's 32-yard line, with Mike Fink returning it to the Missouri 48-yard line. Three plays later, Kansas won the game 7-2.

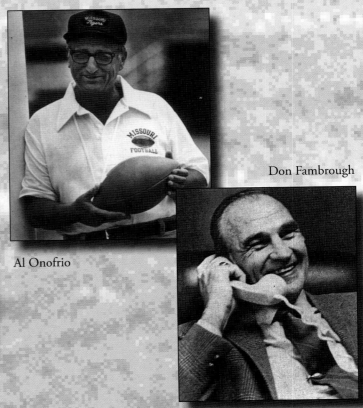

Al Onofrio

Don Fambrough

Don Fambrough (kicking) as a Kansas player in 1946

ON ANY GIVEN SATURDAY

The 1971 game seemed to typify play in the 1970s for both teams, in that many of the games frustrated fans but had their unbelievable moments. To the fans it seemed that the teams to whom they lost, they could have beat, but on any given Saturday, they could be a giant killer, such as in 1972 when a 2-3 Tiger team went to South Bend, Indiana and beat an undefeated Notre Dame team. In 1972, Missouri had the fortune of unexpectedly beating several top ranked teams, which many of the Missouri faithful contend had to do with the luck given them for naming the football field after Don Faurot that year.

In the 1973 game, the two teams battled to a forlorn 0-0 halftime score. In the third quarter, within the span of 1:41, Missouri scored two touchdowns, the first on a 45-yard run by quarterback Ray Smith, the extra point being made, and then again with 2:07 remaining in the quarter when John Moseley made a 53-yard punt return. The extra point was missed on this touchdown, which seemed negligible at the time until the kickoff when Kansas drove 76 yards in eight plays and allowed quarterback Dave Jaynes to pass 14 yards to Bruce Adams for a touchdown. Later, with two minutes left to play on fourth down and two yards needed for a first, Kansas prepared for a short pass to Delvin Williams. Kansas, however, also sent Emmett Edwards long into the end zone, who was the leading receiver at the time in the Big 8. Being covered by Missouri's best pass defender, John Moseley, Edwards cut to the goal post and caught a well-timed pass from Jaynes. Kansas freshman, Mike Love, kicked the game winning extra point, playing in only his fourth game with the varsity. Despite the loss, Missouri still went to their first bowl game in the 1970s, the Sun Bowl, where they proved champions. Kansas, the previous year had gone to the Fiesta Bowl and this year went to the Liberty Bowl, losing both games.

By the end of the 1974 season, after accumulating a 20-24-1 record and beating Missouri three out of four games, Kansas changed head coaches to Robert W. "Bud" Moore. Moore was a native of Birmingham, Alabama and attended the University of Alabama where he played and coached under Coach Paul "Bear" Bryant. In his first year as head coach of the Jayhawks, Moore was able to finish the season with a 7-4 record, beat Missouri, take the team to the Sun Bowl. Moore also earned the Big Eight Coach of the Year award, and lost top honours to Woody Hayes for the National Coach of the Year award.

Three years later in 1977, despite some miraculous wins at opposing stadiums, Al Onofrio was released from Missouri in favour of former Nebraska star player and rising star coach Warren Powers. Powers in his first year at Missouri beat Moore's Jayhawks with his 2-7 Tigers, although at the time the Jayhawks were only 1-9, suffering their worst season since 1969. Despite a 3-7 record, Powers was able to take the Tigers to the Liberty Bowl, winning it. The eventual 1-10 season for Kansas spelled doom for Moore after four years of coaching, causing the return of Don Fambrough as head coach of the Jayhawks. A year later in 1979, Don Fambrough was able to improve the 1-10 Jayhawks to a 3-8 team and the Jayhawks were still playing with lots of young talent, which had been the case the previous year. Warren Powers continued winning at Missouri, defeating the Jayhawks 55-7 and taking his team to yet another bowl game, the Hall of Fame Bowl. With this final victory and bowl game for Missouri at the end of the 1979 season, there seemed to be a bright future ahead for Missouri football and the Border War Game.

Kirby Criswell hugs Don Fambrough in 1979 (left) and more from the game from 1979 (right)

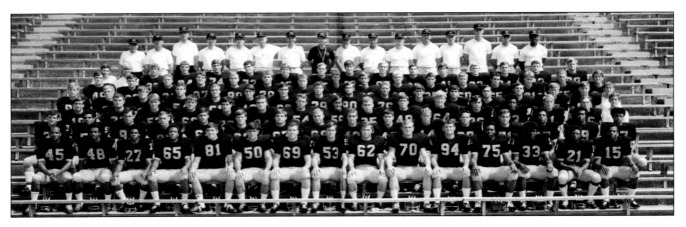

Missouri Football (5-6) - Head Coach Daniel John Devine

Row 1: Moore, Walls, Fountain, Vital, Bennett, Weisenfels, Wallace, Wilson, Kelley, Lowder, Colclasure, Jackson, Harrison, Gray, Hunter.
Row 2: McKee, Britts, Kelley, Borgard, Mizer, Cowan, Kephart, Bell, Buha, Bastable, Farmer, Henley, Stephenson, Brinkley, Glosson, Stuckey. Row 3: Roper, Burns, Moore, Caputo, Matuszak, Luther, Billespie, Mauser, McDonough, Anderson, Dobbs, Washington, Fink, Roth, Manager Moreno. Row 4: Kamradt, Sodergren, Curbow, Henderson, Frost, Pankey, Clark, Kirley, Doak, Gebhard, Kanatzar, Venturi, Tessendorf, Egbert, Bigson, Howard, Manager Pierron. Row 5: Kellett, Colclasure, Nerling, Horton, Paulsen, Schnietz, Saitz, Lindquist, Roley, Lowder, Campbell, Shaw, Beattie, Schnur, Caldwell, Hill. Row 6: Manager McCraith, Manager Carpenter, Gschwender, Manda, Weaver, Schmitt, Dudney, Brown, Schwab, Weber, Hatfield, Schrier, Yanko, Austin, Jaskowiak, McMurry.

Kansas Football (5-6) - Head Coach Franklin C. Rodgers

Missouri Football (1-10) - Head Coach Albert Joseph Onofrio

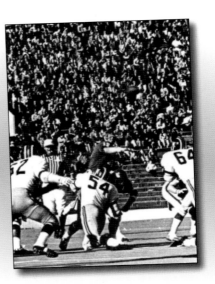

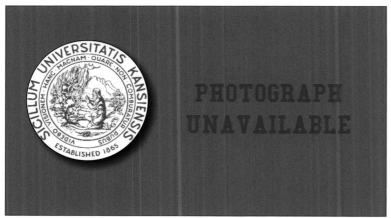

PHOTOGRAPH UNAVAILABLE

Kansas Football (4-7) - Head Coach Donald Preston Fambrough

211

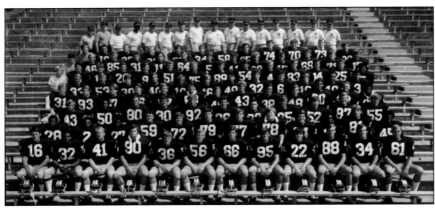

Missouri Football (6-6) - Head Coach Albert Joseph Onofrio
Fiesta Bowl Invitation

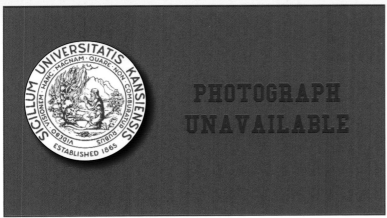

Kansas Football (5-6) - Head Coach Donald Preston Fambrough
Fiesta Bowl Invitation

Missouri Football (7-5) - Head Coach Albert Joseph Onofrio
Sun Bowl Champion

Kansas Football (7-4-1) - Head Coach Donald Preston Fambrough
Liberty Bowl Invitation

Row 1: Bowman, Dillon, Love, Swift, Harris, Norris, Bryant, Miller, Goode, Williams, Hodges, Butler. Row 2: Ross, Turner, Scanlan, Adams, Taylor, Robinson, Kovatch, Skepnek, Clemente, Schmitz, Spear. Row 3: McMichael, Hosack, Mudge, Rome, Lemon, Gardner, Mercer, Jaynes, Englebrake, McDaniel, Winter. Row 4: Edwards, Beeson, Zook, Stockemer, Saathoff, Beggs, Scott, Krattli, Cromwell, Pile. Row 5: Robinson, Weidner, Adams, Towle, Baird, Weger, Boydston, Baker, Smith, Prince, Lewis.

Missouri Football (8-4) - Head Coach Albert Joseph Onofrio

Row 1: Buck, Johnson, Muse, Keeney, Zieger, Evans, Pickens, Sadich, Bybee, Gillick, Vanarsdall, Smith. Row 2: Downing, Cooper, McRoberts, Miller, Yount, Johnston, Gross, Cook, Pisarkiewicz, Miller, Austin, Owens, McDevitt. Row 3: Beckett, Marshall, Marx, Parrott, Goble, Walker, Williams, Davis, Carter, Smith, Galbreath, Fagan, Douglass, Grossart. Row 4: Brown, Towns, Henningsen, Gokin, Cole, Bohner, Billings, Burbridge, Hopkins, Meyer, Frank, D. W. Johnston, Semour, Yearian. Row 5: Gibbons, Garavaglia, Bentlage, Brickey, Kells, Shockley, Smith, Wilson, Demien, Dwyer, Riek, Wefelmeyer, Owens, Carr, Davis. Row 6: Fitzgerald, Phillips, Whitmer, Frisch, Blakeman, Bushell, Dement, Kurka, Bohannon, Hoskins, Engman, Zimmermann, LeBanc, Long, Hodge. Row 7: Culp, Leibson, McDonald, Gourley, Kowalczyk, Hertzog, Putnam, Newman, Williams, Lain, Doyle, Watson, Kirkpatrick, Ghrist. Row 8: Manager Bistline, Bennett, Morrissey, Wright, Miget, Scherman, Blake, Mally, Williams, Banta, Denike, Twellman, Manager Bear. Row 9: Trainer Wappel, Coach Dissinger, Coach Steponovich, Coach Anderson, Coach Warmack, Coach Tobin, Coach Cooper, Coach Onofrio, Coach Kadlec, Coach Jamieson, Coach Snyder, Coach Gautt, Coach Cowdrey, Trainer Proffitt.

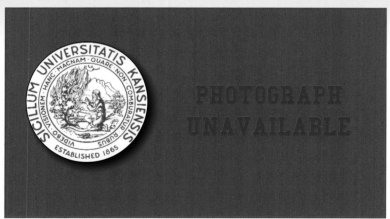

Kansas Football (4-7) - Head Coach Donald Preston Fambrough

Missouri Football (7-4) - Head Coach Albert Joseph Onofrio

Row 1: Carr, Austin, Blakeman, Douglass, Goble, Downing, Galbreath, McRoberts, Owens, Grossart, Garavaglia, Marshall, Cooper, Meyer. Row 2: Bushell, Fagan, Parrott, Owens, Demien, Hodge, Marx, Towns, Hennuingsen, Williams, Culp, Fitzgerald, McDevitt, Brown, Pisarkiewicz. Row 3: Frank, Engman, Whitmer, Smith, Morrissey, Kells, Kirkpatrick, Newman, Yearian, Kowalczyk, Frisch, Cole, Carter, Brown, Banta, Bentlage. Row 4: Bohner, Davis, Downer, Gourley, Helm, Kirkland, Lain, Leavitt, Seymour, Leibson, Taylor, M. Williams, J. Williams, Wepler, Stewart, Doyle, Burbridge. Row 5: Allard, Billings, Blake, Suda, Brickey, Ghrist, Gibbons, Legg, Loving, McBride, McDonald, Shockley, Montgomery, Woods, Phillips, Twellman, Walker. Row 6: Anderson, Boehm, Disselhoff, Gokin, LaBanc, Mally, Newman, McBride, Putnam, Schermann, Shortal, Smith, Wallington, Whitaker, Wolfenberger, M. D. Owens, Watson. Row 7: Hamilton, Wingbermuehle, Klein, Hulett, Clark, Gant, Dansdill, Garlich, Burge, Calabrese, Capra, Lewis, Miller, Winslow, McCormick. Row 8: Manager Bruce, Manager Bistline, Berg, Graham, Toney, Thomas, Gie, Giltner, Guender, Harrell, Bess, Parks, Jones, Petersen, Bekemeier, Manager Manco, Row 9: Trainer Proffitt, Trainer Wappel, Dissinger, Kadlec, Coach McGinnis, Coach Burns, Steponovich, Coach Onofrio, Cooper, Tobin, Coach Hoener, Jones, Jamieson, Cowdrey, Kopay.

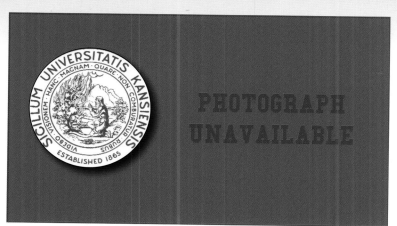

Kansas Football (7-5) - Head Coach Robert W. Moore
Sun Bowl Invitation

Missouri Football (6-5) - Head Coach Albert Joseph Onofrio

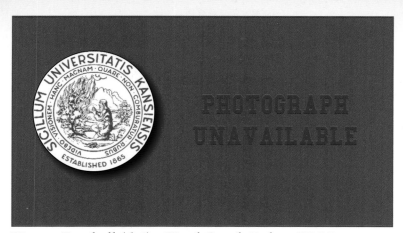

Kansas Football (6-5) - Head Coach Robert W. Moore

Missouri Football (6-5) - Head Coach Albert Joseph Onofrio

Row 1: Sutherland, Leavitt, Legg, Leibson, Taylor, Morrissey, Stewart, Woods, Davis. Row 2: Anderson, Billings, Blake, Blau, Burbridge, Cole, Davis, Twellman, Whitmer, Mally. Row 3: McDonald, Gaddy, Gie, Disselhoff, Dansdill, Newman, Allard, Calabrese, Berg. Row 4: Winslow, Gant, Lewis, Suda, Miller, Giltner, Bess, Garlich, Jones, Parks, Row 5: Hamilton,   Capra, McBride, Owens, Guender, Lauderdale, Petersen, Harrell, Litzenfelner. Row 6: Downer, Toney, Smotherson, Carter, Davis, Wingbermuehle, Bungarda, Montgomery, Burge, Rust. Row 7: Matthews, Velten, O'Neill, Frick, Morgner, Hornof, Keller, Forrest, Clark. Row 8: Forward, Pyatt, Mitchell, Montgomery Lechner, Merriweather, Marx, Moss, Farley, Miller. Row 9: Martin, Hart, Baker, Houston, Howlett, Powell, Gall, Blair, Leonard. Row 10: Baker, Murray, Ray, Gaylord, Ellis, Bekemeier, Dickey, Newman, Massey, Cunningham. Row 11: Scott, Shelp, Simmonds, Brockhaus, Wherle, Leiding, Hughes, Wagner, Devin. Row 12: Stephens, Bradley, Green, Stokowski, Sally, Stecich, Richards, Duff, Wright, Jeffrey. Row 13: Washington, Darkow, Orszula, Sadler, Matchell, Holloway, Poe, Whitaker. Row 14: Coach Cowdrey, Coach Preston, Manager Foster, Manager Athen, Manager Bistline, Manager Simone, Coach Brickey, Coach Venturi. Row 15: Trainer Epps, Jones, Coach Lawrence, Coach Raetz, Coach Kadlec, Coach Onofrio, Coach Reese, Coach McGinnis, Coach Jamieson, Coach Steponovich, Trainer Wappel.

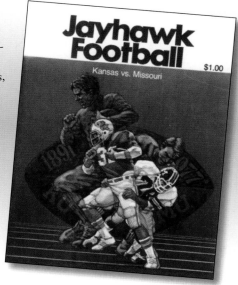

Kansas Football (4-6-1) - Head Coach Robert W. Moore

Missouri Football (4-7) - Head Coach Warren Anthony Powers - Walter Camp Coach of the Year
Liberty Bowl Champion

Row 1: Redding, Reese, Wheeler, Price, Yaralian, Heydorff, Powers, Beechner, Faiman, Thornton, Bratkowski, Epps, Wappel. Row 2: Gant, Gie, Litzelfeilner, Laudersdale, Newman, Downer, Lewis, Winslow, Suda, Montgomery, Dansdill. Row 3: Bungarda, Allard, Calabrese, Owens, Giltner, Harrell, Garlich, Bes, Disselhoff, McBride, Hamilton. Row 4: Forrest, Ellis, Newman, Frick, Carter, Guender, Velten, Jones, Miller, Berg. Row 5: Sanders, Peterson, Miltenberger, Jones, Bekemeier, Hornof, Kelley, Lechner, Dickey, Powell, Jones. Row 6: Bradley, Kuddes, Blair, Matthews, Gadt, Chattin, Schelp, Mottaz, Gaylord, Goodman, Brockhaus. Row 7: Holloway, Green, Stephens, Milla, Verrilli, Jackowski, Pappas, Wagner, Duff, Whitaker, Kennon, Stufflebean. Row 8: Ray, Stakowski, Richards, Jeffrey, Darkow, Anderson, Hyde, Newbold, Potter, Sly, Meyer. Row 9: Gentile, Wright, Richards, Wherle, Sally, Poe, Orszula, Busch, Kirkman, Miller, Boone, Taylor. Row 10: Leonard, Rautman, Wilder, Rogers, Washington, Hughes, Stephens, McNeel, Harlan, Ponder, Edelman. Row 11: Leiding, Sadler, Hill, Vaughn, Scott, Judd, Smith, Houston, Carter, Hairston, Meher. Row 12: Spencer, Leavitt, Morrissey, Whitesides, Clark, Troppman, Finan.

Kansas Football (1-10) - Head Coach Robert W. Moore

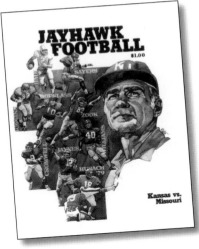

Missouri Football (8-4) - Head Coach Warren Anthony Powers
Hall of Fame Bowl Champion

Row 1: Redding, Beechner, Heydorff, Yaralian, Reese, Powers, Faiman, Price, Wheller, Thornton, Wappel. Row 2: Forrest, Harrell, Miltenberger, Jones, Petersen, Bekemeier, Carter, Berg, Guender, Goodman, Ellis. Row 3: Eldridge, Powell, Hornof, Gaylord, Richards, Lechner, Blair, Newman, Miller, Keller, Brockhaus. Row 4: Poe, Wherle, Bradley, Wright, Stecich, Schelp, Wagner, Duff, Washingon, Pappas. Row 5: Sally, Dickey, Grodie, Chattin, Gentile, Verrilli, Gadt, Darkow, Suntrup, Whitaker, Fellows. Row 6: Leiding, Stokowski, Stephens, Ray, Green, Skillman, Fenlon, Harris, Vaughn, Wilder, Crappo, Hartung. Row 7: Sadler, Hairston, Hoffman, B. Smith, Richards, McDaniel, Sly, Rogers, Potter, Hornof, Jostes. Row 8: Vandenerg, Scott, McNeel, Taylor, Anderson, Hyde, Edelman, Harlan, Miller, Meyer, Lockette. Row 9: Van Matre, Blackwell, Pop, Hill, Mottaz, Ponder, Pelek, Judd, Kirkman, Jennings, Wilson. Row 10: Limbaugh, J. Smith, M. Johnson, Hoover, Lucchesi, Kulich, Laster, Downey, Fletcher, Hirlinger. Row 11: Harrell, Krahl, Gibler, St. Clair, Lortz, Brown, Hawkins, D. Johnson, Crumbacher, Weiss. Row 12: Presberry, Pree, Baron, Macoubrie, Boyer, Shockly, Ekern, Bumgarner, Evans. Row 13: Kurtz, Laderdale, Dansdill, Bratkowski, Finan, Zimmer, Epps, Spencer.

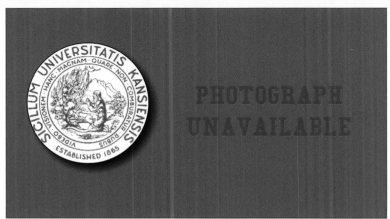

Kansas Football (3-8) - Head Coach Don Preston Fambrough

Oak Springs, Ark.
5 - 8 - 70

Dear Bill:

It is wonderful that at long last you are getting an honor which was due you a long time ago. That, however, is the way of life and people. It is not that people didn't appreciate - they were just slow to act.

More than anyone else, I would like to be at the dinner and believe me, only the five coronary thrombosis attacks are keeping me away. I know you'll understand that.

Bill I'll continue to remember you in my prayers and I'll continue to hope that our paths will cross again

As of old,
Jim Bausch

P. S. Too bad E H couldn't be around for this night.

By James Aloysius Bernard Bausch
Kansas Alumnus 1931
Written Friday, May 8, 1970

(Above) A letter written by Jim Bausch to Bill Hargiss (right) on the ceremony for Bill Hargiss Day in Emporia, Kansas.

JAYHAWK HASH!

In 1972, having upset the sports world by beating Notre Dame and Colorado, a conference foe, we had two consecutive victories against two great teams. Being a senior at Missouri, there were a number of thoughts that crossed my mind during my final game at Faurot Field: Rivalry, pageantry, and… revenge. The rivalry and pageantry of facing Kansas was expressed by Coach Onofrio, the staff, former players, and teammates. Losing to Kansas my junior year, left me with revenge in my heart; I was disgusted and humiliated! Adding fuel to the fire, Mitchell Sutton, one of my teammates with whom I had won a National Junior College Football Championship with two years before, was a Jayhawk. Joining Mitch from the Jnior College Championship team were Curt Nieman and Jerone Hoages. Mitch and I talked by phone from time to time, and Mitch felt they had a better team, which I knew was a bold face lie!

We practiced hard preparing for the game all week. Everyday, I talked to Leroy Moss, my roommate and teammate, about staying focused on beating Kansas. At practice I talked with Tommy Reamon, who was my teammate on that National Junior College Championship team, about beating our feathered foe! There was no way that we were going to let Mitch and our former teammates beat us on our home turf.

The coaches were concerned that we might lose focus and let down against Kansas because of our Fiesta Bowl invitation. Kansas, a spoiler, had little to gain; we were gaining respect with each victory. It was nice knowing that the gamblers in Las Vegas and sports fans were asking "What did Missouri do?"

We spent the night before the game in Jefferson City. On Game Day, we got dressed, had breakfast, and had a quick team meeting. Boarding the bus, all I thought about was beating Kansas. Upon reaching the stadium, traffic was dense, tailgaters were bunched on the Hearne's parking lot and fans were approaching from every direction. We entered the locker room, got taped, dressed, waited briefly, then walked onto the field to stretch and loosen up. I jogged to mid-field and waved to my family, noticed the painted turf, and jogged to the end zone. Running from one end of the field to the end zone was my ritual before every game. The team went through our warm-up drills, John Cherry called the huddle, and everyone was focused on the objective to win. Upon returning to the locker room, last minute adjustments were done. Leroy was seated next to me and I asked him if he was ready. He told me they used to call him "Lunch Meat" because he was always ready!

Coach Onofrio came up for a brief talk and we said a team prayer. Coach Kadlec came around shaking hands and saying "Let's go get those Jayhawks." We walked down to the field and stopped on the edge. The stadium was filled and had a circus like atmosphere. Missouri fans were everywhere. The seniors were announced one by one, when my name was called, I jogged to mid-field, receiving a heartfelt applause that felt like the entire State of Missouri had recognized me for that moment in time! The rest of the team joined us and the game started.

Containing David Jaynes, Delvin Williams, Marvin Foster, and company, proved very difficult, not to mention running into Mitch Sutton all day. Kansas won, and that was the last time I would wear that uniform. I had given my all and would have to live with never having enjoyed that Tiger delicacy… "Jayhawk Hash!"

By Donald Johnson
Missouri Alumnus 1973
Written Thursday, October 2, 2008

SAVITAR 1971 – BORDER WAR 1970

In the season finale, Mel Gray's 97-yard kick return demoralized arch-rival KU, and UMC ended its campaign on a winning note.

SAVITAR 1972 – BORDER WAR 1971

[There is no mention of the game. KU won 28-17]

SAVITAR 1973 – BORDER WAR 1972

[There is no mention of the game. KU won 14-13]

JAYHAWKER 1974 – BORDER WAR 1973

The Jayhawks put the lid on a 7-3-1 season by scoring twice in the fourth quarter to beat Missouri, 14-13. Appropriately, the passing of quarterback Dave Jaynes won the game as he threw touchdown strikes to flanker Bruce Adams and split end Emmett Edwards, both from 14 yards out. Kansas was in the familiar situation of having to come from behind as Missouri jumped out in front 13-0.

The first half was scoreless as turnovers plagued both teams. Missouri scored all its points in the third quarter. Tiger quarterback Ray Smith scored first on a 45-yard run off an option play. KU was forced to punt after the ensuing kickoff and Missouri's John Mosely returned the punt 53 yards for the touchdown.

KU's first break came when Greg Hill missed the extra point. Hill had previously kicked 19 of 19 point-after attempts. Still, things looked bleak for Kansas. Jaynes brought KU right back on a 76-yard march, capping it with the TD-toss to Adams.

The winning touchdown came on a fourth and two play after KU moved from the Missouri 42. Edwards

beat Mosely by a step and Jaynes laid the ball in perfectly. Freshman kicker Mike Love added the point after and KU wound up the regular season on a winning note.

SAVITAR 1974 – BORDER WAR 1973

[There is no mention of the game. MU won 27-3]

SAVITAR 1975 – BORDER WAR 1974

[There is no mention of the game. KU won 42-24]

SAVITAR 1976 – BORDER WAR 1975

[There is no mention of the game. KU won 41-14]

JAYHAWKER 1977 – BORDER WAR 1976

For Kansas and Missouri, little appeared to be at stake the following week at MU, other than a continuation of one of the nation's strongest and oldest rivalries. An added dimension to the game came later in the week, though, when the Sun Bowl announced it would bid Missouri if they won.

Kansas, on the other hand, was playing for pride. The seniors on the squad were especially hungry for this one. A KU victory would give them back-to-back winning seasons and add to another winning campaign four years ago.

The result couldn't have been nicer. After KU fumbled the ball away at the Tiger 10 in the second quarter while trying to extend a 3-0 lead, senior cornerback Skip Sharp intercepted a Steve Pizarkiewicz pass and raced 46-yards for a touchdown. The 'Hawks had just begun.

Campfield scored from 28 yards out, and senior Jim Michaels caught a Vicendese touchdown pass with two seconds left in the half for a 24-0 lead. Mike Hubach set a school record with a 49-yard field goal to start the second half scoring and the 'Hawks breezed to a 41-14 victory, their fifth over Mizzou in the last six years.

SAVITAR 1977 – BORDER WAR 1976

It happened again with Kansas. A dazed Black and Gold squad waded through four quarters for a total of 14 points. The Jayhawks had 41.

SAVITAR 1978 – BORDER WAR 1977

A victory over Kansas might have saved Onofrio's job. However, the Tiger's defensive strategy – which was installed in one week of practice – failed. "We practiced the defense this week, but it was totally different," said Calabrese after Kansas scored 24 first half points in their 24-22 victory. "People weren't sure of what they were doing."

Kansas quarterback Brian Bethke, a 36 percent passer for 120 yards prior to the Missouri game, completed six of nine passes for 180 yards prior to the Missouri game, completed six of nine passes for 180 yards against the Tigers. "We knew Kansas would pass," Onofrio said. "We just didn't expect the passes to be completed."

Onofrio didn't expect to be fired either. As he emerged from the locker room after the KU game, an alumnus whose eyes were as bleary from the effects of alcohol as Onofrio's were from the effects of the defeat, shook hands with the coach.

"Don't worry about it," the man said. "I'll see you at the season opener next year at Notre Dame. Me and you Al, we'll both be there."

Four days later, Onofrio was fired.

JAYHAWKER 1979 – BORDER WAR 1978

COLUMBIA, Mo. - Missouri finally ended the magical spell Kansas held over it and did it in a convincing way, 48-0.

Mizzou didn't waste any time, zipping to a 27-0 halftime lead, with the brunt of the offensive attack coming on the ground.

Kansas, forced to go to the air again because of an anemic running attack, had 286 yards passing. Quarterbacks Harry Sydney and Devin Clinton split time, with Clinton accounting for 165 yards on just nine completions.

Missouri's power backs, James Wilder and Earl Gant, had 160 and 134 yards respectively and Wilder had a school-tying record four touchdowns.

SAVITAR 1979 – BORDER WAR 1978

Sweet Revenge!
Real Tigers Stand Up

The score was Missouri 48, Kansas 0. And, before you start rubbing your eyes or question the credibility of this publication, wait. There's more.

First, it was a day of revenge. Missouri had lost to KU the last three years, twice preventing them from going to a bowl.

Second, it was a day of playful restlessness. With the Tigers grounding out a substantial lead early, the fans resorted to yawns resembling turnpike tunnels and plastic disc-lids fights. Remove lid from soda cup, toss like a frisbee, and see who you can nail.

Third, it was a great day for a search. The search for the real Missouri football team. And, with Earl Gant's 134-yard four touchdown performance and James Wilder's 160-yard game, visions of Missouri's past losses seemed inconceivable.

And, finally, there was a smile on Warren Powers' face, and even talk of - shhhh - bowl games.

"When I got here, all I heard you have to do is beat Kansas, and we beat them," Powers said. "The last two weeks have been very trying for this team. If we beat Nebraska next week, we'll

go to a bowl if I have to pay my way. And I seem to be paying my way a lot lately."

Little did Powers know, though, he would be able to leave his wallet at home.

SAVITAR 1980 – BORDER WAR 1979

Tigers use KU for a whipping post

Psychologists say the best way to relieve frustration is to find an outlet. Scream into a pillow, tear apart a phone book, that sort of thing.

Or, if you're the Missouri Tigers, beat Kansas so badly they think they've been through Dunkirk rather than a football game. This is exactly what the Tiger did in the final game of the season. After a heartbreaking loss to Nebraska and a season marred by dropped passes and missed extra points, the Tigers had frustration to spare. When they took the field in Lawrence, it was time to atone for all the bad memories. It was time to make the rival Jayhawks pay the price for what had been a dreary season.

At halftime the squad led by 14-0. At the end of the third quarter they upped it to 21-0. Then, in the fourth quarter, the deluge began as the Tigers started racking up points with the rapidity of a pinball machine. When the final score of 55-7 lit upon on the Faurot Field scoreboard, the word TILT should have flashed underneath it.

Missouri's statistics were awesome. For the offense, 429 total yards and seven touchdowns. Senior running back Gerry Ellis combined with James Wilder to amass 205 of Missouri's 335 yards rushing – the Tigers' best performance on the ground that season.

For the defense, it was another blue ribbon performance. They put a stranglehold on KU limiting them to 150 yards total offense. Of course, they made their customary contribution to the scoring, too. Reserve linebacker Van Darkow ran back an interception 25 yards for the final score.

"This one felt real good," Missouri's senior flanker Dave Newman said. "This is the first time everything went our way. Frustrated – that's exactly how we felt for 10 games. We had sort of been struggling. It was nice to sit back on the sidelines and smile. It was a good feeling."

In a season marked by the twists and turns of fate, it's not surprising that it would end in irony. After all the disappointments, the 6-5 Tigers were offered a bid to the Hall of Fame Bowl in Birmingham, Alabama. They gladly accepted. "When you're 6-5," offensive tackle Howard Richards said, "you're happy to be going to any bowl."

The decade of the 1980s was referred to as "The Decade of Greed" both with revile and jubilation. In essence, greed became good, at least by those who could obtain wealth. President Ronald Reagan had overwhelming popular support in the United States but he was restrained by a Democratic Congress. The Cold War with the Soviet Union was reaching its finale as the United States declared victory as the Berlin Wall fell in 1989. Everywhere in America appeared a new type of person known as a "yuppie," which was taken from the term "young urban professional preppies," and their counterculture counterparts known as "burn-outs." The popular trends in music at this time were known as "pop," "ska-reggae," and "heavy metal" and vinyl audio records were replaced by a new digital format known as a "Compact Disk" or "CD."

From 1978 to 1983 Warren Powers went to and won three of five bowl games with the Tigers. Kansas finished 1980 4-5-2, but the very next year Don Fambrough improved the team to 8-4. The Border War Game in 1981 was known as an epic battle of the two teams' defenses. With only eight minutes and 56 seconds from the clock expiring in the first quarter of the game, Kansas' starting quarterback, Frank Seurer, dislocated the elbow of his throwing arm, which put him on the sideline for the remainder of the game. As a result, the offense was only able to produce 60 yards of total offense and zero yards rushing in the first half of the game. At halftime, Missouri led the Jayhawks 3-0, which might have been more had Missouri not surrendered the ball four times.

In the second half of the game Kansas scored its first points on a two-point safety when Missouri's center snapped the ball past the end zone. Kansas scored again on an intercepted pass that later turned into a field goal, giving them the lead 5-3 at the end of the third quarter. The game was finally decided in the fourth quarter when Kansas safety, Roger Foote, scored the game's first touchdown on an inter-

Warren Powers

Mike Gottfried

cepted pass which he ran 27 yards to the end zone and Kansas scored again with 9:42 left in the game. A final touchdown was scored by Missouri, to no avail. Despite the loss, Missouri was

Woody Widenhofer

invited to the Tangerine Bowl, where they proved champions and Kansas accepted a bid to the Hall of Fame Bowl, losing that game.

After Kansas' 8-4 season in 1981, the team suffered a 2-7-2 season, which caused the exit once again of Don Fambrough. Mike Gottfried became the new Kansas head coach in 1983 and with a 3-6-1 record; beat the Holiday Bowl bound 7-3 Tigers, 37-27. The Tigers lost in the Holiday Bowl and finished the season with a record of 7-5, which would prove to be the last winning season for either school for the remainder of the decade. After Warren Powers had his first losing season since taking control of the team in 1978, he was replaced as head coach by Robert "Woody" Widenhofer, who was a former Mis-

Bob Valesente

souri fullback. At the time of his hiring, Widenhofer was the defensive coordinator of the Pittsburgh Stealers and was part of the coaching staff that won four Super Bowls and nine postseason appearances. By 1985, after posting a 6-6 season at Kansas, Mike Gottfried was replaced by his assistant coach, Bob Valesente, who in his two seasons at Kansas garnered a 4-17-1 cumulative record. In his first year coaching the Jayhawks, they suffered a tremendous defeat to Missouri 48-0. The game was played in Columbia that year and, although the Tigers had only earned their third win of the season with the victory, the excitement of the win was so great that the Tiger fans razed the goal posts. Because of state of the football programs, towards the end of the decade the *Kansas City Star* proclaimed Missouri, Kansas, and Kansas State the "Bermuda Triangle of college football."

The problems during this part of the decade seemed chronic and insurmountable to fans and were accentuated by the success around them at other Big 8 schools, such as at Oklahoma, Ne-

POINTS OF THE BERMUDA TRIANGLE

braska, and Colorado. On December 30, 1987, Kansas hired an enthusiastic coach, Glen Mason, who had unexpectedly beaten them in the 1987 season with his Kent State Golden Flashes. Glen Mason was born in Colonia, New Jersey and played college football at Ohio State University, served as an assistant coach at the University of Illinois, Ohio State, Ball State, Iowa State, and Allegheny College. He was serving his second year as head coach of Kent State when he beat Kansas and later decided to accept the head coaching job there. Mason brought with him nine assistants and, despite the problems facing the program, was successful in recruiting a talented group of players, who included quarterback Tim Hill, linebacker Paul Friday, and, in 1989, a diminutive but strong and fast running back, Tony Sands. Mason ended the 1988 season 1-10,

Glen Mason

but did so with a team comprised mostly of 17 and 18-year-old players.

The 1988 game was held in Lawrence that year and only had 25,000 in attendance. In the game, Kansas was decimated by Missouri in the second half of the game, eventually losing the game 55-17. Because of his 12-31-1 record at Missouri and general dissatisfaction with the direction of the program, Woody Widenhofer resigned. Missouri administrators, as a result, sought to fundamentally redesign its program as Kansas was now committed, hiring a coach known

Bob Stull

for fixing programs at the University of Massachusetts and at the University of Texas – El Paso, Bob Stull. Robert William Stull is from Davenport, Iowa and later became a three-year football letterman at Kansas State University and was the captain of the 1967 football team, earning both a bachelor's degree and later a master's degree while there.

The 1989 game began in freezing temperatures in Columbia and exhibited a battle between two teams determined to demonstrate their new winning spirits. In the game, the two teams scored a combined 90 points, 56 in the second half of the game and had a combined total of 923 yards of total offense. Despite the rampant scoring, the lead changed only three times and remained close the entire game. At the half, Missouri led the game 21-13, but on the kickoff, Kansas' Charley Bowen returned the ball 47 yards to the Missouri 37 and seven plays later, Tony Sands ran around left end for seven yards, scoring a touchdown that initiated a flurry of scoring for both teams. With three minutes left and a one-point lead in the game, Kansas punted the ball to Missouri's Ron Pointer, who fumbled the ball at the Missouri 13-yard line with only 2:30 left on the clock. Missouri, faced with the prospect of Kansas running the clock and winning the game by default, allowed Kansas to score to allow for their own scoring opportunity. The strategy nearly worked as Missouri received the kick-off and charged 70 yards down the field in less than two minutes to score and possibly tie the game on a two-point conversion. The conversion failed, ending the decade with one of the most exciting finishes in the game's history.

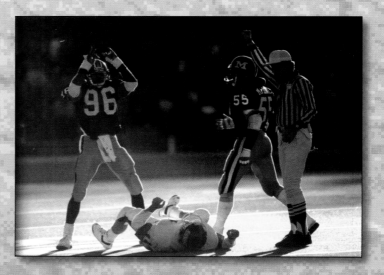

The 1987 Border War Game

Missouri Football (8-4) - Head Coach Warren Anthony Powers
Liberty Bowl Invitation

Kansas Football (4-5-2) - Head Coach Don Preston Fambrough

Missouri Football (8-4) - Head Coach Warren Anthony Powers
Tangerine Bowl Champion

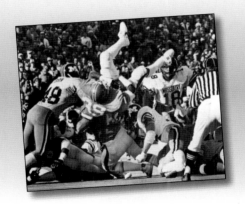

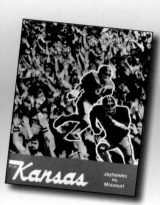

Kansas Football (8-4) - Head Coach Don Preston Fambrough
Hall of Fame Bowl Invitation

Missouri Football (5-4-2) - Head Coach Warren Anthony Powers

Kansas Football (2-7-2) - Head Coach Don Preston Fambrough

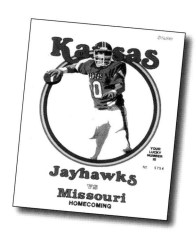

Missouri Football (7-5) - Head Coach Warren Anthony Powers
Holiday Bowl Invitation

Row 1: Trainer Wappel, Doctor McElroy, Coach Powell, Coach Miller, Coach Heydorff, Coach Beightol, Coach Powers, Coach Donnan, Coach Sadler, Coach Schottel, Coach Wynn, Coach Ball. Row 2: Leshe, Krahl, Kramer, Goode, Laster, Bruns, Hornof, Schockley, Driskill, Burns, Wallace. Row 3: O'Hearn, Wilson, Perry, White, Greenfield, Balota, Thomas, Sales, Smith, Bell, Hawkins, Davis, Moorkamp, Manager Stanley. Row 4: Wiese, Shorthose, Llewellyn, Worden, Mack, Carruthers, Harris, Curry, Pearcy, Weinrich, Boyd, Coach McGhee, Coach Wommack. Row 5: Trainer McDonnell, Lewis, Adler, Holloway, Hill, Burditt, Carruthers, Caver, Snowden, Drain, Burch, Erickson, Hooper, Wyrostek, Coach Crumbacher. Row 6: Coach Harlan, Kearney, Bruns, Troyer, Sims, McMillan, Troy, Johnson, Barbosa, Miller, Esson, Brown, Beaver, Bender, Carter. Row 7: Coach Billings, Chapura, McDowell, Schultz, Totsch, Stinson, Opel, Matichak, Thetford, Blackburn, Stachovic, Lockwood, Vollet. Row 8: Svezia, Cathcart, McBride, Pettey, Malvern, Penny, Seitz, Runyan, Kniptash, Hawkins, Clay. Row 9: Coach Rogers, Morgan, Staples, Frazier, Floyd, Richmond, Klohmann, Savage, Sherrill, Suntrup, Zurweller, Hedrick, Close. Row 10: Abernathy, Lattinville, Barbee, Redd, Riley, DeLeonardis, Schulte, Burre, Ricono, Moore, Toben, Frye. Row 11: Kozinski, Runge, Wright, Vestweber, Rigman, Ekern, Chase, Greenfield, Redmond, Peyton, Schrieber. Row 12: Coach Collins, Coach Jones, Herron, Krysa, Henningsen, Keil, Elledge, Deppe, Rosewell, Mundy, Hogan, Morse. Row 13: Hinton, Morris, O'Driscoll, Scott, Mayo, Beaudean, Shepard, Mitchell, Lane, Edwards, Winbush.

Kansas Football (4-6-1) - Head Coach Michael Gottfried

Missouri Football (3-7-1) - Head Coach Warren Anthony Powers

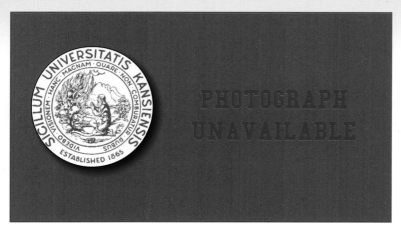

PHOTOGRAPH
UNAVAILABLE

Kansas Football (5-6-0) - Head Coach Michael Gottfried

Missouri Football (1-10) - Head Coach Robert Widenhofer
Sugar Bowl Champion

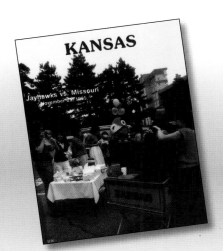

Kansas Football (6-6) - Head Coach Michael Gottfried

Missouri Football (3-8) - Head Coach Robert Widenhofer

Row 1: Coach Miller, Coach Wade, Coach Coe, Coach Anderson, Coach Nelson, Coach Meyers, Coach Widenhofer, Coach McKinley, Coach Zingler, Coach McConnell, Coach Ball, Coach Stanley, Trainer Wappel. Row 2: Romney, Sherrill, Close, Peterson, Justis, Vestweber, Chapura, McMillan, Clay, Pettey, Cathcart, Vollet, Scott, Morris, Esson, Lockwood. Row 3: Coordinator Hudson, Shepherd, Cross, Murphy, Cameron, Overshown, Wallace, Boyd, Caracter, Frye, Moore, Bullard, Whelihan, Ray, Mitchell, Hinton, Coach Rogers. Row 4: Coach Wilson, Redd, Carter, Johnson, Jensen, Boliaux, Vandegrift, Beaudean, Rigman, Henningsen, Van Dyne, Fedak, Schreiber, Bax, Riley, Coach Lathrop. Row 5: Coach White, Hagens, Walters, Coach Bruton, Cockrell, Jones, Ekern, Johnson, Stowers, Delpino, Young, Cook, Reeves, McGhee, Coach McDonnell. Row 6: Coach Zingler, Dryden, Keil, Hodge, Lammers, Walker, MacDonald, White, Lazalier, Slaughter, Stinson, Fletcher, Arneson, Coach McNeel. Row 7: Coach Worden, Trumbull, Paterra, Linthacum, Washington, Monachino, Greenwood, Wilson, Lock, Lamkie, Long, Decker, Mueller. Row 8: Johnson, Ricker, Frenchers, Mitchell, King, Holmes, Rodbro, Scott, Ploesser, May, Taylor, Gadner, Coach Partridge. Row 9: Logan, Rookstool, Pointer, Keough, Baum, LePage, Maupin, Henks, Washington, Ponzer, Grossich.

Kansas Football (3-8) - Head Coach Robert Valesente

Missouri Football (5-6) - Head Coach Robert Widenhofer
Gator Bowl Champion

Row 1: Coordinator Burks, Coordinator Stanley, Coach Coe, Coach McConnell, Coach Wade, Coordinator Anderson, Coach Widenhofer, Coordinator Reese, Coach Zingler, Coach Wheeler, Coach Billings, Coach Ball, Coach Miller, Trainer Wappel. Row 2: Coordinator Hudson, Staughter, Keil, Carter, Mitchell, Delpino, Moore, McMillan, Wallace, Rigman, McGhee, Schreiber, Henningsen, Ekern, Whelihan, Fedak, Taylor, Coach Rogers. Row 3: Coach Worden, Grossich, Johnson, Bullard, Cross, Cockrell, Ballard, Wilson, Stowers, Bax, Boliaux, Lowe, Montgomery, Trainer McDonnell. Row 4: Coach Partridge, Means, Darling, May, Jensen, Corl, Ray, Vandegrift, Johnson, Cameron, Henks, Young, Miller, Stollenwerck, Coach McNeel. Row 5: McKinney, Greenwood, Lock, Hylla, White, Trumbull, Henschel, Bruton, Logan, Holmes, Washington, Brown, LePage, Lammers, Jones, Coach Long. Row 6: Hagens, Murphy, Monachino, Gray, King, Elmore, Foster, Troyer, Weir, Cook, Campbell, Scott, Rodbro, MacDonald, Mueller, Coach Pack. Row 7: Coordinator McKay, Decker, Linthacum, Gardner, Dryden, Patera, Paloucek, Jones, Fletcher, Reeves, Pointer, Leisman, Knippenberg, Rookstool, Smith. Row 8: Bradley, Scrivner, Wilking, Walters, Welch, Williams, White Anderson, Jackson, Van Zant, Williams, Schnare, Russo, Dumas. Row 9: Michalski, Moore, Hamilton, Nolan, Marchitto, Middleton, Leach, Wright, Reiner, Ballard, Herreva, Russell, Plunkett, Thurman. Row 10: Quint, Hall, Childers, Pazell, Parsons, Knight, Pommer, Brown, Colon, Washington, Christensen, Jaquess. Row 11: Oswald, Baker, Wells, Jones, Butner, Boykin.

PHOTOGRAPH UNAVAILABLE

Kansas Football (1-9-1) - Head Coach Robert Valesente

Missouri Football (3-7-1) - Head Coach Robert Widenhofer

Row 1: Coach Pack, Coach Grangoulis, Coach Reid, Coach Fine, Coach Long. Row 2: Coordinator Stanley, Coordinator Hudson, Coach Rogers, Coach Ball, Coach Billings, Coach Wade, Coach Miller, Coach Anderson, Coach Widenhofer, Coordinator Rees, Coach Zingler, Coach Coe, Coach Novak, Coach Cochran, Coach Wheeler, Trainer Wappel, Trainer McDonnell. Row 3: Coordinator Burks, Greenwood, Lammers, Ray, Camerson, King, Lowe, Darling, Vandegrift, Bax, Wilson, Corl, Boliaux, Jensen, May, Henks, Coordinator, McKay. Row 4: Lock, Stollenwrck, Monachino, Scott, Johnson, Washington, Murphy, Jones, Holmes, Young, Anderson, Bryant, Van Zant, Stowers. Row 5: Fletcher, Reeves, Russo, Linthadum, Johnson, Quint, Logan Leach, Weir, Knippenberg, Paterra, LePage, Mueller, Bland. Row 6: Alade'fa, White, MacDonald, Elmore, Colon, Jones, Walters, Decker, White, Russell, Bruton, Washington, Boykin, Gardner. Row 7: Leisman, Miller, Pointer, Campbell, White, Smith, Parsons, Rookstool, Hall, Moore, Pazell, Walters, Dumas, Reiner. Row 8: Trumbull, Lovelace, Roberts, Wilking, Kayhill, Ballard, Harper, Knight, Wright, Christensen, Williams, Plunkett, Elliott. Row 9: Drennan, Baker, Michalski, Goodman, Eagan, Harper, Wells, Petrus, Burke, Condict, Bartlett, Henbrogh, Jacke, Ryan. Row 10: Crowl, Tate, Ryan, Freeman, Paluck, Snisky, Gardner, Maher, Camie, Martin, Funk, Watkins, Smith. Row 11: McCullough, Cole, Gruenberg, Cook, Dougherty, Applegate, Schief, Bradshaw, Wilkins, Honeycutt, Frisch, Hillman, Fisher. Row 12: Noel, Powell, Ringgenberg, McKiney, Scrivner, Fitzmaurice.

Kansas Football (1-10) - Head Coach Glen O. Mason

Missouri Football (2-9) - Head Coach Robert William Stull

Row 1: Coach Reid, Coach Jones, Coach Sally, Coach Sommer, Coach Riley, Coach Frost, Coach Fuller, Coach Frangoulis. Row 2: Coordinator Hudson, Coordinator Stanley, Coach Pack, Coach Toub, Coach Telander, Coach Ward, Coach Lattimore, Coach Koettter, Coach Stull, Coach Church, Coach Flajole, Coach Hoefer, Coach Faulkner, Coach Reid, Trainer Wappel, Trainer McDonnell. Row 3: Washington, White, Reeves, MacDonald, Stowers, White, Greenwood, Scott, Lock, Johnson, Monachino, Gardner, Miller, Mueller. Row 4: Coordinator Burks, Trumbull, Linthacum, Elmore, LePage, Stollenwerck, McKinney, Murphy, Bryant, Jones, Smith, Pointer, White, Leisman, Bruton, Coordinator McKay. Row 5: Fisher, Plunkett, Collins, Titone, Harper, Campbell, Russell, Weir, Michalski, Rookstool, Tabor, Paterra, Fletcher. Row 6: Baker, Scrivner, Dummas, Reiner, Roberts, Colon, Boykin, Hall, Kiefer, Turner, Moore, Jones, Collins, Mays. Row 7: Alade'fa, Van Zant, Applegate, Wells, Washington, Christensen, Russo, Evoy, Wright, Jaquess, Johnson, Trass, McCullough. Row 8: Taylor, Ryan, Ringgenberg, Robertson, Kayhill, Schief, Tate, Leach, Noel, Wilkins, Elliott, Frisch, Worle, Jacke. Row 9: Paluck, Cole, Condict, Hembrough, Crowl, Burke, Martin, Petrus, Watkins, Bartlett, Maher, Ramstack, Gruenberg. Row 10: Huggins, Gardner, Harrison, Alvarado, Louvier, Taylor, Oliver, Holly, Hunt, Bedosky, Hillman, Funk, Freeman. Row 11: Lyle, Pierce, Burgess, Fields, Benson, Jadiot, Engberson, Hamilton, Burke, Livingstone, Chamberlain, Turk, Johnson.

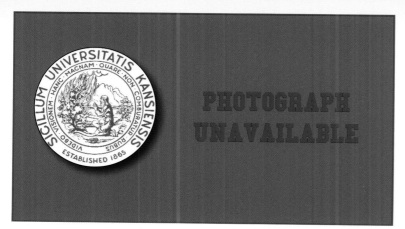

Kansas Football (4-7) - Head Coach Glen O. Mason

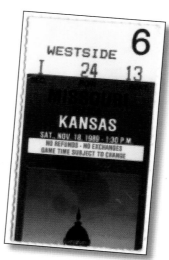

WARREN POWERS
HEAD FOOTBALL COACH

There never was any doubt in Warren Powers mind that he wanted the head football coaching job at Mizzou when it opened up last November.

Never a doubt, even though the Kansas City native was opted for the University of Nebraska's football scholarship offer after his senior year at Lillis high – when Missouri coaches didn't give the smallish, all-state quarterback a tumble.

Nineteen years later, following successful playing careers as a two-way back for the Cornhuskers and a six-year stay as defensive back with the Oakland Raiders, Powers became the applicant for the Tiger vacancy when Al Onofrio was fired on the heels of a 4-7 season.

He was the Selection Committee's choice and accepted the job on December 13. How badly did he want to come? In relinquishing his head-coaching position at Washington State after one season, Powers became the first head coach ever to pay an indemnity ($55,000) in settlement of his release from the WSU contract. Those payments will be made by Powers over a three-year period.

At his first press conference in Columbia, Missouri's new coach announced his goals:

"I came here to win football games, the Big Eight, and go to bowl games," he said.

Power, 37, played offensive and defensive halfback for the University of Nebraska from 1960-62 – and was named the Huskers MVP in his senior season. He then played defensive back for the Oakland Raiders for six years (1963-68), and started for Oakland in the 1968 Super Bowl game. While with the Raiders, Powers led the team in Interceptions for four straight years (1964-1967) and set a club record of 21 interceptions during that span.

In the off season, Powers coached Nebraska's defensive secondary during spring practice – and subsequently spent eight years as a fulltime assistant on the Cornhusker staff from 1969-76.

During these years, the Huskers posted a 78-14-5 record that included national titles 1970 and 1971, and five Big Eight championships or co-championships. All eight teams played in bowl games.

At Washington State in '77, Powers bowed in with a smashing 19-10 upset of his alma mater, Nebraska at Lincoln, earning him Pac-8 and national coach-of-the-week recognition. His pass-oriented attack featured the talents of Jack Thompson, the nation's No. 2 passer and the Cougars finished with a 6-5 record.

Powers was graduated from Nebraska in '63 with a B.S. degree in Business Administration. His wife is the former Linda Hoerig of St. Louis, Mo., a former University student and pompon girl.

The 27th head football coach at Mizzou, Powers was born in Kansas City, Mo. on February 19, 1941.

Written for the Missouri vs. Kansas Souvenir Football Magazine
Printed Saturday, November 11, 1978

Postscript

There is so much to be said about the birth and death of the collegiate yearbook. The *Savitar* and *Jayhawker* were once fabulous historical documents, but as times changed the documentation did also.

Yearbooks until the 1940s were hardcover books that certainly cost the students quite a bit of money to possess. By the late 1940s, yearbooks began to change in format to that of a quarterly magazines that could be collected in an ad hoc spiral binder yearbook hardcover, which was purchased separately of the magazine. In yearbooks prior to the 1950s, full accounts of sporting events were provided along with team photographs. This format persisted until the 1930s, when yearbooks temporarily began to favour portraitures of the players' faces. In the 1950s, yearbooks began to implement styles more akin to magazines and a great amount of detail regarding the seasons was lost as a result. With the magazine format, there were also fewer photographs for sports and student activities overall because they did not fit the format. By the 1960s, the traditional book hardcover format had returned, as did longer accounts of the seasons, but football team photographs had now become stylish photographs of players wearing suits and sitting atop movie theatres and standing in elevator shafts and, heaven forbid, if a game was lost to an undesirable foe, there was no account written whatsoever.

By the 1980s, the yearbook format had shifted to a lot of topical accounts of events and lacked detailed reporting. Additionally, there was a greater effort to account for many more sports and activities than in earlier yearbooks, if only to give all activities equal billing. This also affected how the articles were written because of size constraints within the yearbook.

In the decasde of the 2000s, yearbooks began to fill its pages with photographs with captions and very little written of a journalistic nature. As a result, there really are no accounts in the yearbooks of the Border War Game that are worth mentioning.

The end of the *Savitar* in 2006 is sad and the *Jayhawker* faced the same in 2008. Many universities have yearbooks that not only still survive, but continue to sell well. They may not win journalism awards, but their formats are proven winners that will be enjoyed by alumni and researchers in years to come.

By Shawn Buchanan Greene
Kansas Alumnus 1991
Written Wednesday, September 30, 2009

THE 1990s

The decade of the 1990s ushered in the information and digital age and a great time of prolonged economic prosperity. In the early 1990s, a recession ended that had begun in the late 1980s. The Internet became widely accessible that allowed persons to connect to each other around the world at a fraction of the cost of previous methods. Cellular phones continued to get smaller and were able to hold charges for longer times. Globalization and global capitalism were under way and the North American Free Trade Agreement (NAFTA) was ratified. In the early 1990s, a Seattle, Washington based band, Nirvana, ushered in the age of "grunge rock." The musical genres "rap" and "hip-hop," once considered on the fringe of the music industry, became mainstream, popular music. By the end of the decade, home movie VHS tapes were replaced by a new digital device known as a "Digital Versatile Disk," or "DVD."

In Kansas, Glen Mason slowly began to build the program from his 1-10 initial season. His next two seasons posted records of 4-7 and 3-7-1 and by his fourth season he was finally on the verge of having his first winning season which coincidentally was the one-hundredth year since the first playing of the Border War Game. Because of freezing temperatures, there was a small crowd

Larry Smith

coach who was another person noted for rebuilding programs. Smith was a native of Van Wert, Ohio and had played football with the United States Military Academy. In coming to Missouri, Smith looked to attain immediate results for the program, building upon the work done by Stull. Despite his determination, it took three years for Smith to produce a winning season at Missouri, which finally occurred in 1997. The winning season in 1997 was Missouri's first winning season since 1983 and Smith was also able to take the Tigers to the Holiday Bowl. The following year, in 1998, Smith took the Tigers to the Insight.com Bowl, giving Missouri its first two consecutive bowl appearances since 1981, when Warren Powers coached the team.

On February 25, 1994, the eight schools of the Big 8 Conference merged with four Texas schools of the former Southwest

KU 43 WINS   T-9   MU 47 WINS

A Century of Football

Cartoon from an insert from the 1991 game program

that day at Kansas Memorial Stadium when Tony Sands, playing in his last game as a Jayhawk, broke the University of Kansas, Big 8, and National Collegiate Athletic Association record for total number of yards rushed at 396. Additionally, Sands and the quarterback, Chip Hilleary, broke the National Collegiate Athletic Association record for most combined rushing yards for teammates, 476. Hilleary was credited for 80 yards that day.

In 1993, after five seasons coaching Missouri, the program still had not had a winning season, Stull's total record being 15-38-2. Despite his record, Stull was still respected for his coaching and work with the team and he took a position as assistant athletic director. Missouri then hired Larry Smith as the Tigers new head

Conference: University of Texas, Texas A&M University, Texas Tech University, and Baylor University. However, athletic competition did not begin in the Big 12 until August 31, 1996.

At Kansas, Glen Mason took the Jayhawks to the Aloha Bowl in 1992 and again in 1995. The 1995 season proved to be Mason's best record while at Kansas, posting a final record of 10-2 and earning him the Big 8 Coach of the Year award. That year, in Missouri, Don Faurot passed on October 19 at the age of 93, sending Tiger football fans into mourning. The mourning was further accentuated by Missouri's loss to Kansas in the Border War Game 42-23.

In 1996, Mason finished the season at Kansas 4-7 and he

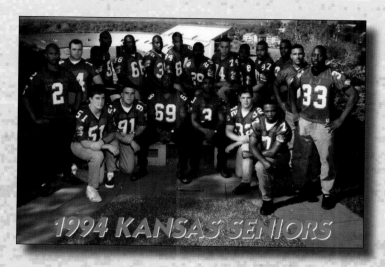

1994 KANSAS SENIORS

12. The reason for the move was to try to increase drama for the game having both teams enter the game unbeaten and untied in Big 12 competition. The game would continue to be scheduled ahead of Thanksgiving week until 2004, when it was returned to the Saturday afterwards.

At Missouri, after his two successive bowl victories in 1997 and 1998, Smith then had a losing season in 1999, posting a record of 4-3. Particularly alarming to Missouri football fans was that Missouri entered the football season 4-0 and proceeded to lose the last three games of the season in successive order, being held scoreless to Kansas, 21-0. The drastic reversal of fortune for the Tigers put into question the future of Missouri football and its future seemed to weigh on the success to be seen for the next season. In fact, both Larry Smith at Missouri and Terry Allen at Kansas expected for the future of their careers at their respective schools to rely heavily on the success of the 2000 season and perhaps, in particular, their success against each other the next season, setting the stage for the 2000 Border War Game.

began to explore options in coaching with another team. Mason eventually took the head coaching position of the University of Minnesota Golden Gophers. Replacing Mason for the 1997 season was Terry Allen, who had been coaching at the University of Northern Iowa. Allen's achievements at Northern Iowa included becoming the winningest coach in Gateway Conference history. Allen was described as a friendly man, but he had difficulty in getting Kansas football to succeed, posting losing seasons of 5-6, 4-7, and 5-7 in his first three seasons at Kansas. Despite his losing record, in the Border War Game, Allen was able win two of three games against Missouri.

The 1997 Border War Game was moved from being the last game of the season to the first game of conference play for the two schools. The move of the game to September 13 made it the earliest game played between the two schools since 1891, until the next year in 1998, when the game was played on September

Missouri underclassmen players await the graduating seniors in 1995

Missouri Football (4-7) - Head Coach Robert Stull

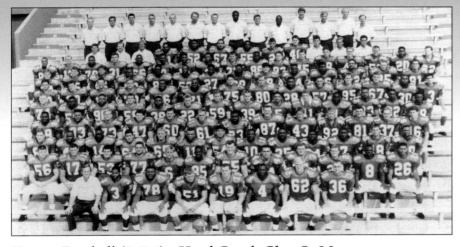

Kansas Football (3-7-1) - Head Coach Glen O. Mason

Row 1: Coach Mason, Hatchett, Oatis, Budde, Moore, Hooks, Walton, Wehrman. Row 2: Bowen, Flachsbarth, Holland, Perez, New, Drayton, Snyder, Zaffaroni, Robben, Priest, Hill, Couglas. Row 3: Tyrer, Dixon, Friday, Nolen, Imwalle, Page, Satches, Terry, Rogan, Sands, Bailey, Hilleary, Johnson. Row 4: Christian, Brown, McCabe, Slyter, Scott, Peebler, Cozzens, Fette, White, Ball, Licursi, Kimerer, Chaffetz. Row 5: Loneker, Mitchell, Howard, Swinford, Vaughn, Bowen, Marcum, Jobbins, Gay, Flynn, Chandler, Ettric, Bell, Belizaire. Row 6: Caudie, Converse, Florell, Liggett, Moore, Stubblefield, Schmidt, Smith Wilson, Ramsey, Moeder, McGee, Rahto. Row 7: Stafford, Bruns, Lambert, Jones, Harris, Harvey, Givens, Harris, Bowen, Britt, Booth, Maumalanga, Thiel, Willeford. Row 8: Wright, Davis, Douglaas, Eichloff, Hempstead, Preston, Thomas, White, Powell, Sanders, Ballard, Bowen, Casey, Vang, Selzer, Scott, Dunn. Row 9: Vidoli, Crocker, Claeys, Brown, Lee, Paddlety, Slaughter, Van Dyne, Williams, Curtis, Gregory, Stanley. Row 10: Heit, Adamie, Warner, Fello, Scalise, Roll, Phillips, Jefferson, Browning, Mitchell, Ruel, Hilles, Himes, Allen.

Missouri Football (3-7-1) - Head Coach Robert Stull

Row 1: Coach LePage, Coach Hardy, Coach Gardner, Coach Klucewich. Row 2: Coach Jones, Coach Mornhinweg, Coach Latimore, Coach Ward, Coach Toub, Coach Flajole, Coach Reid, Coach Koetter, Coach Stull, Coach Hoefer, Coach Faulkner, Coach Telander, Coach Stanley, Trainer McDonnell, Trainer Wappel, Coach Sommer, Video Coordinator Berlin. Row 3: Hall, Scrivner, Wells, Reiner, Leach, Van Zant, Johnson, McCullough, Wright, Jaquess, Trass, Applegate, Washington, Plunkett. Row 4: Maintenance Attendant McKay, Condict, Bailey, Watkins, Martin, Funk, Cooper, Petrus, Snisky, Crowl, Elliott, Gardner, Wilkins, Wiley, Hembrough, Maintenance Attendant Mucha. Row 5: Kayhill, Cole, Schlef, Bass, Burke, Barlett, Ringgenberg, Jacke, Staggers, Noel, Kaminski, Tate, Ryan. Row 6: Maxville, Vogler, Louvier, Jadlot, Harrison, Alvarado, Lyle, Bedosky, Hunt, Johnson, Burgess, Pearce, Benson. Row 7: Mautino, Handy, Sallee, Clay, Adams, Murray, Sanders, Mennenga, Widmer, Fields, Dunn, Holly, Oliver. Row 8: Harris, Wells, Heman, Pooler, Rowland, Parsons, Murray, O'Neil, Pedrotti, Maier, Murtaugh, Blankenship, Sillespie. Row 9: Skinner, Freeman, Baehr, Ivey, Shedden, Dowil, Reagan, Ofodile, Bramon, Barrows, Lyons, Waggoner. Row 10: Madison, McDonald, Jones, Johnson, Walls, Faust, Calvin, Safley, Griggs, Alnutt, Major, Patterson, Adams. Row 11: Campbell, McIntosh, White, Lenhardt.

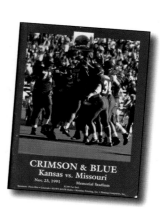

Kansas Football (6-5) - Head Coach Glen O. Mason

Missouri Football (3-8) - Head Coach Robert Stull

Kansas Football (8-4) - Head Coach Glen O. Mason
Aloha Bowl Champion

Missouri Football (3-7-1) - Head Coach Robert Stull

Row 1: Coach McHugh, Video Coordinator Stanley, Manager Montgomery, Coach Flajole, Coach Momhinweg, Coach Hoerfer, Coach Jones, Coach Hall, Coach Stull, Coach Koetter, Coach Iclander, Coach Toub, Coach Cochran, Coach Hegarty, Trainer Wappel, Coach Summer, Coach Jones, Coach Ward. Row 2: Trainer Kistler, Wooden, Brooks, Mortensen, Villarreal, Hunt, Jadiot, Alvarado, Lyle, Bedosky, Harrison, Pearce, Burgess, Holly, Murray, Oliver, Trainer McDonnell. Row 3: Coordinator Burks, Pooler, Stinnett, Handy, Nickols, Pedrotti, Murray, Ofodille, Dunham, O'Neill, Simon, Parsons, Sallee, McDonald, Major. Row 4: Jones, Adams, Lyons, Jackson, Waggoner, McIntosh, Madison, Clay, Wells, White, Singletary, Lenhardt, Blake, Washington, Kottman. Row 5: Alnutt, Walls, Faust, Williams, Griggs, Saffley, Harris, Barrows, Martin, Ivey, Shedden, Dowil, Allen, Keith. Row 6: Boyd, Shepherd, Markel, Jones, Chatman, Love, Cross, Brandon, Corso, Appel, Norris, Lingerfelt, Clark, Johnson. Row 7: Gott, Morris, Sudall, Jones, Janes, Jones, Campbell, Biebel, Sallee, Stewart, Johnson, Woods, Black. Row 8: Brooks, Seymour, Hodson, Faubain, Baker, Miller, Ford, Jenkins, Alvarado, Smith, Lindsey.

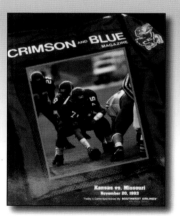

Kansas Football (5-7) - Head Coach Glen O. Mason

Missouri Football (3-8-1) - Head Coach Larry Smith

Row 1: Coach Scesniak, Coach Montgomery, Coach Hiestand, Coach Moeller, Coach Wright, Coach Jones, Coach Hall, Coach Bemdt, Coach Smith, Coach Faurot, Coach Ankney, Coach Hunley, Coach Hoke, Coach McHugh, Coach Toub, Coach Jones, Trainer McDonnell, Trainer Wappel, Coordinator Molyet. Row 2: Chaplain O'Brien, Coordinator Burks, Pooler, Washington, Handy, Frazier, Parsons, Murray, O'Neil, Simon, Pedrotti, Sallee, McDonald, Major, Singletary, Coordinator Cummings, Trainer Kistler. Row 3: Freeman, Waggoner, Madison, Wels, Ivey, Shedden, Allen, Dowil, Buck, Keith, White, Wooden, McIntosh, Lyons. Row 4: J. Jones, F. Jones, Adams, Johnson, Alnutt, Gonzalez, Faust, Sanft, Walls, Blake, Barrow, Safley, Martin. Row 5: Kagan, Jenkins, Markel, Smith, Boyd, Shepherd, Chatman, Love, Cross, Corso, Appel, Norris, Lingerfelt, Terry. Row 6: Murchison, Morris, Seymour, Sundall, Rowe, Janes, Jones, Biebel, Campbell, Williams, Miller, Steart, Baker. Row 7: Libke, Blackwell, Steuve, Henderson, Budgetts, Cracraft, Wyatt, Smith, Niemeyer, Meredith, Faubion, Pohlsander, Ford, Alvarado. Row 8: Wortham, Olivio, Ward, Kerby, Dolan, Haag, Young, Skomia, Morris, Jaegers, Woessner, Reinbold, Gregory. Row 9: Smith, Griffin, Perkins, Key, Sterling, Hill, Daniels, Criss, Benton.

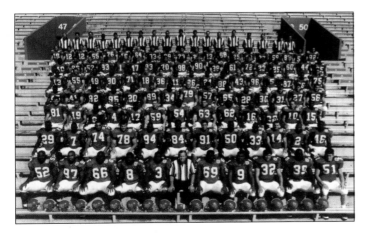

Kansas Football (6-5) - Head Coach Glen O. Mason

Missouri Football (3-8) - Head Coach Larry Smith

Coach Smith, Caoch Scresniak, Coach Montgomery, Coach Becha. Row 1: Trainer Wappel, Coach Wright, Coach Jones, Coach Sommer, Coach McHugh, Coach Moeller, Coach Hiestand, Coach Berndt, Coach Smith, Coach Ankney, Coach Hall, Coach Jones, Coach Hoke, Coach Toub, Coach Mathews, Coach McDonnell, Coach Stanley, Video Coordinator, Molyet, Maintenance Coordinator Burks. Row 2: Williams, Miller Stewart, Adams, Faust, Sanft, Martin, Ivey, Buck, Allen, Dowil, Barrows, Blake, Alnutt, Johnson, Jones, Baker, Maintenance Coordinator Cummings. Row 3: Hickman, Cooper, Chatman, Cross, Gonzalez, Massa, Norris, Appel, Lingerfelt, Douglas, Corso, Haag, Love, Shepherd, Kagan, Alvarado, Simmons. Row 4: Ford, Olivo, Janes, Cracraft, Gilyard, Rowe, Morris, Biebel, Jones, Blackwell, Henderson, Libke, Sundall, Morris, Murchison, Brown. Row 5: Brocke, Scott, Key, Finke, Dolan, Stueve, Skornia, Smith, Meredith, Neimeyer, Reinbold, Whatt, Gregory, Knickman, Binion, Criss, Wisdom. Row 6: Jones, Carter, WilliamsSmith, Londe, Leonard, Daniels, Wortham, Budgetts, Young, Benton, Swander, Slover, Johnson, Geiger, Schmanke, Easter, Scheuring. Row 7: Piersey, Brooks, Valadez, Riti, Keely, Silliman, Springer, Garrison, Heimburger, Ridgley, McArthur, Layman, West, Johnson, Wilder, Johnson, Potter.

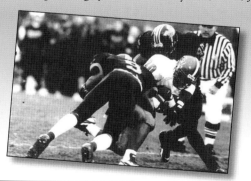

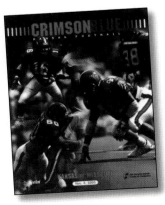

Kansas Football (10-2) - Head Coach Glen O. Mason - Big 8 Coach of the Year
Aloha Bowl Champion

Missouri Football (5-6) - Head Coach Larry Smith

Row 1: Coach McHugh, Coach Toub, Manager Stanley, Coach Hiestand, Coach Moeller, Coach Smith, Coach Hill, Coach Hunley, Coach Hall, Coach Ankney, Coach Smith, Coach Berndt, Coach Jones, Coach Molyet, Coach Stewart, Coach Hoke, Coach Maggard, Trainer Hammons, Trainer McDonnell, Trainer Sharp, Coach Montgomery, Coach Sommer. Row 2: Coach Jones, Olivo, Criss, Baker, Jenkins, Chatman, Cross, Norris, Lingerfelt, Douglas, Appel, Love, Haag, Williams, Miller, Ford, Knickman, Coordinator, Cummings. Row 3: Coordinator McWhorter, Ross, Binion, Coleman, Cracraft, Sundall, Rowe, Jones, Myers, Blackwell, Biebel, Morris, Henderson, Janes, Hawkes, Jose, Morris, Murchison, Coordinator Jackman. Row 4: Simmons, Smith, Piersey, Young, Taylor, Wyatt, Skornia, Neimeyer, Mittelstadt, Mereith, Smith, Heimburger, Bykoski, Stueve, Dolan, West, Johnson, Wisdom. Row 5: Jones, Brooks, Carter, McArthur, Scheuring, Elsayed, Erickson, Marriott, Silliman, Riti, Valadez, Ridgley, Londe, Brocke, Benton, Hickman, Sterling. Row 6: Easter, Potter, Geiger, Schmanke, Haasis, Pitts, Hughes, Wilson, Glauberman, Mazuch, Pipkin, Wilson, McCamy, Hendricks, Bennet, Douglass, Duffy, Toms, Bage, Cooper. Row 7: Kralik, Tucker, Roberson, Posey, Jones, Layman, Black, Angelica, Lewis, Martin, Sebo, Johnson, Proctor, Johnson, Scholten, Weaver, Odom.

Kansas Football (4-7) - Head Coach Glen O. Mason

Missouri Football (7-5) - Head Coach Larry Smith
Holiday Bowl Invitation

(Unordered) Benton, Black, Blakley, Brooks, Carrizal, J. Carter, R. Carter, Colbert, Cole, Crittendon, Crumble, Dausman, Davidson, Deptula, Dolan, Donnelly, Dougherty, Douglass, Duffy, Easter, Elsayed, Erickson, Ford, Foster, Gavins, Geiger, Bigson, Bilpin, Glauberman, Bulliford, Hammerich, Haasis, Harness, Hayes, Heimburger, Hellerstedt, Hendricks, Hill, Hippe, Johnson, Johnson, C. Jones, J. Jones, Jurineack, Kingery, Landers, Layman, Lewis, Long, McAboy, McCamy, McKeown, Marriott, Martin, Mayfield, Mazuch, Meredith, Mingucci, Mitchell, Moore, Nash, Nedimeyer, O'Neal, Odom, Ostendorf, Patton, Payne, Perkins, Piersey, Piper, Posey, Potter, Proctor, Propst, Revard, Rhodes, Riti, Roberson, Ryan, Schmanke, Schober, Scholten, Sebo, Silliman, B. Smith, C. Smith, Sterling, Stueve, Sutton, Tillman, Tookds, Tucker, Valadez, Webber, Weir, D. West, R. West, Whittington, Winston, Wise, Wyatt, Young.

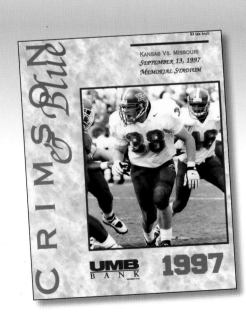

Kansas Football (5-6) - Head Coach Terry Allen

Missouri Football (8-4) - Head Coach Larry Smith
Insight.com Bowl Champion

Row 1: Administrator McHugh, Coach Toub, Manager Stanley, Coach Hiestand, Coach Moeller, Coach Smith, Coach Hill, Coach Hunley, Coach Hall, Coach Ankney, Coach Smith, Coach Berndt, Coach Jones, Coordinator Molyet, Coach Stewart, Coach Hoke, Coordinator Maggard, Trainer Hammons, Trainer McDonnell, Trainer Sharp, Administrator Montgomery, Coach Sommer. Row 2: Coach Jones, Olivo, Criss, Baker, Jenkins, Chatman, Cross, Norris, Lingerfelt, Douglas, Appel, Love, Haag, Williams, Miller, Ford, Knickman, Coordinator Cummings. Row 3: Coordinator McWhorter, Ross, Binion, Coleman, Cracraft, Sundall, Rowe, Jones, Myers, Blackwell, Biebel, Morris, Henderson, Janes, Hawkes, Josue, Morris, Murchison, Coordinator Jackman. Row 4: Simmons, Smith, Piersey, Young, Taylor, Wyatt, Skornia, Neimeyer, Mittelstadt, Meredith, Smith, Heimburger, Bykoski, Stueve, Dolan, West, Johnson, Wisdom. Row 5: Jones, Brooks, Carter, McArthur, Scheuring, Elsayed, Erickson, Marriott, Silliman, Riti, Valadez, Ridgley, Londe, Brocke, Benton, Hickman, Sterling. Row 6: Easter, Potter, Beiger, Schmanke, Haasis, Pitts, Hughes, Wilson, Glauberman, Mazuch, Pipkin, Wilson, McCarny, Hendricks, Bennet, Douglass, Duffy, Toms, Barge, Cooper. Row 7: Kralik, Tucker, Roberson, Posey, Jones, Layman, Black, Angelica, Lewis, Martin, Sebo, Johnson, Proctor, Johnson, Scholten, Weaver, Odom.

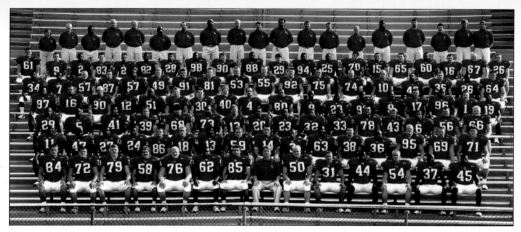

Kansas Football (4-7) - Head Coach Terry Allen

Missouri Football (4-7) - Head Coach Larry Smith

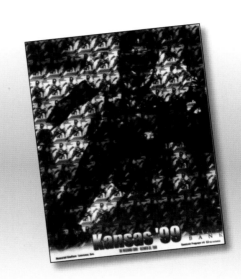

Kansas Football (5-7) - Head Coach Terry Allen

RUNNING BACK CAPS CAREER WITH RECORD BREAKING DAY

For one eventful Saturday afternoon, senior running back Tony Sands captured the nation's spotlight: 396 yards on 58 carries.

With those numbers, Sands rewrote both the KU and NCAA record. Even so, the 5-foot six-inch, 175-poounder said he had yet to achieve all that he aspired.

"It's just another step toward the next level," Sands said of his record-breaking day as a Jayhawk. "The N.F.L. is where I want to be, and I feel I will achieve that goal."

Those who followed Sands' career knew he would carry through on his ambitions.

Growing up in Fort Lauderdale, Fla., Sands learned to be responsible at an early age. He credited his achievements then and today to the lessons he learned from his religious faith.

"Religion has helped me a great deal along the way," Sands said. "One of the most important things it has taught me is perspective. I knew at a young age that my parents had faith in me to make my own decisions. They let me choose my own path, and it' helped me adjust to life much better."

That sense of perspective and adjustment allowed Sands the means to struggle through some rough times during his first year at KU.

Recruited by then first-year coach Glen Mason, Sands enjoyed only one victory coupled with ten defeats in his first season.

Meanwhile, schools such as the University of Miami and Florida State, which offered Sands chances to play in his home state, were busy winning bowl bids and national championships.

Yet as an integral part of the rebuilding process at KU, Sands led his teammates to an improved record each of his four years. The end result was the 1992 Jayhawks, a team that finished 6-5 and gave KU their first winning season since 1981.

"You really can't pinpoint one thing and give it credit for our turnaround," Sands said, "We all just believed in the team, went out and worked hard and dedicated ourselves to wanting it done. It's all about commitment."

Although one person cannot be credited with the Jayhawks' improvement, Sands could certainly be given a lot of the credit. Amassing 3,688 career rushing yards, the most in KU history, Sands guaranteed himself a spot in the KU record books for years to come.

Besides breaking NCAA single game marks for rushing yards and carries and the KU career mark for total yards, Sands also set KU records for touchdowns and attempts. He was named first team all Big Eight, Big Eight Player of the Year and third team All-American.

No KU player ever did so much with so little. However, Sands was by all means only small in size. He would be remembered not only as a player but [as] a person as well. During his career at KU, Sands managed to achieve as much from a personal and academic standpoint as he did on the field.

Sands, who had a wife and two children, devoted his stay at KU to working toward a career in the Drug Enforcement Agency, a goal he said he hoped to capture after his football days were over.

He also kept the proper perspective with regards to his family. Sands' philosophy at home and in the classroom was an echo of what he practiced on the field.

"I know I have to be aware of my situation" he said. "When I am at home, school and football are put aside. I am a father and a husband. I

Tony Sands and Coach Glen Mason at the post-game press conference

don't take football home."

In his home, Sands employed many of the same beliefs he felt helped him succeed. He expected his children to learn that hard work paid off and vowed to let them taste success, but they would earn it for themselves.

Sands tasted success and looked forward to more. This was evident in his sense of wholeness.

When looking back on his four years at KU, Sands brightened. This could have been due to his memories or to the prospects of the future.

"I feel I've gained respect and that I've grown up a lot, "he said, "but if there's anything that I've learned, I think it's the knowledge that those who love you love you when you do good, when you do bad, and whenever. Those are the people who help you out."

Sands surprised everyone with his accomplishments at KU. Through good and bad times, he never eased his dedication to excellence. As the fans in Memorial Stadium witnessed him romp for 396 yards that Saturday against Missouri they were shown there is a lot to learn from Tony Sands. More importantly, they were shown that there was more on the way.

By Chad Ernest Bryan
Kansas Alumnus 1992
Written for the 1992 Jayhawker *Yearbook*

THE ACHIEVEMENT OF
ONE
SHARED BY ALL

Over the years, I must have talked to 50,000 people who claimed to be at the 1991 Missouri game, when "Tuxedo" Tony Sands set the NCAA Single Game Rushing record with 396 yards. The funny part is that it was so bitterly cold that there was only an estimated 28,000 in attendance that day... but I was there and I had an interesting perspective. I was the one who handed the ball off to that diminutive (5 foot 6 inch, 175 pound) [168 centimetres, 79 kilograms] running back 58 times.

Many things still come to mind when I think of that 1991 Kansas-Missouri game... the determination in Tony's eyes as he addressed the team the night before in the team meeting, the fact that we needed a win to secure the first winning season in over a decade. What I do not recall was any part of our game plan that day, including handing the ball off to Tony so many times. I believe that just evolved as the game progressed. Our running game really seemed to click and behind that little number 24 and his energy, we were hard to stop.

I remember we jumped out to a 10-point lead at the end of the first quarter. Then Mizzou rolled back to a 25-22 halftime. By the end of the third quarter, we managed to break away from the Tigers by building a 46-29 lead and it was about then that the team began to believe that this day was going to be truly special.

Tony had carried the ball around 40 times for almost 300 yards and I remember looking at Tony in the huddle and you could just tell he had plenty of gas left in the tank. We were just feeding off his energy every play. I am sure it was about then that the coaching staff on the sidelines recognized that Tony was approaching the Big 8 Rushing record; 342 yards.

It was one of those moments, looking at the guys around the huddle, then down at T. Sands. The only responsibilities that I had at that point were to receive the signal from Coach Mason on which side to hand the ball off (right or left) and then call the play and snap count.

After that record was obtained, we just kept giving him the ball. It was Tony's last carry as a Jayhawk that broke the NCAA Single Game Rushing record. With 20 seconds left on the clock, before I could even reach a referee for a time out, our linemen had Tony on their shoulders, carrying him off the field in celebration.

We were all sharing the same feelings inside – all the hard work through training together for that reward – the achievement of one shared by all. That is one of the wonderful things about football being a team sport. Yes, Tony deservedly got the recognition that day, but we also were some proud teammates and friends that shared a brotherhood bond forever.

Once a Jayhawk, always a Jayhawk... Go KU!

By Chip Hilleary
Kansas Alumnus 1993
Written Friday, October 2, 2009

(Left-Right) Bret Pomrenke, Chip Hilleary, Dan Schmidt, Wes Swinford, and "Tuxedo" Tony Sands (kneeling)

"Tuxedo" Tony Sands got his nickname for wearing his tuxedo to formal affairs

Chip Hilleary

...NEITHER HAD I

The night before the game with Missouri, the team had a meeting. At the meeting, all the seniors were given an opportunity to speak before the team. The first player to speak was an offensive lineman named Chris Perez, and the second player to speak was me. I started my speech wanting to say something about "commitment," so I said, "It takes a group of men to make a commitment to see success through…" That is exactly what we did when we started the season. Then I spoke about love. I talked about how every guy in that room loved each other and how the players, coaches, and the University showed my family (Calandra, my wife, and my sons Maxie and Deshaun) love. While I was speaking, I sensed a feeling of power coming through the room. Both players and coaches started crying and the feeling that we were going to be successful came over the room. After the rest of the seniors finished, the coaches ended the meeting. I then started thinking about how successful I wanted to be the next day.

The game started and both teams were having success on the field. During half-time, Chaka Johnson came over to my locker and said, "You have about 25 carries and 150 yards at half-time." I really did not understand the significance of what he was saying because winning the game was the only thing on my mind. At some point in the third quarter, Coach John Jefferson told me that I was close to a school record and then, in the fourth quarter, I was told that I was close to a Big 8 record. Once the records started posting on the big jumbo screens, the fans started going crazy, not just because we were winning, but because history was being made at the same time; and I still only wanted to win the game. Finally, I passed the record, the NCAA single-game rushing record! My teammates grabbed me and carried me off the field.

After the press conference, I can remember getting dressed and walking out of the locker room to a sea of fans. I stood, signing autographs, for at least an hour and a half. Later, when I was in our truck with my wife, she said she had left the game because it was too cold, but returned to the stadium when she heard on the radio I was setting a record. She said how important it was for her to get back to the game, so my boys could see their father break a record.

Later that night, I had friends in the military call from Germany, telling me that I was on television there - in Germany. My brother Shaun called and said he couldn't believe it. Well, neither had I. It was at that point when I really understood what had just happened to me.

I would love to thank the University of Kansas, my teammates, and the fans for their commitment to me and their love.

I hope they show the same love and commitment for my son, Deshaun, as they showed me, now that he too is a Jayhawk.

By Tony Sands
Kansas Alumnus 1992
Written Thursday, October 15, 2009

The first decade of the new millennium was heavily influenced by the attack on the World Trade Center. Mathematicians lamented the celebration of the new millennium on the eve of December 31, 1999, knowing that there was no such thing as a year "0" and, therefore, also knowing that the new millennium would start in 2001. "Hip-hop" was now the most popular music genre of the time and a University City High School graduate, Nelly, from University City, Missouri, in suburban Saint Louis, had a string of hits being played on radios around the world. Across the state, from Blue Springs, Missouri, in suburban Kansas City, David Cook sang a string of hit songs to eventually win American Idol, a nationally televised contest. Also, having learned from previous wars, Republicans and Democrats struggled to find a way to debate aspects in favour and in opposition to the wars in Afghanistan and Iraq, without undermining the troops that were bringing the President's policy to action.

Both the Missouri and Kansas coaches, Larry Smith and Terry Allen, went into the 2000 Border War Game expecting for the loser of the game to lose his job as head coach of his team; it not mattering that the Border War Game was scheduled earlier in the season on October 14. Both Missouri and Kansas entered the game that year with identical records of 2-3, but Kansas got the better of Missouri, dominating in total offense 453 yards to 247 and causing five turnovers of the football. The Jayhawks won a lopsided victory against the Tigers, 38-17 and, as was predicted, Larry Smith was released as head coach of Tigers football at the end of the season. Missouri brought in as his replacement Gary Pinkel, who had been the head coach of the University of Toledo. At the University of Toledo, Gary Pinkel spent 10 years developing a caliber program recording an overall record there of 73-37-3, becoming the school's winningest coach.

The 2000 victory extended Allen's stay at Kansas but he had ended the season 4-7 and the next year ended the season 3-7, losing the Border War Game to Gary Pinkel's 3-7 Tigers team. With three games left in the 2001 season, Allen was released as head coach. It was at this point that Kansas desired to hire a coach tutored in running a traditionally top-tier collegiate football program. The school hired Mark Mangino who had first worked as an assistant coach at Kansas State University under Bill Snyder and then at the University of Oklahoma, where he

Gary Pinkel in 2007 holding the Lamar Hunt Trophy

was an offensive coordinator for the team that won the National Championship in 2000.

In his first year at Kansas, Mangino finished the season with a 2-10 record. However, Mangino improved the team to a 6-7 record, winning both the Border War Game and taking the team to the Tangerine Bowl, which they subsequently lost. The appearance, though, was the first bowl appearance for Kansas since 1995 and Mangino was already showing significant improvements for the Kansas program. Despite the 2003 Border War Game loss, Gary Pinkel's Tigers ended the season 8-5, also appearing in the Liberty Bowl.

In 2004, administrators at Missouri and Kansas decided that the name "Border War" for the game seemed inappropriate in light of the wars being conducted in Afghanistan and Iraq. As such, the game was renamed the "Border Showdown." Both schools had losing records that year and Kansas won the first Border Showdown Game. Despite their losing records from the previous season, in 2005 both coaches ended the season with 7-5 records and each won a bowl championship; Missouri, the Independence Bowl and Kansas, the Fort Worth Bowl. Again, in 2006, Missouri was invited to a bowl game – the Sun Bowl, where they lost. Kansas ended the season 6-6, losing the Border Showdown 42-17 but incredible circumstances were building for the next season in 2007.

For the first time since 1945, the game returned to Kansas City with great help and influence by Lamar Hunt, owner of the National Football League Kansas City Chiefs. Hunt passed in 2006 and it was decided to introduce the Lamar Hunt Trophy to the game in his honour. The game was held at Arrowhead Stadium, where the Kansas City Chiefs play, and the crowd was the second-largest in that stadium's history. The Tigers came into the game ranked fourth in the nation with one loss to Oklahoma and Kansas was an undefeated team ranked second in the nation. In a spectacular game, Missouri proved victorious with 12 seconds left in the game when Lorenzo Williams sacked Kansas quarterback Todd Reesing in the end zone, ending a Kansas rally that might have won them the game. The previous day, number one ranked Louisiana State University lost to Arkansas, propelling Missouri to the number one position in the country. A loss a week later to Oklahoma, who had beaten Missouri previously in the season, caused them

THE BORDER SHOWDOWN

to lose the Big 12 Championship and removed Missouri from the Bowl Championship Series Championship Game. Additionally, the Tigers were slighted because they won no bid to the Bowl Championship Series, whereas Kansas, who had just lost to the Tigers, received an invitation to the Orange Bowl, which they won. The 2007 Tigers accepted an invitation, instead, to the Cotton Bowl, which they also won. The Tigers finished the season 12-2 and Kansas 12-1, the highest win totals in both school's histories.

Because of the achievements of the 2007 season, Mark Mangino was honoured with numerous National Coach of the Year awards, which came from: the Associated Press, ESPN/ABC, The Sporting News, the Football Writers Association, the Walter Camp Football Foundation, the National Sportscasters and Sportswriters Association, the American Football Coaches Association, the Maxwell Football Club George Munger Award, and the Woody Hayes Award. Additionally, Mangino was named the Big 12 Coach of the Year by the Big 12 coaches and the Big 12 Co-coach of the Year by the Associated Press. With these achievements, Mangino became the only National Collegiate Activities Association coach in history to win Frank Broyles Award as the nation's top assistant coach and all of the major national Coach of the Year awards.

The next year in 2008, both schools had winning records and bowl appearances, Missouri went to the Alamo Bowl and Kansas, the Insight Bowl. The Border Showdown Game was just as exciting as the previous year, with Kansas edging Missouri 40-37. The game was the last Border Showdown for the two quarterbacks that significantly contributed to both schools' successes; Chase Daniel, of Missouri and Todd Reesing, of Kansas; then, just as suddenly as their meteoric rise, disaster began to loom.

In 2009, Missouri had a good year, ending with an 8-5 record. Kansas did not faire as well, ending the season 5-7. Many viewed the Kansas season as unmotivated and it was particularly disconcerting to supporters that after winning their first five games, the team proceeded to lose their next seven in successive order. The spectre left from the season was exacerbated by rumours concerning Mangino's questionable treatment of players. After an inter-

The 2007 Border Showdown Game

nal investigation was begun, Mark Mangino resigned his position with the team. On December 13, 2009, it was announced that Turner Gill, the third year coach of the University of Buffalo, would be the new head coach of the Kansas Jayhawks.

In June of 2010, much speculation ensued that the Big 12 Conference was on the verge of dissolution. It was speculated that half of the members might join the Pac 10 Conference, while the other half might join the Big Ten. On June 10, the University of Colorado accepted an invitation to join the Pac 10 Conference as its eleventh member, which was to become effective in 2012. The next day on June 11, the University of Nebraska applied for and was unanimously accepted into membership of the Big 10 Conference as its twelfth member. Rumours persisted that Texas, Texas Tech, Texas A&M, Oklahoma, and Oklahoma State were soon to join the Pac 10 Conference, leaving Missouri, Kansas, Kansas State, and Iowa State without a conference and further rumours suggested that Missouri might also join the Big 10 Conference without Kansas, which might terminate the Border Showdown Game in future years.

On June 14, Texas, Texas Tech, Texas A&M, Oklahoma, and Oklahoma State officially declined the Pac 10 invitation and committed themselves to staying in the Big 12 with Missouri, Kansas, Kansas State, and Iowa State as a ten member conference. The departure of the University of Nebraska may spell doom to several longstanding rivalries that it held with members of the Big 8. While the future of the Border Showdown rivalry for now is secure, one wonders if it will be forever.

The 2001 Border War Game

Missouri Football (3-8) - Head Coach Larry Smith

Kansas Football (4-7) - Head Coach Terry Allen

Missouri Football (4-7) - Head Coach Gary Robin Pinkel

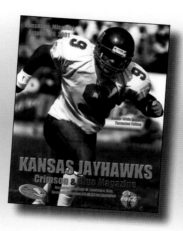

Kansas Football (3-8) - Head Coach Terry Allen

Kansas team photo by Jeff Jacobsen

Missouri Football (5-7) - Head Coach Gary Robin Pinkel

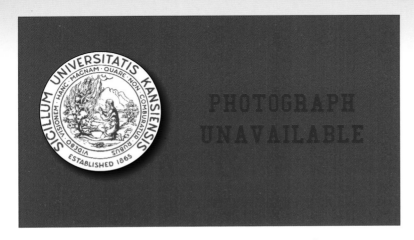

Kansas Football (2-10) - Head Coach Mark Thomas Mangino

Missouri Football (8-5) - Head Coach Gary Robin Pinkel
Independence Bowl Invitation

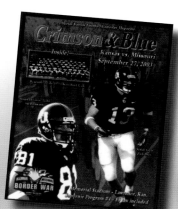

Kansas Football (6-7) - Head Coach Mark Thomas Mangino
Tangerine Bowl Invitation

Kansas team photo by Jeff Jacobsen

Missouri Football (5-6) - Head Coach Gary Robin Pinkel

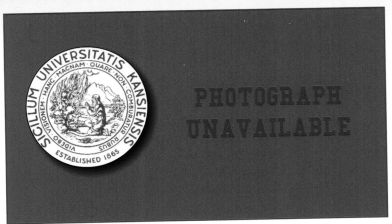

Kansas Football (4-7) - Head Coach Mark Thomas Mangino

Missouri Football (7-5) - Head Coach Gary Robin Pinkel
Independence Bowl Champion

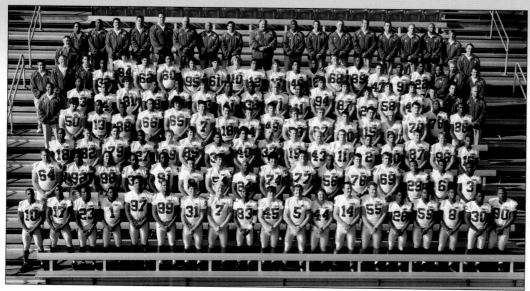

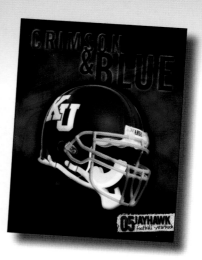

Kansas Football (7-5) - Head Coach Mark Thomas Mangino
Fort Worth Bowl Champion

Kansas team photo by Jeff Jacobsen

Missouri Football (8-5) - Head Coach Gary Robin Pinkel
Sun Bowl Invitation

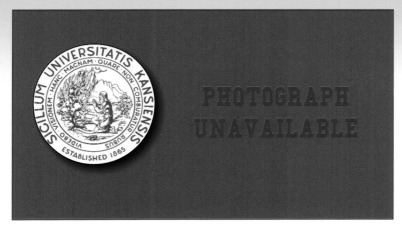

Kansas Football (6-6) - Head Coach Mark Thomas Mangino

Missouri Football (12-2) - Head Coach Gary Robin Pinkel
Cotton Bowl Champion

Kansas Football (12-1) - Head Coach Mark Thomas Mangino
Orange Bowl Champion

Kansas team photo by Jeff Jacobsen

Missouri Football (10-4) - Head Coach Gary Robin Pinkel
Alamo Bowl Champion

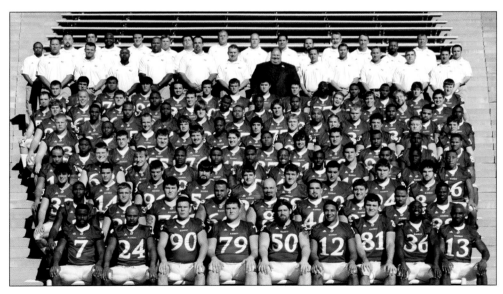

Kansas Football (8-5) - Head Coach Mark Thomas Mangino
Insight Bowl Champion

Kansas team photo by Jeff Jacobsen

Missouri Football (8-5) - Head Coach Gary Robin Pinkel

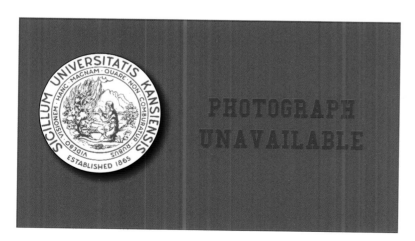

PHOTOGRAPH
UNAVAILABLE

Kansas Football (5-7) - Head Coach Mark Thomas Mangino

Missouri Football - Head Coach Gary Robin Pinkel

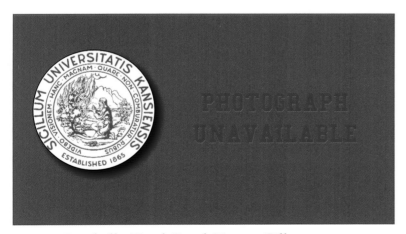

Kansas Football - Head Coach Turner Gill

MISSOURI

ALL-AMERICANS

Ed Lindenmeyer	T	1925
Paul Christman	QB	1939
Darold Jenkins	C	1941
Bob Steuber	RB	1942
Harold Burnine	DE	1955
Danny LaRose	DE	1960
Ed Blaine	T	1961
Conrad Hitchler	DE	1962
Johnny Roland	DB	1965
Francis Peay	OT	1965
Russ Washington	OT	1967
Roger Wehrli	DB	1968
Mike Carroll	OG	1969
Scott Anderson	C	1973
John Moseley	DB	1973
Henry Marshall	WR	1975
Morris Towns	OT	1976
Kellen Winslow	TE	1978
Bill Whitaker	DB	1980
Brad Edelman	C	1981
Jeff Gaylord	DT	1981
Conrad Goode	OT	1983
John Clay	OT	1986
Justin Londoff	TB	1997
Rob Riti	C	1999
Justin Smith	DE	2000
Martin Rucker	TE	2007
Jeremy Maclin	AP	2007, 2008
Chase Coffman	TE	2008
Danario Alexander	WR	2009
Grant Ressel	K	2009

RETIRED JERSEYS

Johnny Roland	23
Roger Wehrli	23
Brock Olivo	27
Bob Steuber	37
Darold Jenkins	42
Paul Christman	44
Kellen Winslow	83

KANSAS

ALL-AMERICANS

Ray Evans	RB/DB	1947
Otto Schnellbacher	WR	1947
George Mrkonic	OL	1951
Oliver Spencer	OL	1952
Gil Reich	DB	1952
John Hadl	RB	1960, 1961
Gale Sayers	RB	1963, 1964
Bobby Douglass	QB	1968
John Zook	DB	1968
David Jaynes	QB	1973
Bruce Kallmeyer	K	1983
Anthony Collins	OL	2007
Aqib Talib	DB	2007

RETIRED JERSEYS

John Hadl	21
Ray Evans	42
Gale Sayers	48

Austin McRae
1890

Hal Reed
1891

E. H. Jones
1892

Jake Robinson
1893-1894

Pop Bliss
1895

Frank Patterson
1896

Charles Young
1897

Dave Fultz
1898-1899

Fred Murphy
1900-1901

Pat O'Dea
1902

John Mclean
1903-1905

Bill Monilaw
1906-1908

Bill Roper
1909

Bill Hollenback
1910

Chester Brewer
1911-1913

MISSOURI

Indian Schulte
1914-1918

John Miller
1919

Jimmy Phelan
1920-1921

Henry Garrity
1922

Gwinn Henry
1923-1931

Frank Carideo
1932-1934

Don Faurot
1935-1942
1946-1956

Chauncey Simpson
1943-1945

Frank Broyles
1957

Dan Devine
1958-1970

Al Onofrio
1971-1977

Warren Powers
1978-1984

Woody Widenhofer
1985-1988

Bob Stull
1989-1993

Larry Smith
1994-2000

Gary Pinkel
2001-2009

BORDER WAR COACHES OF

Will Coleman
1890

Ed Hopkins
1891

Al Shepard
1892-1893

Hector Cowan
1894-1896

Wylie Woodruff
1897-1898

Fielding Yost
1899

Charles Boynton
1900

John Outland
1901

Art Curtis
1902

Harry Weeks
1903

Bert Kennedy
1904-1910

Ralph Sherwin
1911

Arthur Mosse
1912-1913

Henry Wheaton
1914

Herman Olcott
1915-1917

Jay Bond
1918

Leon McCarty
1919

Phog Allen
1920

KANSAS

Potsy Clark
1921-1925

Frank Cappon
1919-1922

Bill Hargiss
1928-1932

Ad Lindsey
1933-1938

Gwinn Henry
1939-1942

Henry Shenk
1943-1945

George Sauer
1946-1947

Jules Sikes
1948-1953

Chuck Mather
1954-1957

Jack Mitchell
1958-1966

Pepper Rodgers
1967-1970

Don Fambrough
1971-1974
1979-1982

Bud Moore
1975-1978

Mike Gottfried
1983-1985

Bob Valescente
1986-1987

Glen Mason
1988-1996

Terry Allen
1997-2002

Mark Mangino
2003-2009

Turner Gill
2010

GAME RECORDS AND STATISTICS

Date	Day	City	Field	MU	KU
1891-10-31	Saturday	Kansas City	Exposition Park	8	22
1892-11-24	Thursday	Kansas City	Exposition Park	4	12
1893-11-29	Thursday	Kansas City	Exposition Park	12	4
1894-11-31	Thursday	Kansas City	Exposition Park	12	18
1895-11-28	Thursday	Kansas City	Exposition Park	10	6
1896-11-26	Thursday	Kansas City	Exposition Park	0	30
1897-11-25	Thursday	Kansas City	Exposition Park	0	16
1898-11-24	Thursday	Kansas City	Exposition Park	0	12
1899-11-30	Thursday	Kansas City	Convention Hall	6	34
1900-11-29	Thursday	Kansas City	Association Park	6	6
1901-11-28	Thursday	Kansas City	Association Park	18	12
1902-11-29	Thursday	Kansas City	Association Park	5	17
1903-11-26	Thursday	Kansas City	Association Park	0	5
1904-11-25	Thursday	Kansas City	Association Park	0	29
1905-11-30	Thursday	Kansas City	Association Park	0	24
1906-11-29	Thursday	Kansas City	Association Park	0	0
1907-11-28	Thursday	St. Joseph	St. Joseph's League Ball Park	0	4
1908-11-28	Thursday	Kansas City	Association Park	4	10
1909-11-25	Thursday	Kansas City	Association Park	12	6
1910-11-24	Thursday	Kansas City	Koppel Stadium	5	5
1911-11-25	Saturday	Columbia	Rollins Field	3	3
1912-11-23	Saturday	Lawrence	McCook Field	3	12
1913-11-22	Saturday	Columbia	Rollins Field	3	0
1914-11-21	Saturday	Columbia	Rollins Field	10	7
1915-11-25	Thursday	Columbia	Rollins Field	6	8
1916-11-30	Thursday	Lawrence	McCook Field	13	0
1917-11-29	Thursday	Lawrence	McCook Field	3	27
1918-11-28	Thursday	NO GAME - INFLUENZA QUARANTINE			
1919-11-27	Thursday	Lawrence	McCook Field	13	6
1920-11-25	Thursday	Columbia	Rollins Field	16	7
1921-11-24	Thursday	Lawrence	Kansas Memorial Stadium	9	15
1922-11-30	Thursday	Columbia	Rollins Field	9	7
1923-11-29	Thursday	Lawrence	Kansas Memorial Stadium	3	3
1924-11-27	Thursday	Columbia	Rollins Field	14	0
1925-11-21	Saturday	Lawrence	Kansas Memorial Stadium	7	10
1926-11-20	Saturday	Columbia	Missouri Memorial Stadium	15	0
1927-11-19	Saturday	Lawrence	Kansas Memorial Stadium	7	14
1928-11-24	Saturday	Columbia	Missouri Memorial Stadium	25	6
1929-11-23	Saturday	Lawrence	Kansas Memorial Stadium	7	0
1930-11-22	Saturday	Columbia	Missouri Memorial Stadium	0	32
1931-11-21	Saturday	Lawrence	Kansas Memorial Stadium	0	14
1932-11-12	Saturday	Columbia	Missouri Memorial Stadium	0	7
1933-11-30	Thursday	Lawrence	Kansas Memorial Stadium	0	27
1934-11-29	Thursday	Columbia	Missouri Memorial Stadium	0	20
1935-11-28	Thursday	Lawrence	Kansas Memorial Stadium	0	0

Date	Day	City	Field	MU	KU
1936-11-26	Thursday	Columbia	Missouri Memorial Stadium	19	3
1937-11-25	Thursday	Lawrence	Kansas Memorial Stadium	0	0
1938-11-24	Thursday	Columbia	Missouri Memorial Stadium	13	7
1939-11-25	Saturday	Lawrence	Kansas Memorial Stadium	20	0
1940-11-21	Saturday	Columbia	Missouri Memorial Stadium	45	20
1941-11-22	Thursday	Lawrence	Kansas Memorial Stadium	45	6
1942-11-26	Saturday	Columbia	Missouri Memorial Stadium	42	13
1943-11-20	Thursday	Lawrence	Kansas Memorial Stadium	6	7
1944-11-23	Saturday	Kansas City	Ruppert Stadium	28	0
1945-11-24	Thursday	Kansas City	Ruppert Stadium	33	12
1946-11-28	Saturday	Columbia	Missouri Memorial Stadium	19	20
1947-11-22	Thursday	Lawrence	Kansas Memorial Stadium	14	20
1948-11-25	Saturday	Columbia	Missouri Memorial Stadium	21	7
1949-11-19	Thursday	Lawrence	Kansas Memorial Stadium	34	28
1950-11-23	Saturday	Columbia	Missouri Memorial Stadium	20	6
1951-12-01	Saturday	Lawrence	Kansas Memorial Stadium	28	41
1952-11-22	Saturday	Columbia	Missouri Memorial Stadium	20	19
1953-11-21	Saturday	Lawrence	Kansas Memorial Stadium	10	6
1954-11-20	Saturday	Columbia	Missouri Memorial Stadium	41	18
1955-11-19	Saturday	Lawrence	Kansas Memorial Stadium	7	13
1956-12-01	Saturday	Columbia	Missouri Memorial Stadium	15	13
1957-11-23	Saturday	Lawrence	Kansas Memorial Stadium	7	9
1958-11-22	Saturday	Columbia	Missouri Memorial Stadium	13	13
1959-11-21	Saturday	Lawrence	Kansas Memorial Stadium	13	9
1960-11-19	Saturday	Columbia	Missouri Memorial Stadium	7	23
1961-11-25	Saturday	Lawrence	Kansas Memorial Stadium	10	7
1962-11-24	Saturday	Columbia	Missouri Memorial Stadium	3	3
1963-11-23	Saturday	Lawrence	Kansas Memorial Stadium	9	7
1964-11-21	Saturday	Columbia	Missouri Memorial Stadium	34	14
1965-11-20	Saturday	Lawrence	Kansas Memorial Stadium	44	20
1966-11-19	Saturday	Columbia	Missouri Memorial Stadium	7	0
1967-11-25	Saturday	Lawrence	Kansas Memorial Stadium	6	17
1968-11-23	Saturday	Columbia	Missouri Memorial Stadium	19	21
1969-11-22	Saturday	Lawrence	Kansas Memorial Stadium	69	21
1970-11-21	Saturday	Columbia	Francis Field	28	17
1971-11-20	Saturday	Lawrence	Francis Field	2	7
1972-11-25	Saturday	Columbia	Faurot Field	17	28
1973-11-24	Saturday	Lawrence	Kansas Memorial Stadium	13	14
1974-11-23	Saturday	Columbia	Faurot Field	27	3
1975-11-22	Saturday	Lawrence	Kansas Memorial Stadium	24	42
1976-11-20	Saturday	Columbia	Faurot Field	14	41
1977-11-19	Saturday	Lawrence	Kansas Memorial Stadium	22	24
1978-11-11	Saturday	Columbia	Faurot Field	48	0
1979-11-24	Saturday	Lawrence	Kansas Memorial Stadium	55	7
1980-11-22	Saturday	Columbia	Faurot Field	31	6
1981-11-21	Saturday	Lawrence	Kansas Memorial Stadium	11	19
1982-11-20	Saturday	Columbia	Faurot Field	16	10
1983-11-19	Saturday	Lawrence	Kansas Memorial Stadium	27	37

273

DATE	DAY	CITY	FIELD	MU	KU
1984-11-17	Saturday	Columbia	Faurot Field	21	35
1985-11-23	Saturday	Lawrence	Kansas Memorial Stadium	20	34
1986-11-22	Saturday	Columbia	Faurot Field	48	0
1987-11-21	Saturday	Columbia	Faurot Field	19	7
1988-11-19	Saturday	Lawrence	Kansas Memorial Stadium	55	17
1989-11-18	Saturday	Columbia	Faurot Field	44	46
1990-11-17	Saturday	Lawrence	Kansas Memorial Stadium	31	21
1991-11-23	Saturday	Lawrence	Kansas Memorial Stadium	29	53
1992-11-21	Saturday	Columbia	Faurot Field	22	17
1993-11-20	Saturday	Lawrence	Kansas Memorial Stadium	0	28
1994-11-19	Saturday	Columbia	Faurot Field	14	31
1995-11-04	Saturday	Lawrence	Kansas Memorial Stadium	23	42
1996-11-23	Saturday	Columbia	Faurot Field	42	25
1997-09-13	Saturday	Lawrence	Kansas Memorial Stadium	7	15
1998-09-12	Saturday	Columbia	Faurot Field	41	23
1999-10-23	Saturday	Lawrence	Kansas Memorial Stadium	0	21
2000-10-14	Saturday	Columbia	Faurot Field	17	38
2001-10-20	Saturday	Lawrence	Kansas Memorial Stadium	38	34
2002-10-26	Saturday	Columbia	Faurot Field	36	12
2003-09-27	Saturday	Lawrence	Kansas Memorial Stadium	14	35
2004-11-20	Saturday	Columbia	Faurot Field	14	31
2005-10-29	Saturday	Lawrence	Kansas Memorial Stadium	3	13
2006-11-25	Saturday	Columbia	Faurot Field	42	17
2007-11-24	Saturday	Kansas City	Arrowhead Stadium	36	28
2008-11-29	Saturday	Kansas City	Arrowhead Stadium	37	40
2009-11-28	Saturday	Kansas City	Arrowhead Stadium	41	39

Kansas 55 - Missouri 54 - Tied 9

BORDER WAR RIVALRY COACHING RECORDS

Kansas

Coleman	0-0	.000	McCarty	0-1	.000	Valesente	0-2	.000
Hopkins	1-0	1.00	Allen	0-1	.000	Mason	5-4	.555
Shepard	1-1	.500	Clark	2-2-1	.500	Allen	3-2	.600
Cowan	2-1	.666	Cappon	1-1	.500	Mangino	4-4	.500
Woodruff	2-0	1.00	Hargiss	2-2	.500	Gill	0-0	.000
Yost	1-0	1.00	Lindsey	3-2-2	.571			
Boynton	0-0-1	.500	Henry	0-4	.000			
Outland	0-1	.000	Shenk	1-2	.333			
Curtis	1-0	1.00	Sauer	2-0	1.00			
Weeks	1-0	1.00	Sikes	1-5	.166			
Kennedy	4-1-2	.857	Mather	2-2	.500			
Sherwin	0-0-1	.500	Mitchell	1-6-2	.250			
Mosse	1-1	.500	Rodgers	2-2	.500			
Wheaton	0-1	.000	Fambrough	4-4	.500			
Olcott	2-1	.666	Moore	3-1	.750			
Bond	0-0	.000	Gottfried	3-0	1.00			